Books by David J. Rothman

Conscience and Convenience: The Asylum and its Alternatives in Progressive America (1980)

Doing Good: The Limits of Benevolence (Co-author, 1978)

The World of the Adams Chronicles (Editor, 1976)

The Sources of the American Social Tradition (Co-editor, 1975)

On Their Own: The Poor in Modern America (Co-editor, 1972)

The Discovery of the Asylum: Social Order and Disorder in the New Republic (1971)

Politics and Power: The United States Senate, 1869–1901 (1966)

Conscience and Convenience

CONSCIENCE AND

David J. Rothman

Scott, Foresman and Company
Glenview, Illinois   Boston   London

CONVENIENCE

*The Asylum and its Alternatives
in Progressive America*

ISBN 0-673-39350-X

I H G F E D C B

BP

FOR SHEILA
WITH LOVE

CONTENTS

IV THE WORLD OF MENTAL HEALTH

V DREAMS DIE HARD

ACKNOWLEDGMENTS

THE OPPORTUNITY TO THANK the people and organizations that helped and encouraged me to complete this book is most gratifying. The National Institute of Law Enforcement and Criminal Justice provided the bulk of research funds (Grant 75-NI-99-0054); I also received support from the National Institute of Mental Health (Grant RO1-MH-23543). Both of these agencies were altogether mindful of the integrity of research, concerned only that my study be as exacting and compelling as I could make it. The Center for Policy Research supplied an environment that in all ways furthered this work.

My research was facilitated by the year I spent as Robert Pinkerton Visiting Professor at the School of Criminal Justice, New York State University, Albany. I also had the pleasure of delivering the annual Samuel Paley lectures at Hebrew University in 1977, and the opportunity to explore and discuss these issues was very rewarding. My colleagues at Columbia not only demonstrated a lively interest in this project, but encouraged me to integrate my research and teaching responsibilities. I must note, too, the education I received in criminal justice during the course of my several years of service on the Field Foundation sponsored Committee for the Study of Incarceration.

Several friends reviewed the manuscript, offering useful suggestions. Robert Fogelson, Jay Kaplan, Sheldon Messinger, Charles Rosenberg, and Andrew von Hirsch were generous with their assistance; once again, Oscar Handlin provided me with an important and challenging critique. Somehow or other, Mildred Schneider was able to decipher my handwriting, put up with innumerable changes, and assist me in countless ways to prepare the manuscript for publication.

My obligation to the staffs of libraries and archives is great. In particular, I wish to acknowledge the help of those at the National Archives, the Columbia University libraries (especially the Social Work division), the Rockefeller Archive Center, and the State Libraries at Albany, Boston, Lansing, Oklahoma City, Sacramento, and Saint Paul.

My most significant debt is to my wife, Sheila M. Rothman. As is true of almost everything that I have written, her assistance both in the archives and at the editor's desk was indispensable. Indeed, her own research and writing in history and social policy exerted a compelling influence on the structure of the arguments that follow. Our children, Matthew and Micol, tolerated the innumerable dialogues that took place between us, never certain where the lines of one book ended and the other began. The chance to dedicate this book to her gives me more pleasure than even she may imagine.

D.J.R.

Barnard, Vermont
June, 1979

INTRODUCTION

IN THE OPENING DECADES of the twentieth century, new ideas and new programs transformed public attitudes and social policies toward the criminal, the delinquent, and the mentally ill. The innovations are well-known for they have dominated every aspect of criminal justice, juvenile justice, and mental health right through the middle 1960's. They include probation, parole, and the indeterminate sentence; the juvenile court and the outpatient clinic; and novel designs for the penitentiary, the reformatory, and the insane asylum. Yet we know surprisingly little about the origins and initial consequences of these procedures: how they were conceived, how they were translated into practice, and how they actually worked.

This gap in our knowledge is all the more glaring because we are today in revolt against inherited wisdom and established programs. For the first time, vigorous debate is challenging the legitimacy of each of these measures. Should criminal sentences be open-ended or fixed? Should the authority of the juvenile court be narrowed? Should prisons and mental hospitals be dismantled and juvenile institutions be abolished? The goal of this book is to inform both history and social policy, to analyze a revolution in practice that has an immediate relevance to present concerns.

To a remarkable degree, American historians have ignored these programs for the criminal, the delinquent, and the insane. There is not a single history of probation or parole or indeterminate sentences, not more than two or three accounts of prisons, mental hospitals or training schools in the twentieth century, and only a handful of studies of juvenile courts or outpatient clinics. Perhaps the fault rests with the substance of the story. One French student of the Parisian underworld in the mid-nineteenth century counseled a friend to avoid the subject, to leave to others the "warts and pustules" of his society. But the problem goes deeper, in many ways reflecting the obfuscating character of the term "reform." All of the measures that this book will be analyzing carried that label and were prominent on the Progressive agenda. Their enactment appeared so appropriate, so logical a step forward in humanitarian and scientific progress, that their principles did not have to be analyzed in depth. But in the longer history of the response of the public to the deviant, reform is an altogether misleading designation. To the Jacksonians, who in the decades following 1820 first created the prisons, insane asylums, and reformatories (a phenomenon I explored in *The Discovery of the Asylum*), those institutions were reforms. Then, to the Progressives, inherited procedures seemed so inadequate that they had to undertake reform; and now, in turn, Progressive solutions appear to stand in need of reform. In brief, reform is the designation that each generation gives to its favorite programs.

To recognize the repetitive quality of this process makes the subject more fascinating and clarifies the essential questions to be addressed. How does each generation arrive at its reform program? What elements come together to earn a proposed innovation the title of reform? Who makes up the cadre of reformers? Perhaps even more important, where do they find their constituents? How do their programs win enactment? And then a second order of questions emerges: what difference do the programs make? How consistently are they translated into practice? Put more forcefully, why is it that reforms so often turn out to be in need of reform? With these types of inquiries in mind, this book is ultimately about the enterprise of reform.

Two words, "conscience" and "convenience," point to the dynamic and tension that are at the core of the analysis. We begin first with conscience, for the Progressive programs were the invention of benevolent and philanthropic-minded men and women and their ideological formulations were essential to promoting change. Coming from the world of the college, the settlement house, and the medical school, the Progressive reformers shared optimistic theories that at once clarified the origins of deviant behavior and shaped their efforts to control it. They marched under a very appealing banner, asking citizens not to do less for fear of harm, but to do more, confident of favorable results.

Their principles can be summarized succinctly. Progressives aimed to understand and to cure crime, delinquency, and insanity through a case-by-case approach. From their perspective, the Jacksonian commitment to institutions had been wrong, both for assuming that all deviants were of a single type, the victims of social disorder, and for believing that they could all be rehabilitated with a single program, the well-ordered routine of the asylum. To Progressives, knowledge about and policies toward the deviant had to follow a far more particular bent. The task was to understand the life history of each offender or patient and then to devise a remedy that was specific to the individual.

In that effort, two seemingly different approaches competed for favor among Progressives. Some reformers were environmentalists, locating the roots of the individual's problem in one or another of the wretched conditions of the immigrant ghetto. Others adopted a psychological explanation, looking to the mind-set of the deviant for the causes of maladaption. But whatever the orientation, the two schools agreed that each case had to be analyzed and responded to on its own terms. One offender was best treated in the community — and hence the need for probation. Another offender would have to be incarcerated until he proved himself able to reenter society — and hence the propriety of an indeterminate sentence to a prison or training school that would resemble a "normal" community. Yet another patient might best be treated at home — and hence the need for outpatient clinic care; or require short-term intensive treatment — hence, the psychopathic hospital; or need long-term care — which the mental hospital would provide. In effect, all Progressive programs assumed one outstanding feature: *they required discretionary responses to each case.* Rules could not be made in advance. Every person had to be treated differently. Fixed codes or set procedures were both unfair and ineffective.

That these measures would expand the power of the state, enlarging the freedom of action of public officials, did not disturb reformers. To the contrary, another distinguishing mark of the Progressive mentality was its willingness to increase the scope of state action and widen its exercise of power. Julia Lathrop, Hull House resident and later Chief of the Children's Bureau, summarized the credo well: "The success of our future civilization lies in government adding to their responsibility and taking on work which people have not hitherto been willing to entrust to them." Thus, Progressives were eager to relax the formal rules under which juvenile court judges, probation officers, parole boards, wardens, superintendents, and psychiatrists operated. In this way, the needs of justice and the aims of therapy, the welfare of the individual and the security of society would be satisfied.

But conscience is only one part of the record. To understand the speed with which the new measures took hold, one must reckon with convenience as well. Progressive proposals found a favorable response among the administrators of criminal justice and mental health — indeed, a much more favorable response than among the public at large. Wardens, district attorneys, judges, mental hospital superintendents, and directors of child care agencies welcomed the enlargement of their discretionary authority. The innovations brought them numerous practical advantages, enabling them to carry out their daily assignments more easily and efficiently. For operational reasons, they supported the Progressive innovations with enthusiasm. Accordingly, the process of reform is far more complicated to trace in the twentieth century than in the early nineteenth. In the Jacksonian era, one can rightly describe *a* reform position without especial attention to the special interests of its advocates. In the Progressive decades, the cast of characters is longer and their particular agendas much more varied.

These distinctions are all the more important because convenience assumed a critical role in determining the outcome of the new measures. For reform proposals to find a constituency among administrators may well be a precondition for the success of any movement. What is most important, however, is that this Progressive alliance undercut the aims of the original design. What remained was a hybrid, really a bastard version — one that fully satisfied the needs of those within the system but not the ambitions of reformers.

Although it is simple and almost fashionable now to talk about the inevitable "failure of reform," to insist that nothing works, the story here raises more complicated considerations. Clearly, the label of "failure" is often attached to a program too quickly and uniformly; the question should be, "failure, or success, to whom?" As we shall see, the administrators of criminal and juvenile justice and mental health in the decades 1900–1940 did not define the Progressive measures to be failures at all. To the contrary, the innovations satisfied them in countless ways, from helping them to clear crowded court calendars, to maximizing their control over inmates and patients, to buttressing the legitimacy of their institutions.

From the perspective of the designers of the system, the programs did appear to be failures; that is, they did not meet expectations. The architects recognized all the flaws and cracks that appeared when blueprint became structure. But what conclusions follow for us from this finding? Should we use the occasion for whipping the reformers, for denigrating the effort to do good, for bolstering the judgment that doing nothing may be the only sensible public policy? Or does the result become the text for preaching on the evils of modern society, for lamenting that good intentions do not produce good results, for making the reformers into tragic heroes? Or ought we to step back and view the whole enterprise with a detachment that borders on wonderment, to analyze the weaknesses of reform theory as though its proponents were attempting to fly by flapping their arms? Or finally, ought we to recall the horrors of the nineteenth-century prison and asylum and then go on, more or less complaisantly, to conclude that the legacy in corrections and mental health was so grim that anything reformers did to try to improve conditions must be applauded? Undoubtedly some readers will adopt one or another of these positions, discovering ample evidence here to support their inclinations. Nevertheless, this list of choices is incomplete and must be expanded.

There is little arguing that the reform effort should be evaluated in light of the social context and the state of knowledge available at the time. The horrors of the jails, prisons, and asylums were real enough to encourage a belief that any change would be for the better; to fault reformers for not having stronger weapons at hand with which to combat deviant behavior would not only be unfair but presumptuous, considering that we are now not well equipped either. Yet, these points made, we must also recognize that Progressives never paused to reckon with their own limitations. They never considered whether, given their knowledge, they should move more cautiously and circumspectly in implementing their policies; whether it was right for them to leave the deviant so helpless before their desire to treat and cure. Reformers, to a fault, were enthusiasts, so certain of their ability to achieve success that they were unwilling to qualify or to moderate their programs, to protect the objects of their wisdom from the coercion of their wisdom.

Moreover, for all their awareness of how great the gap was between the rhetoric and the reality of programs, Progressives were unable to perceive any of the underlying causes for failure. They never understood, for example, the nature of the alliance that linked them to the administrators of the system. In this respect, the Progressives active in criminal justice were at one with their co-reformers who were attempting to regulate the corporations: neither group could appreciate how the very parties that were to be regulated might capture the regulating agency or turn ostensibly corrective legislation to their own advantage. As a result, throughout the 1920's and 1930's, criminal justice and mental health reformers never reconsidered the premises of their programs. Failure, they believed, reflected faulty implementation, not underlying problems with theory or with politics; incompetent administrators and stingy legislators, not basic flaws within the design, undercut the strengths of the innovations. Hence, reformers responded to disappointment in one-note fashion: they urged better training for probation and parole officers; better programs for prisons and training schools; more staff for juvenile courts and more attendants for mental hospitals. Do more of the same so that the promise of these innovations would be realized. So however sympathetically one may respond to reformers' initial determination to improve the system, it is more difficult to condone their die-hard unwillingness to review their own record, to ring the bell on their own policies.

Finally, is it true that whatever else, Progressive innovations were better than the procedures that they replaced? Whatever their weaknesses, were the new practices improvements on the old? The book will provide the evidence for resolving the issue; the data are too complex for rapid summary. One needs to know first a good deal about the implementation of probation, parole, the juvenile court, and outpatient programs; and about their effects upon prisons, reformatories, and mental hospitals — all of which makes up the substance of the chapters that follow. Yet let it be clear from the start that the answer to the question may well be, no, that Progressive reforms did not significantly improve inherited practices. To raise but one theme to which we will frequently return, innovations that appeared to be substitutes for incarceration became supplements to incarceration. Progressive innovations may well have done less to upgrade dismal conditions than they did to create nightmares of their own.

For all this, the most interesting and important enterprise remains that of appreciating the dynamics of reform, not in order to denigrate or applaud the would-be reformer but to analyze the strengths and weaknesses of the movement. This commitment may well reflect a sense that those who would attempt to do good today have much to learn from the history of reform, in terms of why ambitious programs were not realized and how men and women of good conscience responded to the course of events. In this spirit, it becomes relevant to understand that a peculiar reading of history made Progressives fearful that alternatives to their own program inevitably would be harsh and cruel. For another, they were not about to give any appearance of being allied with hard-line critics of these new measures who considered them ways of coddling the criminal. Even more important, reformers were never deeply disturbed by the fact that administrative convenience had become so well served in their programs; for they were convinced that their innovations could satisfy *all* goals, that the same person and the same institution could at once guard and help, protect and rehabilitate, maintain custody and deliver treatment. They perceived no conflict between these goals, no clash of interest between the deviant and the wider society, between the warden and his convicts, between the hospital superintendent and his patients, between the keeper and the kept. The "friend" or social worker who did probation work could simultaneously be an "officer"; the juvenile court judge who was charged to protect society could also be a parent to the delinquent. This belief was among the most fundamental in the reformers' canon, and in retrospect, perhaps the most dubious. The study of the past does not give license to predict the future, but it is more than a little tempting to argue that such goals can never be satisfied together, that they are too diametrically opposed, at least in this society, to be joined. More modestly it can be said that the Progressive effort to link them failed. In the end, when conscience and convenience met, convenience won. When treatment and coercion met, coercion won.

However disappointing the outcome of Progressive efforts, the analysis here is far more favorable to the prospects of constructive change within the systems of criminal justice and mental health care than might be at first imagined. The point is perhaps most easily demonstrated by contrasting the perspective that emerges from this study with that offered by a writer like Michel Foucault. In *Discipline and Punish*, the prison, from the 1820's to the 1970's, in France as well as in England and the United States, is an unvarying form of discipline; it assumes an inevitability in capitalist societies that makes reform at best foolhardy, at worst deceptive. But this approach is entirely static and thus misleading. As we shall see, prisons in particular, and criminal justice procedures in general, do have a history that Foucault's mode of analysis cannot illuminate. The prison did not descend once and for all from some capitalist spirit. The more one understands the alterations within the system, the more one explores motives, designs, and alliances, the less an air of inevitability hangs over the practice of punishment and the less compelling arguments of economic determinism become. Choices were made, decisions reached; and to appreciate the dynamic is to be able to recognize the opportunity to affect it.

Moreover, Foucault's analysis never enters into the everyday world of criminal justice. It is one thing to claim that the goal of surveillance dominated the *theory* of punishment, quite another to examine what actually happened when programs were translated into *practice*. Then the historian parts company with the ideologue to complicate the story in much more interesting and, ultimately, energizing ways. In Foucault's world, the fit between a capitalist society and the prison is tight, as though rationality dominated throughout. In fact, the fit was much looser and procedure less systematic. And this gap is important both for getting the story straight, for knowing what did or did not happen, and, again, for opening up the prospects for innovation, for breaking out of constructs that are confining, even self-confirming. None of this, let it be clear, suggests a platform for reform or posits an optimism about results. But it does say that change is possible and may be significant without being total. There is much more room for maneuver than a Foucault could ever imagine or allow.

Let me reiterate one point to elucidate the character of this study. When I began this book, I not only intended to complete the story that I traced in *The Discovery of the Asylum* (that is, to take the account from the 1870's and 1880's down to 1940), but I believed I would be examining the rise of alternatives to incarceration. The *Asylum* volume had analyzed the origins of institutions. This book would analyze their decline. My initial orientation reflected my awareness in the early 1970's of the declining rate of incarceration not only in mental hospitals but in prisons and training schools. I also had the notion that probation, parole, juvenile courts, and outpatient clinics were frankly efforts at community placement, that they were the forerunners, in spirit and in practice, of the present-day commitment to deinstitutionalization, as though Progressives had a fundamental quarrel with the principle of incarceration. In fact, my starting assumptions were far too simple. The Progressives were anti-institutional in a very special way. Their quarrel was not so much with the institution per se, as with uniformity and rigidity. They were not so much struggling to return the offender to the community (although that theme does appear in one form or another) as attempting to individualize treatment. Their perspective was substantially different from that of the 1970's, so different that I am comfortable in taking the period 1900–1965 as one, labeling it "Progressive," and conceiving of the post-1965 period, our own, as post-Progressive — indeed, anti-Progressive.

This recognition of the differences is critical if one is to examine the Progressive program on its own basis and not impose on it a later ideology. Moreover, a complicated view of Progressive measures does illuminate many of the problems and possibilities that current action faces. Let me here suggest two of them. First, Progressives believed that institutions (be they prisons or mental hospitals) could coexist with, and even sponsor, non-institutional programs. As we shall see, they were wrong. Institutions dominated the system so as to make other options almost impossible to realize. Second, Progressives imagined that non-institutional programs might take away some clients from the institutions, that probation might spare an offender from a term in a state prison, that a community clinic might spare a patient from a stay in a state hospital. In fact, they were wrong again: innovations often became add-ons to the system, not replacements. Probation probably brought more people under the authority of the state than it kept out of prisons; by the same token, parole may well have increased terms of incarceration, not shortened them. Hence, the past record does alert us to some of the most urgent present-day policy concerns. Can institutions allow for the development of alternatives? Can alternatives become genuine alternatives? In the field of criminal justice and mental disabilities, these two questions are the most significant that our society now confronts and our answers to them will determine the fate of our own innovations.

I

The Nineteenth-Century Legacy

CHAPTER ONE

Coping with Evil

EVERY OBSERVER of American prisons and asylums in the closing decades of the nineteenth century recognized that the pride of one generation had become the shame of another. The institutions that had been intended to exemplify the humanitarian advances of republican government were not merely inadequate to the ideal but were actually an embarrassment and a rebuke. Failure to do good was one thing; a proclivity to do harm quite another — and yet the evidence was incontrovertible that brutality and corruption were endemic to the institutions. Nevertheless, despite the relative novelty of incarceration (the buildings, after all, were often only thirty to forty years old and many citizens might still remember opening ceremonies), and despite its many obvious abuses, very few observers, whether members of reform societies or of state legislatures, challenged the root principles of the system. Horror stories could spark efforts at piecemeal amelioration but not at fundamental change; one or another practice might be modified, but the principles themselves remained appropriate and legitimate. In other words, the post–Civil War generation had a series of strategies for coping with evil which kept the institutions at the core of the public response to the deviant.[1]

The awareness of the gross inadequacies of prisons and asylums was widespread. Newspapers, state commissions, and philanthropic societies reported the evidence in vivid detail. The prisons had degenerated from the rigid discipline of the solitary system at Pennsylvania or the congregate system at Auburn into more or less lax, corrupt, and brutal places. At Sing-Sing, which had become famous in the 1830's for the march-shuffle that was the lock step, investigators in the 1870's discovered that "dealers were publicly supplying prisoners with almost anything they would pay for; convicts sitting and lying about under the trees, or congregated in groups in cool places, without keepers, [were] playing all sorts of games, reading, scheming, trafficking ... numerous shanties scattered about the grounds, affording lounging places for convicts." Other investigators uncovered examples of labor contractors and guards supplying prisoners with contraband, wardens exploiting convict labor for their own gain. Like contemporary Mexican prisons, the yard had something of the atmosphere of a village about it.[2]

Not surprisingly, laxity and brutality went hand in hand. Wardens in the 1830's had been able to impose order by strict military routines, rules of silence, and one-man-to-a-cell arrangements. Their successors, however, confronted serious overcrowding and understaffing, as well as the intrusive authority of private contractors who purchased the right to inmates' labor from the state. Under these circumstances prison life turned chaotic and wardens had regular recourse to amazingly bizarre punishments. From their perspective, this was the only way to maintain authority over the convicts. To anyone else, the solutions were unquestionably cruel and unusual.

To begin with the more medieval devices, state prisons in the post–Civil War decades designed a "pulley" mechanism. "By means of a cord ... bound about both wrists brought together, and drawn upon an overhead system of pulleys," the convict was lifted "entirely from the ground, with his whole weight suspended upon the small cord." The duration of this punishment ranged from two minutes or less to an hour. A variant on the pulley was "tying up": a cord was fastened around the inmate's wrists and attached to an overhead fixture. The tension was then adjusted according to the degree of pain to be inflicted: the milder form allowed the subject to keep his toes on the floor; the severe case was hoisted into the air. As one guard informed a New York State committee: "If Mr. Moon [the principal keeper, or warden's assistant] told me to hang them up pretty good, so as to stretch them some, I would stand them up on a box . . . and then would take the box from under them." Sing-Sing had its own particular mechanism, a "tying up" device that suspended prisoners by their thumbs instead of their wrists. "This is a very severe punishment," reported another New York investigator. "Men have been kept raised so long as to cause bleeding from the mouth, before the doctor would order the prisoner taken down."[3]

Wardens also had recourse to the iron cap or "cage" (shades of the iron mask), "worn on the shoulders by an iron band around the neck, the cage part extending some fifteen inches or more, within which the head is enclosed by small rods or bands of iron, weighing from 6½ to 8 pounds." And they used "hooks," another kind of pulley device; the inmate's wrists were handcuffed behind him and then attached to hooks set in the wall about chest high. "It had the effect," one prison official noted, "to raise the man in such a way, his weight comes most upon his toes," causing excruciating pain in the arms, shoulders, back, and legs. In addition, of course, there were the lash and the paddle, the number of strokes set to fit the offense. In New York, the paddles were made of "two thicknesses of sole leather . . . three to four inches wide on the blade . . . about 28 inches long." The blows were administered to "bare flesh of the buttocks of the subject, who was in position bent across a frame called a chair or horse, with his face downward, his feet encased in fixed shoes at the base on one side, his arms secured by wristlets attached to a bar about one foot from the ground on the other side, and his thighs and back fastened with leather straps." In most cases, the number of blows remained below thirty, but "it was not an extraordinary occurrence in which a prisoner received 40 or 50 blows," and one investigation turned up a case of 100 blows.[4]

More modern punishments were in use too, particularly solitary confinement to the "dungeon," as it was known. Inmates were locked in totally dark cells furnished only with a bucket ("not even a board having been provided") and fed on "short rations," that is, four ounces of bread and one-quarter of a pint of water daily, usually for periods of up to a week, but occasionally for three to six weeks, or more. Straitjackets were another popular punishment, and so was the brick bag — the convict who would not work was forced to wear it until he changed his mind.[5]

Perhaps the most incredible torture instrument of the period was the "water crib," in use at the Kansas prison. The inmate was placed in a coffin-like box, six and one-half feet long, thirty inches wide, and three feet deep, his face down and his hands handcuffed behind his back. A water hose was then turned on, slowly filling the crib. The effect was of slow drowning, with the inmate struggling to keep his head up above the rising water line. As one keeper boasted to an investigatory committee, the crib was marvelously efficient: "You take a man and put him in there and turn the water on him and that wilts him at once. He wilts and says he will be good. It might take days in a blind cell [solitary] until his system was all deranged." The committee had several questions for him:

> Q: Do they know how soon you are going to quit with the crib?
> A: No.
> Q: Isn't the only value of the water cure the shock?
> A: Yes sir, I never saw a man show any temper.
> Q: Do they get any water in their lungs?
> A: I don't know. I suppose so if they open their mouths and try to.
> Q: Do they ever open their mouths?
> A: Yes sir.
> Q: You always see them spit water out, don't you?

A: Not always.

Q: When they don't spit water out, is it because they are so far gone they can't spit, isn't it?

A: I don't know.

Q: Did you ever have to turn them over and let the water run out?

A: Never saw that done.[6]

In the asylums for the insane, as in the prisons, the decline from the ambitions of the Jacksonian founders was dramatic. Once again, indifference and abuse were joined. Neglect was rampant — and how could it be otherwise when a handful of physicians had responsibility for hundreds, even thousands of patients? That the great majority of inmates were the chronic and aged insane made any serious effort to deliver treatment even less likely. The staunchest critics (who often came from a training in neurology as opposed to a career in institutional administration) found asylums and prisons to be practically indistinguishable. "It is too common a belief," one of them pointed out, "that the hospitals are prisons, and the superintendents only keepers; and the friends of the insane will look for every other help before they will trust an insane asylum." Asylum superintendents were hardly enthusiastic in their own defense. They freely admitted to "a gradual yet inevitable accumulation of the chronic and incurable class in hospital populations" which inevitably "affected their reputations unfavorably as agencies of cure." More, they acknowledged that "we are coming to the idea that very few people do get well." As one of them concluded: "I find that recoveries are much less likely to occur than I once believed. . . . I do not believe that more than twenty-five of every hundred get well," a very different statement from the claims in the 1830's and 1840's of 80, 90 and even 100 percent cures.[7]

Custodial care was generally not humane care. Part of the problem was violence between patients, with staffs either too small or too uninterested to intervene. The records were filled with such entries as: "Fourth Ward, April 6, 1882. C.S. received a blow on the nose from Mr. C.; Mr. C. was sitting on a bench in the yard when S came up to him and kicked him; Mr. C. then struck him on the nose; witnessed by attendant E.A. Williams." Part of the problem, too, was that staff members themselves often abused the inmates, and the supervising physicians had neither the time nor the inclination to correct the situation. The accusation of a patient was generally not worth very much against the denial of an attendant. But everyone knew just how pervasive the brutality was. One state investigation of conditions at the Utica, New York asylum revealed the "bleaching out" process: "When a patient is kicked, of course, there are black marks on him — bruises — and to put him into cold water and to keep him there, why, it will take the discoloration out of his skin." Or, in answer to the investigator's question: "In what way did the attendants usually punish patients?" came this attendant's response:

A: With their hands and feet; when an attendant was attacked by a patient, he defended more with his feet than with his hands.

Q: How did he use his feet?

A: In a natural way — kicked with them, generally kicked the fellow in the stomach and the ribs.

Q: Why was that done?

A: In some cases the patients were so bad that the attendants had to protect themselves as best they could; there is no man that will allow a madman to attack him without defending himself. . . . A madman would kill you if he got the chance, and you must not let him get the chance.

Q: Can you recall any other instances where you saw patients struck by attendants?

A: I saw them struck most every day.[8]

The well-ordered asylum had become the madhouse. It was not treatment of the inmate but survival of the staff that was at stake.

Worse yet, asylums that were overcrowded and merely custodial typically relied upon a series of restraint mechanisms which fell short of the cruelty of prison devices but were still gruesome enough. There was the "waist belt," for "passing around the body and around the back of a chair"; the patient's wrists were enclosed in leather straps which, in turn, were attached to a ring on the waist belt "sufficiently loose to allow them to feed themselves ... by bending the head." In use, too, were "leather mittens" for patients who mutilated themselves; the mittens, made without thumbs, "were fastened around the wrist by a lock." Then came the "camisole, which is generally made of canvas and restrains the hands and arms, preventing the patient from getting into mischief or doing damage." And the "muff" — "the hands are placed into it; the camisole ... is a little better, but some patients will tear the camisole with their teeth which they cannot do with the muff." Finally, asylums used "the covered bed; that is, to all intents and purposes, a child's crib; it is large enough for an adult patient and is well-ventilated: the cover fastens on to it by means of hinges and will lock on; the covered bed is a necessary restraint ... to keep a patient in a horizontal position." The New York committee investigating Utica learned that "on some wards we have some patients who sleep constantly in covered beds." The asylum was practicing solitary confinement on the wards.[9]

The list of institutional inadequacies could be easily extended, but rather than draw out the indictment (which no one would dispute), let us consider how this generation of keepers, politicians, and would-be reformers responded to these facts. How did Americans in the 1870's, 1880's, and 1890's react to the knowledge of pervasive brutality? Or, to put it more sharply, what kept such institutions alive?

Since inmates and patients were typically the immigrant and the poor, incarceration seemed a convenient policy, at least to a society that was acutely apprehensive about alien hordes and dangerous classes. Already in the 1850's and 1860's, the prisons and asylums were becoming the special preserve of the foreign-born and the poor, and over the next decades this trend accelerated. In 1890, the penitentiary population in such an industrial state as Illinois was 60 percent foreign-born or second-generation immigrant, essentially German and Irish; less than one-third of the inmates had completed a grammar school education and only 5

percent a high school or college education. The great majority of
inmates were men who held unskilled or at best semiskilled jobs;
typically laborers, farmers, brakemen, barbers, saloon keepers,
shoemakers, coachmen, miners, teamsters, and waiters. Similarly,
in California, 45 percent of the prisoners were foreign-born (Chi-
nese and Mexican as well as Irish and German) and again, laborers, waiters, cooks, and farmers composed the majority of the
group.[10]

Asylum inmates shared these same characteristics. In 1890, 40
percent of all those incarcerated in state mental institutions were
foreign-born or the children of the foreign-born. In the industrial
regions, of course, the percentage was still higher. In Illinois, half
of the patients in these institutions were aliens (in the Cook
County Hospital the number reached 77 percent). In Massachusetts, the Worcester asylums held 50 percent first or second generation; at Danvers the figure was 51 percent and at Northampton, 53 percent. (By contrast, in Boston's private and exclusive
McLean Hospital a bare 10 percent of the patients were immigrants.) In New York, the Utica asylum population was 50 percent foreign-born, the New York City Asylum for the Insane at
Blackwell's Island, 86 percent. (Again, by contrast, the Bloomingdale Asylum, New York's equivalent of McLean, held only 31
percent immigrants.) By the same token, the great majority of
patients in state facilities were working class. The Illinois asylum
inmates were typically farmers, laborers, and domestics; in Connecticut, they were laborers, factory employees, farmers, domestics, housekeepers, and mechanics. Indeed, when Connecticut
identified patients by sources of financial support, the "paying"
inmates were a tiny fraction of the total (some 6 percent), while
the "indigent" and "pauper" class made up the rest.[11]

Under these circumstances, substandard institutional conditions came to be accepted as something less than scandalous. The
places might not be all that they should be, yet (the thinking
ran) they were good enough for the immigrant. Or, in a variation
on this theme, the aliens had only themselves to blame for the
decline of the asylum, for they were untreatable or unmanage-

able. The well-ordered institution might effect cures among the native-born, but it could do little for the foreign-born. To Americans in the post–Civil War decades, aliens were at best frightening figures, crowded into their strange and separate ghettos. Should the alien turn deviant, incarceration, whatever the quality of care, seemed the right response. A policy of exclusion and banishment, so the public might be rid of the offender and done with the insane, appeared altogether appropriate.

These judgments also affected the various official supervisory bodies established to monitor institutional operations. Every prison and asylum had its board of visitors or board of managers who in turn reported to a state board of charities and correction, or occasionally to a special commissioner of lunacy or of corrections. Ostensibly these groups would ferret out abuses and help to bring about reforms. In the overwhelming majority of cases, however, the boards were not equal to the task of insuring decent care, let alone quality care. And they were certainly not going to challenge the system of incarceration.

The list of causes for this disappointing performance is long. The board positions were usually not full-time or salaried, so that members were in no position to fulfill their duties diligently. Appointments were honorific — the type of post that the governor awarded as political patronage (to be sure, it was not high on the list), a post that a businessman might seek so as to express his philanthropic impulses. Thus, the board of managers of the Utica asylum in the 1870's was composed of a local manufacturer (the chairman), two bankers, a grain merchant, two other manufacturers, two lawyers, and two more businessmen. Not only did their own affairs keep them from visiting the institution very frequently, but as amateurs in the field, they had little inclination or skill to go beyond the superintendent's word. They took their major task to be financial oversight, advising on purchases. But they would not go beyond the books of the institution to do or say very much about inmate treatment. Those serving on the state boards were no different, as witness the following legislative examination of one New York State Board of Charities member:

Q: Are you a physician or have you ever been?
A: No, sir.
Q: Never read medical works as a profession?
A: No sir.
Q: What has been your calling?
A: A teacher.
Q: What would you say to the practice of putting an insane person in a chair, and strapping them into that chair . . . and keeping them there without exercise, the entire day?
A: The answer depends upon the circumstances of the case.
Q: In your opinion would it not be injurious to the health of that person to be strapped in the chair the entire day?
A: It depends entirely on the physical and intellectual condition of the patient. I am not a physician and cannot answer it as an expert in managing insane people or asylums, consequently, my opinion on such a subject would be worth very little.

This sense of amateurishness and deferential attitude, this belief that a layman was not fit to pass judgment on strapping the insane to a chair, meant that the boards would not be likely to confront the authority of a superintendent. Should a scandal erupt, the board was inclined to defend the superintendent, to blame an attendant, perhaps to request a change in one procedure or another, but not to question the design itself.[12]

The alliance rested on an even more solid foundation: the board members identified with the superintendent as one of their own as against the inmate, that alien figure in every sense of the term. The visiting board member spoke with the superintendent gentleman to gentleman, as befit members of the same club and class. When evidence of malfeasance surfaced, the board turned to the superintendent to correct it, assuming his good faith and competence. The board would not take up the cause of the immigrant or the lower-class deviant against the superintendent. It would certainly not examine conditions of incarceration from the perspective of the kept as opposed to the keeper. Hence, at best, the boards attempted to counter one particular abuse or another. At worst, they simply ignored whatever failings they could and tried to minimize the import of those that they could not. In short, the boards were a mechanism perpetuating the legitimacy of incarceration, giving the system the aura, but not the reality, of objective oversight.

The financial cost of incarceration also seemed modest, especially in light of its conveniences. In the post–Civil War decades, most prisons operated under a contract arrangement: the state sold inmate labor to the highest bidder. All the parties liked the arrangement. The state had the guarantee of an income without incurring risks or capital costs: it was the contractor who supplied the machinery, the goods, and the supervisory personnel. In return, the contractors had a cheap supply of labor for manufacturing goods to be sold on the open market. In 1885, the total value of goods produced in the prisons was $24 million, of which the contract system was responsible for $17 million. And in a state's budget, the returns could be considerable. Few states (outside of the South) profited from the system, but the returns from contract labor in these years went far toward reducing costs. In Ohio, for example, prison contracts in 1883 brought in $250,600, almost covering total prison expenditures of $325,000. The only losers in the scheme (and there was much debate as to whether they were actually losers) were manufacturers and workers in competing industries; but through the 1880's, neither group was able to mount sufficient political pressure to eliminate the arrangement. So in effect, state legislatures and taxpayers had little cause to quarrel with the financial aspects of criminal incarceration. Costs did not run counter to the convenience of confining offenders.[13]

Insane asylums certainly did not yield such handsome returns, but over these decades the states, as opposed to the localities, assumed an ever-increasing share of the expenditures. County care of the insane in almshouses gave way to state care in asylums — a policy which, as we shall soon see, seemed the more humane, and which not incidentally meant that counties transferred the expense to state budgets. To be sure, the taxpayer ultimately paid the bill, and expenditures for the institutions did constitute a major part of the budget in many states — in Ohio, for example, the appropriations amounted to $655,000 in a budget of $2,500,-000, or one-quarter of the total. Still, several considerations made the burden less noticeable when the state bore the costs. For one, some states, like New York, enjoyed windfall returns from sources other than property taxes, so that individual taxpayers were not particularly conscious of the costs of asylum care. For another, citizens were less informed about state than about local expenditures, making protest about asylum costs that much less likely. Even more important, when a county supported one of its insane in a local almshouse, the expense was both immediate and controllable. The greater the number of the insane that the county cared for, the higher the costs. But once the state took responsibility, this simple equation no longer held. The rate of state taxes would not vary with the decision of any one county to commit or not to commit a particular person. The tax rate would reflect all county decisions about commitment — as well as a host of other considerations which had nothing to do with caring for the insane (public works, economic growth, and so on). Thus, the state's assumption of the costs of asylum care effectively removed the financial aspects from public attention. There would be no protest against the system because it was expensive. To the contrary, from the vantage point of the citizen, state asylums seemed a reasonable and prudent mode of support.[14]

Functional considerations were only one, and probably not the most important one, of the reasons why institutions in particular, and policies toward the criminal and the insane in general, did not undergo significant change during these years. Not only anti-immigrant sentiments and taxpayers' complacency kept prisons and asylums alive. A group of reformers continued to justify the idea of incarceration for negative reasons, that is, for fear of what a sustained attack upon the institutions might produce. However wretched the current state, conditions would degenerate still further if the institutions were abolished.

In criminal justice, the reformers' sense of history confined them. They looked back to the period before the penitentiary — with its gallows, whipping posts, and edicts of banishment — and reasoned that the abolition of the prison would inevitably restore such horrid practices. Instead of taking inspiration from the fact that incarceration was a relatively recent invention and therefore properly approached with skepticism, they believed that all that stood between barbarism and civilization was the prison itself. As one warden expressed it: "When one studies the history of crime and its punishments up to the middle of the Eighteenth Century, he must be struck with the gruesome fact that the law of crime punishment and penal progress has made its way over dead bodies. . . . With such a fiendish record of crime punishments lying behind us, who shall dare to assert that the world is not growing better." Hence, the appropriate task was to reform incarceration, not to launch a fundamental attack upon it.[15]

The superiority of asylum care to other ways of handling the insane seemed even more obvious. If not for the asylums, lunatics were certain to suffer the same fate as their colonial predecessors, to be locked in attics or jail cellars. The task was not to design alternatives to incarceration but to extend the reach of institutions, specifically by transferring the insane from county almshouses to state facilities. Better the asylum than the almshouse — and reformers had little trouble in making the case.

One of the first and most influential statements on behalf of state care came from the New York Commission in Lunacy. Established in 1889, its first report offered persuasive details about the miserable fate of the insane in poorhouses. "The most that can justly be said in behalf of the poor-houses," the Commission declared, "is that they are custodial in character. In truth, the treatment accorded to the [insane] inmates is scarcely better than that which be given sane paupers." No physician supervised the insane; a "keeper" was in charge. Only a few almshouses had medical supplies and none of them used a "proper system of classification," or maintained a "proper case record"; physical restraints were commonly applied "at the will of an untrained attendant." The Commission also discovered massive neglect. "In many instances, the mattresses were literally reeking with filth, and evidently were not dried from one day's end to another." More, "the practice which prevails in many instances of compelling two patients to sleep together cannot be too strongly condemned." Sanitary conditions were so primitive that "it is a common practice at most of those places to bathe three or more patients in the same water." Obviously no provisions were made for inmates' amusement, exercise, or occupation, or even for their obtaining fresh air.[16]

After these general indictments, the Commission recounted a few specific horror stories, echoing the reports of Dorothea Dix fifty years earlier:

> Within a small room in an old and dilapidated wooden building suitable only for an outbuilding . . . was found a demented old woman. She was in a state of turbulent dementia, scantily clad, barefooted, exceedingly filthy. . . . The floor was wet and otherwise soiled with excrement, the odor from which was exceedingly offensive. In fact, it smelled more like a privy vault than a place for the confinement of a human being.

> In another institution a woman was discovered sitting in a strong wooden chair, secured to the floor. . . . The keeper . . . said that the patient was an exceedingly filthy one; that unless thus confined, she would defile the whole place in the course of a few hours.

> On the woman's ward of another institution the scene presented was that of veritable bedlam. In this ward were found, indiscriminately huddled together, paupers, children, vagrant and insane, all in a state of extreme disorder.

Confronting these nightmarish scenes, the Commission recommended "that all of the insane in the county poorhouses . . . be transferred at the earliest possible date to State asylums," and that "the State assume the entire expense, not only of clothing and maintaining the insane, but also of removing them to and returning them from the asylums." The Commission was not about to ponder whether conditions might be no less shocking in state facilities. Evils were best faced one at a time.

This sense of the institution as the lesser of possible evils constituted only one source of its legitimacy in the late nineteenth century. Reformers also expressed a very positive and enthusiastic commitment to the idea that prisons and asylums could accomplish rehabilitation and cure. The prospect of doing good, not merely the desire to avoid greater harm, ultimately bound another generation of well-meaning observers to the practice of incarceration.

A keen optimism about the penitentiary's ability to rehabilitate the criminal continued to dominate the thinking of the prison reformers in the post–Civil War period. By 1870, Enoch Wines, Franklin Sanborn, and Zebulon Brockway, among others, were meeting in a National Congress of Penitentiary and Reformatory Discipline, and the resolutions they enacted became the chief planks in the reform agenda for the next several decades. Facing glaring institutional abuses, the group did not attempt to revive and purify the original Jacksonian arrangements. Rather, they came up with a new design. The goal remained "moral regeneration" through the penitentiary, but now in a different type of penitentiary.

As the Congress's 1870 *Declaration of Principles* explained in very traditionally Jacksonian terms, crime was "a sort of moral disease," and therefore the "great object [of] . . . the treatment of criminals . . . should be his moral regeneration . . . the reformation of criminals, not the infliction of vindictive suffering." To achieve this end required novel means. "Neither in the United States nor in Europe, as a general thing, has the problem of reforming the criminal yet been resolved"; the majority of inmates still went out "hardened and dangerous." Clearly, then, "our aims and our methods need to be changed, so that practice shall conform to theory."[17]

Accordingly, the *Declaration* offered two new principles for the organization of the institution. First, "the prisoner's self-respect should be cultivated to the utmost, and every effort made to give back to him his manhood." Second, "the prisoner's destiny should be placed, measurably, in his own hands; he must be . . . able through his own exertions, to continually better his own condition. A regulated self-interest must be brought into play." These postulates represented an initial approximation of some of the ideas that would characterize the twentieth-century program. The regimen of the Jacksonian system, from fixed sentences and the lock step to the rules of silence and isolation, now seemed to debase and humiliate the prisoner and to rob him of initiative. The post–Civil War reformers wanted to substitute a much more open-ended sentencing code: "Preemptory sentences ought to be replaced by those of indeterminate length," declared the *Declaration*. A "proof of reformation" should replace the "mere lapse of time" in winning an inmate release. And such reformation would at once be encouraged and demonstrated through a "progressive classification of prisoners based on character and worked on some well-adjusted mark system." Taking its inspiration from the Irish system as developed by Sir Walter Crofton (in which prisoners moved up grade by grade until they finally earned a "ticket of leave"), the *Declaration* insisted that this arrangement would well suit American prisons. "Yankee ingenuity is competent to devise some method whereby this . . . system . . . may receive practical application among us."

The themes announced in the 1870 *Declaration* marked reformers' statements (but, as we shall see, not state practice) over the next twenty years. The Conference on Prison Reform in 1877 and the annual meetings of the National Conference of Charity and Corrections frequently endorsed the policies of prison classification, marks, and tickets of leave. Yet however different these approaches were from Jacksonian precepts, still they looked primarily, indeed exclusively, to the penitentiary, its internal organization and routine, to effect rehabilitation. Inmates should be given their manhood, but behind walls; inmates should move up grade by grade, but from prison tier to prison tier. Thus the *Declaration* could insist in all good faith: "Reformation is a work of time; and a benevolent regard to the good of the criminal himself, as well as to the protection of society, requires that *his sentence be long enough for reformatory processes to take effect.*"[18] The best-intentioned observers in the post–Civil War decades remained committed to reform through incarceration. They opted to reconstitute the prison, to correct it from within. Import a grading system and link prisoners' self-interest to their improved behavior, and then prisons would realize their rehabilitative purpose.

To substantiate these opinions, reformers enthusiastically cited the experience of one "model" institution, the Reformatory at Elmira, New York. Here was a real-world example that demonstrated the efficacy of their proposals. Elmira was the experiment that revealed the rightness and the practicality of their notions, making it the proper successor to the Auburn and Pennsylvania penitentiaries.

Opened in New York in 1877 and dominated for the next twenty years by its superintendent, Zebulon Brockway, Elmira was the most ambitious attempt to fulfill the 1870 *Declaration of Principles.* As a reformatory, it held first-time felons between the ages of sixteen and thirty who, in the estimation of the sentencing judge, were capable of reformation. Its inmates, in other words, were both in terms of age and in terms of seriousness of offense midway between those in the juvenile houses of refuge and those in the state prisons. Brockway's design incorporated the precepts of the new penology. Elmira adminstered a form of indeterminate sentence: the judge committed the offender to Elmira and its managers then determined his date of release, subject only to the rule that inmates could not be held longer than the maximum term that the legislature set for the particular offense. "It is only by this means," insisted Brockway, "that every avenue of hope for release from imprisonment, save the single one of *personal fitness for further liberty,* can be closed to the prisoner . . . and his mind be turned . . . to the matter of preparing himself for restoration to citizenship."[19]

A highly elaborate grading system accompanied the indeterminate sentence. Brockway established three classifications: the inmate entered at grade two and if he behaved himself well (fulfilling work and school assignments and committing no disciplinary infractions), he could earn up to nine marks a month; thus, six months or fifty-four marks later, he could win promotion to grade one — the only grade from which he could be released into the community. On the other hand, an uncooperative inmate was demoted to grade three, "for either of three reasons":

(1) Crookedness . . . when it reveals the continued criminality of the man.
(2) Quarreling, when it culminates in an assault or fight.
(3) Such disregard of rules or proprieties as shows indifference to progress or great want of self-control, if continued for three months or more.

After three months of satisfactory behavior in grade three, an inmate would be promoted to grade two, and so on.

The grades also determined privileges within the institution. Inmates in the first grade wore "neat blue uniforms with navy cap, they have better rooms, dine at tables in a great dining hall, and have the privilege of conversing with each other during meals. Men in this grade move in larger platoons under command of a captain of their own grade. They can write and receive letters every week." By contrast, third grade inmates wore "clothing of red color, their rooms bereft of all, save bed, blankets and bucket." They could not write or receive letters or have visitors; they marched about in lock step. Conditions in the middle grade fit between the two extremes: the rooms had cupboard, chair, and gas light; the beds had sheets; and inmates were allowed to write a letter once a month. Those whose behavior could not be controlled under this system were confined to solitary, or given assignments to hard labor, or, finally, transferred to a state prison. Elmira was the elite setting, relying upon the back-up sanction of a tougher and less desirable institution.[20]

Elmira's publicists declared the design a resounding success and a proper model for widespread emulation. "This institution," Brockway announced, "based upon the indeterminate sentence and the marking system, constitutes an ideal reformatory prison," exemplifying "the possibility . . . of a successful reformative treatment for criminals. The high ground taken by the Reformatory, not in an ideal sense, but in its practical application . . . properly supplements the recommendation for an extension of the work in operation here to other prisons." Indeed, Elmira's annual reports offered statistical support for these judgments (provided that one did not scrutinize them too carefully). Eighty-one percent of the inmates discharged underwent "probable reformation," — a figure arrived at by assuming that those not rearrested within six months and half of those who had been "lost sight of" were law-abiding.[21]

Elmira's claims were taken at face value and its organization came to represent the reform ideal. The editorial pages of *Science* said of Elmira's 1886 annual report: "Every page of it is of the greatest interest. It is the record of the progress of an attempt . . . to make good and useful citizens out of a class of men usually given over altogether by society as dangerous. How well Mr. Z. R. Brockway, the superintendent, has succeeded in his task of reformation, is well known to students of our penal institutions." The *North American Review*, as well, publicized Elmira's system. Inmates at other institutions, it claimed, had a sullen and depressed appearance, constituting "a most depressing and dispiriting sight." By contrast, at Elmira, a "great industrial and educational establishment," the inmate was eager "to work out his own salvation." Accordingly, he moved with "alertness and vigor. . . . Stupidity and hopelessness have given place to intelligence and ambition. The change is astonishing." In this same spirit, one writer in the *Journal* of the American Social Science Association, who wondered "How Far May We Abolish Prisons?" answered, to the degree that we put men into reformatories like Elmira. After all, "Elmira reforms more than 80 percent of those who are sent there."[22]

What all these claims and respectful citations constituted was an endorsement of incarceration for rehabilitating the deviant. To post–Civil War American reformers, Elmira proved that prisons, if properly designed, could fulfill their original promise.

Hence, incompetence and abuse were not the inevitable result of institutionalization, but the fault of one particular warden or guard; failure reflected individual inadequacy, not a flaw in the concept of the penitentiary. The ideal of an institution that cured was practical and realizable — and if reality fell short, then the problem rested with one or another administrator.

Indeed, these postulates seemed so persuasive that even scandals at Elmira itself did not dampen enthusiasm for the model. In 1894 an executive investigation into charges that Brockway practiced "cruel, brutal, excessive, degrading and unusual punishment of inmates" finally exonerated him. But the hearings revealed that discipline at Elmira was certainly not, as promised, consistently mild or encouraging. Brockway had frequent recourse to the strap (some 30 percent of the inmates felt it and a whipping occurred on the average of twice a week); that the twenty-two-inch-long leather whip was, ostensibly, first soaked in water to soften the blows was not much of a mitigating circumstance. Brockway also used solitary confinement regularly, with the convict shackled by his hands or his feet to the cell door — and again, the fact that "in no case within the past ten years has a convict been shackled both by his hands and his feet at the same time" did not amount to a very powerful qualification.[23]

Despite these exposes at Elmira, or the even more obvious examples of corruption in other prisons, well-meaning observers continued to cite Elmira as evidence that failings were idiosyncratic to an institution or its managers, not evidence that the concept of incarceration itself might demand rethinking. The impact of the Elmira model was not to spawn imitations; neither it nor the 1870 *Declaration of Principles* affected American prison routines during these years. Rather, Elmira appeared to justify contentions that incarceration, properly redesigned, should remain at the center of the criminal justice system.

Perhaps the most sustained and significant attack on the concept of institutionalization emerged in the field of insanity. In the 1870's and 1880's, leaders in the new discipline of neurology launched a major critique of medical superintendents and their institutions that at times almost challenged the very idea of incarceration. Yet, when one looks beneath the bitter rhetoric to the substance of their recommendations, it turns out that the neurologists had little to offer as alternatives to institutionalization. More often than not, their proposals aimed to give the laboratory a place in the asylum, not to alter the system of care. The results of their recommendations would have been somewhat smaller, better supervised, and more research-oriented facilities. But institutions would have continued to be the mainstay of the system.

To the leading neurologists of the period, such as Edward Spitzka and William Hammond, the study of mental disease had to be a part of the study of normal psychological functioning. As historian Charles Rosenberg has explained, neurologists believed that "the same mechanisms that governed ordinary mental life also determined the manifestations of mental illness." This belief had a very particular consequence for them: the focus of investigation was to be almost exclusively anatomical. Progress in understanding and treating insanity would come from the laboratory and the dissecting room, not from observing the behavior of the insane or from analyzing the excessive mobility of American social life. Insanity, as Spitzka argued, could not be fathomed apart from the "whole nervous system. . . . Psychiatry is but a subsidiary branch of neurology. . . . The study of insanity should be considered a subdivision of neurology."[24]

These postulates underlay the neurologists' unrelieved disdain for the asylum and its keepers. The superintendents, charged Spitzka, had produced "nothing worthy of notice . . . in the fields of pathology and clinical observation. . . . One is justified . . . to deploy the strongest terms of censure in characterizing the apathy and ignorance manifested by those concerned in this dereliction of scientific duty." Moreover, asylum superintendents had excluded the neurologists from their institutions, thus not only failing to carry out their own scientific duties but preventing others from doing so as well. They also failed to keep clinical records or to provide therapeutic programs, instead dispensing excessive doses of drugs. Indeed, Spitzka's scorn for them was so great that he would not even credit them with being decent administrators.

"Judging by the average asylum reports," he declared, "we are inclined to believe that certain superintendents are experts in gardening and farming (although the farm account frequently comes out on the wrong side of the ledger), tin roofing (although the roof and cupola is usually leaky), drain-pipe laying (although the grounds are often moist and unhealthy), engineering (though the wards are either too hot or too cold) . . . in short, experts at everything except the diagnosis, pathology and the treatment of insanity." In the end, the neurologists were convinced that asylum care was not only crude and incompetent, but cruel and inhumane. It relied too heavily on restraining devices and seclusion rooms. "We do not think," concluded Spitzka, "that the crib-beds constitute the 'proper treatment which the patient has a right to claim.'" Medical superintendents, in a word, were despots and not benevolent ones at that.[25]

Not surprisingly, the neurologists went on to urge a reduced reliance upon institutionalization for the mentally ill. In contrast to the pleas of medical superintendents that patients come to the asylum at the onset of symptoms, they argued that many patients could be treated as well, perhaps even better, at home. "The medical profession," declared William Hammond, "is, as a body, fully as capable of treating cases of insanity as cases of any other disease, and that in many instances sequestration is not only unnecessary but positively injurious." Hammond, in fact, was very conscious that incarceration meant a loss of freedom to the patient — which in itself had detrimental effects. Supporters of institutionalization "fail entirely to appreciate the strength of the passion for liberty which is in the human heart. . . . All the comforts which the insane person has in his captivity are but a miserable compensation for his entire loss of liberty . . . the mighty suffering of a lifelong imprisonment." Asylum care was appropriate for "those who cannot be properly taken care of at home." But for others, "the violent rupture of social and family ties is especially injurious," as was "the association which they are compelled to have with lunatics."[26]

Nevertheless, for all their sensitivity to claims of liberty and to the damaging effects of confining the mad to the world of the

mad, the neurologists were far more articulate about the faults of
the existing system than they were capable of designing alternatives. On the attack, they were cogent and precise; as naysayers
they were brilliant. But as soon as they moved to their own
programs, language and thought became much more general,
abstract, and even muddled. They knew well what they did not
like. But given the infancy of their own discipline, they had very
little to offer that was innovative.

Thus, the bulk of the recommendations that neurologists offered aimed to improve institutional conditions. To make asylums over into something other than houses of detention, Spitzka
recommended banning the crib; reducing restraint "to the greatest possible minimum"; providing patients with employment;
keeping fuller statistics; enlarging boards of trustees (with doctors and lawyers represented); expanding the power of commissions in lunacy (ideally composed of two doctors and one lawyer); and, of greatest significance, conducting systematic research
into the physiology of insanity through regular autopsies (which
should be made "compulsory by legal enactment" in asylum laboratories). The list was long but not especially novel. It aimed
more at preventing abuses than at delivering treatment; it attempted to bring more observers into the asylum but it was not
directly relevant to the substance of treatment. The program was
most specific about limiting the power of the superintendent, but
most general about improving the lot of the patient — and the
one goal would not necessarily promote the other. The suggestion
of making more occupational programs available for the insane
was a lame one, and whatever promise the autopsies had was
speculative. In many cases it appears that all the neurologists
really wanted was space in the basement, with very little of substance to offer about the therapies to be administered on the
floors above.[27]

As might be expected, then, medical superintendents did not
have much trouble with these proposals; and, invective aside, one
or another of them made similar recommendations, only with
more sympathy for the difficulties that administrators faced. Yes,
restraints were to be regretted, but they were, after all, necessary

for the protection of some self-abusive patients — and therefore the equipment should remain under the superintendents' tight control. Yes, cottages and wards should become more homelike and the numbers of inmates and degrees of overcrowding should be reduced — but always remember that the insane were better off in the asylum than in the almshouse. Yes, lunacy commissions were not to be avoided altogether — still, the meddlesome quality of the state should never be underestimated. Care at home for the insane was a good idea — except that the family was often totally ignorant of how to control the person and could be even more restrictive and punitive in its approach than the asylum. As one superintendent noted: "Those surrounding an insane person often conduct themselves with little judgment, and sometimes without humanity. . . . They either oppose indiscriminately every tendency to activity, good or bad, or else yield to the most fantastic and unreasonable whim in the hope of pacification. . . . Patients are often brought to the hospital barbarously bound with ropes or handcuffed, when such restraint is unnecessary; even punishment and cruel beatings are resorted to." Not for the last time would a recitation of horrors (real or imagined) in the community be used to justify the perpetuation of institutions.[28]

In sum, the reputation and the performance of post–Civil War asylums reveals that institutional abuse and failure, inadequacy and incompetence, would not in and of themselves necessarily or inevitably promote innovations or alternatives. Not only were the conveniences of asylum care attractive, but the most benevolent-minded citizens of the period continued to subscribe to the notion that institutions were the lesser of the evils or, more enthusiastically, that they could be upgraded and redesigned to accomplish good. Rehabilitation remained so appealing a goal that its prospect sustained the legitimacy of both penitentiaries and insane asylums. Hence, institutions survived this second round of scrutiny. The children of the founders, with much less cause than their parents, continued to justify incarceration if less for its present performance than at least for its future promise.

II

The World of Criminal Justice

CHAPTER TWO

Individual Justice:
The Progressive Design

THE PROGRESSIVE ERA marked a major divide in attitudes and practices toward the deviant, creating new ideas and procedures to combat crime, delinquency, and mental illness. Americans in the period 1900–1920 set out to design and implement alternatives to incarceration, a change that had a very particular meaning to them. Institutions did not so much represent buildings with walls but a style of operation that was rigid, inflexible, and machine-like. The Progressives were anti-institutional, not in that they intended to break down buildings and walls or even to return the majority of deviants to the community, but rather in that, by implementing open-ended, informal, and highly flexible policies, they were devising an individual, case-by-case strategy for rehabilitation.

Thus, Americans enacted probation, parole, and indeterminate sentences for adult offenders, established juvenile courts for delinquents, and founded outpatient clinics for the mentally ill. In this same spirit, and without fear of self-contradiction, they redesigned prisons, reformatories, and insane asylums. To be sure, one can locate precedents for some aspects of this movement in such documents as the 1870 *Declaration of Principles* or in the history of the Elmira Reformatory. But what is remarkable is how much more ambitious and influential this Progressive agenda was. In genuinely novel ways, it substituted discretionary authority for uniform rules in all programs affecting the deviant.

The Progressive character of the new measures in adult criminal justice is readily apparent. Probation, the immediate post-conviction release of offenders into the community under supervision with limitations upon personal liberty, became common between 1900 and 1920. The idea itself was certainly older — in the 1850's, John Augustus, a Boston shoemaker, persuaded some judges to give him custody over juvenile offenders. But not until the Progressive period did probation become a popular courtroom disposition. In 1900, only six states provided for probation. In 1915 alone, thirty-three states created or extended the procedure; and by 1920, every state permitted juvenile probation and thirty-three states, adult probation.[1]

At the same time, the indeterminate sentence with release through parole altered the character of prison sentences. Before 1900, judges set the precise term of incarceration for adult offenders. After 1900, judges levied the minimum and maximum terms, leaving it for parole boards to decide upon the moment of release and the conditions of post-release supervision. This revolutionary change was accomplished with incredible speed. In 1900, only a handful of states allowed for parole, generally reserving it for young first offenders in reformatories. By 1923, almost half of all inmates sentenced to state prisons were under an indeterminate sentence, and a little over half of all releases were under parole.[2]

The rapidity with which these transformations occurred, the fact that criminal justice assumed a new character within twenty years, reflected the broad nature of the supporting coalition. State after state passed probation and parole legislation with little debate and no controversy. Concerned citizens, settlement house workers, criminologists, social workers, psychologists, and psychiatrists stood together with directors of charitable societies, judges, district attorneys, wardens, and superintendents. To find a common goal uniting such a diverse group is itself surprising. When one remembers the stake that many of these groups had in existing practices, the harmony of views becomes still more astonishing. Judges were supporting a procedure that transferred their sentencing power to a parole board; wardens were almost unanimously in favor of measures that appeared to be anti-institutional. Traditionally hard-line, "no-coddling-the-criminal" types such as district attorneys also backed programs that could be seen as being distinctly soft on the offender. And that settlement house workers and social workers agreed with directors of charitable societies was no less unprecedented.

As might be expected, each group in this diverse coalition had its own reasons for supporting the measures, and these must be carefully sorted out. As we shall see, ideological considerations played a critical role. The events of the 1870's and 1880's had made it eminently clear that institutional abuses need not spark change, that is, unless they are perceived in novel ways. So too, operational considerations assumed a vital importance: many of those who held power within criminal justice had substantial self-interested reasons for prompting these innovations. Succinctly put, an alliance did take place between self-styled reformers and administrators, between the ideal and the practical. We must understand, then, how such a partnership occurred, and, perhaps most important, what became of it, what were the actual results — and this question brings us to the essence of Progressivism, possibly to the essence of most efforts to do good.

In the beginning was the idea, and it was a bold and hopeful one. A number of students of deviant behavior, who for reasons of clarity we will simply call reformers, were convinced that they understood the complex causes of crime and were capable of designing a program to eradicate it. Their certainty is all the more striking for they did not minimize the difficulty of the challenge. To the contrary: these Progressive reformers prided themselves on recognizing the deeply rooted character of social issues which their predecessors had ignored or dismissed. Progressives believed, for example, that the origins of poverty went deeper than the immorality of the poor; it was not merely bad habits that were responsible for dependency. Indeed, the confidence of these reformers seems all the more difficult to account for when one remembers just how disturbed they were about the hordes of immigrants flocking to American shores, about the anonymity of the city, and about the new size and strength of American corporations. It might even seem reasonable to address Progressivism in terms of a panic, an effort to retrieve the status of the once-dominant middle class or the values of an older and homogeneous rural America. But the burden of analysis here must be to explain the sources of optimism, the willingness to strike out in new directions with an inordinate self-assuredness about the results.

Reformers' special approach to social problems reflected, first, the influence of the new social sciences. They were typically the graduates of the new colleges and universities whose curriculums included courses on the "punishment of criminality" and "public and private charities." By 1890, as a survey of the just-organized American Social Science Association discovered, a wide variety of state universities (from Indiana to Southern California), prestigious private universities (Harvard, Brown, and Columbia), and men's and women's colleges (Amherst, Franklin and Marshall, Vassar, and Bryn Mawr) were offering such courses. And the lessons that they taught were invigorating. To understand and solve a social problem, students were instructed to go out and gather all the "facts" of the case. Armed with the data, they would then be able to analyze the issue in "scientific" fashion and discover the right antidote. At the same time, the data would provide them with all the necessary arguments for persuading a legislature to enact remedial measures. Clearly, more than a touch of naivete clung to this method; a youthful enthusiasm elevated the power of a positivistic approach, as though the facts would speak for themselves, both to would-be reformers and to politicians. But this perspective meant that the social sciences were disseminating a very heady message.[3]

The organization that best exemplified this Progressive outlook was the settlement house. The city, or rather the slum, was, as Richard Mayo-Smith, one of the first professors of sociology, explained, "the natural laboratory of social science"; and the mission of the settlements was to gather and analyze its data. To Vida Scudder, a founder of Boston's Dennison House, and to other settlers, ghetto life was "a sociological laboratory where the patient, accurate and sympathetic observer [note the rankings of the traits] may get at the truth." Or, as she explained more fully: "He who would combat effectively the ills of our body politic: ignorance, poverty, crime, political corruption and moral disease — must see things as they are and reason from intimate and comprehensive knowledge as to cause and cure." There is no exaggerating just how prevalent and characteristically Progressive this perspective was. As Jane Addams observed, those who came to settlements in the 1890's were likely to say: "We must do something about the social disorder." Those who came after 1900 were prone to exclaim, with no less enthusiasm: "We want to investigate something."[4]

The quality of these investigations emerges in Robert Hunter's classic text, *Poverty* (1904). Hunter, the son of a prosperous Indiana manufacturer and a graduate of Indiana University, spent several years living at Hull House before moving to New York in 1902 to become head social worker at University Settlement. There he led the successful agitation for a state child labor law and then, building on his first-hand knowledge of social conditions, published *Poverty*. In true Progressive fashion, Hunter opened with a statistical analysis of the problem. The facts were that 14 percent of the population in good times and 20 percent in hard times, to a total of at least 10 million Americans, lived in poverty. And to Hunter these facts did speak for themselves: they demonstrated the inadequacy of a moralistic interpretation of dependency. The major causes of poverty were unemployment, sickness, work accidents, and below-subsistence wages that did not permit a worker to "maintain a state of physical efficiency." Conceding that some among the poor might be victims of their own indulgences (the pauper class), Hunter was most intent on demonstrating that "there are also many, many thousand families who receive wages so inadequate that no care in spending, however wise it may be, will make them suffice for the family needs." In a phrase, the dependent were "victims of our neglect."[5]

Despite these grim observations, Hunter's tract exuded a sense of confidence, which points to the second critical component in the Progressive mind-set: an ultimate confidence in the benefits of the American system. Hunter contrasted two possible reform strategies: the one, which he immediately rejected, was the "Tolstoyan" way, "a voluntary return to nature . . . abandon the great city and the factory," celebrating "the extinct industrial order of previous centuries"; the other, Hunter's way, "has faith in the wisdom of our economic development, however much it may deplore the misery at present incident to it." The great task of reform, Hunter concluded, was "equalizing opportunity." The change would not be accomplished quickly: "We are impatient and restless at the delay." Nevertheless, he was certain that "the time will come when an awakened social conscience will insist upon these necessary social measures."[6]

In effect, Progressives had no intention of turning their backs on the marvels of American industrialism. They had no fundamental quarrel with the American economic and social system, and no inclination to offer radical prescriptions. Instead, they were convinced that the enactment of some specific reforms would enable all citizens to enjoy a high standard of living and opportunity for upward mobility. Certain greedy businessmen and speculators would have to give up excess profits and be curbed in their activities, but no one's true or real interests, as reformers defined them, would have to be sacrificed. The poor need not rise up against the rich or tear down the machines in order to obtain a fair share.

Progressives were equally convinced of the viability of cultural uplift and of the supreme desirability of middle-class life in cultural as well as material terms. No crisis of values divided them; no agonizing debates pitted their life styles against those of the immigrant or the poor. The model was clear: all Americans were to become middle-class Americans. Everyone was to become hard-working, to abandon Old World vices, to respect and accumulate private property. "It is fatal for democracy," argued that leading Progressive, John Dewey, "to permit the formation of fixed classes," and a host of Progressive organizations, from the settlement houses and the playgrounds to new-style public schools and health clinics, set out to bridge the gap between the classes. Of course, the traffic across that bridge would run in only one direction: from them to us, from alien to American, from lower class to middle class. Taken together, these assumptions made the Progressives altogether certain that the stability of American society was at one with the welfare of all its citizens. Social cohesion and individual betterment went hand in hand. Public interest and self-interest coincided.[7]

But this coincidence did not mean to the Progressives that some invisible hand would automatically produce the common well-being from the sum of individual self-interested actions. Progressives, to come to the third and perhaps most distinguishing feature of the movement, opposed this nineteenth-century doctrine. As they saw it, the state would have to exercise its authority to correct imbalances, to bring about equality, to realize the common good. The "awakened social conscience" and the "necessary social measures" that Hunter called for would have to be achieved through state action. Herbert Croly, probably the most outstanding Progressive theorist, made this argument still more powerfully in *The Promise of American Life*. For Croly, the nineteenth-century faith in an invisible hand had died with the rise of the cities, the factories, and the corporations. "No pre-established harmony can then exist between the free and abundant satisfactions of private needs and the accomplishment of a morally and socially desirable result." Rather, he insisted, "the American problem is a social problem"; the nation was in need of "a more highly socialized democracy." To realize the promise of American life, the public sector would have to guide, even dominate, the private sector. The state, not the individual, would define the social good and take final responsibility for its fulfillment.[8] In sum, for Progressives, only the state could make the individual free. Only its enlarged authority could satisfy the particular needs of all citizens.

Armed with these principles, reformers set out to explore and respond to the problem of deviant behavior. They were confident that they knew how to analyze the causes of criminality, what should constitute the proper kind of treatment, and how it should be implemented. Their answers can be put briefly and then explicated: the origins of deviancy had to be uncovered through a case-by-case study, an individual approach. Ameliorative action had to be fitted specifically to each individual's special needs, and therefore required a maximum of flexibility and discretion. Finally, the state could be trusted to carry out these precepts; indeed, the state had the obligation to act in the best and mutual interest of the offender and the community. The maxims were coherent and powerful, reflecting Progressivism at its most ambitious and promising to yield effective results.

The most critical component of the Progressive attempt to understand the causes of crime was not an agreed-upon answer but an agreed-upon method. There was no single all-embracing explanation that dominated professional or lay thought during these years. To some analysts, environmental considerations were most important; others looked to psychological elements and still others emphasized biological principles. Whatever the specific explanation, all of them endorsed a case-by-case approach. The point was to understand the facts of each offender's life history. The investigation was to focus not on the questions of personal guilt, a matter which all the schools dismissed as irrelevant, but on the individual circumstances of the offender. Indeed, the method held the key to rehabilitation. In the diagnosis would be the prescription. To understand the particulars of the case was to solve it.

The most popular and influential interpretation of deviant behavior in the opening decades of the twentieth century was the environmental interpretation. Seemingly, there was nothing novel about such an approach; the Jacksonians, too, had faulted society for crime. But there the similarities ended. The Jacksonians had focused on the apparently pervasive moral weaknesses of the community. Viewing their world against the model of a tight and self-enclosed eighteenth-century village, they found their own society to be corrupt and corrupting. Extraordinary social and geographic mobility undermined such institutions as the family and the church and disrupted every force for stability. Not surprisingly, then, the morally weak citizen moved inexorably from the tavern to the theater to the gambling den, and on to the prison. The Progressives, taking their point of departure from the social sciences, traced criminality to specific social and economic causes. The problem lay not in the fundamental structure of American society but in one particular aspect. The fact was that the promise of the system did not extend evenly to all segments of the society: it did not penetrate the ghetto and the slum. Thus, an understanding of the etiology of crime demanded a very close scrutiny of conditions in these special enclaves.

The most influential and elaborate statement of this position appeared in Sophonisba Breckinridge and Edith Abbott, *The Delinquent Child and the Home*. Both women were leaders in the field of social work, which in this era was indistinguishable from sociology in their mutual concern for solving social problems. Both authors were also settlement house residents and participated in practically every major social welfare campaign. From this background they traced the roots of delinquency directly to the immigrant's social and economic circumstances. The very process of immigration, they explained, could produce deviants. Immigrant parents were ignorant of truancy laws designed to keep children in school; they did not understand that picking up coal from railroad yards was not the same thing as going over a field to glean what harvesters had left behind. Breckenridge and Abbott described how the condition of poverty produced delinquency. Desperate need could cause children to steal; the demands and routine of factory work could prompt a girl to search for easier ways to make a living. Unsatisfied economic ambitions could often lead immigrant parents to exploit their children — and the pressure to bring home money might tempt

them into crime. Also, mothers were often so busy working that
they were unable to supervise their children; and illness and industrial accidents caused frequent deaths among parents, forcing
homeless children to take up a life in crime. In short, ghetto
poverty created delinquents and delinquents grew up to become
criminals.[9]

To be sure, Progressives did not altogether abandon traditionally moralistic judgments. Robert Hunter's analysis of poverty
included a condemnation of the "pauper" and Breckinridge and
Abbott, too, linked deviancy to depravity. Criminality was inevitable when children were raised in homes "in which they have
been accustomed from their earliest infancy to drunkenness, immorality, obscene and vulgar language, filthy and degraded conditions of living." But just as Progressives took as their primary
responsibility the identification of the environmental causes of
poverty, so they offered a checklist of ghetto inadequacies that
composed the causes of crime. One examination of the "conditions in New York City that are conducive to criminality" noted
that in the ghettos the population was "enormously congested,
living conditions are unspeakably bad, and proper sanitation and
fresh air are at a premium." So too, "conditions of employment in
the sweat shops and loft manufactories . . . [and] the seasonal
fluctuations of labor are provocative of unrest and lawlessness."
Another tract located the origins of both crime and poverty "in
wretched living conditions, in child labor, in the wrong kind of
education, in orphanhood, in unsupervised street life. . . . We see
the slums . . . and the street life of city urchins, and we subcon-
sciously question what we would have become, perhaps, under
like conditions. We know that the environment has prevented
many a man now a criminal from starting right."[10]

Yet in the minds of these analysts, as with Hunter and other
Progressives, such considerations bred confidence, not despair.
The problem was manageable: it could be located spatially in the
ghetto and it could be solved, given the right programs. The bad
news all related to the immigrant slums. The good news was that
the rest of American society was strong, prosperous, and stable.

Thus, the goals for reform were obvious and eminently practical: to bring the benefits and values of middle-class life to the poor, to incorporate the poor within the promise of American life, to make the newcomer over into the native-born, with the appropriate life style and standard of living. While no one can read this message fifty years later without being struck by its facile and even smug optimism, in fact the Progressives thought the task altogether realizable. Supremely confident of the preeminence of their economic system and social values, they shared a missionary's vigor and zeal.

Progressives adopted two strategies, one designed to treat the broader causes of crime, the other to rehabilitate the deviant himself. They actively lobbied before municipal boards and state legislatures to correct ghetto deficiencies, from congested living arrangements (through tenement house reform) and unsupervised street life (through the organization of playgrounds and clubs) to dangerous work places (through accident compensation laws) and unhealthy conditions (through municipal bureaus of hygiene). At the same time, they looked to respond to the offender directly, in a case-by-case fashion. They were predisposed to such an approach because of their belief that social classes should be brought closer together, in an immediate as well as a long-term sense. To this end, settlement houses were located in the midst of the slums and their residents tried to act the role of good neighbors. But more, reformers believed that the environmental causes of crime were so varied that no one general prescription could fit all cases. Only a one-to-one approach could uncover the slum's effects on the offender.

Most important of all, Progressives were certain that an environmental interpretation of crime made a mockery of personal culpability. No one who was raised in a slum could be held strictly accountable for his actions. The wretchedness of the social setting was so great that responsibility could not be assigned in uniform and predictable fashion.[11] Elemental fairness dictated that the offender be treated as an individual. It was not merely a sensible and effective principle, but a just one. Any other method was vengeful. In sum, the Progressive's environmental interpretation of crime led directly to a highly discretionary system of justice.

There was a second approach to the origins of deviancy that gained credence in the Progressive period and even greater popularity in the 1920's and 1930's, an interpretation that emphasized psychological over environmental considerations. This explanation looked more closely to the mental state than to the social circumstances of the offender — and yet it too, for different reasons, promoted an individual and discretionary response to the deviant. Whatever conceptual differences divided the two schools, they both came together to create a peculiarly Progressive system of criminal justice.

The work of the psychiatrist William Healy demonstrates how neatly the two perspectives came together. Healy began his medical training in Chicago, went on to direct the Psychopathic Institute of the Chicago juvenile court, and eventually headed up the Judge Baker Foundation child guidance clinic in Boston. In 1915 he published one of the most influential statements on the crime problem, *The Individual Delinquent,* or as its subtitle put it, *A Text-Book of Diagnosis and Prognosis for All Concerned in Understanding Offenders.* Healy was confident that a detailed knowledge of the individual offender and a close examination of the dynamics of each case would clarify the causes of deviant behavior. He was certainly not an environmentalist: "Poverty, and crowded housing, and so on, by themselves alone are not productive of criminalism. It is only when these conditions in turn produce suggestions, and bad habits of mind, and mental imagery of low order, that the trouble in conduct ensues." For Healy, "all problems connected with bad environmental conditions should be carefully viewed in the light of the mental life."

It was the roots of the "bad habits of mind" and "mental imagery" that he set out to explore. His terminology owed much to the work of the child study expert, G. Stanley Hall; his notion of mental imagery carried a debt to Freud. (Healy was an early reader of Freud, but his grasp of Freudian principles was weak.)

But the most notable feature of Healy's approach was its very eclecticism. He was trying to offer psychological explanations of criminality without accepting or promulgating one psychological theory. He had, in other words, no set of organizing principles to mind, convinced instead that a devotion to the "individual case" would clarify the causes of deviant behavior.[12]

The results of this approach were evident throughout Healy's tract. His summary of the "causative factors" of criminality ranged from mental abnormalities and defective home conditions to mental conflict, improper sex experiences, bad companions, and defective interests. (In fact, the list was reminiscent of the charts on the origins of insanity that mid-nineteenth-century medical superintendents included in their annual reports.) And Healy's efforts to refine the categories did not proceed very far. He attempted to differentiate between "major causes" and "minor causes," but beyond his own personal judgment he offered no criteria for making such distinctions. His results, then, were self-confirming. He believed that mental abnormalities were more determinative than the environment and thus the one, predictably enough, scored higher than the other on his "scale of significance." Healy did finally acknowledge that although causation was intricate, the links could be plotted in a diagram. But the result was a scattering of lines here and there across a page.[13]

Despite these problems, Healy's work, and that of like-minded psychiatrists, quickly won an enthusiastic following in the Progressive era. For one reason, the psychiatrists were confident that criminality could be successfully treated. Case studies would not only define causes but produce effective prescriptions. The mental set of the criminal was as easily corrected — perhaps even more easily corrected — than the noxious environment of the slum. For another, psychiatrists also had little patience with the concept of culpability. Like the environmentalists, they talked much more of finding cures than assigning moral blame. Finally, and most telling, their actual suggestions for "treatment," the advice that they offered, repeated and confirmed the proposals of the environmentalists. Despite the novelty of their language, their remedies were identical to those that settlement house residents offered. The psychiatrists used different labels and terminology, but they intended to combat the same enemies with the same weapons.

As a case in point, take Healy's approach to Mary Doe, age eighteen, a shopgirl who repeatedly stole from department stores. Healy traced her difficulties to the fact that she had "poor educational advantages"; she had been kept away from school so much as to have "a dearth of healthy mental interests." Moreover, Mary Doe suffered from "mental conflict over sex affairs" as a result of "no guiding hand" instructing and protecting her. The environmentalists were completely comfortable with such an analysis — terms like "mental conflict" might be unusual, but the ill effects of department stores, bad companions, and school truancy were very familiar arguments. Healy's recommendations for treatment were equally familiar. Mary Doe would improve "if some good woman will give her a helping hand. . . . Change of occupation, friendship with some woman competent to become her confidant, adviser and helper, and development of healthy mental interests, we feel sure, will do what is needed." Just the task for a settlement house resident.[14]

Healy's psychological interpretation of deviancy also fit well with other Progressives' confidence in the soundness of the American system. If mental conflict was at the root of the problem, then social conflict was not. It was sex, not capitalism; it was images, not reality. How Healy's line of interpretation reinforced the reformers' faith in the promise of American life.

Both the environmentalists and, even more obviously, the psychiatrists found in the prestige and progress of medical research still another reason to promote a case-by-case analysis of the deviant — and to anticipate successful treatments. It is difficult to sort out to what degree the medical approach inspired the reformers and to what degree they were using the medical experience to give legitimacy to ideas already conceived. In any event, for all Progressives the most popular metaphors in criminal justice were medical. Just as doctors approached each patient individually and scientifically, concerned not with moral guilt but with the source of the illness, so those in criminal justice should approach each offender. "Diagnosis," argued Warren Spaulding, one of the most active reformers in Massachusetts, "is as necessary in the treatment of badness as it is in the treatment of illness." Instead of focusing upon culpability, the system had to investigate the offender's "past character and conduct, surroundings, associates, and tendencies . . . what family the offender has; whether he works regularly and supports those dependent upon him, whether he has habits which lead him into criminal ways, etc. . . . All these things, and many others, must be known by the court before it can pass intelligently upon questions relating to the disposal of a criminal case." In a similar vein, Edward Devine, editor of *Survey*, a leading Progressive social welfare publication, explained that criminal justice reformers "take the position which the physician takes toward his patient, who is not trying to form some moral judgment as to what he has done, but who puts himself in sympathetic relation with the difficulty as it now stands and is primarily concerned with trying to get at the root of the trouble." For Devine, this perspective represented the novel contribution of the movement: "Our new attitude . . . toward the criminal is not one of forming moral judgments against him, but it is intelligently finding out what the trouble is and putting into operation those influences and agencies . . . that will restore him to society."[15]

This same analogy and conclusion pervaded Progressive legal theory. One prestigious committee of the newly organized American Institute of Criminal Law and Criminology (a committee of which Roscoe Pound, the most important legal theorist of the period, was one member) opened its argument on behalf of reform by contrasting old-fashioned medical practice, with its reliance upon the calomel pill and bloodletting lancet, to modern practice, which searched for "the causes of disease . . . various, but distinguishable by diagnosis and research," and then prescribed treatment, finding "specific modes . . . for specific causes or symptoms." Criminal justice had to follow this route. It could no longer be "indiscriminate and machine-like, but must be adapted to the causes, and to the man as affected by those causes." The science of penology should emulate the science of medicine — and that premise enlarged reformers' expectations. "The extinction of the criminal class and the ultimate abolition of prisons," one reformer concluded, "are ideals to be kept in view, just as the elimination of disease must be the perpetual aim of medical sciences."[16]

Even those Progressives who were attracted to a third type of explanation for deviancy, that is, to the doctrines of eugenics, linked their views on heredity to the larger principle of individual diagnosis and treatment, and they did it with some optimism. To Thomas Mott Osborne, whose reform activities at Sing-Sing will be explored later (Chapter 4), heredity was one more factor that made it all the more necessary to investigate the particulars of each case rather than simply to allocate guilt. "A man's actions are the resultant of many forces. His heredity, his environment, his training, all react upon that mysterious something — the man's own individuality. If the influences which really form a man's character are hard to determine, it is still harder to find adequate reason to blame him for the conduct which results. He is certainly not responsible for his heredity . . . he is certainly not responsible for an unfortunate environment." Hence, Osborne concluded, " 'Judge not that ye be not judged' . . . is . . . not only good ethics, it is sound penology."[17]

Progressives even managed to take the arguments of Cesare Lombroso, the outstanding late-nineteenth-century continental theorist on crime, whose findings (at least as popularly read) seemed to prove the notion of the "born criminal," and use them to support their own views. They cited Lombroso's "born criminal" as one more reason to differentiate among offenders, to respond to the criminal and not to the crime. But they also noted, and correctly, a shift in his position. Lombroso's earliest writings were devoted almost exclusively to the role of heredity in criminality; his later works gave more attention to environmental causes. Thus, when the Progressive-minded American Institute of Criminal Law set out to translate the writings of the great European criminologists, their first choice was Lombroso. His work, the Institute maintained, would encourage Americans to "study all the possible data that can be causes of crime — the man's heredity, the man's physical and moral make-up [the old Lombroso view], his emotional temperament [the psychiatrists' contribution], the surroundings of his youth, his present home [the perspective of settlement house workers], and other conditions — all the influencing circumstances." The Institute in particular and Progressives in general had little difficulty in joining all the theories together, because all of them finally substantiated the conclusion that "the great truth of the present and future for criminal science, is the individualization of penal treatment — for that man, and for the case of that man's crime."[18]

As was apparent to every proponent of the new criminology, an individual approach to the offender had to be highly discretionary. To respond to the criminal and not the crime demanded flexibility and room for maneuver. A case-by-case analysis could not fit with set principles and a strict uniformity. After all, why compile the facts and study the personal history if not to determine the particular and appropriate response? Indeed, one of the major reasons why the Progressives so commonly offered a medical analogy was to justify giving criminal justice administrators an unprecedented latitude of action. No one compelled a physician to prescribe in advance for the patient — and no one should compel an official to prescribe in advance for the offender.

Rather than pause to consider all the potential consequences of such a principle, Progressives quickly and comfortably moved to endow the state with all the necessary powers. One reason for their rather complacent attitude was that they were, by their own as well as by everyone else's definition, reformers, scientific and expert reformers, attempting to benefit the criminal and the society. With more than a touch of pride, Progressives contended that their predecessors had pursued a primitive aim of vengeance; they, on the other hand, were committed to the more advanced goal of rehabilitation. Clearly, as Charlton Lewis put it, fixed sentences to miserable prisons, "the method of apportioning penalties according to degrees of guilt . . . is as completely discredited and as incapable of a part in any reasoned system of social organization, as is the practice of astrology or . . . witchcraft." To "return evil for evil," as nineteenth-century practices had done, was but to fulfill a "crude instinct." Instead, "as an embryo civilization grows toward its birth [America at 1900?] the time will come when the moral mutilations of fixed terms of imprisonment will seem as barbarous and antiquated as the ear-lopping, nose-slitting and hand amputations of a century ago."

Perhaps a more balanced view would have disheartened or discouraged reformers. If they had seen their predecessors as genuinely devoted to doing good, then Progressives would have had to reckon seriously with the possibility of their own failure. If an earlier criminal justice design had been well-intentioned but corrupted, so their own designs might deteriorate, and this thought was too dark for men and women with a new mission to consider. In brief, Progressives were confident that their programs had such a humanitarian quality that a grant of vast authority to the state was eminently proper.[19]

But the matter went deeper. The most distinguishing characteristic of Progressivism was its fundamental trust in the power of the state to do good. The state was not the enemy of liberty, but the friend of equality — and to expand its domain and increase its power was to be in harmony with the spirit of the age. In criminal justice, the issue was not how to protect the offender from the arbitrariness of the state, but how to bring the state more effectively to the aid of the offender. The state was not a behemoth to be chained and fettered, but an agent capable of fulfilling an ambitious program. Thus, a policy that called for the state's exercise of discretionary authority in finely tuned responses was, at its core, Progressive.

One final consideration made reformers all the more comfortable with enlarging the state's discretionary authority. As we have seen, they perceived no conflict of interest between the needs of the deviant and the needs of the community. They could simultaneously promote the general welfare (in this instance public safety) and the individual welfare (making offenders law-abiding) without sacrifice to either side, without engaging in complicated trade-offs. Thus, the state could be trusted with expanded powers because the problem of crime, as of poverty, was merely a managerial one: to make certain that the benefits of American society reached all citizens. Just as Progressives were confident that no war needed to be waged between social classes, so they were certain that no war needed to be waged between offender and society. Or to translate this into the language of criminal justice, reformers saw no reason to circumscribe narrowly the discretion of the state because there was no opposition between its power to help and its power to police. By attempting to adjust the offender to society, the state was providing the offender with the optimal circumstances for realizing his own well-being.

From these principles Progressives moved logically and consistently to design and promote probation, parole, and the indeterminate sentence. Each innovation endowed the state with the discretion to accomplish the individualization of criminal justice, to bring a new spirit of humanitarianism and a new capacity for rehabilitation to every stage of the post-conviction process.

Let us walk the offender through the novel Progressive procedures step by step, beginning with the moment when a jury pronounced him guilty or a judge accepted his plea of guilty. The first requirement of the system was to gather all the details of the offender's life, to compile the facts of the case — in court language, to carry out a pre-sentence investigation and compose the pre-sentence report. This major task belonged to a new and altogether Progressive official, the court-appointed probation officer. As one court official aptly described the assignment: "Narrowly defined, it is the complete record, chronological and topical, of every contact, direct and indirect, with the offender. . . . More broadly defined, it is more than the mere record, it is the actual facts . . . the history of the case." Accordingly, "the investigation should be comprehensive enough to give a clear picture of the offender, his traits, habits, abilities, and tendencies. . . . To this end it is essential to discover such causal factors involved in the case as the social, economic, moral, mental, hereditary, etc." Or, as one leading criminologist of the period, Edwin Sutherland, noted: "Whatever throws light on the offender's heredity, environment, character, and activities is pertinent to the investigation."[20]

The pre-sentence report itself, to follow the outlines used in both California and New York, was to open with a description of the crime: not what the offender was indicted for or pleaded guilty to, but the "real" facts of the case, what in contemporary federal parole jargon would be called "offense behavior" as opposed to "offense conviction." Then the report was to describe the offender's PERSONAL HISTORY (vital statistics, place of birth, residence, immigrant status); EDUCATION AND EARLY LIFE (truancy record, response to discipline, injuries, early associates, habits of indulgence and repression, parental control, grudges, ambitions); FAMILY AND NEIGHBORHOOD (grandparents, parents, and sibling history, from their education to the causes of their deaths as well as "a final space to indicate influence on the offender"); and HOME SITUATION (including the number of boarders, economic status, and moral condition). Then it was to provide an INDUSTRIAL HISTORY of the offender (being certain to include any prior police or prison record) and an analysis of his PERSONALITY. Finally, the report was to offer an ETIOLOGY OF MALADJUSTMENT (habit of thought, mental conflicts, behavior pattern) and close with a SUMMARY and RECOMMENDATION.[21]

To complete this exhaustive schedule, probation officers were to interview the offender (preferably not in his jail cell but in a quiet and private office); visit his home in order to talk with parents, neighbors, and friends; go to his school to interview his teachers; then visit his place of employment to speak with fellow workers and supervisors. Finally, the probation officer was to arrange for the physical and mental testing of the offender and incorporate the examiner's findings into his recommendation. On the basis of this report the judge would decide what was best for both the offender and the society.

In effect, the Progressives created the modern criminal dossier, going well beyond the casual biographical sketches the nineteenth-century wardens included in their annual reports, to a much more systematic and thorough compilation. Now the criminal really did have a record! Reformers did not so much as conceive of the possibility of a mischievous result, the possibility that the state should not be allowed, or had no right, to investigate every detail of the offender's life and of his family. Perhaps even more important, they did not doubt the relevance of this information to sentencing decisions. Here was an entirely new conception of what judges should know in order to sentence properly.

With this record before him, the judge decided between probation and incarceration. "The new system," explained Warren Spaulding, "divides convicted offenders into two great classes — those who will and those who will not 'reform without punishment.'" In the Progressive model, the personal characteristics of the offender, not the actual crime, were to guide the decision. On the negative side, "there are many who must be imprisoned because they are not fit for liberty; unbalanced, abnormal persons ... who cannot be allowed to be at large." So too, "there are large numbers of men who must be imprisoned for their own good, for discipline and training. They can be taught obedience and their relations to society in no other way." Further, "there are others who are distinctly criminal in character — some of them by birth, some from a great variety of other causes. ... And there are large numbers of incapables who do not know how to get an honest living and [therefore] resort to crime." On the positive side, however, there were a group of offenders who demonstrated a strong likelihood of rehabilitation and a low risk of recidivism. They were the right candidates for probation, properly coming under the supervision of a probation officer.[22]

What was to constitute this supervision? What should characterize the face-to-face encounters between probation officer and offender? Everyone agreed that something of a police function was appropriate. Although the probationer is " 'at large,' he is not 'free.'" Probation did entail a loss of liberty: "It takes away some of the rights which belong to the man who has not been convicted. ... The state is justified in assuming an oversight and direction of his conduct," perhaps requiring him to "shun evil companions; to keep away from the saloon ... to work steadily and support those who are dependent upon him." But everyone also agreed that probation was much more than police work, that the probation officer "must watch over and not merely watch" the offender. It was no easy matter to define or give substance to this second aspect. Uncovering details was one thing; translating them into an effective treatment quite another. And this problem, as we shall find again and again, frustrated Progressive reform programs.[23]

The first Progressive thrust, especially popular in the years 1900–1915 among the environmentalists, was to cast the probation officer in the role of "friend." The ideal officer, as depicted in the early language of the New York State Probation Commission, gained the "confidence and friendship" of his charges through "helpful oversight and encouragement," through "friendly admonition and encouragement," by "an expression of confidence in his ability . . . and friendly advice." To the New York Magistrate's Court, "the probation process is in its very essence one of education by constructive friendship. It presupposes an intense personal interest in, and an intimate personal relation on the part of the probation officer to his charge."[24]

However vague the term "friend," it conveyed a number of special meanings to Progressives. It recalled the duties of nineteenth-century "friendly visitors," the middle-class women who entered the homes of the poor on behalf of the private charities. The volunteer friendly visitor, as Josephine Shaw Lowell (the major architect of the program) had explained, was to "raise the character and elevate the moral nature." Her impact would come through "personal influence," which means that "a constant and continued intercourse must be kept up between those who have a high standard and those who have it not, and that the educated and happy and good are to give some of their time regularly and as a duty, year in and year out, to the ignorant, miserable and the vicious." In fact, in many jurisdictions, the first probation officers were volunteers who might actually be serving in both capacities, on one day visiting the poor and on the next visiting offenders on probation. And criminal justice reformers often composed lists of personal attributes for probation officers that came dangerously close to the requisites for educated sainthood. In order to influence by example, they were to be themselves "persons of good character and education, exceptional intelligence, sympathetic temperament, tact, good judgment and strong personality."[25]

But the model of probation officer as friend also had a distinctly twentieth-century quality, linking it to the settlement house worker. The comparison was obvious insofar as investigative responsibilities were concerned: both the probation officer and the settler were to be expert in the gathering of facts, the one to educate the court and the other to educate the legislature. And the similarity extended to the style of personal intervention as well. Both were to have a more ongoing presence in the ghetto and a more intimate relationship with their clients than was expected of friendly visitors.

Still more significant, the probation officer, like the settler, was to be comprehensive in approach, going well beyond lessons in morality to a systematic effort at rehabilitation. As one *Manual for Probation Officers* (1913) expressed it: "He is expected to befriend those under his care, to win their confidence, and to study their temperament, abilities and special needs. He should also aid them in thinking out their problems . . . inspire laudable and practicable ambitions; and suggest practical ways of bettering their surroundings and manner of life." In essence, the officer's charge recapitulated the Progressive agenda: to win confidence (like the settlers who resided in the ghettos); to inspire practical ambitions (so as to promote social mobility); to secure employment (to raise the standard of living); to promote recreation (in keeping with the need to build playgrounds); to recommend proper medical care (just as settlers did for immigrant mothers and children at the newly established municipal bureaus of health); and to encourage opening a bank account (so as to make certain that everyone realized the promise of American life).[26]

In all of this, the probation officer was not to lose sight of the duty of upgrading the community. He or she was to become, as one Chicago probation officer put it, "a neighborhood factor, being looked upon as a 'general utility man.' . . . She must be prepared to respond to calls; enter into consultations and give advice to children, parents, relatives, principals, teachers, socie-

ties, clubs, institutions, and police departments." In effect, probation "stands not only for the solution and treatment of crime but
most valuable of all is its preventive force."[27]

Progressives found considerable advantages in bringing this
model into criminal justice. The probation officer as friend rendered the notions of punishment and vengeance obsolete. In the
most tangible way, the ideal of friendship would infuse court
sanctions with a new spirit of humanitarianism. At the same time,
the probation officer as friend at once promoted and justified the
need for unfettered discretion. One did not tell a friend under
what circumstances to enter a home, or what questions to ask —
so constitutional strictures about search or self-incrimination
were irrelevant. The model of friend also fit well with individualization of treatment. One was not a friend to a crowd but to a
person; a friend could respond to particular needs, unencumbered
by rules of uniformity. In all these ways, the "friend" that was the
probation officer fulfilled the spirit of Progressivism.

An alternate model for probation work appeared around World
War I and gained even more popularity during the 1920's and
1930's. Reflecting the impact of psychological approaches to criminality, it made the probation officer into a social worker. To be
sure, distinctions between friend and social worker had never
been iron-clad. At some point in the 1920's most settlement house
residents moved themselves from one category to the other. In all
events, the appeal of the new model was great. In 1916, Homer
Folks, who spearheaded many Progressive campaigns in child
welfare as well as in criminal justice, expressed some of the dis-
satisfactions that made probation's turn to social work seem so
appropriate. Clearly Folks could not accept probation as mere
police work: "I do not understand that probation is a substitute
for discipline." And he was no less unwilling to depend upon the
brilliance or compassion of a few saintly types: "It is not necessary nor is it desirable, in my judgment, to look upon probation
work as something mysterious or unusual." And yet, Folks could
not define a more rigorous method. "There are not many books,"
he conceded to a gathering of probation officers, "that can be of
much help to you. The art and science of assisting those who get

into trouble in the courts yet remains to be written." Under these circumstances, Folks took refuge (as William Healy did) in the notion that investigation in and of itself would provide prescriptions, that the case history would yield clues as to the right cure. Once again, the medical model buttressed the case. "Just as diagnosis is two-thirds of medicine," Folks argued, so "in probation the work of investigation . . . is two-thirds of the battle." The search would generate the answers. "I have known a good many physicians," Folks concluded, "and it seems to be that the most successful . . . are those who have no particular theory about the philosophy of medicine, but who are very shrewd, close, keen observers, and who remember everything."[28]

Soon enough, reformers did have a book to assign to probation officers — and it came from the social work shelves: Mary Richmond's *Social Diagnosis* (1917). Edwin Cooley, chief probation officer in New York's Magistrate's Court, was among the first to make a connection that would become standard. "*Social Diagnosis*," he declared in 1918, "should be in the hands of every probation officer," precisely because it was "a very definite step in the development of social case technique. We have passed the day in probation work when perfunctory and superficial investigation and supervision of a defendant will suffice. We must go to the root of the trouble." Hence, "we must train ourselves to become capable of observing the causes and effects of human conduct and of recording the manner in which probationers respond to the various methods of treatment. . . . We must correlate the results of our experience." Yes, the probation officer "must be to each probationer what our best friends have been to us," but he must also be certain that each probationer received a full battery of psychological tests and the full benefits of psychological counseling. Without this effort, "no satisfactory probation work can be accomplished."[29]

Joining the role of counselor to that of friend was a relatively simple step, at least insofar as reform rhetoric was concerned. Psychological insights promised to move criminal justice from retribution to helpfulness; social workers were not less committed to a case-by-case approach — indeed, faith in this method underlay the entire discipline. By the same token, discretionary procedures were, if anything, still more appropriate for social workers and psychologists, who more closely approximated the expertise of physicians (and they did all that they could to confirm this resemblance), so that the legitimacy to be borrowed from a medical model was that much greater. Thus, whether one chose to follow a version of environmental causation or to mix it with psychological considerations, whether one thought of the probation officer as friend or as social worker, probation held a secure place as a worthy reform.

With similar force and logic, reformers advocated the indeterminate sentence and parole for incarcerated offenders. Although the indeterminate sentence had European roots and was first adopted here in the post–Civil War reformatory, not until 1900–1920 did it cover most inmates in state prisons. Reformers justified the practice in very Progressive terms. The fixed sentence was retributive, crude, and unfair. "The origin of it," as one of them explained, "was the native impulse to return evil for evil. . . . Any penal code which attempts to inflict penalties commensurate with offenses [as flat time did] . . . is but organized lynch law." Determinate sentences, another argued, exemplified "the old idea . . . that it is the business of the State to take vengeance upon the wrongdoer, to get even with him, to pay him back in his coin, to take an eye for an eye and a tooth for a tooth." Their reasoning was straightforward: to establish in advance a formula of so much time for such an offense "was based upon the theory that the amount of guilt connected with each crime was a definite and ascertainable quantity." But, reformers insisted, "it is absolutely impossible to determine with a fair approximation to accuracy the amount of guilt involved." Why? Because no one could measure culpability, because no one could distinguish the contributory influences of the environment or the state of mind or heredity from simple willfulness — and thus it was improper and unjust to apportion blame so uniformly. Or, as one judge friendly to the movement phrased it, "Justice cannot be measured by a yardstick or any fixed standard known to science."[30]

Moreover, fixed sentences could not be rehabilitative in intent or practice. "We endeavor," declared one writer in the Progressive journal, *Charities and the Commons*, "to cure crime by a system childishly futile. As well might we sentence the lunatic to three months in the asylum, or the victim of smallpox to thirty days in the hospital, at the end of these periods to turn them loose, whether mad or sane, cured or still diseased." Rather, "offenders must be dealt with as individuals, not as a class."[31]

Each of these contentions justified indeterminate sentences. An open-ended period of confinement would allow officials to consider all the individual characteristics of the offender — his degree of guilt as well as his potential for rehabilitation. "There is no criminal *class*," insisted Warren Spaulding. "There are classes of criminals, but that is a different matter. . . . Each criminal is an individual and should be treated as such." Further, to establish how much more effective this sentencing principle would be, reformers quoted William Gladstone's dictum, "It is only liberty that fits men for liberty," and then contended that indeterminate sentences would encourage each offender to seek his own reform. As we shall see later, this notion did have major implications for prison organization; suffice it to note here that reformers justified the procedure by noting that the inmate's "destiny is placed largely in his own hands." He learns that "liberty can never come except through himself." In short, with this change "the prisoner becomes the arbiter of his own fate. He carries the key to the prison in his own pocket."[32]

Reformers also joined provisions for parole with the indeterminate sentence to thereby heighten the program's attractions. Parole administration was to mirror probation. Both had an essential investigatory function: the parole board, like the probation officer, would examine the criminal's case history, including his behavior within the prison as well as his earlier record (with the help of the pre-sentence report), to determine his fitness for release. And both had a supervisory function: the parole officer, like the probation officer (and often these were one and the same person), would at once watch and watch over the parolee. Thus all of the arguments that proponents advanced on behalf of probation reappeared to buttress parole. All of the pieces in the

Progressive design for criminal justice seemed to fit together. The puzzle had been solved.[33]

Once again, reformers paid no attention to the possible dangers of reaching sentencing decisions on a case-by-case basis. The chance that the state might abuse such discretion, that it might exercise power in discriminatory ways, did not worry them. To the contrary, many Progressives went so far as to advocate the extreme indeterminate sentence — from one day to life — finding the minimum and maximum term structure too narrow a compromise. "The same paternalistic spirit," noted one advocate, "which empowers the State to take possession of the child and to place him in school for a number of years, must empower the State in like manner to hold the weak and the unfit," even if it were for life. And those who knew well that indeterminate sentences were far less popular among European reformers, precisely because of "the difficulty of safeguarding individual liberty," did not find such a concern appropriate here. In Europe, "untold suffering has been occasioned by prolonged and unjust imprisonment for political and other reasons." Europeans had good reason to distrust the state. But Americans enjoyed a different history, free from gross intrusions by the state. Thus, to the question: how under an indeterminate sentence "shall individual liberty be protected?" the response seemed obvious. All one needed was an intelligent parole board and conditional reviews at regular periods of time.[34] In the end, the question of individual liberty was so easily resolved, actually dismissed, because Progressives trusted the state to act in the best interest of all.

Proponents of the new system were not reluctant to buttress their case with some very practical arguments. They were eager to report that probation, for instance, would be "a paying investment in terms of dollars and cents." In 1910, they estimated the cost of one year's imprisonment at $220, the cost of one year on probation at $22, and immediately concluded: "The most promising method for the reduction of the cost of crime is found in the adoption of the probation system." And there were other, less easily calculated, savings too, as when a rehabilitated offender became "a productive member of society," not a burden to it; "a taxpayer and hence a source of revenue to the state," not a drain on it. In all, they were happy to conclude with Warren Spaulding that reform principles "are of as great interest to the taxpayer as they are to the philanthropist."[35]

More important, reformers were not embarrassed to note the tougher features of their programs, particularly in the indeterminate sentence. Doing good was not at odds with protecting society, not only because rehabilitation was ultimately the best guarantee of safety but because the new measures did not coddle the criminal. With rather remarkable aplomb, Progressives pointed out that a sentence of "one day to life" cut two ways: if some offenders would be released quickly, others, the incorrigibles, would remain incarcerated for long, very long, periods of time, without regard, let it be clear, for the nature of the offense itself. And the list of incorrigibles was not a short one. There was the professional criminal who in cold calculation decided to earn his living through theft and burglary. There were also some individuals, according to Dr. Bernard Glueck, the head of the psychiatric clinic at Sing-Sing, who "because of their psychological make-up . . . are absolutely or permanently incorrigible." Prominent, too, on the list, indicating the popularity of eugenic concepts, were the mentally deficient, the "feeble-minded" as they were called. For the "hopeless defectives," no type of treatment would be effective — and estimates placed them at 20 percent or more of all prison inmates. Indeed, as Charles Hoffman, a Progressive-minded Cincinnati judge, insisted: "A great part of the crime wave of which we hear so much, is caused by weak-willed, psychopathic or feeble-minded individuals who are unable to resist the impulses of the moment."[36]

Reformers took careful note of these categories and drew their conclusions coldly. Probation, declared one of its most vigorous champions, was out of the question for "those who are suffering from feeble-mindedness, dementia praecox [schizophrenia], and other forms of insanity, drug addiction disease, and the different types of degeneracy." On the other hand, indeterminate sentences which stretched on — without end? — were very appropriate for a variety of cases. "The incorrigibles," declared Bernard Glueck, "have to be dealt with in only one way, and that is permanent segregation and isolation from society." Charlton Lewis, another champion of the innovation, condemned fixed sentences because "human brutes and vermin . . . are then set free to plague the community. . . . Nothing but universal custom could blind us to the folly of such a practice." As the influential clergyman and reformer Samuel Barrows concluded: "It is just as important for society that the incorrigible offenders should be detained as it is that the corrigible offenders should be released."[37]

Perhaps the most striking feature of these statements is not the Progressives' suggestion of permanent confinement itself — many people carry a list of those who should be excluded from the community, from four-time rapists to two-time murderers — but their confident readiness to incarcerate, specific crime aside, those diagnosed as defective, irredeemable, or incorrigible. Perhaps the confidence of the reformers was founded upon their secure sense of themselves as humanitarians — and their sense that therefore they could decide who should and should not be released into the community; or perhaps it was founded upon their faith in psychological expertise and the medical model. "It borders on the ridiculous," declared Judge Charles Hoffman, that "in the light of all that science and medicine has revealed on the line of pathological and psychopathic states as affecting conduct . . . our criminal courts still continue the farce of trying the offense and not the offender." Or perhaps long terms seemed fair because the offender held the key to his liberty — and those who did not earn release deserved to remain incarcerated. But whatever the reason, Progressives were prepared to promote their measures as tough-minded as well as benevolent. In their world, there was no need to come down finally on the side of helping or on the side of hurting.[38]

However persuasive the Progressives' rhetoric, the rapid acceptance of their proposals also testified to the program's practical appeal to the major actors in criminal justice. Wardens, judges, and district attorneys rallied to the reforms for a series of essentially self-interested reasons. Some among them, like

Thomas Osborne, might be as high-minded as the most dedicated philanthropist. Nevertheless, the new procedures offered those inside the system very tangible and practical benefits. For reasons of personal advantage, they were prepared to march under the Progressive banner.

One need not emulate Progressive historians in their near fixation with hidden motives to appreciate just how vital this element was to the enactment of probation and parole. The combination of outsiders' idealism and insiders' self-interest may be a prerequisite for the adoption of many new programs. But the alliance here exacted a price of its own — and it was a heavy one. The full price will emerge when we analyze what happened as probation and parole were translated into practice. Still, given its critical importance, we must recognize from the outset the personal stake that administrators had in expanding the discretionary quality of criminal justice.

No group more enthusiastically supported the indeterminate sentence than prison wardens. Meeting in 1900 at the annual Congress of the National Prison Association, they unanimously and "heartily" resolved in favor of "the principle of the indeterminate sentence; that, in the opinion of this body no other penal system yet devised supplies to the offender so many motives and opportunities for reformation, erects so many barriers against crime as an occupation, and affords society so effective protection against the incursions of the habitual criminal." The wardens' stake in the change, however, went well beyond the language of the text. As remarks at this and subsequent meetings suggested, they recognized substantial benefits that would accrue to them as prison managers. First, they anticipated that indeterminate sentences would reduce inmates' discontent and make them more tractable — not because, as reformers insisted, the prisoner could now win his own freedom, but because parole boards might well equalize sentence length. The wardens were looking to uniformity through parole, aware that a convict serving a five-year term for the identical crime for which his cellmate was serving eighteen months "considers himself the most abused man on the face of the earth," and behaved accordingly. To the degree that a parole board treated men alike, to that degree the prison would be easier to control.[39]

Second, and more important, wardens understood that indeterminate sentences would supply them with a genuinely powerful weapon: the authority to determine inmates' release time. Heretofore, wardens could exert some slight influence over sentence length; "good time" laws allowed them to reduce the period of incarceration. But the amount of time was small (typically one day for every month on good behavior), the allotment was fixed through legislation, wardens could not increase time, and inmates tended to assume that the time was coming to them. In effect, wardens met more difficulties in revoking good time than rewards for allowing it. On the other hand, indeterminate sentences entailed substantial amounts of time (years, not days); and it was obvious from the outset that wardens would play a determinative role in parole decisions — either through direct service on the boards (as was the case in the opening years) or through notations on the dossiers that parole boards could not ignore (such as "dangerous inmate, many disciplinary infractions, do not release"). In effect, reformers had delivered into their hands a disciplinary mechanism far more potent than the lash, and not insignificantly, far more legitimate. Rather than discipline in covert ways and run the risk of legislative investigations, wardens could now act in forthright fashion — and yet be capable of rewarding favorites and punishing recalcitrants. Indeterminacy enhanced *their* discretion and they rushed to endorse it.[40]

Wardens may also have welcomed the new legitimacy that the reforms gave their institutions. They could now, more deftly than before, shuttle back and forth between incapacitative and rehabilitative rationales for their programs. They could present themselves as in the business of confining very dangerous offenders: the minor offender had ostensibly gone off on probation and the redeemable criminal was out on parole. What remained was the hard-core incorrigible, for whom custodial care, without frills, was entirely appropriate. Yet, whenever it served their purposes, they could present the prison as a reformatory that tested the fitness of the inmate for release. Thus, probation and parole presented prison administrators with the option of speaking grandiosely about the challenge of doing good or adopting an effective fall-back position and talking about the tough but necessary job of confining the menace to society.

The favorable judicial response to the Progressive innovations was even more critical to their popularity. It is easy to understand why most judges so readily approved probation. That they also welcomed the indeterminate sentence and parole, measures which, after all, involved a wholesale transfer of sentencing power from the courts to an executive and administrative body, is more surprising. In both instances, however, the courts did not create constitutional barriers to the implementation of the reforms. With one exception (a Michigan court decision on parole which was quickly reversed in that jurisdiction) judges consistently upheld the constitutionality of the new procedures.

Probation, both in concept and in practice, extended the discretionary authority of the judiciary and in no way restricted its prerogatives. Judges determined who would and who would not receive this sentence, and there was no appealing their decision. They appointed the probation officers (sometimes from a civil service list, sometimes not), set their schedule, and supervised their activities. Given the inherent difficulties of deciding an appropriate sentence, judges also found the added information of the pre-sentence report useful; while in no way restricting them, the data could help them reach a decision. Judges also welcomed the option of probation as an alternative to the suspended sentence. Instead of delivering a stern lecture and then turning the offender loose on his own, they could now assign him to a probation officer, put him under a series of restrictions, and require him to report periodically. Thus, probation facilitated judges' work in ways that guaranteed their enthusiastic and wholehearted support.[41]

Parole, to the contrary, did severely circumscribe their authority. Not judges, but a parole board now determined release dates; the authority that judges had exercised for a century was given over to an administrative body — and one that they would not appoint or supervise, or even review. That judges permitted this loss of power and abdicated their traditional role in sentencing, seems puzzling.

They certainly had ample occasion to strike down the new laws. A series of cases brought before state courts in the Progressive period contested the constitutionality of the indeterminate sentence — but whether the opposing briefs cited the judges' constitutional obligations or the fundamental rights of offenders, the courts upheld the statutes. Judges noted that since the legislature had the power to establish in criminal codes the length of punishment for any particular crime (indeed, since it defined what was a crime), it could surely implement a parole system. Moreover, judges were convinced that this delegation of authority to parole boards was entirely consistent with the states' right to organize and oversee their prison systems. Nor would judges accept the contention that the indeterminacy of the sentences represented cruel and unusual punishment, or that parole boards might be so arbitrary in their decision making as to violate the due process rights of an inmate.[42]

Running through all the court decisions was the belief that the new measures were reforms. Judicial findings consistently reiterated the Progressive rhetoric. To label parole a cruel and unusual punishment, said the Indiana court, would be "to turn back the hands on the dial of human progress a hundred years." The Ohio court was convinced that parole "marks a new experiment in the management and discipline of prisoners. . . . It is evidently prompted by a desire to reform, as well as to protect society." And a higher Michigan court overruled the judicial decision against parole by declaring unequivocally that "the design of the indeterminate sentence law is to reform criminals and to convert bad citizens into good citizens." To be sure, a few judges, in dissenting opinions, insisted that "so-called humanitarians" had made the prisoner into "the servant and slave of the prison board." The board's "discretion is not reviewable by the courts; it is arbitrary." This legislation gave "unheard of power to four men, not elected by the people." But their protests were drowned out in the chorus of approvals.[43]

Judges' predilection for taking reformers at their word points directly to the critical role of Progressive ideology in legitimating the innovations. But at the same time, judges shared some pragmatic considerations of their own. The indeterminate sentence was especially useful to state magistrates facing periodic reelections. In the nightmare case when a released prisoner immediately committed an offense that provoked community outrage, the sentencing judge could now pass the blame to the parole board. Citing the spread in a minimum-maximum sentence, he could claim that he had authorized, say, a ten-year maximum, but that the parole board had decided on release after five. In fact, parole boards became the whipping boy of the criminal justice system; throughout the 1920's, as we shall see, the boards came under bitter attack as countless newspaper headlines screamed PAROLEE COMMITS ROBBERY, or MURDER, or RAPE. But these headlines, of course, spared the judge from attack, which he would especially appreciate at election time.

Judges, and other criminal justice administrators as well, may also have welcomed the discretionary authority of the Progressive innovations because they were facing the most heterogeneous collection of offenders ever to appear before American courts. It may not be coincidental that sentencing practices became most flexible just when immigration reached unprecedented proportions. Now judges could distinguish among criminals not in terms of what they had done but in terms of who they were — and they may have found this leeway necessary in dealing with a bewildering variety of aliens. Thus, to offset the diminution of judicial authority, judges gained both political advantage and added freedom to dispense justice as they saw fit.

Local district attorneys, for the most part, accommodated themselves easily to the Progressive programs. If they did not lead in the crusade for their adoption, they did not organize or lend support to opposing campaigns. At most they took a firm line to the effect that probation had to be "meaningful," that supervision should be rigorous. "Unless probation is real probation," declared one of them, "the criminal escapes punishment and learns deception as well." They did not, however, attack the fundamental principles or goals of the reforms, and given their influence among legislators, this stance represented a notable victory for the reformers. Perhaps their very familiarity with lockups, jails, and prisons, made district attorneys more willing to experiment with alternative procedures; or perhaps they too preferred probation supervision to suspended sentences. But probably the most significant consideration was that probation and parole made their own jobs easier to carry out.

During the Progressive period, court calendars became desperately overcrowded. The growth in urban populations outstripped the extension of court facilities; the dockets swelled, most probably because of a rise in the absolute numbers of those coming under the courts' jurisdiction (as opposed, for example, to a rise in police efficiency). In Chicago in 1915, 110,000 persons were arrested; and while most of them were charged with trivial offenses, the very size of the group put an unprecedented burden on the administration of criminal justice, particularly on the prosecuting attorneys who were most responsible for moving people through the system. As we will explore in more detail later, prosecutors turned with increasing regularity to plea bargaining, to obtaining admissions of guilt from those charged with crimes. And probation and parole were valuable assets in this effort, for they gave room to negotiate. Now prosecutors could offer the option of probation, and many persons, perhaps even most, faced with a choice between probation and a trial with the possibility of a prison sentence, would accept the bargain: better to suffer the inconvenience of reporting to a probation officer than to risk incarceration. District attorneys could also use indeterminate sentences to advantage: the promise of a low minimum sentence might induce a guilty plea, and so might the threat of a very high maximum. In brief, it is difficult to think of anyone in the system who would delight more in discretionary authority than the district attorney.[44]

Unlike the total unanimity which had greeted the Jacksonian impulse to institutionalize the criminal, some opposition did develop to Progressive efforts, most notably from the ranks of the police. To release convicted offenders on probation, without a jail or prison term, seemed to them to denigrate their own efforts, to generate "disrespect [for] the police authorities," to treat the action of the police "as a joke." As one chief of police in New Haven angrily charged, the daily newspapers were reporting a mounting number of burglaries and then complaining, "What is the matter with our police? Are they asleep? What are we coming to? . . . Why don't the police and detectives capture the thieves?" To which he responded that the police were doing their job well — the problem was with the judges who let criminals off on probation, to return to their neighborhoods "where they become heroes." Moreover, policemen themselves found probation demoralizing. "What have the officers accomplished . . . ? What satisfaction is there for the officers who may have worked faithfully . . . to clear up a number of burglaries?" For a convicted criminal to forego a prison sentence meant that policemen "have accomplished nothing and their work has gone to naught." To make matters even worse, probation officers, not the police, supervised the offender. With no sense of history, but with much frustration, the Jersey City police chief declared: "Police control of all offenders has been in practice since the advent of civilization itself. . . . It does not seem possible that these duties could be performed better by others who never had actual experience in that profession."[45]

Police forces were no happier with parole. From their perspective, it put hardened criminals back on the street too quickly. Prisons, the chiefs argued, were not a valid testing ground for future conduct. "The worst outside," insisted the Pennsylvania police chief, "is quite frequently the model prisoner inside." And again they complained that released prisoners came under the supervision of parole officers, not policemen, and that many parole agencies were unwilling to provide local police departments with a list of parolees. The agencies feared that the police would round up their charges every time a crime was committed. To the police, however, the refusal meant that felons whose exact whereabouts were unknown, could plague the community. Not surprisingly, for all these reasons, police chiefs in their annual meetings vigorously condemned parole. "It is the sense of this convention," they resolved as early as 1897, "that it is not in conformity with justice, nor with the best interests of our people and society, to parole prisoners committed to the penitentiary, on a ... crime of felony."[46]

There were other attacks, more individual than formal and organized, on the Progressive measures. From the start, many prisoners detested the indeterminate sentence, both for psychological reasons — to undergo a period of incarceration without knowing when it would end was exceptionally painful — and for practical ones too: they did not want their guards and wardens exercising such extraordinary power over their lives. As one anonymous inmate noted in an article for the *Atlantic Monthly* magazine: "The lawbreaker prefers the five minutes' gamble with fate before a magistrate, to an indefinite, soul-racking jugglery at the hands of Jim Crow political beneficiaries." But such protest, of course, only made the reform seem all the more desirable: if prisoners did not like the medicine, it must be especially good for them.[47]

Opposition also came from some hard-line judges and district attorneys who simply would not accept the proposed reforms as anything other than ways of coddling the criminal. To one New York district attorney, probation and parole represented an "overindulgence to the offender." In similar spirit, a Chicago municipal judge defined parole as giving the dog two free bites instead of one. And one group of Boston citizens, the Massachusetts Civic Alliance, distributed flyers proclaiming: "Don't Hurry to Pass the Parole Bill for the theories of punishment are fickle and still unsettled." Rather than rehabilitate the deviant, they argued, the new program "exposes society to the mercy of criminals."[48]

Occasionally too, a conceptual and philosophical attack on indeterminacy and discretion appeared, especially from European visitors. The President of the English Prison Commission, Sir Evelyn Ruggles-Brise, was astonished that of all people, the Americans should have moved from a fixed to an indeterminate sentencing scheme. "Certainty and fixity of punishment ... seems so obvious, and to result so naturally from the necessity of maintaining the system of social rights, that one is puzzled to account for . . . the indifference on the part of the American public as to any proportion between the crime and the penalty." The use of the medical model to justify such a departure particularly disturbed Ruggles-Brise. "They talk and write wildly and loosely about the absurdity of releasing a patient from [a] hospital before he was fully cured. . . . It is almost impossible to take up a journal in America which, in writing on prison reform, does not adopt dogmatically the analogy between crime and disease, without thinking or knowing that the relation between the two is one of the most subtle and the most difficult, and almost indiscoverable of all relations."[49]

But these naysayers did not and could not dampen enthusiasm for the reforms. The Progressives had too many ready answers and the administrators too clear a stake. Dissenters, whether police chiefs or European critics, made little impact against such an alliance. The new system of criminal justice fit too well with current ideas and needs.

CHAPTER THREE

Watching Over the Offender: The Practice of Probation

NO MATTER HOW INTRIGUING it may be to trace a reform impulse to its diverse sources or to explore all the nuances of a new ideology, the final test of a reform is in its record of implementation. A program must ultimately be judged by results, what actual benefits it brings, what degrees of mischief it creates. Clearly, one would not wish to slight the motives of the reformers. As George Eliot put it in *Daniel Deronda*: "Ignorant kindness may have the effect of cruelty; but to be angry with it as if it were direct cruelty would be an ignorant unkindness." But however well turned the phrase, the critical issue remains: was the effect cruelty? Were the consequences, however unintended, a good deal less than satisfactory? On the whole, historians have all too often failed to confront this issue. Yet if one is to begin to understand the implications of such a Progressive innovation as probation, then practice must be compared with promise.

That something of a gap should have separated the rhetoric advocating probation and the reality of the measure was altogether predictable. The program was so ambitious and optimistic that a dilution and diminution in day-to-day practice would inevitably set in. Nevertheless, despite this expectation, the record of probation in the opening decades of the twentieth century is still filled with surprises. For one, the gap was simply enormous: the translation bore very little resemblance to the original text. For another, the translation, however inadequate, remained popular, in the sense that probation continued to be widely used in the courts and consistently advocated in reform tracts. How shall we understand this persistence in the face of failure, this reliance upon and support for a program that had little correspondence to the original design?

Of the facts of the case there is no dispute. Investigatory committees of all types, whether composed of legislators, social workers, district attorneys, blue-ribbon grand jurors, or concerned citizens, returned a similar verdict: probation was implemented in a most superficial, routine, and careless fashion, as "a more or less hit-or-miss affair," a "blundering ahead." True, almost every county and city seemed to have its own way of doing things; diversity, and not uniformity, prevailed. But for all the variety, the common practice of probation was notably haphazard.[1]

The measure never did take root in rural areas or small towns. Reformers had national ambitions for their program, but in fact only densely populated areas established probation departments. By 1930, the federal government and thirty-six states had adult probation laws on their books, including every major industrialized state and every state with an important city. But there were blank spots, particularly in the southwest (from Kentucky and Tennessee to Texas and New Mexico) and in the mountain states (the Dakotas, Nevada, and Wyoming). Moreover, within the states, probation was most often found only in the heavily urbanized regions. Legislatures typically compelled the cities to establish probation departments, but allowed the more rural areas discretion as to policy. Thus, in Illinois, some 20 percent of all offenders in the state were released on probation, but in the rural counties, the figure reached only 8 percent. In brief, probation was always more of an urban than a rural practice.[2]

More important, even in the urban areas, probation officers' credentials, case loads, pre-sentence reports, and post-sentence supervision never approximated the reform criteria. In the Progressive period, and with increasing emphasis through the 1920's and 1930's, proponents had looked to a skilled and professional corps of workers to implement probation. In their minds, it was the very training of staff which was to give probation its impact: this was not to be an amateur foray into doing good, but rather a systematic effort to improve the social environment and adjust individual behavior. Accordingly, probation officers were to complete an undergraduate course in sociology and psychology, go on to graduate study in social work, master the skills of case work, gain experience in a community group, and then join a probation department. In this way the staff would grasp "the modern conceptions of human behavior" that had to underlie the program.[3]

Judged by such standards, the actual results were pitiful. With monotonous regularity observers complained of the inadequate training of most probation personnel. In smaller cities, the majority of the staff were district attorneys, sheriffs, policemen, well-meaning volunteers, or the sentencing judges themselves. In Oregon, for example, probationers were typically given over to "a friend, a parent, the sheriff, the district attorney, the Veterans of Foreign Wars, American Legion, Salvation Army, or perhaps to the Oregon Prison Association." The fact that metropolitan regions had specially appointed and salaried probation staff was no guarantee of better quality. Observers credited the probation organizations in New York State and Massachusetts with operating the best systems in the country. Yet one witness after another conceded to a New York investigatory committee that the probation officers lacked credentials. As the head of the State Probation Commission, Fred Moran, testified: "The probation officers . . . have not the training, most of them, that they ought to have to do probation work today, and if we conceive of probation work as a system of changing habits . . . they are not equipped to do it."[4]

Investigations in other jurisdictions returned similar findings. The nationwide survey of criminal justice release practices that the Attorney General's office carried out in 1935–1936 concluded that fully half of the metropolitan districts studied set no qualifications at all for probation staffs. Its investigators again and again sent back reports noting a "poorly trained staff." In Chicago, for example, the chief probation officer had served as sheriff of Cook County until his appointment; before that he had been an Army captain. Why his selection? "The Chief probation officer," noted the investigator, "has political connections." So too, the Advisory Committee to the National Commission on Law Observance and Enforcement, known, for its chairman, as the Wickersham Commission, put its findings succinctly: "Probation officers, in general, have been . . . untrained and chosen with little eye to their fitness."[5]

Critics had no difficulty in accounting for the failures of the probation system, and their points, as far as they went, were well-taken. For one, in the great majority of jurisdictions judges had complete authority to select their probation officers; and since many judges were uninformed about or unimpressed by the technical skills of social workers, they felt free to disregard professional considerations in favor of personal or political ones. Hence, a relative, friend, or political supporter could be rewarded with a job in probation work, and the judge, if challenged, could always respond that personal characteristics, insight, and empathy compensated for a lack of formal training. A minority of jurisdictions (ten states, as of 1930) did place probation appointments under civil service; and their formal requirements for eligibility were more rigorous, calling for some college education as opposed to just a high school diploma or a few years' experience. But even these requirements fell below professional standards. More, the civil service tests were hardly exacting, being mostly variations on the theme of "list probation's major goals," and judges generally had the final say on which of the eligibles would receive the appointment anyway. When a group of reformers in Chicago did offer examinations and compose a list of qualified candidates, the judges simply declined to make appointments from the list.[6]

Moreover, observers understood that persons with training could not be attracted to the low paying probation positions. Several state commissioners repeated Fred Moran's complaint in

New York: "Unfortunately we cannot attract social workers who have the training, because of the lack of compensation." Probation officers' salaries ranged from $900 to $2,500 a year, with most falling at the lower end of the scale — this at a time when unskilled factory labor earned about $1,200 a year. Because of these inadequate salaries "men and women with desirable educational qualifications and with specialized training are entering other fields of social service."[7]

In effect, both in terms of appointment and in terms of salaries, probation was a part of the court system, and as a result its personnel were chosen and paid as though they were clerks. In administrative and in practical terms, the officers were the judge's assistants, not by any stretch of the imagination his partners. They were the amateurs, he was the professional.

The conditions of probation work also made recruitment difficult. The courthouse rooms in which probation officers were to carry on their duties were as overcrowded with people as they were bare of amenities. How involve oneself in an intimate and sensitive relationship with a client without even the privacy of an office, when one was seated in a hall with desks abutting each other and where the noise level from many conversations was high? Moreover, the case loads themselves were so burdensome, the number of persons to be investigated and supervised so large, that no one who was eager to do serious case work would find a probation position acceptable, let alone attractive.

Which brings us to the second major disparity between reform goals and probation realities. Designers of the system had anticipated that the intensive character of probation would restrict to a minimum the number of clients per officer. The ideal ratio was 50:1. But almost no jurisdiction met it. Given the diversity of conditions, one cannot talk realistically of a national average; and data on the number of clients must also take into consideration how many other miscellaneous and unrelated tasks an officer might have to fulfill — from dispensing gun licenses to administering widows' pensions. Still, it is clear that probation staffs carried impossible loads, impossible in the sense that reformers' expectations could not be met. "It is admitted by all concerned," reported the Wickersham Commission, "that probation services are almost everywhere understaffed . . . In many jurisdictions 'the case load' is many hundreds of cases." Investigators for the Attorney General's survey analyzed case loads in several hundred courts and confirmed this finding. In Newark, New Jersey, to choose but one example, 37 field workers had responsibility for some 5,800 cases, a load of 150 per worker. Other researchers reported similar results. The National Probation Association, examining conditions in Milwaukee, discovered that three officers had charge of 839 cases, "making an average burden of about 280 cases to each . . . an overload of about 400% on the basis of from 50 to 75 cases to each officer."[8]

This overload gave compelling testimony to the inability of probation to fulfill either of its two major assignments: to establish the suitability of convicted offenders for probation or to conduct intensive post-sentence supervision. The officer's first obligation was to advise the judge on the propriety of probation, following an extensive and thorough investigation of the offender's life history. What came of this in practice? Again, one confronts an incredible diversity of conditions. "In no state," noted the Attorney General's survey, "is the administration of probation of the same quality and standard throughout the State." Frequently "a splendid, well administered probation department" operates right next to "a notoriously 'black spot' on the probation map." Moreover, "even within the limit of a single metropolis a wide variation in probation procedure may be observable." Nevertheless, a generalization that highlights the weaknesses and inadequacies of the system subsumes the great majority of cases. The Attorney General's survey could identify only three states within whose boundaries a probation department carried out intensive investigations. Of the 108 departments that it analyzed, only 16 "could be classified as offering the prospect of good investigation with fair regulation." Sixty-three departments delivered pre-sentence reports of middling to minimal thoroughness; in 13, the sheriff or police composed the report; and in another 16, the probation department did no investigation at all.[9]

Every imaginable variation of investigatory style appeared as one moved from jurisdiction to jurisdiction. In Hartford, Connecticut, the state attorney's office composed probation reports; in Boise, Idaho, the judge himself conducted personal inquiries. In Brooklyn a group of county detectives took charge, forming, as one observer put it, "a species of secret service."[10]

Some probation officers did submit lengthy reports to their judges, but the way that they gathered and analyzed the data revealed the distance that separated even the most diligent workers from the program's designs. When one reads over the six-page, single-spaced typewritten pre-sentence report from a Buffalo probation officer, or the four pages that his counterparts in Minneapolis, Detroit, and St. Louis composed, it becomes immediately apparent that probation officers commonly took a series of shortcuts to complete their assignments. Generally, they based most of their reports on a single interview with the defendant; they could find the time to take one trip to the jail or see in their office someone released on bail. It then became a simple matter to learn and to record where he was born, educated, and employed, and to set down his version of the event in question. Some probation officers also did ask the local police department or social service clearing house about the man; and the most energetic officers did make inquiries to the references that the defendant supplied. But at best, a pre-sentence report constituted a brief biographical sketch together with the more or less crude impressions of the probation officer. For instance, the St. Louis officer entered under Personality: "A. has a salesman's manner and attitude. He is neat and clean in appearance. The references suggest good breeding." The Minneapolis worker concluded: "Does seem to have enjoyed a good reputation. It appears that he was a capable and competent businessman. . . . He doesn't need punishment but he probably needs some sort of treatment." And the Detroit officer told the judge: "In general personality he impresses one as being rather unstable, definitely lacking in insight and judgment and manifesting a rather poor appreciation of social and personal relationships. Some measure of disciplinary treatment is indicated." In sum, the probation officers, confronting the need to complete ten to fifteen pre-sentence reports a week and lacking familiarity even with the jargon of social case work, let the defendants speak for themselves, and then proceeded to pass judgment, telling the judge what impressed or bothered them. The pre-sentence report, intended to be an analytic device, had become a form of gossip.[11]

Not very much more could be claimed for probation supervision after sentencing. The ideal remained highly ambitious and well-publicized. "Mere custodial care" of the probationer was not contemplated. Rather, as the head of the service in New York declared: "The minimum standard for the work of this Division is social case work in accordance with the best practices in use in recognized social service agencies." His counterpart in Boston first cited the definition of Mary Richmond: "Social case work consists of those processes which develop the personality through adjustment . . . individual by individual," and went on to suggest that "one would substitute the term 'probation work' for social case work."[12]

In practice, however, probation supervision turned out to be quite different. The grand promises of treatment were almost everywhere reduced to printed and sometimes childish "conditions." Listed on a typed sheet, which the probationer had to sign, were such stipulations as:

1. You are not to engage or work where alcoholic beverages are sold. You are not to buy or drink alcoholic beverages.
2. Do not loaf in so called saloons, cigar stores or pool rooms.
3. Work steady.
4. Obey all laws and conduct yourself as a good citizen.
5. Do not leave the city to work or live without the consent of the Probation Officer.
6. Failing to report will be considered a violation of probation.
These instructions are for your good and the Probation Officer will give you all the help he can.

Many jurisdictions, of course, added their own favorite rules. Wilmington, Delaware, ordered probationers to attend some church and to be home not later than eleven o'clock. Jackson County, Missouri, would not allow probationers to marry if single, or to divorce if married.[13]

It is doubtful whether these conditions were widely enforced, let alone whether the more extensive goals of supervision were implemented. In an all too common complaint, Brooklyn's chief probation officer told the very tough-minded New York State Crime Commission that "Probation officers in this City will have often up to 400 cases . . . scattered to the winds . . . under supervision. There is nothing but a moral thread holding [clients], and they expect a few probation officers to do what the Almighty did not do. . . . Our contact with [probationers] may be less than 10 minutes a year." And yet somehow "we are expected to return them to society perfect." In the same vein, the Cleveland Crime Commission described how the probation office "was continually crowded. . . . Three probation officers were attempting to carry on investigation, work with individuals, receive reports, collect money, make out receipts, and at the same time keep track of the courtroom. . . . Obviously, the adult probation work is lacking in efficiency." Worse yet, "each probation officer must be his own clerk, as no clerk or typist is provided. The record work is crude and unsatisfactory. . . . The chief probation officer is without a constructive plan, but makes an effort day by day to meet the problem of that day. In view of the absurd conditions under which he undertakes so vast a work, the wonder is that he does anything at all." And performance could be still more inadequate. The probation office in Chicago, as an investigator for the Progressive-minded National Probation Association (NPA) learned, had no idea where many of their probationers were, no idea even where their records in the office were.[14]

Probation officers rarely visited a client at home, and clients rarely visited their officers in person either. When the NPA field secretary observed the Milwaukee probation office, he noted that on a given day only forty-seven of the eighty-five persons due to report appeared, and even that turn-out made it impossible for the officer to devote anything but the most perfunctory attention to each client. "Reporting consists . . . of the asking of a few stereotyped questions, the marking of a card, or a lecture on the virtue of promptness in the making of reports." The Oregon State probation officer confessed to a researcher from the Attorney General's office that "where he is asked to supervise an individual, about all that he does is to watch the man's record for future arrests." Those judges who preferred to do their own probation work, to conduct "bench supervision," fared no better: "There is in fact no supervision. At most it consists of writing once a month to the judge, or meeting him on the street and giving him an oral report."[15]

Performance in Massachusetts, despite that state's reputation for administering one of the best programs, was just as inadequate. In Roxbury, as one investigator found, "When the chief is out, Probation Officers play cards, chew the rag, etc. . . ." Reporting was routine and supervision lacking. In the Suffolk County court, there was only "superficial" periodic check-ups. On the whole, probation supervision operated "in a vacuum without use or regard to other agencies and available resources."[16]

Such conditions not only made the fulfillment of case work principles well nigh impossible, but also prevented probation from carrying out a meaningful police function. Probationers could abscond at will; nothing but a "moral thread," as that Brooklyn probation chief had noted, tied the probationer to his officer. Indeed, as we shall see, when probation departments reported a high rate of "success," with 70 to 80 percent of clients completing probation without being returned to prison, they were, in effect, conceding that supervision was a sham. Since no services were being provided to the probationer, it is hard to credit a "success" rate to anything else except a basic ignorance of the probationer's activities.

Not merely the logic of the situation points to such a conclusion. The Attorney General's survey of probation undertook a painstaking review of some 19,000 case records from all over the country. Their data made clear not only that revocation of probation occurred in a minority of cases (19%), but that the great majority of revocations were for new offenses, not for violations of probation conditions (by a proportion of almost 2:1). In such cases, the police, not the probation officer, detected the probationer's crime. Thus, the probation worker turned out to be no more effective a police officer than he was a social worker. If presentence investigations mixed hearsay with impressionistic evidence, post-sentence supervision was little more than an empty formality that seemed to serve no purpose at all.[17]

Although there is little that is controversial in this negative conclusion and contemporary observers would not have quarreled with it, it does raise some fundamental questions. First, why did probation fail so quickly and so uniformly? To say that the fault lay with too few probation officers or workers, too low salaries, or too heavy a case load, is merely to reframe the question; for why were there so few workers and so heavy an overload? Second, in light of the dismal performance, why did the system persist? Seemingly it serviced no one — and the few thousand probation workers on the rolls hardly had the political influence to keep the program going. In fact, the two questions are intimately connected. The very reasons for the deterioration were integral to the survival of probation.

To begin with, the program was incredibly ambitious. Even an occasional reformer did confess that the original formulation had been too grandiose. Harvard University Law Professor and Criminologist Sheldon Glueck, for example, conceded that probation had overclaimed its case. As for the probation worker: "All we ask of her is perfection. . . . All she needs is the wisdom of the serpent, the gentleness of the sucking dove, the skin of a rhinoceros, and the constitution of an ox."[18] But while such a view might explain a limited gap, it could not account for the full extent to which practice did not measure up to design.

More significant was the flimsy quality of reform theory — an understandable weakness, since our own explanations of deviancy may be no more compelling; but whereas today's social policy analysts are becoming more and more modest about the goals of intervention, the Progressives were anything but modest. Proponents of probation (like their colleagues in the field of mental health) believed that a mass of data could substitute for effective theory, that the concept of "individualization" justified an almost random collection of information. This perspective appeared in the writings of William Healy and, not by coincidence, in those of the psychiatrist and reformer Adolf Meyer. But when the dictums of a Healy were translated into practice, the results were bound to be unsatisfactory. To tell a probation officer to complete pre-sentence reports that were all-inclusive was to tell him that no categories or types of information were more significant than others. And instructions to omit nothing are not instructions — not knowing what to exclude is precisely the same as not knowing what to include. The task of reporting on an offender's environ-ment and heredity; his youth and maturity; his schooling, work record, and police record; his grandparents' history; and his par-ents' and siblings' history, is not a difficult task, it is a meaningless task. And no one should have been surprised to discover that meaningless tasks were not performed.[19]

On the basis of such a potpourri of knowledge, what could be expected of treatment? The advice and training that probation workers received on how to "adjust the maladjusted" were vague and inchoate, at best commonsensical, at worst irrelevant. Since the cause of the deviancy might rest anywhere in the mass of data, then the cure might also come from any sort of intervention. To attempt to respond to each client as an individual was to sink into therapeutic helplessness. The probation worker, therefore, might well take refuge in card playing, in paper work, in printing "probation conditions," or in explanations that blamed failure on an overcrowded calendar and work load.

It was very rare for a contemporary critic to voice this charge — one does not often find skepticism about widely accepted truths — but an occasional commentator did make the point. A law school professor, Jerome Michael of Columbia University, speaking at one of the innumerable New York conferences on the crime problem (this one sponsored by Governor Herbert Lehman in 1935), dared to ask an assembly full of proponents of proba-tion how they could distinguish the incorrigible from the corrigible offender. What was their basis for dispensing probation and, no less critical, "where does the knowledge exist . . . which will enable judges in cooperation with probation officers to reform or rehabilitate the corrigible offender?" Michael went on to note, with all false modesty: "I pretend to have no more than a very superficial acquaintance myself with the various fields of knowledge in which it is said it is possible to find them: psychiatry, sociology, et cetera. I must confess I don't know where it is." The answers he received were as lame as were to be expected. "You have to take chances," was one response. "Nobody needs to tell us how hard our job is," was another. "I don't know the answer, but at least we are trying to learn that answer by comparison, by evaluation, by study of similar cases," was still another. The question was too fundamental to be confronted. In the end, respondents had to take comfort in the thought that "At least we are dealing with the problem."[20]

Political realities as well as theoretical limitations distorted the practice of probation. The system was administered on a local basis, with each county or municipality responsible for funding and organizing its own department. Reformers had not anticipated this feature; they had been unconcerned with just where probation would fit in a government bureaucracy. Rather, the local character of the system had grown more or less naturally from probation's attachment to the county and city courts. Just as localities paid their own judges, so they would pay their own probation staff. The result, however unexpected, was an almost bewildering diversity of probation procedures. Because hundreds of jurisdictions each had charge of its own system, reformers' ambitions for implementing a coherent and uniform program were bound to be frustrated.

Local responsibility also undercut probation in a more vital way: it pitted the financial self-interest of the municipality against the probation system. The state government paid the costs of incarceration in state prisons, but the locality paid the costs of release on probation. Most reformers missed this distinction. They tended to emphasize instead the general point that probation was cheaper than institutionalization, since the price of maintaining a person on probation was one-tenth of the cost of confining him. But despite the probable accuracy of this claim, the calculation had to be recast in terms of: "cheaper for whom?"

Some students of probation did recognize that conflict. Baltimore Judge Joseph Ullman, a devoted advocate of the new program, conceded that his reformist dream "probably will not come true." Why? Because "the Probation Department is supported by the city [of Baltimore] — the penal institutions, except the jail, by the State. Therefore, if the city should spend an additional $6,000 in order that the State might save $16,000, there wouldn't be any financial advantage accruing to the city." A 1934 Virginia commission on criminal justice also reported that the state probation law "leaves the financing of probation to the local communities. It is not difficult to understand why there has been little use of this form of penal treatment when one realizes that a community may send its lawbreakers to jail or prison at the expense of the State but must itself bear the burden of placing them on probation." And New York's Governor Al Smith told his state's Crime Commission that probation would never improve in quality unless local communities met their responsibilities. Still, it was not until the 1960's, when the state of California gave probation subsidies to its counties, that any change occurred in the allocation of fiscal responsibility. Throughout the pre–World War II period, the implementation of probation was not in the best financial interests of any given community.[21]

The effects of this fiscal fact of life helped to shape the history of probation. For one, rural communities, usually poorer and more tax-conscious than their urban counterparts, were especially reluctant to incur probation costs — and here was one more reason why probation was more prevalent in the city than in the countryside. Moreover, state legislatures, dominated in these years by rural interests, permitted rural areas to avoid practicing probation, but then mandated it for the cities. And many cities responded as one might expect. They obeyed the letter of the law, not the spirit of the program: they hired too few probation officers and let the case loads swell. A full funding of the system — an honest attempt to maintain, let us say, a fifty-to-one ratio —

would have added a considerable burden to municipal budgets. By the same token, cities were eager to use probation primarily where it would reduce their own expenses, that is, as an alternative to commitment to local jails. Cities did have a financial incentive to use probation for misdemeanants who might have ended up in their own lock-ups; they had no financial reason to use probation for felons who could be sent to the state-run prisons.[22]

So although reformers had expected sentence disposition to be based on the character of the criminal, in actuality probation was often reserved for those who had committed a minor crime — and one reason for this outcome was the special distribution of costs. To the extent that municipalities placed petty offenders on overcrowded probation rosters, they were acting with a clear sense of their budgetary self-interest.

If such considerations help to clarify the dismal condition of probation, they make still more difficult the question as to why the system persisted. Surely it was not because of the intellectual power of the theory or because of any expected financial windfalls from the practice — or, let it immediately be said, because of a deep or pervasive popularity of the program. To the contrary, to the extent that one can, in the absence of systematic surveys, gauge public opinion, probation, like many other of the Progressive innovations in criminal justice, stood in marked disfavor. It did not attract the vitriolic denunciations that characterized public responses to parole. But one would hardly describe the reputation of probation in positive terms.

By the mid-1920's legislators were making frequent attempts to abolish the program altogether. Even in Massachusetts, one of the model states, bills were introduced "very sweeping in their character — which tended to do away with all the modern devices of reformation . . . to reduce the whole process of dealing with the criminal and the offender of all kinds to a strict rule of thumb." As the state's deputy commissioner of probation recounted in 1925, "We were all of us pretty much abolished by the proposed legislation." Generally, proponents of probation fought back successfully and won legislative battles. But these confrontations pointed to a persistent and widespread hostility to the program's principles.[23]

Supporters, trying to locate the sources of opposition, faulted the citizenry for a crude and simple desire for vengeance. "Retribution forms the basis of the public's accepted belief of the purpose of the criminal law," one probation officer noted; but reformers "insist upon individualization in order to determine who . . . may be reformed without punishment." Others denounced the press, furious that every time a probationer committed a crime, the headlines read: "Man on probation does . . ." Why did the newspapers never note how many probationers were leading law-abiding lives?[24]

Still others noted, accurately, that probation was seen as being soft on the criminal. Opponents in the New York legislature, for example, declared: "The whole thing comes down to this, whether there would have been very much less crime if these fellows that are out committing crime had known that they would not be coddled, but would get sentences and get them surely." According to this line of thought probation had the priorities all wrong: "Protect society first, and then take care of the criminal, if you can."[25]

These hard-line attitudes became all the more widespread in the 1920's because the country seemed to be in the midst of a fierce crime wave. Reformers again blamed the press for fostering such attitudes, insisting that crime had not increased disproportionately to the rise in population. "'The crime wave,'" insisted Charles Chute, General Secretary of the NPA, "is a reportorial phrase. It seems evident that certain newspapers, lacking the sensational war news which filled the press and sold out papers by the millions, have exaggerated sensational crimes for ulterior motives." Given the inadequacies of the crime statistics, the issue cannot be resolved, but newspaper headlines did report every gang war and shoot-out in bold type, and editorials frequently analyzed why America should be afflicted with so much lawlessness. One of the more easily identifiable villains was, of course, probation: "The crime wave . . . has been encouraged by the . . . soft heartedness of judges in placing on probation men who have been convicted of serious crimes." And these criticisms persisted through the 1930's as well. One of the purposes of the Attorney General's study of release procedures was to explore whether or not the public's hostility to probation was justifiable. Thus, whether the crime wave was real or imagined, probation did appear to many to be too easy on the offender.[26]

With probation proving to be so ineffective, costly, and unpopular, how could it persist under such unfavorable circumstances? The answer rests not in the sentiments of the reformers or the general public, but in the specific interests of those who administered criminal justice: the prosecuting attorneys, the judges, the criminal lawyers. Probation, as it actually functioned, facilitated their work in critical ways. This group of supporters, the very ones who might have been expected to oppose a "coddling" approach, indeed the ones who might have had the political influence to abolish it, were instead among its most adamant defenders.

The operational convenience of probation emerges clearly as soon as one examines who actually received probation. Reformers had expected an "individualized" decision based on the potential for rehabilitation of each offender. In practice, however, a very different set of criteria ruled. The first distinguishing characteristic of probationers was that they had pleaded guilty to a lesser offense than the original indictment. Put most simply, probation went to those who plea bargained or, to use the vernacular, copped a plea. Not their "offense behavior" but their, and their lawyers', "office behavior" was the critical element.

Given the covert and unrecorded character of plea bargaining negotiations, a surprisingly impressive body of evidence establishes their links with probation. That plea bargaining itself flourished in the 1920's and 1930's, and particularly in urban areas, there is no doubt. As the Illinois Crime Survey Commission reported, "The conviction cannot be escaped that in Cook County for the most part, criminal administration has ceased to be a legal matter of the trial and conviction of offenders, but has become a highly specialized system of jockeying and bargaining." So too, "In the State of New York," the New York State Crime Commission declared, "the most common plea is 'guilty of another lesser offense,'" and not surprisingly the practice was most rampant in New York City. "The average percentage of pleas of guilty of another offense outside of New York City is about 10. The percentage for New York City is nearly 50."[27]

The function of probation was to facilitate this plea bargaining process, which it did remarkably well. The Illinois Crime Survey could not, of course, find written evidence that those under indictment had agreed to plead guilty in return for a sentence of probation, but there were "strong inferences that those were the facts." Probation "has become merely an additional bit of machinery for manipulation by both the criminal and the law enforcing agencies." The various state attorneys were remarkably frank in admitting this to the Crime Survey committee. "We very rarely have a plea of guilty to any serious offense," noted one prosecutor, "unless the defendant has a very reasonable chance to be put on probation, and, in my opinion, I think the great majority of pleas of guilty are induced by the opportunity or hope in a release on probation." Another declared: "I find that in nearly every case the criminal will plead guilty if he is promised probation." And another even noted that "if the defendant fails to get probation he almost always will ask leave to withdraw his plea of guilty and enter his plea of not guilty, and without cost."[28]

Harder data linking probation to plea bargaining emerged from other investigations. The New York Crime Commission reported that "a comparison of suspended sentences [on probation] with the nature of pleas in criminal cases indicates that pleas of guilty are much more likely to win suspended sentences than pleas of not guilty." In the entire state, "pleas of guilty result, in about one-third of the cases, in suspended sentences. Among the 'not guilty plea' cases which result in convictions, only about 14 percent result in suspended sentences. . . . This is especially true in New York City where apparently a willingness to plead guilty to a lesser offense is very much more likely to result in a suspended sentence." And if one examined only the practices in larger cities, leaving aside rural areas, the correlation between a guilty plea and probation was even stronger.[29]

Not only places like New York and Chicago, but counties all over Texas revealed this same dynamic. The Attorney General's survey analyzed a sample of cases placed on probation in Texas in 1934 and 1935 and discovered that in the overwhelming majority of instances, those who avoided incarceration had entered guilty pleas. So cause and effect were easily identified: "The District Attorneys agree with the defendants, or their counsel, that if they will plead guilty a suspended sentence will be recommended."[30]

To check the reliability of these findings, the Attorney General's survey staff sent a questionnaire to some 270 federal and state judges who presided over criminal trials (most of them in courts of general criminal jurisdiction), asking them directly whether guilty pleas affected their sentencing decisions. The answers were unambiguous. Ninety percent stated that "a plea of guilty in most cases resulted in their imposing a more lenient sentence than they would have imposed if the criminal had stood trial." Many of the judges "emphasized that they are much more inclined to grant probation when a prisoner pleads guilty." A few of them even admitted that they refused to grant probation "to any offender who has put the State to the cost and inconvenience of a trial."[31]

As one might expect, there was no shortage of denunciations of plea bargaining. The Attorney General's report condemned the practice out of hand: "It is subject to grave abuses . . . confuses the guilt finding process with sentencing process." It undermined the "impartial administration of justice," put people on probation who were bad probation risks, and "might even increase their disrespect for the law. . . . 'Beating the rap' by way of 'copping a plea' . . . and 'begging probation' are phrases used by the professional criminal in describing his methods of circumventing the processes of criminal justice." The verdict of the Illinois Crime Survey was equally severe: "There seems to be no justification for such wholesale reductions as one encounters in Cook County."[32]

What is more surprising is the ease with which district attorneys and sentencing judges responded to these complaints, sometimes even bringing reformers' rhetoric to their own defense. The

most popular retort was that a plea of guilty had become a prerequisite for probation precisely because it demonstrated that the
criminal had begun the process of reformation. As one Minneapolis court administrator explained, probation was properly
reserved for those who plead guilty: "In very few instances is the
convicted offender granted probation, the theory being that probation is for the penitent offender." Or, to turn the point around,
anyone found guilty at trial was not merely guilty of the specific
crime but also of perjury — and therefore, he surely did not deserve probation. Thus, an Illinois prosecutor could openly and in
direct contradiction of the law declare that in the case of a felon
convicted at trial, "it is apparent that he has testified falsely
[and] he is never released on probation."[33]

A second defense was to present plea bargaining as another
method of individualizing justice. One New York prosecutor, testifying before the Crime Commission, boldly insisted that the
district attorney as well as the judge had to fit the indictment to
the offender, to exercise discretion. "I have accepted [pleas to]
lesser degrees," he noted, "and I expect to do so in the future, in
the interests of justice and decency and mercy. . . . Don't let us
get to the point where we are to make . . . cast iron [rules] and
give no discretion to the judge or the district attorney." And what
is more, the committee credited his reasoning, admitting he had
raised a proper ethical and legal problem.[34]

In sum, the administrators of criminal justice were content with
the practice of probation. Pre-sentence investigations might be
crude and post-sentence supervision superficial; the rehabilitative
promise of the system might be far from realized; but their ability
to use probation for their own ends was in no way diminished,
and, perhaps, even increased. (Indeed, a rigorous pre-sentence
report or psychiatric examination might have restricted their
freedom to maneuver.) In view of the burgeoning number of
criminal cases, plea bargaining arrangements were not merely
convenient but necessary. Probation clearly facilitated the process, and thus seemed made to order for an overburdened system.

To be sure, some trade-offs were called for in this arrangement,
but those in charge of criminal justice were prepared to make

them. Prosecutors were opting to maximize the number of guilty pleas at the price of minimizing the severity of the individual punishments. From their vantage point, however, the trade-off was worthwhile. They would be credited with courtroom victories — the total number of convictions would be very high — and if the punishments appeared too lenient, they could say that the fault lay with judges or probation personnel. Small wonder, then, that district attorneys defended probation against legislative attack. When the Illinois Crime Survey polled the state's prosecutors, twenty out of twenty-three came out staunchly in favor of the system.[35]

Judges were even more steadfast in their endorsement of probation, although again some considerations could have dampened their enthusiasm. Since they were the ones who actually sentenced offenders to probation, public criticism at their seeming coddling of the criminal could come back to haunt them at election time. More, plea bargaining did represent something of an abdication of their own authority; the prosecutor and the defendant's lawyer reached agreement and the judge did little more than rubber stamp the bargain.

But counter-considerations prevailed. For one, it was their court calendars that were overfilled and their interest in clearing them was as great as the prosecutors'. For another, in any given case they could refuse to accept the plea bargain, thereby preserving at least the appearance of authority.

More important, judges enjoyed the vast discretionary authority that probation allowed them. They could, and did, dispense justice almost as they saw fit, so that those who examined their decisions were stunned by the variation in practice. "Each court acts separately," reported the Illinois Crime Survey, "and is governed in the main, only by its discretion." In Oregon, noted another investigator: "It is impossible to formulate any set practice." It was all a matter of "the policy of the judge." The same conclusion emerged from Arizona: "Different judges follow varying practices. . . . On the whole, the judges do not follow any set practice." True, even under nineteenth-century laws judges had been able to suspend sentences, to allow the offender his freedom without any supervision at all. But they found probation a preferable alternative. In many jurisdictions, the legality of suspended sentences had never been clear and the propriety of turning a convicted offender altogether free appeared at least somewhat dubious. Probation, on the other hand, secured the judge's right to pass a non-incarcerative sentence and allowed him the rhetorical justification that the released offender would be under close supervision. Accordingly, every judge queried in the Illinois Crime Survey favored the program. A similar study in Wisconsin learned that "the judges are almost unanimous in their support of probation." "I know of no better forum," concluded one judge, echoing his colleagues' sentiments, "in which to entrust this question [of probation or incarceration] than the court before whom this case has been tried and who is familiar with the facts and circumstances involved."[36]

But what use did the judges make of this familiarity? Beyond permitting the prosecuting attorneys to complete their plea bargains, to what ends did judges use their discretion? The obvious variety of practices precludes an altogether satisfactory generalization; still, it does appear likely (and the tentative quality of this language is purposeful) that the exercise of judicial discretion helped to effect a dual system of criminal justice: one brand for the poor, another for the middle and upper classes. Judicial discretion may well have promoted judicial discrimination.

It is probably not coincidental that probation gained popularity among administrators of criminal justice precisely at the moment when they confronted not only a crowded docket but an altogether alien collection of offenders. A judge sitting in New York or Boston or St. Louis or Minneapolis watched a parade of immigrant types pass before him, from first-generation Russians to second-generation Slavs to third-generation Irish — to say nothing of the native-born rural migrants who had just moved into the cities. Under these circumstances, judges may well have been particularly enthusiastic about a procedure that allowed ample room for distinctions among offenders, not on the basis of the crime, but on the basis of the person.

Did judges, in fact, grant probation in discriminatory fashion?

To offer a fully satisfactory and firm answer is, at least for now, impossible. Yet some evidence, albeit of an impressionistic kind, does suggest that many judges were prone to exercise their discretionary authority in class-biased ways.

Recognizing the free hand that judges had in dispensing probation, investigators at times asked judges to list the considerations that guided their decisions. Judges typically responded that the offender's age and prior criminal record were very relevant criteria. A youthful first-time offender was far more likely to gain probation than an older recidivist. (It was never clear whether judges considered age and record a mitigating circumstance or a predictive device, whether they were attempting to reduce the rigors of the criminal law or trying to calculate risks to the community. In all events, they did generally define probation as a marked and generous gift of leniency.) Judges also declared themselves more prepared to use probation when offenders came from a "good background" or from "good social background": when they had "good educational background," a "favorable family history," a proper "family influence and surroundings," a "suitable home," or "proper home environment and good job prospects." Although judges rarely defined these phrases precisely, such criteria obviously were biased in favor of the middle classes, of those who in social class and background most resembled the judges themselves. The youngster from the good family, with good job prospects, but who had made a misstep, warranted probation. His counterpart from the slums, whose father might have a criminal record and whose mother might have had several brushes with the law, would be much less favored.[37]

Certainly the rhetoric of the pre-sentence reports confirms this bias. Discovering that one offender lived with foster parents who owned their own farm, the probation officer declared: "They are excellent type people and highly regarded in their community . . . The defendant resides on a small farm in an ideal neighborhood." No one would have made such a claim for tenement life. Because another offender had belonged to the Boy Scouts and then later to the Junior Chamber of Commerce, his pre-sentence report indicated "good use of leisure time." And it seemed appropriate to note that he was also "neat and clean in appearance . . . [of] good breeding."[38]

Occasional bits of evidence confirm the links between social standing and probation. One researcher for the Attorney General's survey reported that "there is much evidence in Oregon that . . . sons of prominent families . . . local citizens, members of the white race . . . have a better chance of obtaining some form of judicial release than do prisoners conversely situated." The director of adult probation in California, expressing his enthusiasm for the new system, frankly noted that heretofore, "we have been accustomed to treat all members of our anti-social class alike, whether white or negro . . . mentally normal or sub-normal." Because under the old system, "they all look alike," it was assumed that they "should be treated accordingly. . . . Thus we have been traveling in darkness for years; and what is more, we shall drift further than ever in the 'Sea of Ignorance' unless we take time and endeavor to learn more about the individual criminal." Apparently, individualization was to permit an escape from outmoded notions that those who committed crimes should be treated alike, that distinctions as to the color of the offender were irrelevant to criminal justice. Or, as a judge from Baltimore argued, uniformly depriving serious offenders of the opportunity for probation was wrong: "I have [given probation] in manslaughter cases, burglary and in other cases where the criminal charge was a felony," and with good success — because "many of these young men come from the great middle classes who are good citizens." All they needed was help in obtaining a job. "This system works," he concluded.[39]

It is not claiming too much to assert that such biases were rooted in the very heart of the theory of probation. If judges were seeking the offender's readjustment, how much easier to treat someone who had less distance to travel in his readjustment; and how much more complicated to take an offender from the slums and turn him into a hard-working, law-abiding citizen. If they were attempting to predict lawful behavior, the likelihood seemed greater that someone from a comfortable and respectable family would return to the straight and narrow than someone from a broken family mired in poverty. Indeed, since judges often recognized that probation supervision was a sham, they may have been all the more conservative in their choices, or, put another way, more ready to gamble on a middle- than on a lower-class offender.[40] Even if judges were attempting to be lenient, surely it seemed likely that someone from a substantial background had made a (forgivable) trespass, whereas someone from the dangerous lower classes was embarking on a life in crime. The very existence of a system designed to transform "them" into "us" meant that those already more like "us" were bound to be favored. Once consideration shifted from the crime to the criminal, class distinctions came almost inevitably to assume new significance when punishments were meted out. Such distinctions, it is true, did not have to await the coming of probation; the policeman on the beat undoubtedly made similar judgments and so did the prosecutors in court anterooms. Still, the introduction of probation brought these kinds of discrimination to still another level of criminal justice, to sentencing decisions as well.

Finding so many advantages to probation, prosecutors and judges vigorously defended the measure in public forums and legislative hearings. The task, however, was not easy. They did reiterate the reform ideology — but this rhetoric would not satisfy hard-line critics, particularly as the evidence of inadequacies in implementation mounted in the 1920's and 1930's. Nor could the administrators explain the real grounds for their support of probation: self-interest. Plea bargaining, for example, was in such bad repute that to note its link to probation would have been foolhardy. And it would never do to suggest to a middle-class audience that it might benefit from the discretion that probation allowed; such a contention was well beyond the boundaries of acceptable political argument. Therefore, prosecutors and judges were often compelled to conclude treaties with the opposition, to make compromises satisfactory to both sides (if not to the reformers). The framework for these agreements was relatively simple: the legislative codes narrowed the criteria for probation eligibility, but without seriously restricting the administrators' discretion.

Although few states, even in the first enthusiasm for probation, had given judges a blank check, more and more of them in the 1920's and 1930's extended the list of crimes for which probation was not allowed. In 1926, to the dismay of the National Probation Association, Massachusetts enacted a statute forbidding the courts to give probation to anyone guilty of a third felony; that same year, New York, again over the opposition of the NPA, prohibited probation for anyone convicted of committing an armed felony. "There has been a fear," noted the Executive Secretary of the NPA, "to give too much discretion to judges in applying a system which mistakably was thought to be one of leniency."[41]

Nevertheless, the restrictions increased year by year and state by state. After its own review of probation in New York in the late 1920's, the Crime Commission recommended, and for the most part saw enacted, statutes that ruled out probation for those guilty of murder, arson, burglary, rape, first-degree robbery, kidnapping, armed felony, a second felony conviction, or a second conviction "of any of the eight misdemeanors connected with professional crime," such as possession of burglary tools, illegal entry, and unlawful ownership of a pistol. In 1928, California and Michigan disallowed probation for second felony offenses. The Illinois code of that year excluded murder, manslaughter, rape, kidnap, willful and corrupt perjury, arson, larceny, embezzlement of over $200, incest, burglary of an inhabited dwelling, and any conspiracy against the state's election laws. Whatever the variation, the statutes attempted to restrict the use of probation to the less serious crimes.[42]

Yet these limitations were not nearly as important to the administrators of the system as one might suppose. Judges frequently ignored the statutes, granting probation to offenders who were technically ineligible. Investigators uncovered frequent cases in which a judge simply refused to take into account a past criminal record — and there was no way to alter his decision. A more important fact was that legislative restrictions did little to hamper the ability of prosecutors to plea bargain. The codes merely set the terms and the boundaries within which negotiations would take place. If armed burglary was an exempted crime, the plea would have to be reduced to simple burglary; if robbery in the first degree was ineligible, the offender would plead guilty to robbery in the second degree. In fact, the tougher the law, the easier it might be for the prosecutor to obtain his guilty plea. An offer to the offender to reduce a charge below the felony level in return for a guilty plea not only might have favorable consequences for him in this crime, but was an opportunity to avoid being a two- or three-time loser. More, anyone brought up on a third felony charge would be eager to cop a plea for a misdemeanor. (This was precisely what happened when legislatures mandated life sentences for third-time felony offenders; on the third offense they were understandably ready to plead guilty to a misdemeanor.) In sum, legislative restrictions were a cheap price to pay for the survival of the system.[43]

When prosecutors were not using probation for their own purposes, judges, especially in the lower courts, were typically dispensing it to minor offenders. Reformers had not expected so narrow an application: although they had not designed the system for the hardened professional criminal, still they considered it a potent intervention, appropriate for at least some felons as well as some misdemeanants. More precisely, they had hoped for case-by-case decisions in which the individual himself, and not the formal and legal character of his act, would determine eligibility. But, as we have seen, local magistrates preferred to use probation for those guilty of petty larceny, disorderly conduct, minor burglaries, motor vehicle infractions, drunk or disorderly conduct, and cases of non-support. In a state like New York, a little over 90 percent of probationers in 1914 were misdemeanants and only 10 percent felons; in fact, the percentages did not vary much over the next decades. By 1926, for example, the numbers on probation had increased enormously, but still 90 percent of the rolls were composed of those guilty of less than felony offenses.[44]

Other jurisdictions were no different. The Attorney General's analysis of some 19,000 cases on probation in twenty-four different jurisdictions pointed to a similar pattern. Reformers, to be sure, protested these practices. Frank Wade, head of the New York State Probation Commission, was hopeful that "opposition to the use of probation in offenses less than felonies is rapidly disintegrating." But, he conceded, "the extension of probation for felonies still encounters strenuous antagonism and distrust." And such distrust would persist through the pre–World War II period.[45]

This judicial behavior was by no means irrational. Aware that pre-sentence reports were not accurate predictors and that post-sentence supervision was farcical, judges preferred probation for those who seemed to need little more than a slap on the wrist. Occasionally they would acknowledge making this calculation. In Baltimore, one judge conceded that the judiciary selected probationers on a " 'hand picked' basis of persons who probably do not need supervision anyway." A candid New York magistrate wondered whether those probationers reputed to have "made good" and to represent a victory for the system would not have succeeded even without it. "I am convinced," he testified, "that of the 65 percent who have made good without criminal record, 33⅓ percent, and I think that is very conservative, would have made good anyway, whether placed on probation or not."[46]

To speculate on what sentences judges would have passed without a probation system is risky, but some evidence does permit a few suggestions. The use of probation for petty offenders, and the reluctance to apply it to serious offenders (a reluctance that may have been even greater in the case of lower-class serious offenders), hint that reformers' ambitions aside, judges probably seldom resorted to probation for offenders who otherwise would have been incarcerated. Advocates had presented probation as an alternative to the penitentiary, but the program did not work that way. Plea bargaining may have spared some offenders from a prison term, but as we shall see in more detail later, their numbers were probably not great enough to have a notable impact on the total prison population.

Probation may have helped to reduce the numbers in local jails.

All sorts of variables, ranging from the efficiency of the police to the willingness of jurors to convict to reliance on other types of institutions (such as almshouses or workhouses), all determined the size of a jail population. Still, in states like New York and Massachusetts, probation may have been a contributing element. Between 1908 and 1914, for example, the New York jail population climbed more slowly than the general population (going from 3,508 to 3,935) — and over the same period, the probation rolls mounted (from 1,648 to 8,141). The rates of commitment to jails in Massachusetts also dropped as the use of probation expanded (from 898 per 100,000 in 1910 to 280 per 100,000 in 1923).[47]

But probation may have had another and more important effect: it may have served as a substitute for a suspended sentence. Rather than think of probation (as the reformers did) primarily as an alternative to the prison or the jail, it seems most appropriate to conceive of it as an alternative to doing nothing at all. In effect, probation may have been a supplementary and add-on program, increasing the number of persons brought under the aegis of the criminal justice system.

The New York experience again is instructive. On January 1, 1908, the total adult population under court or correctional oversight was 16,344 (some 4,000 in state penitentiaries, some 1,600 on probation, and the rest in reformatories and local jails); by 1914, the number had climbed to 25,015 — 5,000 in state prisons and 8,140 on probation. Over the six years when probation was taking root in the state, the number of persons under criminal justice jurisdiction jumped by 50 percent, with much of the increase due to the expansion of probation rolls. And this trend, once begun, was not reversed. In 1907 the New York courts committed 12,053 persons (adults and juveniles combined) to correctional institutions and placed another 1,672 on probation; twenty years later they dispatched 17,373 persons to correctional institutions and put 23,154 on probation. Thus, the total number of persons under state supervision had risen dramatically (from 14,000 to 40,500), with probation leading the way. Or to demon-

strate still more vividly the "add-on" quality of probation, between 1908 and 1926, 240,000 adults in New York State went on
probation — and given finite facilities and tax-conscious legislators, it would not have been possible for most or even many of
them to have been incarcerated. In brief, the new system allowed
the state to exert a legal authority over a group of people who
otherwise would have been left to their own devices.[48]

The supplementary character of probation is also evident in
Massachusetts. In 1900, the state placed 6,201 persons on probation and sentenced another 27,809 offenders to state or local incarcerative facilities — exercising control over 34,010 people. In
1929, it placed 32,809 persons on probation and committed another 19,650 to prisons and lock-ups, exercising control over
52,451 people. Thus, even a drop in the numbers incarcerated
could go hand in hand with a rise in the numbers under state
jurisdiction. In Massachusetts, probation reduced the jail population and simultaneously expanded the network of oversight.[49]

A few contemporaries glimpsed this truth and tried to make
political capital out of it. The New York State Crime Commission
expressed keen dissatisfaction with the implementation of the system but, given the political lineups, recommended improving, not
abolishing, probation. "It is an interesting fact," argued the
Commission, "to be noted by those who are critics of probation
on the ground that it 'encourages' leniency that in New York
County where probation is probably most highly developed and
most completely administered the rate of suspended sentence is
the lowest in the state." In the rural districts which lacked probation systems, twice as many offenders went off on suspended
sentence, completely free of oversight, than in New York County.
Even leading reformers, like Hastings Hart and Frank Wade,
occasionally made similar remarks. Before probation, declared
Hart, "Judges have been accustomed to suspend sentence, but the
fellow went out and he [the judge] had no means of keeping
track of him." Then came the new system: "Every time a man
was put on probation and had to make return to an officer from
time to time . . . and was liable to be brought back into court if he

did not go straight, you can see that you had a much tougher purchase upon him." In other words, to vote for probation was not to vote for coddling the criminal but for policing him.[50]

In the end, contemporaries did not take this argument terribly seriously. Probation continued to be understood not only among the public at large, but in legislative and judicial circles, as a grant of leniency. A powerful and self-reinforcing dynamic set in: to define probation as leniency meant that those on the rolls were not in need of close supervision; since they were not in need of close supervision, there was less reason to worry that probation officers were overworked, underpaid, and undertrained. But, of course, since probation officers were obviously ill-equipped to handle the serious offender, it was appropriate to enact legislation restricting probation eligibility; and so one came around the circle to using probation for those who did not require supervision anyway.

However little attention contemporaries paid to the "add-on" quality of probation, it well warrants our attention. Here was an innovation that in dramatic ways expanded the scope of state action and state surveillance. When one notes, too, the enlarged definition of what constituted relevant court information (in the pre-sentence report), appropriate probation conditions, and the investigatory powers of the probation officer (in the guise of friend), the point becomes still more significant. To be sure, probation's potential for coercion was never realized in a sweeping way. Most probation officers were far too overburdened with clients and responsibilities to be intrusive in systematic fashion. Nevertheless, probation did have serious consequences for civil liberties. Whatever its overall effects, the individual probationer could never be certain that his would not be the unusual case, the exception to the general rule of neglect. His probation officer might have the time or the inclination to misuse authority; his revocation might come because he ignored a probation condition. That the system's potential for coercion was never fully realized does not mean that all probationers escaped from the arbitrary exercise of power.

Further, we are not accustomed to think of the parsimony of

our legislatures as protective of civil liberties — yet in the case of probation such a judgment is warranted. The opportunity for coercive state intervention was present. Probation officers did not need warrants to enter a client's house; their right to search and to question was not restricted; indeed, clients typically could not even be represented by counsel in their dealings with probation departments. What were the counterbalancing elements? A crowded work schedule; the need to report to the court on investigations of new cases while simultaneously having to carry out supervision of older cases; a very low salary scale that did not attract the energetic to the system; the dead-end quality of the job. All of these elements were related to probation's unrealized potential to do mischief — so that tax-consciousness may have been more relevant to preserving civil liberties than heretofore imagined.

How did the reformers themselves react to the distortion of their original designs? The answer is simple and straightforward: they continued to advocate probation and to promote individualized and discretionary justice. At no point in the pre–World War II period (or, really, before the mid-1960's) did reformers pause to wonder whether the gap between rhetoric and reality should lead them to abandon the program. They did not ask the structural question: if the administration of probation was not satisfying the reformers themselves, was it actually serving other and very different groups and interests? The faulty administration of the program in 1920 or in 1930 or in 1940 did not spark a reconsideration of the assumptions of the program. Reformers blamed stingy legislatures and poor administrators, not the concept itself.

That for a generation reformers doggedly defended their original principles is not difficult to explain. It was not merely a case of good intentions dying hard, of eagerness to do good outstripping ability to do good. Rather, first, the intellectual premises of probation grew all the more powerful and persuasive. Throughout the 1920's and 1930's, psychological explanations for all types of human behavior gained popularity, especially with the mounting reputation of Sigmund Freud. As a result, to anticipate the "readjustment" of the deviant; to contend, as one New York probation officer did, that "crime is attributable to deep rooted psychological processes"; and to deny the "impossibility of separating the individual from the physical and social forces which condition his development" seemed to make eminent good sense. Only an intervention based on psychological insights could alter deviant behavior, and probation represented that intervention. In other words, reformers were not about to abandon a psychological orientation just when that perspective was capturing the national imagination.

Proponents also remained loyal to the principles of probation precisely because its administration was so inadequate. Since the ideas of the program were valid and the practices so faulty, clearly the problem lay with implementation. If only the case loads would shrink, if only the training of the officers would improve, then the system would function effectively. To give up the theory in light of the glaring inadequacies of performance seemed premature and unwarranted.

Moreover, the opponents who lined up against probation appeared so crude in their thinking that reformers thought it impossible to do anything except line up against them. When the alternative to probation seemed to be to lock up and throw away the key on all criminals, small wonder that men of good faith stuck to their innovation. Since the only counterproposals that they heard were to get tougher with the offender — to pass out longer sentences, to confine three- or four-time felons for life — a defense of treatment goals and individual approaches seemed both the more humane and the more promising strategy. In short, how could reformers dare attack probation when it might stimulate a massive increase in retribution? It is not unusual to support a program on the basis of the enemies it makes, and from the reformers' perspective probation had made the right enemies.

Reformers were also reluctant to give up on probation because, in their calculations, it was at least in a few jurisdictions delivering effective treatment. This judgment did not result from a close study of the case records (for such a study would have put to rest any notion that treatment was taking place anywhere), but from the subsequent police records of probationers. Within six months to a year after their sentences, a majority of probationers had not been recommitted to jail. Reformers delighted in a New York City study (331 cases, 87 percent "success") and a Massachusetts study (2,000 cases, 88 percent "success").[51] The pitfalls of measuring probation effectiveness by subsequent arrests did not occur to them. They did not ask whether low re-arrest figures might reflect bad policing, or bad record keeping; more important, they generally did not ask whether the success rate would have been identical if probation had not been used. To the degree that probation was reserved for the "easy" cases, for those who might otherwise have received a suspended sentence, a "success" rate had no connection to the effectiveness of the program. Enthusiasts, however, are not likely to look far beneath the surface of data that seem to confirm their key thesis.

In the end, all of the arguments in favor of probation made good sense to reformers because of their underlying Progressive belief in a harmony of interests within American society. An effort to do good for the offender and simultaneously to protect the social order, to serve the individual and the community, would ultimately succeed, or (put in its least ambitious form) could not produce harmful results. How much better for the offender not to be the object of vengeance, but benevolence; how much better for the society to rehabilitate criminals than to punish them. Unable to imagine that the effort to do good might subject the offender to arbitrary or excessive state action, or conversely, that an open-ended criminal justice system might not be protective of a society's safety, reformers saw no reason to lessen their support of probation.

In much the same way, reformers could not begin to sort out the complex character of their relationship to the administrators of criminal justice. Trade-offs were not part of their perspective and they did not imagine that the operational needs of district attorneys or judges might be in conflict with their own aims, and even subvert them. To understand such considerations, reformers would have had to entertain notions of one narrow self-interested group competing with another. But they could not see their system that way. To Progressives, discretionary justice carried no costs. It was in everyone's best interest.

CHAPTER FOUR

Up Against
the Prison Wall

PROGRESSIVES WERE EAGER to extend the premises that underlay probation to the design of the penitentiary. Acutely dissatisfied with existing conditions of incarceration but convinced that some offenders would have to be confined, they were confident of their ability to effect rehabilitation behind as well as outside the walls. In fact, their proposals represented the second grand reform program in the history of the prison, the successor to the founding ideology of the Jacksonians.

Both generations of reformers believed that the penitentiary could cure the criminal. Their strategies, however, differed markedly. The Jacksonians had conceived of the ideal prison routine as an antidote to the community. Certain that the roots of deviancy could be traced to the chaotic and exceptionally mobile quality of American society, they tried to create a utopian alternative: a highly disciplined and regimented routine which would at once reform the prisoner and inspire the community to emulation. The inmate was to be isolated from all contaminating influences (not only of the society at large but of his fellow prisoners) so as to come under the perfecting influence of bell-ringing punctuality and steady work habits. Rules of silence, the lock step, long work hours and longer periods of isolation, restrictions on mail and curtailment of visits, all became the distinguishing characteristics of American prisons of the Jacksonian era.

The Progressives reversed these principles. For them, the lines of influence had to run not from the prison to the community but from the community to the prison. Rather than serve as a model to the society, the penitentiary was to model itself on the society; it was not to be an antidote to the external environment, but a faithful replication of it. "The conception of the prison as a community" was the organizing formula. "Temporary exile into a temporary society as nearly as possible like normal society on the outside would seem the best solution."[1]

Such an orientation appeared first in the 1870's, with the *Declaration of Principles* of the National Congress. But the Progressives enlarged on these ideas and made them relevant to the operation of all types of prisons. Persuaded of the essential soundness of the American system and committed wholeheartedly to the notion of individualizing criminal justice, they labeled the traditional prisons "machine-like," and criticized them as failures at rehabilitation. How could it be otherwise when they prescribed the same medicine to all inmates and did not prepare them to reenter society? "The old prison system," noted one reformer, "exists in terms of suppression and isolation of the individual and in a denial of a social existence." It was absurd to compel a prisoner to follow ironclad rules in the institution when he should have been helped to adjust to the democratic quality of community life. The prison had to be redesigned to meet individual needs and to faciliate an eventual return to society.[2]

The task may well have appeared formidable. After all, every state prison held anywhere from one thousand to three thousand inmates in an environment that at best resembled a factory. But Progressives were certain of their ability to individualize and democratize the prison. They wished to abolish such inherited practices as the lock step and the striped uniforms. They encouraged liberalized correspondence and visitation rules; to maintain contact with the outside society would facilitate the inmate's later adjustment. Further, they detested the rule of silence; inmates were social creatures and should be so treated. Progressives also looked to introduce amusements into the prison routine. Sports, exercise, movies, bands, and orchestras, all now seemed appropriate. And so did commissaries, where prisoners could purchase the small but significant amenities that would heighten their sense of a more ordinary life.

The design that best exemplified Progressive ambitions was the Mutual Welfare League, an attempt to introduce the startling concept of inmate self-government into the penitentiary. Thomas Mott Osborne was its chief architect and publicist. In 1913, as the head of the New York Prison Reform Commission, he took the unprecedented step of spending a week anonymously as an inmate at the Auburn penitentiary. Participant-observation has since become commonplace, but Osborne may well have been the first reformer to practice it. Some Progressives went to live in the slums; Osborne went to live in the prison.

Auburn seemed to Osborne to violate every precept of common sense, that is, common sense to a Progressive. Its regime was unnatural and therefore ineffective. He found the rule of silence cruel. "Fourteen hundred men sitting at dinner — and no sound of the human voice; — it is a ghastly thing." And he could only wonder at its invention: "How students of penology . . . would imagine that human beings can be healthy in body, mind or soul, except by natural relations through the power of speech with their fellow human beings, passes understanding." The practice of total isolation was no less bizarre. Osborne calculated that he spent fourteen consecutive hours of confinement daily in a tiny, cage-like cell, and six days of this was almost more than he could bear. So then "how about those who must look forward to an endless series of nights, month after month, year after year, five, ten, fifteen, twenty years, life? How do they ever stand it?"[3]

In a regimen of constant confinement, insisted Osborne, particularly in an all-male setting, "certain natural immoral acts are bound to arise, because of the essentially unnatural social conditions." Jacksonians had expected isolation to spark redemption, but Osborne was convinced it encouraged masturbation and perversion.[4]

The inevitable consequence of such a system had to be pervasive brutality. "The nervous condition of the men, caused by the silence, the monotony . . . carries with it an equally nervous condition of the guards." Predictably, the guard became "irritable and severe. . . . His fear engenders brutality; and brutality breeds revenge," which in turn provokes "more nervousness and greater fear; and so the vicious circle is complete." The inhumanity was thus integral to the old design. "Every generation or so there is a revelation of prison tortures; and a scandalized community forces the legislature to pass a law forbidding some special form of punishment." But the only result of such piecemeal responses was "to have some new cruelty devised to take its place." For Osborne, prisons had to be totally revamped. "The prison system," he concluded, "endeavors to make men . . . virtuous by removing temptation; to make them respect the law by forcing them to obey the edicts of an autocrat . . . to give them individual initiative by treating them in large groups; in short, to prepare them again for society by placing them in conditions as unlike society as they could well be made."[5]

Osborne was at one with other Progressive reformers in looking to abolish the remnants of the nineteenth-century prison routines. But he offered something more when he extended the concept of the prison as a community into the arena of prison government. Inspired in part by similar kinds of effort among juvenile delinquents at the George Junior Republic, of which he was a trustee, and perhaps in part by the work of the settlement houses (whose clubs diligently tried to teach the immigrants democratic procedures and parliamentary rule), Osborne wanted to make the inmates responsible for their own conduct. Here again, the motto was Gladstone's: "It is liberty alone that fits men for liberty."

As set forth by Osborne (and to a degree implemented by him when he became warden of Sing-Sing in 1914), the Mutual Welfare League was to be the major governing body of the prison. Inmates would elect a Board of Delegates, who in turn would elect an Executive Board. This Board would constitute the prison's rule-making and enforcement body, subject to review by the Delegates. Its members would supervise the inmates in the shops and in the yard. It would organize various fund-raising events, and use the proceeds to provide movies and more recreation facilities. It would also select a judiciary board to hear cases of infractions and levy penalties. In ideal form, it would not necessarily abolish the jobs of the wardens and the guards, but it would certainly circumscribe them. More, the Mutual Welfare League would present inmates' grievances before the public and the legislature. In sum, the League would make inmates "not good *prisoners*, but good *citizens* . . . [and] fit them for the free life to which, sooner or later, they are to return."[6]

Progressive reformers greeted Osborne's ideas enthusiastically. Frank Tannenbaum, later to become one of the outstanding Latin American scholars in the United States, began his career as a prison reformer. His book, *Wall Shadows* (1922), one of the most popular reform tracts of the period, owed a clear debt to Osborne. "Prison Democracy," Tannenbaum proclaimed, was *the* answer. The inmate "forgets, one might almost say, that he is in prison. His whole life tends to become vibrant with an altogether new set of values and new set of experiences." Osborne was also the hero of the 1920 Prison Survey Committee Report to the New York State legislature. The traditional prison, concluded the Committee, was "merely a mechanism for keeping men docile and obedient to rule while in prison. Mr. Osborne shifted the point of view toward the question of how to send them out." The Committee recognized that the implementation would be difficult. "But it is better to have problems and mistakes come out of trying to establish democracy in prisons than to have no problems and abundant errors as the results of the present isolation and desocialization of the prisoner."[7]

The broad Progressive intention to redesign the prison on the model of the community persisted as a favorite precept for reformers through the 1920's and 1930's. When two leading criminologists, Edwin Sutherland and Thorsten Sellin, organized a conference in 1931 on "The Prisons of Tomorrow," this theme dominated. Edward Cass, the president of the National Probation

Association, insisted that the "treadmill quality" of a highly disciplined prison routine "is not a proper preparation for the resumption of a varied social life." Prisoners were expected to function "in a complex social environment — but the institution does little . . . to augment their ability to do this." The head of the National Society of Penal Information was equally certain that the "excessive regimentation of prison life, at best unnatural and abnormal, is in no way a preparation for social life after release." And the psychiatrists present, such as William Allison White, also had kind words for the community model. "Prisons for the most part are literally horrible places," declared White, because "the prisoner can find little or no self-expression, few or none of the satisfactions of life." Unless the prison setting became more normal, rehabilitation could not be achieved.[8]

Psychiatrists, however, were not completely satisfied with this formulation and they brought a second model to prison reform, the model of the prison as hospital. Reflecting their own belief in psychological as opposed to environmental causes of deviancy, they looked to transform the institutions into treatment centers which would diagnose the ailment and deliver the appropriate antidote. On the face of it, the hospital model did not fit with the community model. Whatever else they may be, hospital routines are not those of a free society; or in other terms, what precisely did inmates need, training in democratic habits or therapeutic encounters? But in prison reform as in probation or, for that matter, in Progressive schools, the distinctions were blurred and the programs did become blended together. In the 1920's, for example, school reformers moved to introduce John Dewey's notions of democratic practices into the classroom and at the same time, to bring child guidance counselors onto the school staff. Students were to be trained in self-government through classroom routines (again, the similarity to Osborne's Mutual Welfare League is obvious) and simultaneously to take a battery of psychological and vocational aptitude tests, so as to learn where they best fit. This same perspective carried over into the prison: it too could serve both as a laboratory for democracy and a laboratory for science.[9]

The first goal of the psychiatrically-minded reformers was to establish diagnostic centers or clearinghouses for all new inmates. It was not the judge's task, they insisted, either to set the term of confinement (hence the indeterminate sentence) or to decide on the type of institution in which an inmate should be treated. These tasks belonged to psychiatrists, psychologists, and social workers. They would interview, examine, and test the inmate, determine his aptitudes and his potential for rehabilitation, then assign him to an appropriate place.

Accordingly, these reformers urged the establishment of a variety of institutions, each to serve the special needs of a class of offenders. "The prison system," announced William White, "must develop different types of institutions for different types of individuals." His colleague, Dr. H. E. Allison, contended: "The public schools are graded. . . . Our general hospitals are divided." And so too, "specialization in our penal institutions must not be delayed if we desire to make progress."[10]

Two California psychiatrists, Ernest Hoag and Edward Williams, proposed just such a system, using New York's institutions to illustrate their points. Criminals, they explained, fit into five broad categories: those capable of learning a trade, those best suited for agriculture, the insane, the defective, and the psychopathic. A reception station (located at Sing-Sing) with medical, psychiatric, and educational departments would diagnose and assign each inmate. The prisons at Clinton and Auburn would serve as the industrial centers and Great Meadow as the farm; Dannemora would hold the criminally insane and the psychopathic; and a new institution would be built for the defective.

There were other, more simple, schemes, under which prisoners could be classified according to their potential for rehabilitation. Those most likely to be reformed would enter a minimum security prison; the less amenable would go to a medium or maximum security setting. The particular system of classification was almost not as important as the idea of classification itself. One way or another, the inmate had to be treated as an individual, not as part of a mass.[11]

The psychiatrists' agenda for the prison fit well with the goals of other reformers; it also appealed to wardens, not only because of the legitimation that a hospital analogy provided but because the program might simplify the business of custody. Classification promised to remove the troublemakers from the general prison population, thereby isolating the hard-core offender. "In every penal institution," William White himself noted, "there are a few, perhaps not more than four or five in a thousand, who cannot be influenced. . . . It is not right, not fair, not desirable that the other nine hundred and ninety-five should be treated by a standard set by them. Because, for example, four or five might abuse the privilege of freedom of speech [note "privilege," not right], the nine hundred and more should not be deprived." In other words, a prison community, like a normal community, should be purified, and classification would serve this end.[12]

So too, the psychiatrists' program seemed fully protective of community safety because they were prepared, perhaps even more than other reformers, to confine the untreatable for very long periods of time. Psychiatrists saw no barriers, either legal or medical, to identifying and segregating "defective" or "psychopathic" criminals. Doctors Hoag and Williams, for example, insisted that classification schemes distinguish carefully between "socially adaptable" and "socially unadaptable" offenders: "Practical solution consists in . . . segregating . . . those who are permanently unfit to take their places in the life of the outside world." Indeed, "the total number of this class is extremely large." William White, for his part, thought the number much smaller but had no difficulty with the propriety and fairness of permanent segregation. "I believe fully," he declared, "in society's right to segregate the dangerous anti-social types so long as they continue dangerous. Individuals who are so constructed that they cannot function effectively and safely as social units should be removed from society . . . [so that] society can be protected from their depredations." Once again, the reform program did not seem to demand trade-offs. Rehabilitation and protection went hand in hand, without social costs or compromises.[13]

Psychiatrists' attention to the details of classification did not carry over into any meticulous description of the content of the rehabilitative programs themselves. The question of diagnosis practically monopolized their writings; and when they did occasionally offer specific programs, they were more comfortable talking about vocational education and schooling than they were describing psychological counseling or therapeutic intervention. The void, as we shall see again in the mental hospital (Chapter Ten), was not accidental. In the prison, as in probation and in the mental hospital, most attention went to diagnosis because psychiatrists remained uncertain of how to translate their understanding of the deviant into specific recommendations for cure. For all their allegiance to a medical model, they had no medicines to prescribe.

This inability to design programs helps to account for the readiness of a psychiatrist like William White to devote the bulk of his prison writings to criticism of the traditional principle of uniformity and emphasis on the importance of individualization, and then to end his tracts with a plea for the prison as a research center. White's books and articles right through the 1920's and 1930's invariably trail off into vague declarations promoting the idea of prisons as institutions "for sincere scientific study and research and conscientious endeavor," as though sincerity and conscientiousness would compensate for ignorance. He looked to "the gradual transformation of prisons into laboratories for the study of human behavior and the conditioning of human conduct," but how that conditioning was to occur, he could not say. White reiterated the need to give up "archaic methods of thinking and acting." But what was to be substituted in their place? "A system calculated to produce the greatest possible results of social value from the material at hand." Not for the last time, good intentions were to substitute for knowledge.[14]

The inability of psychiatrists to move beyond diagnosis to treatment actually brought them closer to other prison reformers.

Just as Healy's prescriptions on how to treat a maladjusted girl in the community were identical to the recommendations of the settlement house workers, so all reformers, regardless of training, agreed upon the ideal prison routine.

Everyone supported classification. The Massachusetts Civic League in 1922 made "thorough psychiatric examination and observation, that the mental condition may be diagnosed and treated," one of the first planks in its agenda, followed immediately by "classification for treatment of the reformable cases" and "permanent segregation of those hopelessly criminal and dangerous to society." The Wickersham Commission concurred.[15] Education, vocational training, and work routines would rehabilitate those inmates who could be rehabilitated. Prisons had to offer, according to one advocate, Austin MacCormick, "fundamental education" for the illiterate," starting from zero or from a grade so low that they will have to go through the very arduous processes that should have been completed in childhood." In New York, the investigatory committee chaired by Alfred Lewisohn supported this view: "The greatest field for 'schooling' in prison is in overcoming illiteracy." For those already literate, the prisons were to provide vocational education, whose benefits, MacCormick noted, "are too well understood to require discussion." Vocational education was linked to opportunities for work within the prison. "The two go hand in hand," declared MacCormick. "The industries of the institution . . . should offer a wide variety of skilled and semiskilled operations that should match the production, standards and pace of outside industries." The Lewisohn Committee called for seven hours a day of labor with pay: "Work is to be the foundation around which every activity revolves in every prison."[16]

Such programs would not only train the inmates but revolutionize the quality of prison life. Here was the way to change prisons into communities, for now a prisoner's initiative could be rewarded. He would move up in school grade and work ranks, practically earning his way out of the prison. Such procedures would also alter the character of prison discipline. Demotions and loss of privileges, instead of brutal physical punishments, would become the major sanctions. Just how many privileges could be withdrawn, just what rights the prisoner, however refractory, enjoyed, reformers did not discuss. They focused on the top of the ladder, not its bottom rungs.

All of these principles, from normalization to classification to education, constituted the new prison design. "The day must be filled with as much interesting activity in the form of work, play, education, and conversation as possible," declared the Wickersham Commission. And the Lewisohn Committee provided the timetable:[17]

Daily Schedule

5:30	Reveille
5:45	Setting up exercises
6:15	Make up quarters
6:20	Sick call
7:00	Breakfast
7:30–11:30	Shop, power on, every man working
11:30–11:45	Wash for dinner
11:45	Recall
12:00	Dinner
1:00–4:00	Shop, power on, every man working
4:00–6:00	Washing up, liberty in yard, baths, shaves, purchases, calls, visits
6:00	Recall
6:15	Supper
7:00–9:00	Classes, entertainments
9:30	Taps

In sum, reformers believed that they could transform a nightmarish prison, dedicated to punishment, into a community that would at once prepare the inmate for release and serve as a testing ground for society. The prisoner who functioned well behind walls could function well outside them. The inmate who succeeded in promoting himself through the ranks was ready to graduate into free society. Since in this new prison "they would be learning to play the game according to the rules," they would be ready upon release to continue playing by the rules. Prison adjustment had become social adjustment — the good inmate, the good citizen.[18]

The Progressives' design for the penitentiary did alter the system of incarceration. Their ideas on normalization, classification, education, labor, and discipline had an important effect upon prison administration. But in this field, perhaps above all others, innovation must not be confused with reform. Once again, rhetoric and reality diverged substantially. Progressive programs were adopted more readily in some states than in others, more often in industrialized and urban areas, less often in southern, border, and mountain regions. Nowhere, however, were they adopted consistently. One finds a part of the program in one prison, another part in a second or in a third. Change was piecemeal, not consistent, and procedures were almost nowhere implemented to the degree that reformers wished. One should think not of a Progressive prison, but of prisons with more or less Progressive features.

The change that would have first struck a visitor to a twentieth-century institution who was familiar with traditional practices, was the new style of prisoners' dress. The day of the stripes passed, outlandish designs gave way to more ordinary dress. It was a small shift, but officials enthusiastically linked it to a new orientation for incarceration. In 1896 the warden of Illinois's Joliet prison commented that inmates "should be treated in a manner that would tend to cultivate in them, spirit of self-respect, manhood and self-denial. . . . We are certainly making rapid headway, as is shown by the recently adopted Parole Law and the abolishment of prison stripes." In 1906, the directors of the New Hampshire prison, eager to follow the dictates of the "science of criminology" and "the laws of modern prisons," complained that "the old unsightly black and red convict suit is still used. . . . This prison garb is degrading to the prisoner and in modern prisons is no longer worn." The uniform should be grey: "Modern prisons have almost without exception adopted this color." The next year they proudly announced that the legislature had approved an appropriation of $700 to cover the costs of the turnover. By the mid-1930's the Attorney General's survey of prison conditions reported that only four states (all southern) still used striped uniforms. The rest had abandoned "the ridiculous costumes of earlier days."[19]

To the same ends, most penitentiaries abolished the lock step and the rules of silence. Sing-Sing, which had invented that curious shuffle, substituted a simple march. Pennsylvania's Eastern State Penitentiary, world famous for creating and enforcing the silent system, now allowed prisoners to talk in dining rooms, in shops, and in the yard. Odd variations on these practices also ended. "It had been the custom for years," noted the New Hampshire prison directors, "not to allow prisoners to look in any direction except downward," so that "when a man is released from prison he will carry with him as a result of this rule a furtive and hang-dog expression." In keeping with the new ethos, they abolished the regulation.[20]

Concomitantly, prisons allowed inmates "freedom of the yard," to mingle, converse, and exercise for an hour or two daily. Some institutions built baseball fields and basketball courts and organized prison teams. "An important phase in the care of the prisoner," declared the warden of California's Folsom prison, "is the provisions made for proper recreation. Without something to look forward to, the men would become disheartened. . . . Baseball is the chief means of recreation and it is extremely popular." The new premium on exercise and recreation was the penitentiary's counterpart to the Progressive playground movement and settlement house athletic clubs.[21]

This same orientation led prisons to introduce movies. Sing-Sing showed films two nights a week, others settled for once a week, and the warden or the chaplain usually made the choice. Folsom's warden, for example, like to keep them light: "Good wholesome comedy with its laugh provoking qualities seems to be the most beneficial." Radio soon appeared as well. The prisons generally established a central system, providing inmates with earphones in their cells to listen to the programs that the administration selected. The Virginia State Penitentiary allowed inmates to use their own sets, with the result that, as a visitor remarked, "the institution looks like a large cob-web with hundreds of antennas, leads and groundwires strung about the roofs and around the cell block."[22]

Given a commitment to sociability, prisons liberalized rules of correspondence and visits. Sing-Sing placed no restrictions on the number of letters, San Quentin allowed one a day, the New Jersey penitentiary at Trenton permitted six a month. Visitors could now come to most prisons twice a month and some institutions, like Sing-Sing, allowed visits five times a month. Newspapers and magazines also enjoyed freer circulation. As New Hampshire's warden observed in 1916: "The new privileges include newspapers, that the men may keep up with the events of the day, more frequent writing of letters and receiving of letters from friends, more frequent visits from relatives . . . all of which tend to contentment and the reestablishment of self-respect." All of this would make the prisoners' "life as nearly normal as circumstances will permit, so that when they are finally given their liberty they will not have so great a gap to bridge between the life they have led here . . . and the life that we hope they are to lead."[23]

These innovations may well have eased the burden of incarceration. Under conditions of total deprivation of liberty, amenities are not to be taken lightly. But whether they could normalize the prison environment and breed self-respect among inmates is quite another matter. For all these changes, the prison community remained abnormal. Inmates simply did not look like civilians; no one would mistake a group of convicts for a gathering of ordinary citizens. The baggy grey pants and the formless grey jacket, each item marked prominently with a stenciled identification number, became the typical prison garb. And the fact that many prisons allowed the purchase of bits of clothing, such as a sweater or more commonly a cap, hardly gave inmates a better appearance. The new dress substituted one kind of uniform for another. Stripes gave way to numbers.

So too, prisoners undoubtedly welcomed the right to march or walk as opposed to shuffle, and the right to talk to each other without fear of penalty. But freedom of the yard was limited to an hour or two a day and it was usually spent in "aimless milling about." Recreational facilities were generally primitive, and organized athletic programs included only a handful of men. More disturbing, prisoners still spent the bulk of non-working time in their cells. Even liberal prisons locked their men in by 5:30 in the afternoon and kept them shut up until the next morning. Administrators continued to censor mail, reading materials, movies, and radio programs; their favorite prohibitions involved all matter dealing with sex or communism. Inmates preferred eating together to eating alone in a cell. But wardens, concerned about the possibility of riots with so many inmates congregated together, often added a catwalk above the mess hall and put armed guards on patrol.[24]

Prisoners may well have welcomed liberalized visiting regulations, but the encounters took place under trying conditions. Some prisons permitted an initial embrace, more prohibited all physical contact. The rooms were dingy and gloomy. Most institutions had the prisoner and his visitor talk across a table, generally separated by a glass or wire mesh. The more security-minded went to greater pains. At Trenton, for example, bullet-proof glass divided inmate from visitor; they talked through a perforated metal opening in the glass. Almost everywhere guards sat at the ends of the tables and conversations had to be carried on in a normal voice; anyone caught whispering would be returned to his cell. The whole experience was undoubtedly more frustrating than satisfying.[25]

The one reform that might have fundamentally altered the internal organization of the prison, Osborne's Mutual Welfare League, was not implemented to any degree at all. The League persisted for a few years at Sing-Sing, but a riot in 1929 gave guards and other critics the occasion to eliminate it. One could argue that inmate self-rule under Osborne was little more than a skillful exercise in manipulation, allowing Osborne to cloak his own authority in a more benevolent guise. It is unnecessary, however, to dwell on so fine a point. Wardens were simply not prepared to give over any degree of power to inmates. After all, how could men who had already abused their freedom on the outside be trusted to exercise it on the inside? Administrators also feared, not unreasonably, that inmate rule would empower inmate gangs to abuse fellow prisoners. In brief, the concept of a Mutual Welfare League made little impact on prison systems throughout this period.[26]

If prisons could not approximate a normal community, they fared no better in attempting to approximate a therapeutic community. Again, reform programs frequently did alter inherited practices but they inevitably fell far short of fulfilling expectations. Prisons did not warrant the label of hospital or school.

Starting in the 1910's and even more commonly through the 1920's, state penitentiaries established a period of isolation and classification for entering inmates. New prisoners were confined to a separate building or cell block (or occasionally, to one institution in a complex of state institutions); they remained there for a two- to four-week period, took tests and underwent interviews, and then were placed in the general prison population. In the Attorney General's *Survey of Release Procedures: Prisons* forty-five institutions in a sample of sixty followed such practices. Eastern State Penitentiary, for example, isolated newcomers for thirty days under the supervision of a classification committee made up of two deputy wardens, the parole officer, a physician, a psychiatrist, a psychologist, the educational director, the social service director, and two chaplains. The federal government's new prison at Lewisburg, Pennsylvania, opened in 1932 and, eager to employ the most modern principles, also followed this routine. All new prisoners were on "quarantine status," and over the course of a month each received a medical examination, psychometric tests to measure his intelligence, and an interview with the Supervisor of Education. The Supervisor then decided on a program, subject to the approval of its Classification Board. All of this was to insure "that an integrated program . . . may lead to the most effective adjustment, both within the Institution and after discharge."[27]

It was within the framework of these procedures that psychiatrists and psychologists took up posts inside the prisons for the first time. The change can be dated precisely. By 1926, sixty-seven institutions employed psychiatrists: thirty-five of them made their appointments between 1920 and 1926. Of forty-five institutions having psychologists, twenty-seven hired them between 1920 and 1926. The innovation was quite popular among prison officials. "The only rational method of caring for prisoners," one Connecticut administrator declared, "is by classifying and treating them according to scientific knowledge . . . [that] can only be obtained by the employment of the psychologist, the psychiatrist, and the physician." In fact, one New York official believed it "very unfair to the inmate as well as to the institution to try and manage an institution of this type without the aid of a psychiatrist."[28]

Over this same period several states also implemented greater institutional specialization. Most noteworthy was their frequent isolation of the criminal insane from the general population. In 1904, only five states maintained prisons for the criminally insane; by 1930, twenty-four did. At the same time, reformatories for young first offenders, those between the ages of sixteen and twenty-five or sixteen and thirty, became increasingly popular. In 1904, eleven states operated such facilities; in 1930, eighteen did. Several states which constructed new prisons between 1900 and 1935 attempted to give each facility a specific assignment. No state pursued this policy more diligently than New York. It added Great Meadow (Comstock), and Attica to its chain of institutions, the first two to service minor offenders, the latter, for the toughest cases. New York's only rival was Pennsylvania. By the early 1930's it ran a prison farm on a minimum security basis; it had a new Eastern State Penitentiary at Grateford and the older Western State Penitentiary at Pittsburgh for medium security; and it made the parent of all prisons, the Eastern State Penitentiary at Philadelphia, the maximum security institution. Some states with two penitentiaries which traditionally had served different geographic regions, now tried to distinguish them by class of criminals. In California, for instance, San Quentin was to hold the more hopeful cases, Folsom the hard core.[29]

But invariably, these would-be therapeutic innovations had little effect on prison routines. They never managed to penetrate the system in any depth. Only a distinct minority of institutions attempted to implement such programs and even their efforts produced thin results. Change never moved beyond the superficial.

The presence of psychiatrists and psychologists on the prison payrolls was of more symbolic than real importance, their credentials lending a legitimacy to incarceration without their services altering routines. For one reason, the number of institutions that hired full-time professionals remained small; in 1926 there were only twenty-nine *full-time* psychiatrists on the prison staffs of thirteen states, and five of them were in New York. For another, even the most advanced states employed only one psychiatrist and perhaps two psychologists per institution. They were to interview and classify every entering inmate (say five to seven hundred a year), record the progress that all inmates were or were not making (another fifteen hundred a year), and give recommendations on the propriety of release. Clearly, the numbers alone made the task impossible. With such a ratio of professional to inmate, the impact of psychiatric and psychological work within the institutions was almost nonexistent.[30]

Nor did the skills that the new professionals brought to the institutions prove very helpful. Not only numbers but the state of the art rendered them, and their programs, ineffective. As we have already noted, their classification schemes were static and descriptive, not dynamic or analytic. Whether put forth by Harvard Business School professor Dr. Elton Mayo or Dr. Edward Doll or the Wisconsin Psychiatric Field Service (to choose three outstanding efforts), they offered a fourfold division: the improvable inmate, the professional criminal, the mentally defective, and the psychologically defective. In essence, there were only three categories: the better sort, the hardened, and the defective — or the hopeful, the dangerous, and the hopeless. But such divisions were of little use. There was nothing that any warden could do with them, really nothing that the professionals themselves could do with them. They fit offenders into boxes but did not explain how they came to enter such a box, nor how they could be moved out of it. They did not provide specific advice on how a hopeful case could be trained to enter the community, or how a professional criminal could be transformed into a hopeful case.

A few contemporaries recognized these limitations. The Attorney General's analysis concluded that "classification has demonstrated that the division of the prison population into groups . . . is a sterile procedure." The categories were not "translated into action in the lives of the individual criminals." At best, the classifications "help the professional prison worker to keep the ultimate objective in view in spite of the jungle through which he gropes." The astute commissioner of prisons for England and Wales, Alexander Patterson, concluded his report on American prisons in the mid-1930's with the observation that "Americans were suffering from the illusion that when every offender has after examination been relegated to a type, a problem has been solved." Unfortunately, "the work of these scientists ends as a rule when classification has followed examination." Diagnosis simply did not lead to prescriptions for treatment.[31]

Even if specific prescriptions had been forthcoming, there is little reason to imagine that they would have been followed. The plea for specialization among institutions was not generally heeded and prisons made little effort to segregate types of offenders within a facility. Some among them relied upon administrative segregation, in separate cell block areas, to lodge homosexuals or troublemakers. But beyond such divisions, obviously carried out for reasons of security and not treatment, prisoners were all housed together. "The congregate prison," concluded the Wickersham Commission, "has made even these crude classifications useless in practice."[32]

The implementation of other reform programs was equally disappointing. Educational offerings were unimpressive. Most institutions provided some kind of schooling (sixty-nine of eighty-five institutions so reported to the Attorney General), and typically employed an "educational director" (forty-seven of the sixty-nine). But the quality of teaching and the number of inmates served were unimpressive. The Attorney General's survey identified only twelve state prisons that offered satisfactory programs.

Austin MacCormick, probably the foremost expert on prison education, was still more critical. "Save for a few exceptions," he concluded in 1929, "we are tolerating a tragic failure. There is not a single complete and well-rounded educational program in all the prisons and reformatories for adults in America." The facilities were inadequate: "The schoolroom is a dimly lighted, smelly mess hall, a chapel with a sloping floor . . . the lower corridors of a cell block, or a room in the basement . . . or a remote and inaccessible building in the prison yard." And the techniques were worse: "A few illiterates are learning to read from a book that tells how Tommy and Susie went out to catch butterflies. . . . A few strays . . . are studying arithmetic or history or geography from ancient and dog-eared textbooks written for juveniles." The teachers themselves were inmates, under the nominal direction of the supervisor. The students, generally the illiterate inmates, as often as not failed to enroll in or to complete whatever courses were available. As one prison investigation concluded: "Not only is the head teacher expected to make bricks without straw, but he is not given, figuratively speaking, any clay with which to work. That is, if an inmate is very much needed in the shops, he is not expected to attend school. On the other hand, if he is no good anywhere else around the prison he is sent to school."[33]

To examine what were supposed to be the best-run programs suggests conditions in more ordinary ones. The New Jersey State prison was exceptional in hiring an educational director and five full-time teachers, and in compelling illiterates to attend school. Yet out of a population of some 1,700 inmates, there were only 346 enrolled; of these, 217 dropped out and a mere 129 completed a course. At Auburn, with an inmate population of 1,200, only 99 were enrolled; at Sing-Sing, with 2,100, only 394 were in a school program (taught by a staff of four teachers and 24 inmates). San Quentin boasted the highest percentage — some 1,680 of the 6,000 inmates enrolled, but the institution employed only one full-time teacher and used 56 inmates. The verdict of the New York Lewisohn Committee in 1920 holds for the decades that followed as well: "Every condition which should make prison education stagnant, uninspired, unprogressive, exists to-day."[34]

The prisons fared even worse in providing vocational educa-tion. Formal offerings were few; only thirty-four prisons even reported having such programs. The Attorney General's survey estimated, probably liberally, that less than 10,000 prisoners out of 106,000 received vocational training, and most of them were probably inmates in reformatories, not state prisons. MacCormick was certain "that no prison has more than scratched the surface in the field of vocational education." And what could pass for voca-tional training was all too evident in conditions at the Colorado Penitentiary. "The warden's conception of vocational work and vocational education," reported an investigator, "is the establish-ment of industrial shops." These shops trained inmates to make road signs, automobile license tags, and knitted goods; but Col-orado had no knitting mills, and only the prison made tags and signs. The program might help the warden's budget, but it had no relevance to vocational training.[35]

To all observers, whether reformers, legislators, or wardens, the prison's greatest failure was its inability to keep inmates em-ployed, to provide steady labor. No goal had been more funda-mental to the prison from its very moment of inception a hundred years before. The Wickersham Commission spoke for everyone when noting: "Without work convicts waste physically and suffer in morals and mentality. . . . It is a facile descent from idleness to mischief and worse." And yet, no goal was more elusive. Try as they would, most prisons simply could not give work to their charges.[36]

No one doubted that idleness pervaded the prisons, but esti-mates differed as to just how rampant it was. Prison reports were unreliable. Wardens were aware that tax-conscious legislators would look first at the entry in the annual report on numbers of men employed (and monies earned) and judge the prison admin-istration at least in part by its success in maintaining a good employment (and financial) record. Hence, wardens exaggerated the number of jobs provided or assigned several men to do tasks that one could perform alone. In 1923 the Department of Labor estimated that a little over 6 percent of the prisoners were idle, but most observers reckoned the true figure to be much higher. The Wickersham Commission in 1928 put the number at 16 percent; that same year, the New York prison commission estimated its unemployment at 25 percent; Howard Gill, in his study of prison labor for Sutherland and Sellin's *Prisons of Tomorrow,* juggled returns around to reach 39 percent. But probably the most accurate estimate came from the Attorney General's study. Determined to get behind wardens' registers, and knowing that in some institutions "prisoners have been assigned to shops and marched to work at regular hours, even though the machinery had long since been removed from the factories," the investigators tried to calculate the number of prisoners at work by the amount of goods produced. Allowing 25 percent employment for institutional maintenance, they concluded that fully 60 percent of inmates were idle. Out of a total prison population in 1935–36 of 106,800, 24,300 men held productive jobs, 26,700 were involved in maintenance work, and 55,800 had nothing to do. Put another way, in forty-seven of eighty-five state prisons more than half of the inmates were unemployed, and in another nineteen more than 40 percent were unemployed. Only four prisons "provide even average employment for all their prisoners throughout the year."[37]

Widespread idleness made most prisons unprofitable and no one was happy with this fact. Legislators complained about making sizeable annual appropriations to the prisons. Reformers too, if somewhat more ambiguously, were disappointed. Although they did not want cost accounting to determine the propriety of a rehabilitative program, still, they were unwilling to concede that reform might be financially burdensome. Doing good was not supposed to entail heavy costs. Nevertheless, the returns were all too clear. In 1928, only eight prisons of the fifty-nine that the Wickersham Commission surveyed showed a profit. And by the mid-1930's, with the Depression in full swing, the annual reports of only three state systems could still do so.[38]

Reformers and legislators were all the more disturbed by these findings because, as they well knew, their own interventions had exacerbated the problem. In response to prevalent abuses as well as to the political pressures exerted by free labor, states had dismantled the nineteenth-century prison industries system. The convict lease, contract, and piece work arrangements, which had generally employed convicts and returned profits, no longer seemed acceptable. The difficulty, however, was that the states had not been able to come up with financially sound alternatives.

The abolition of the convict lease system had been the first victory. In 1885, thirteen states, almost all of them Southern, had turned their inmates over to private contractors to work in sugar or other types of agricultural production. By 1923, no state allowed this practice. The transformation was in many ways testimony to the power of the reform ideology, for in purely financial terms, the shift was costly. The contractors had paid the states handsomely for inmate labor and at the same time spared them all administrative costs. Nevertheless, the system could not survive into the twentieth century. In state after state reformers, backed by solid public opinion, put an end to the arrangements.[39]

The stages that the Texas prison system moved through exemplified the general trend. Beginning in 1870, Texas allowed private contractors full control over inmates, including their upkeep and discipline, in return for sizeable payments. By the early 1880's, investigations began to reveal horror stories of cruelty, confirmed by a high number of deaths in the work camps; and in 1883 the state, haltingly and incompletely, began to expand its control. It assumed responsibility for the walled facility at Huntsville, hired and paid the prison guards, and soon took on the task of feeding the inmates. Still, the contractors set the work schedules, and the death rate remained very high. Between 1886 and 1888, 223 inmates died, and while some of the deaths could be explained away because Negroes ostensibly were already carrying "the seeds of disease," state inspectors agreed that at least some contractors "violate the rules and sometimes are guilty of inhumane treatment." By 1898 dissatisfaction was more acute, and the warden at Huntsville recommended terminating all leases: "After long experience I am thoroughly convinced that no sort of supervision can be inaugurated that will absolutely prevent abuses under the contract system." Still the leasing of convicts went on. As late as 1909 more than 1,000 prisoners were working under lease, bringing the state an annual return of about $800,000.[40]

The abolition of the system, appropriately enough, came in the middle of the Progressive era, under the governorship of James Colquitt. In 1909 an investigatory group returned another shocking report of brutal treatment, together with a recommendation to end leases, which the next legislature accepted. No one doubted the ultimate reason for the change: "The sentiment of the people," declared a state committee, "found expression in a demand for the abolition of the lease contract system." The new law, enacted "in the name of humanitarianism," was the product of "the widespread feeling of antagonism to the lease system throughout the State." To confirm this judgment, the prison system itself adopted many Progressive measures. The warden reported that he eliminated "the embarrassing, degrading garb of stripes"; entering inmates now received a physical examination and, however rudimentary, a classification; parole also became part of the Texas procedures. The state had finally, in the best Progressive tradition, recognized that "no institution owned by the State should be permitted, even for a day, to pass from under the control and direction of the State."[41]

It did not take long to discover just how costly this principle was. Neither reformers nor legislators had anticipated a problem: if private contractors had profitably employed inmates in agricultural production, why could not the state? To be sure, an immediate investment in good farming land was necessary; but the returns should be forthcoming. Nevertheless, the Texas prison system incurred a huge debt in 1911 and 1912 and a legislative investigatory committee was immediately appointed. Its findings gave little comfort; all it could say was that humanitarianism was proving expensive. Moreover, the ledgers looked no better as time progressed; through the 1920's and 1930's, the state-run prisons ran a deficit of about $800,000 a year. Since the older system had brought in that same amount in income, reform was actually costing some one and a half million dollars annually.

There was no shortage of efforts to explain the financial disaster — almost every annual report of the Texas prisons tried to account for it. Some charged that "the suspension of the long-used method of punishment in the penitentiary — the strap — has resulted in decreasing the productive efficiency of convict labor in a very large degree." Others blamed one contingency or another — a fire this year, excessive rains at time of planting that year; they cited the rundown condition of cotton-ginning equipment or increased expenditures due to a greater number of inmates. But none of the arguments proved particularly useful and the ledgers continued to show heavy losses. Perhaps the only consolation for the Texas legislators was that their situation was anything but unique. Almost every other state that moved from convict leasing to state-run prisons also ran a substantial deficit.[42]

The second major reform in prison industries also represented a shift from private contracting to state control. Here the villain was the nineteenth-century practice of having companies pay the state for the right to bring raw materials, machinery, and foremen into the prison and then use inmate labor to manufacture the goods for sale on the open market. While reformers objected to the abuses which accompanied this practice — contractors bribed guards to make the men work longer or rewarded inmates with contraband — the more vigorous opposition came from manufacturers and labor unions who denounced the arrangement as unfair competition. The protests did not meet quick success. New York outlawed the system in 1894, but as late as 1923, 40 percent of all goods manufactured in prison were made under the contract system and 60 percent of all prison goods were sold on the open market. Most states, it seemed, were able to reach a compromise with their own special interests: prisons would manufacture goods not already made in the state, or would sell their products elsewhere. A neighboring state could do nothing to protect itself from the sale of these goods, since prohibitions were interpreted as violating rights of interstate commerce. Not until

1929 did the necessary federal legislation outlaw such practices; the Hawes-Cooper Act removed the interstate character from prison products, subjecting them to state law at their point of destination. The effects were immediate. By 1932 only 16 percent of all inmates worked for private contractors, and by 1940 the practice had practically disappeared. So too, the bulk of prison goods, with some important exceptions, were no longer sold on the open market.[43]

Once again, reformers and their allies anticipated that the prisons themselves would successfully employ inmates. A state-use system, wherein all prison products would be purchased by the state, not only eliminated charges of unfairness but would provide a ready, indeed captive, market for the products. Under this arrangement, prisoners could also manufacture auto license tags as well as raise agricultural produce and manufacture textiles so as to feed and clothe themselves and other inmates. Moreover, the state could employ prisoners on public works projects, such as highway-building programs. Reformers were quite enthusiastic about this prospect, finding the road camp preferable to a maximum security penitentiary. And in fact, the states did take up all of these programs. By 1932, 42 percent of employed inmates were working under state-use and another 23 percent on public works. But for all of this, prisons proved thoroughly incapable of keeping men busy or running self-sustaining operations.[44]

Again and again investigators attempted to understand the sources of failure. They had no difficulty in composing a long list of causes; what they could not do was overcome them. Every ten years another New York committee took up the issue — in 1910 a Moreland Commission, in 1920 the Lewisohn Committee, in 1929 the State Crime Commission. Each of them agreed that the market for prison goods in the state agencies was immense but was not being tapped. The Moreland Commission noted that New York City institutions alone consumed sixteen million dollars worth of goods — and yet the prison industries returned a profit of only $158,000. Lewisohn's committee estimated a market worth twenty million dollars in the state — and yet prison industries showed a profit of only $235,000. Meanwhile, the prisons were costing the state over two million dollars a year. And just as the dismal reports repeated themselves, so did the roster of problems. The equipment was "antiquated and second hand"; the "shops in prison dark, poorly heated, dismal, poorly ventilated," producing substandard work. The foremen were so badly paid that it was impossible to attract knowledgeable men to the job; the prisoners lacked requisite skills. State agencies avoided, by one subterfuge or another, purchasing the second-rate prison goods. The state lacked a uniform cost accounting or, more broadly, compelled the superintendent of prison industries to function "on a 'hand to mouth' policy because [of a] lack of business policy on the part of the State." And New York's troubles were anything but unique. "The attempt to develop a prison labor system within high walls which will produce enough to pay for the maintenance of the institution," concluded the Wickersham Commission, "has failed. The prison system of factory administration does not ordinarily have behind it either the investment, skilled management, space, marketing facilities, adaptability to changing needs or labor which successful administration on the outside needs and secures." In sum, one more reform hope was disappointed.[45]

There is no shortage of explanations to account for failure of reform efforts to make over the prison into a community, a school, a hospital, or a profitable business. In many instances, the concepts themselves were flawed; the classification systems and the treatment programs were crude. Moreover, the tasks that reformers set for the prison were often beyond the capability of the society to achieve in any setting. There were not sufficient psychiatrists to staff the mental hospitals, let alone the prisons. Dewey's principles of democratic procedures were not realized in most schools, and vocational education proved as ineffective in trade high schools as in prisons. So too, the failure to administer profitable industries behind walls was at one with the general failure of government agencies to administer efficient public works programs, whether in a few municipalities in the 1920's or on a grander scale in the 1930's. Clearly reformers' programs for incarceration were overly ambitious, outstripping both the powers of their own theory and the available social and technological resources.

But the matter goes deeper, and the causes for the failure of reform are linked to the perpetuation of the system. Well-meaning observers, whether from schools of social work or from state legislatures, insisted that rehabilitation and custodial care could go hand in hand. "The function of the penal institutions," declared the Wickersham Commission, "is protection of society. To this end all efforts must be bent and all administrative methods be adapted." How were prisons to accomplish this goal? "There seems to be but one answer possible — by the reformation of the criminal."[46] Neither this Commission, nor any other one, ever imagined that because all prison administrative methods had to be bent to protect society, reform programs would be warped. But in fact, a fundamental opposition divided the two goals, an opposition that finally proved fatal to the reformers' designs.

It may well be that a system of incarceration, by its intrinsic nature, can never serve both the aims of incapacitation and rehabilitation. It can be said that confining men against their will in company not of their choosing for twenty-four hours a day over a period of time creates abnormal situations that do not permit rehabilitation. Yet, whatever the merits of such a theoretical statement, historical analysis must pursue a different line of argument. Perhaps Progressive reforms were doomed from the start by the inherent character of incarceration, perhaps not. But in the actual implementation of the system, the goals of custody and rehabilitation proved to be conflicting. More, the conflicts were always resolved in one direction only: the needs of incapacitation took precedence over reform. If wardens defined an innovation as consistent with the security needs of an institution, they were prepared to endorse it in theory (even if they would not or could not see to its effective translation into practice). If, on the other hand, a new measure seemed to run counter to the security needs of the institution, wardens vigorously opposed it and blocked any chance for implementation.

Thus, prison managers had no quarrel with a change in uniforms — it was irrelevant to internal security and might bolster the legitimacy of their operation. The argument that a striped costume facilitated capture after escape was obviously bogus: stripes would not keep a man in prison, which was the warden's primary consideration, and anyone able to mount the walls would be able to obtain civilian clothing. By the same token, the assorted privileges introduced into the prison, from movies to baseball to freedom of the yard, were effectively incorporated into the general scheme of discipline. Classification carried no dysfunctional side effects; to the contrary, wardens did not object to a procedure that might spare them responsibility for insane inmates. Eating in mess halls was somewhat more complicated and an occasional warden did complain about it; but guards armed with tear gas or rifles on a suspended catwalk seemed a sufficient deterrent to trouble. The idea of a school program posed no difficulties. Wardens could always keep troublemakers out of the classroom; indeed, the more cautious among them, apprehensive about letting any inmates out of their cells after dark, curtailed drastically the hours for study; and if they, in effect, scuttled the program, nevertheless they were preserving their own priorities. Wardens also preferred to keep men employed. A busy inmate might stay out of mischief, after all. More important, so long as almost all prisons operated at a loss, each warden was more or less protected from legislators' wrath. In this way, they could continue to give first precedence to holding men securely, not profitably. And better to assign three men to a job that one could do than run an industry that might pose a risk to institutional order. One Progressive reform that wardens did consider a threat to security, the Mutual Welfare League, made no headway at all. A program that might alter the balance of power, on a psychological if not an actual level, between guard and captive could not be supported.[47]

The custodial character of the penitentiary was at once reflected in and perpetuated by the character of its personnel. In terms of recruitment and service, from warden down to guard, prison work was police work. The staff was qualified to fulfill one task only: holding the inmates.

Prison wardens from all parts of the country were almost without exception qualified to do nothing other than superintend a custodial program. Career line information is available on nineteen wardens in the mid-1930's. Eight began their careers with a significant period of police work; three followed an army career; four started out as guards and painstakingly worked their way up the ladder. San Quentin's warden, appointed in 1936, had been a county sheriff for eight years, chief of police for sixteen, then warden at Folsom for ten; his replacement at Folsom had worked in the California prison system for twenty-two years. Warden Lewis Lawes at Sing-Sing, author of several popular books about the prison, first worked as a guard at Clinton and Dannemora, then served as superintendent at two New York reformatories, and finally moved to Sing-Sing. His colleague at Auburn started out as a policeman and served as chief of police in Troy, New York, for twenty-seven years. His counterpart in Oregon was first a police officer, then a guard, and after twenty-three years in the system, a warden.[48]

Recruitment to the chief supervisory positions within the prison — the assistant warden, captain of the guard, or principal keeper — followed a similar pattern. In a sample of fifty-eight of this group serving in twenty-three institutions, 29 percent came to prison work after a lengthy police career; 57 percent began as guards and slowly made their way up the chain of command; and the average length of service was twenty-two years. Clearly, the tone and style of the institution were set by those with experience exclusively in maintaining security.[49]

We know less about the career lines and personal characteristics of the rank and file guards, but on the basis of their low wages and abysmal working conditions, it seems fair to conclude that prison work had to be a last resort for the unskilled and uneducated. Even the top posts were not particularly well-paying: the average warden's salary in the late 1920's was $4,700 — supplemented, to be sure, by room and board and a practically unlimited opportunity to use inmate labor for personal assignments. The situation was far less favorable for the guards. "The pay is so low," declared the Wickersham Commission, "that it is impossible to secure any but the least competent." Of seventy-five prisons reporting wage scales to the Attorney General's *Survey of Release Procedures*, 44 percent paid between $535 and $1,000; the rest, between $1,100 and $2,000. Nor did these figures merely reflect Depression conditions. In the late 1920's, the maximum salary for guards in 19 percent of the institutions had been below $1,000; in another 46 percent, between $1,000 and $1,500; only 11 percent offered salaries over $2,000. And in return, guards served particularly long hours. The Wickersham Commission calculated that 70 percent of them worked ten hours a day or more. Conditions had improved slightly by the mid-1930's — 35 percent of the prisons had instituted a forty-eight-hour work week. But another 30 percent still kept guards at their jobs seventy to eighty-four hours a week. As one Illinois investigatory body concluded: "The position of the guard is well nigh intolerable. His salary is ridiculously low and far less than that which can be earned even by the most incompetent mechanic. His hours of labor are very long. . . . He is himself virtually a prisoner."[50]

Under these circumstances, about one-third of the staff turned over rapidly. Men entered, found the situation not to their liking, and after a year or two, left. At the same time, others, with either fewer options or less ambition, stayed on and on. By the 1930's most states included guards on civil service lists, so that political party turnover no longer forced wardens to hire or fire staff members. In only a minority of states, no more than twelve, did every change in political administration spark a house cleaning. In the majority, including such states as Massachusetts, New York, Pennsylvania, Ohio, Colorado, and California, two-thirds of the prison guards had served for five years or more; indeed, some 15 percent of this group had been serving for over fourteen years. As would be expected, a good part of the prison guard staff were over forty years old. Alexander Patterson, the English visitor, correctly observed that "many old men [were] in charge of American institutions."[51]

The custodial orientation of the prison was no less evident in the selection of auxiliary staff for farm or shop operations. Some prisons did hire skilled managerial types to run their industries. But even more commonly, certainly in maximum security institutions, recruitment came from the ranks of guards. In Folsom prison, where complete personnel files survive, the foreman of the shoe and tailor shop, the steward of the mess, the chief engineer, the garage mechanic, the four electricians, and even the educational director had all begun their careers as prison guards. More, the low level of salaries for these positions made the recruitment of skilled workers almost impossible. The average salary paid to prison farm superintendents in the late 1920's was $1,754, while an accountant made $2,446. Only a prison guard would find taking such a job a promotion.[52]

By the same token, prison personnel received practically no training either before assuming their duties or while holding them. Three states briefly experimented with training programs, but in effect the only instruction the staff received was in using firearms. In fact, the only qualification for the job was a knowledge of firearms. As the Wickersham Commission observed, "The prison is looked upon not as a professional problem of the highest complexity, requiring men of great knowledge and ability . . . but rather as an institution for the repression and control of the dangerous." And with all sarcasm intended, Howard Gill concluded: "We can never professionalize reformatory effort until we recognize the importance of the job sufficiently to pay for it in a manner commensurate with other scientific endeavors," that is, with "a salary at least as large as that of a plasterer or a bricklayer."[53]

Nowhere was the clash between rehabilitative and custodial goals more evident than in the exercise of prison discipline. Reformers recognized that "discipline is crucial in all penal administration. . . . It sets the mood and the temper of all other activities." And precisely because it was so vital, they hoped that it would be fair, humane, and intelligent. The administration of the law inside the institution should approximate the workings of the law in the community so that inmates would be learning preparatory lessons.[54] Yet whatever the inequality in the distribution of justice in the outside society, the capriciousness and cruelty of prison discipline was a thing unto itself. The goal was to maintain order to the exclusion of all other considerations. Security, not justice, dominated.

Prison rules, if one can call them that, were so incredibly arbitrary and inclusive that the inmate was liable to punishment at any time. The Iowa State Penitentiary, for example, printed 105 regulations in twenty-eight pages, including prohibitions against "fighting, grimacing, hands in pockets, hands or face not clean, hair not combed, having contraband article on your person or in your cell, impertinence to visitors, insolence to officers, insolence to fellow inmates, inattentive at work, in line, or at school, laughing and fooling, loud talking in cell, not out of bed promptly, bed not properly made, not in bed promptly, not at door for count, not wearing outside shirt, profanity, quarreling, refusal to obey, shirking, spitting on floor, staring at visitors, stealing, trading, throwing away food, wasting food, writing unauthorized letters." And the list of offenses for which inmates at Sing-Sing were actually punished was not very different: "dirty cell, fighting, assault, refusing to work, speaking disrespectful to officer, making home brew, being drunk, having a straight razor or knife, malicious destruction of property, agitating, sending out improper or uncensored letters, attempted escape, and being abusive to the parole board."[55]

Not surprisingly, the Wickersham Commission observed that "the enforcement of rules against 'gaping about,' 'staring,' 'inattention,' 'laughing,' 'making signs,' 'silliness' and 'profanity' would tax the patience of a Job and the wisdom of a Solomon." Their only purpose was "that they make possible the maintenance of order, the prevention of escapes." The Attorney General's survey compiled its own list of absurdities (including "Banish from your mind all evil thoughts") and concluded that such regulations hardly offered "a realistic approach to the very difficult problem of changing the attitude of a murderer, a robber, or a rapist." What they did represent was the prison's efforts to set down in ostensibly legitimate and formal terms, rules that would control an inmate's every action.[56]

The regulations under which the prison guards worked (sometimes not very much briefer or more precise than those for the inmates) also made clear that a wide open definition of security was at the system's core. The Illinois penitentiary rule book first commanded guards: "Preserve order, maintain discipline and prevent escapes at all hazards." The New York rules opened by instructing guards to help in "securing the reformation of the inmates," but then went on to regulations that touched on no other matter save prison order. Rule 10 conveys their spirit well: "Armed guards hold the key to the safety of the officer and to the security of the inmate. Therefore, it is essential that their attention shall be concentrated on their duties."[57]

Prison rules prohibited the guards from doing anything except guarding the inmates. Whatever ideas reformers advanced about prison staffs counseling inmates were actually forbidden by formal regulations. Guards were not to converse with inmates except to issue commands for immediate tasks. "No officer or employee," declared the New York regulations, "shall chat with inmates or convey to them any articles, letters, newspapers . . . nor shall they listen to their history. . . . They shall, however, when occasion requires, instruct the inmates in the rules necessary for their government." Some institutions even declared: "No officer or employee shall take any action toward securing funds or employment for any inmate . . . without consent of warden." The Wickersham Commission argued, with full justification, that "all of these rules are bent to the end of discipline" and to that task only. The Attorney General's survey noted that the relationship between keeper and kept "borders upon the relationship of members of a caste and the 'untouchables.' . . . Either guards are not trusted to understand the prisoners with whom they deal or are not expected to do so. In either case, the pious hope that the prison 'intends their reformation, if possible' seems rather remote." The overriding concern was to prevent a possible collusion between guard and inmate, to keep the castes separate so that captive and captor would never conspire to undermine the security of the prison.[58]

The actual exercise of prison discipline, like the rules themselves, could not satisfy even a minimal standard of justice.

Reform programs did alter some procedures, but here too their substantive effects were limited. By the 1920's most prisons provided for some sort of preliminary hearing: the guard reported an infraction and the inmate had the opportunity to defend himself. But the defense generally took place before a board of one — the principal keeper or the deputy warden or the captain of the guards — the person, in other words, with front-line responsibility for prison security. Some institutions (less than one-quarter) established a disciplinary board, which included the chaplain, the psychiatrist, and some members of the classification committee. But the principal keeper always chaired the sessions and the boards did little to restrain arbitrary authority. Nowhere was the inmate allowed to call witnesses for his defense; nowhere could he cross-examine a guard. Minimal due process protections seemed to pose too basic a threat to the fundamental order and security of the institution. To give the inmate the right to question his guard would disturb the chain of command and alter the balance of power. Prison justice did not dare to approximate community justice.[59]

As for the punishments themselves, wardens manipulated the new prison privileges to the ends of discipline. They would deprive a disobedient inmate of freedom of the yard or of attending a movie or of writing his letters or using the commissary. And they, like their nineteenth-century predecessors, took away "good time" allotments. But none of these deprivations seemed sufficient to maintain security. Every prison had resort to stronger sanctions, which returns us to the essentially custodial character of the institution.

The exercise of prison discipline, then as now, was shrouded in secrecy. Wardens would deny investigators the necessary access; many of them did not keep records; others maintained inaccurate ones. The Wickersham Commission was one in a long line of groups complaining that "the method of discipline is the most difficult thing to uncover because the prison officials are sensitive about it and the prisoners are intimidated from testifying."[60] Nevertheless, several points are clear and all of them indicate that once again the system's dedication to its own security could not and did not coexist with a rehabilitative program.

First, despite all the mystery, there is simply no question that prisons were places of pervasive brutality, so pervasive as to make a Progressive model of community, school, or hospital less than relevant to their functioning. It is true that regulations outlawing corporal punishment of inmates did become prevalent in the twentieth century. By the 1930's, most systems prohibited the use of the whip as well as the ingenious nineteenth-century torture devices. Instead, solitary confinement became the permissible punishment of last resort, that is, at least officially. Lacking a calculus for pain, it is not always easy to measure one kind of punishment against another. But in no simple sense can the substitution of solitary for the whip be automatically considered a "reform."

There were in fact two kinds of solitary: administrative segregation, where the prisoner was locked into a regular cell (lighted and ventilated, equipped with a bed, blanket, and toilet facilities), fed three regular meals a day, and confined in this way for long periods of time, months rather than weeks. Then there was "solitary confinement" proper, the "hole" or the "pit" or the "cage" or the "dungeon," as prison jargon called it. Every prison had one: the inmate was kept in a starkly bare concrete cell, unlighted and unventilated, and fed bread and water; at most, he received blankets and a bucket for his bodily needs. Confinement here was supposed to last for shorter periods — a week or two. Some regulations placed an upper limit of six or seven consecutive days in solitary, but wardens often violated them, in spirit if not in letter. They would keep prisoners in the hole for six days, release them for one, then put them back into the hole again for another six days, and the routine could stretch for months. Thus, even prisons nominally obeying formal regulations administered a punishment that was hardly humane.[61]

How often were the formal regulations themselves obeyed? How frequently did prison guards and wardens inflict punishments that the state had defined as cruel and unusual? Although no quantitative answer is possible, it is useful to explore one incident in detail, the response to a food strike in San Quentin. Not that the beatings there are an index to beatings elsewhere. Rather, the underlying assumptions of the prison staff, presented in defense of their actions, reveal with remarkable clarity how in the name of institutional security all punitive measures became legitimate: how, ultimately, a custodial prison was unable to exercise fair or humane discipline.

In 1939, forty-one inmates in San Quentin went on a hunger strike to protest the quality of the institution's food.[62] They would not enter the mess hall or go to work until they had the chance to talk with the captain or warden. Punishment was immediate and the principal keeper sent them to solitary; what happened to them there became the subject of investigation. The San Quentin prison Board first conducted closed hearings and exonerated all the guards of charges of brutality. But then the state's prison director reopened the case, and in November of that year, the governor himself heard testimony. No one, guards, inmates, or prison Board, disagreed on what had actually taken place; a number of the strikers were removed from solitary and forced to stand in a circle twenty-two inches across, and those who refused to follow this order were beaten. And no one denied that the California constitution prohibited cruel and unusual punishments in general, and corporal punishments specifically. But then how had such a violation occurred and why had the Board not taken more vigorous action?

The defense that guards and Board members offered is significant not as an accurate statement of motives, but as a presentation of a line of argument that they believed to be creditable and legitimate. Without such harsh action, the Board insisted, San Quentin would have become a "circus prison." To discharge any of the guards who administered the beatings would "not only shatter the morale of every reformatory in California, but will undermine the discipline of every prison in the United States." Were a new warden to be appointed, "he will inherit a situation where he must fight for the mastery of his prison or surrender to the convicts." Indeed, "certain gang leaders within the walls are already celebrating their coming victory over rules and discipline." And the guard responsible for the beatings was no less adamant in making this point. Had the core of troublemakers not been beaten, "it would have encouraged others to have done the same thing until there would have been a general disregard of the rules." The issue was simple: "Was the prison to be run by the Warden or by the prisoners?"[63]

Moreover, the very fact that the governor was now holding an open meeting threatened the good order of the prison. "A public hearing," argued the defense lawyer, is "probably the most dangerous type of hearing that could be held . . . because of its effects on the convicts, on the prisoners, and on the people all over the State." The Board had been right to hold its earlier investigation in secret; the most that the governor should do was to meet privately with prison managers. Calling inmates to testify weakened the internal security of the prison, and at the same time reduced its legitimacy among the general public.

Further, the governor lacked the authority to hold such a hearing, for the Board and its warden had "complete jurisdiction" over the prison. No one could second-guess them. "There is no authority by which you can limit the amount or the severity of the punishment, provided the circumstances in the original instance required it or justified it." Such a doctrine as cruel and unusual punishment had no meaning within a prison: everything depended upon the amount of provocation and the staff's need to maintain control.[64]

To buttress these contentions, the guard in charge of solitary, one Lewis, explained the dynamics behind the escalation of punishment. A back-up sanction was always necessary behind the walls. If one penalty did not work, a harsher one had to come next — and this was true not only for this riot, but in the daily administration of the institution. When Lewis first arrived at San Quentin, solitary had been too lax: "It had been a failure . . . the men had no fear of solitary. . . . The men would lay back in there; they would talk and laugh and raise all the trouble that they cared to. . . . Solitary to them was a joke." When the warden put him in charge, "the only orders I received was to keep order in solitary. I went at it very slowly and carefully." First he instituted a rule of silence, then he took away all reading material, then the right to smoke. Still "they didn't mind solitary." So he "pinched down a little harder." Beds were to be made in military fashion and could not be sat upon during the day. "But I still found that some men would stay there week after week." So he tried an experiment: drawing a twenty-two inch circle and having the men stand in it for five hours a day, without turning about. "They were made to stand all in one [way] — facing in one direction."[65]

These procedures, seemingly adequate for ordinary circumstances, were not sufficient in the extraordinary case. Thus, when the food strikers sent to solitary refused to enter the circle, the only thing to do was to whip them. The circle too, in other words, needed a back-up, and that was flogging. Accordingly, Lewis beat them until they would stand on the spots. "If I had failed for one minute down there, we would have had rioting and bloodshed in San Quentin." For final effect, he added a "thank-you" theory. "Even Ted Burns — one of the lowest degenerates here — two days after I had trouble with him, he called for me, and he said: 'Mr. Lewis, I am almost glad you gave me that licking; in fact, it made me think; I haven't been respectful to officers here, but I will be from now on.' And he didn't come back to solitary any more."[66]

The Board concurred with the thinking in this presentation. When the governor asked one member directly if whipping was a good prison practice, he responded: "I couldn't let you put that in my mouth, Governor; but I can tell you this. I think that any restraint that the guards administered to the prisoners to the point of compelling them to obey the rules is justified, and that no prison can be conducted otherwise." The argument had come around again to the good order of the prison.[67]

Neither the assumptions nor the practices revealed in this case were unique to the California system. The need for a back-up sanction to solitary was felt almost everywhere. The Kentucky penitentiary abolished corporal punishment in 1920; but the National Society of Penal Information visited the institution nine years later to discover that the dozen men in solitary "were 'in chains,' that is, standing with one hand cuffed to the cell door and the other cuffed to the post supporting the upper gallery. They remained in that position throughout the working hours for periods of 5 to 20 days." In Rhode Island, the Wickersham Commission reported that inmates "are cuffed by one arm to a ring in the wall about shoulder high. A strait jacket may be used." In Joliet, Illinois, and Stillwater, Minnesota, inmates in solitary "were cuffed to the door of the cell about 12 hours a day." Another popular practice was to confine men to a semicircular cage so tight that they could not sit down or move about. The solitary cells, reported an investigator of the Jackson, Michigan, prison, "are equipped with so called 'cage doors' in addition to the solid steel plate forming the outer door. The cage door is a semi-circular, barred affair, so constructed that a person may be placed between it and the outer door of the cell. With both doors closed the victim is forced to stand upright, can't turn around, or crouch." The Ohio penitentiary at Columbus had a similar solitary and cage arrangement. "Confinement alone has never proved very effective," observed the Attorney General's survey, but prison administrators were well equal to the task of devising supplementary punishments.[68]

The idea that prison officials ought to be free to run their institutions as they chose prevailed through the pre–World War II period and right up to the mid-1960's. Even before the recent prisoners' rights movement, inmates had petitioned the courts for relief from one or another disciplinary practice, but judges invariably dismissed their cases, adhering strictly to a "hands off" policy. As late as 1951, a federal judge hearing an appeal on a prisoner's right to correspond summarily declared: "We think it is well settled that it is not the function of the courts to superintend the treatment and discipline of persons in penitentiaries, but only to deliver from imprisonment those who are illegally confined." Courts assumed not only that wardens had administrative expertise but that prisoners enjoyed "privileges," not "rights." The courts had neither the inclination nor, as they saw it, a cause to intervene.[69]

Prison boards generally were unwilling to challenge the wardens' authority. They took their primary task to be appointing the right man to the warden's job and, thereafter, supporting him in his work. When one California Board member was asked: "Did you consider it a part of your function . . . to inquire as to whether or not the warden was carrying out the duties that were required of him by law?" he responded: "I never made such inquiry. . . . I assumed that everything was going along all right." When his interrogator continued: "You assumed that having appointed Mr. Smith as warden that he was going ahead and performing the duties that were required of him?"—the Board member answered simply, "Yes." And state legislators were no more willing or eager to penetrate the closed world of the prison. After all, whom could they trust to expose conditions accurately? Surely not the inmates or, for that matter, the guards. Almost by definition, any staff member who criticized the institution was a disgruntled employee, trying to settle a personal grievance through public attacks.[70]

In effect, the state and the prison had struck a mutually agreeable bargain: As long as the warden ran a secure institution which did not attract adverse publicity (through a high number of deaths or riots or inhumane practices becoming publicly known), he would have a free hand to administer his prison as he liked. And most of the time, wardens fulfilled their side of the arrangement. The number of escapes from the state prisons was low. In the mid-1930's, no breaks occurred from Attica or Clinton or Sing-Sing, or from Western Pennsylvania, Connecticut, Minnesota, Colorado, or Folsom. Less than five prisoners on the average escaped from Auburn, Menard in Illinois, Virginia, Eastern Pennsylvania, Maryland, Huntsville in Texas, or San Quentin. To be sure, wardens could not always prevent prison riots or the circulation of horror stories about cruel and inhumane punishment. But in the end, it was security that counted, not rehabilitation; and the prison administrators knew it, fashioned their routine accordingly, and survived in power.[71]

The image that captures the essence of the American prison in these decades, then, is not one of inmates exercising in the yard or attending classes or taking psychometric tests, but of the physical presence of the walls. And the walls were incredible, rising twenty to thirty feet above the ground and going down another five to twenty feet below the ground, with anywhere from five to fifteen towers jutting out above them. The occasional legislator who questioned the enormous expense of erecting these structures was told in no uncertain terms that thirty feet was better than twenty-five feet for preventing inmates from scaling the walls, and that every extra foot below the ground was a necessary safeguard against their tunneling out. In the end, reformers, with all their grand hopes of transforming the institution, were up against the wall.

CHAPTER FIVE

A Game of Chance:
The Condition of Parole

NO CHANGE THAT Progressives brought to criminal justice had more significant consequences than the system of parole under an indeterminate sentence. With impressive rapidity, discretion replaced fixity both in courtroom dispositions and prison releases. Yet the parole innovation was undoubtedly the most unpopular of all reform measures. Parole became the whipping boy for the failures of law enforcement agencies to control or reduce crime. Whenever fears of a "crime wave" swept through the country, or whenever a particularly senseless or tragic crime occurred, parole invariably bore the brunt of attack.

And it was a bitter and pervasive attack. Practically every crime commission and investigatory body in the 1920's and 1930's began its examination of parole with a statement conceding massive public opposition, really disgust. Clair Wilcox opened his 1929 report of the Pennsylvania Parole Commission by noting the outpouring of denunciations of parole for turning hardened criminals loose to prey on society. In similar tones, Professors Andrew Bruce, Ernest Burgess, and Albert Harno, in their 1928 report to the Illinois Parole Board, not only noted that deep public opposition had sparked their investigation, but that the public was convinced that parole represented nothing more than coddling the criminal. And ten years later, the Attorney General's *Survey of Release Procedures* observed how discontented Americans seemed with a practice that appeared to be little more than a grant of leniency to professional criminals.[1]

One has only to glance at the newspaper coverage of crime stories to confirm parole's dismal public image. Cartoons vividly revealed the quality of the opposition. The front page of the *Chicago Daily Tribune* (January 15, 1937) carried two sketches: above, the arm of the parole board giving "A Death Sentence for the Innocent Citizen," with, below, the convict shooting a man point blank. In a variation on this theme, cartoons depicted the parole board opening the prison gates to release various beasts, each labeled "burglar," or "thief," or "habitual criminal." The caption for the drawing: "Turning the Killers Loose."[2]

Press accounts of crime incidents reiterated the lesson. "Parole Man Kills Girl and Ends Own Life," announced one *Denver Post* headline (September, 1936); the story went on to tell how Ira Marshall, aged forty, "paroled last November from the state penitentiary, where he was serving a term for grand larceny" committed the murder. Another *Denver Post* story recounted how "Walter Meyer, 22 year-old paroled convict, is reported by Chicago police to have confessed the murder of a suburban policeman." The gloss of the story was self-evident: "The number of murders and other crimes of violence committed by paroled criminals shows there is something rotten with the administration of our parole system." Or take the following editorial from the Cleveland *Plain Dealer* (April 24, 1921): "PAROLED: Throughout the record of the men implicated or suspected of implication in the Sprotsky murder appears time after time one all-significant word: Paroled! . . . Most bandit gangs are made up in large part of paroled men — men who have been turned loose on the public by some board given more to sentimentalism and leniency than to justice. If parole abuse were curbed the keystone of the arch of banditry would fall." One enterprising reporter, Martin Moody, even published a book entitled *The Parole Scandal* (1939), which informed readers: "Parole is the nation's Public Scandal No. 1. . . . Paroled men are being released to rob, murder and kidnap. You will not notice the few lines of print which will herald the killer's release. The next time you hear of him it will be when he *again* uses a gun and holds up — who? Maybe *you*, or someone you love." No one less than J. Edgar Hoover delivered the verdict on parole which the press regularly repeated: its practice, the FBI head announced, "approaches a national scandal. . . . Prison sentences are not sentences, but problems in division and subtraction."[3]

How are we to understand the simultaneous triumph of parole and the persistently angry attacks on it? How did a procedure take hold and perpetuate itself right down through the 1960's while suffering from such popular disdain? Clearly parole, by being last in line in criminal justice practices, did pay for all the inadequacies in the system. In the standard case, the police captured the offender, the district attorney helped convict him, the judge sentenced him, the prison confined him — and then the parole board released him, so it was to blame when he victimized society once again. Judges could answer charges of leniency by pointing to the high maximums in their sentences that the offender probably had not served out; wardens could cite their having incapacitated the inmate during his term. It was the parole board that broke down prison walls and therefore deserved all blame for whatever happened next. But then, given such buck-passing, how and why did parole survive? If it was so vulnerable to attack, what made it so invulnerable to change or abolition? What sustained a program that had to carry such a heavy, if perhaps unfair burden? To answer these questions, we must first explore the internal operations of the system, how it functioned, whom it served, and with what effects. Here too, we will be tracing the links between reform ideology and administrative convenience; we will see how grand hopes and operational needs combined to sustain and perpetuate a procedure, despite disappointments, inadequacies, and in this case especially, a deep and enduring public opposition.

No sooner does one plunge into the realities of parole than the question of its persistence is further complicated, for one uncovers almost everywhere a dismal record of performance. Neither of the two essential tasks of parole, the fixing of prison release time or post-sentence supervision, was carried out with any degree of competence or skill. Amateurs on parole boards reached their decisions hastily and almost unthinkingly, while overworked and undertrained parole officers did little more than keep a formal but useless file on the activities of their charges. Whatever the reasons for the survival of parole, they will not be found in the efficient or diligent administration of the system.

The composition and procedures of the parole boards reveal all too clearly the weaknesses of release practices. By the mid-1930's, most states had established central agencies to fix release time; parole decision-making powers did shift from the institution itself (the warden together with the board of managers) to a special board of three to five men, appointed by the governor. But the creation of these independent agencies was of little import and gives a misleading sense of how specialized their functions were. In practical terms, the boards were often composed of those already charged with other state government responsibilities. The Idaho Parole Board, for instance, was made up of the Governor, the Attorney General, and the Secretary of State; in Wisconsin the duty belonged to the Board of Control (in charge of supervising all state institutions) sitting under another name. "The granting of parole," accurately concluded the Attorney General's survey, "is looked upon merely as a minor incidental function which can be taken care of by a State official when he can squeeze in a few hours a few times a year."[4]

Even where parole was the work of a full-time board free of other state functions (as was true in some dozen states), the members usually had no particular qualification for the task, save perhaps their party loyalties. The statutes set down no criteria for their selection, and governors made their choices with political considerations most in mind. Since the posts were not under civil service requirements and the salary levels were, on the average, $5,000 a year, the patronage was substantial. Typically, the governors looked to achieve an ethnic and regional balance, and they were always certain to include one representative of law enforcement agencies. Thus, the chairman of the Minnesota parole board in the 1930's had served for eleven years as an assistant county attorney in Minneapolis; one of his colleagues was an accountant and businessman from St. Cloud, and the other was president of the Minnesota American Lutheran Church. The Washington parole board in the early 1930's was composed of a wholesale jeweler from Spokane (as chairman), an insurance broker, and the "farmer member of the board," who actually ran a general store in Palouse, the center of the state's wheat belt. Parole from Pennsylvania's Eastern Penitentiary was in the hands of an ear, nose, and throat doctor (as chairman), together with a lawyer-businessman (from a rural section), a produce merchant (from the Italian community), a director of a physical education program, a university criminologist, and two businessmen. In Massachusetts, where one might have expected to find the most professional board operating, the members were a former member of Congress (Richard Olney), the black secretary of the Boston Urban League (Matthew Bullock), and the former Assistant to the Commissioner of Corrections.[5]

If board members had no particular qualifications for determining when an inmate ought to be released, the dockets that they received on each case could do little to enlighten them. Reformers had not only anticipated that "experts" would decide parole, but that detailed information on the state of rehabilitation of every inmate would be available. Both expectations, however, proved illusory. In three-fourths of the states, parole dockets were threadbare documents, supplying little more than a brief family history (married, parents living), past criminal record (arrested here, jailed there), and prison conduct (so many times punished for infractions). Almost all boards asked the prosecuting attorney and the sentencing judge about the propriety of parole for their cases. But again the results were thin. Usually these officers failed to respond at all. When they did, they merely jotted down a sentence declaring that the inmate should or should not be given parole.[6]

Some thirteen states compiled a fuller parole dossier, including descriptions of present family circumstances as well as information on medical and psychiatric examinations. Still, in the case of at least one of them, Illinois, a state investigatory committee found that although the dossier contained an enormous amount of data, much was irrelevant, and no effort was made at discrimination. "Frequently the Committee found the 'jackets' tremendously bulky, filled with letters from relatives and friends, political personages, lawyers and physicians, lengthy petitions signed literally by the members of whole communities and various other items . . . statements drawn by the trial judge and the state's attorney, mental health reports by the psychiatrist, and reports of hearings given the prisoner by the Supervisor and his assistants." Hence, the committee reported, "often it took a member a day, sometimes two or even three days, to disentangle the mass of material in one of these jackets, to rearrange it, and to read and digest it." Three or four days, as we shall see, was more than the parole boards could devote monthly to a consideration of all cases. Further, the professional reports in the dossier were usually diagnostic, not predictive; they labeled an inmate or presented a detailed case history, but did not offer predictions or even the grounds for predictions on how the inmate would fare in the community.[7]

The deficiencies in the dockets were overshadowed by the speed with which parole boards examined them. The boards' standard practice was to hold a monthly hearing at an institution; at these hearings, members would simultaneously read the docket, interview the inmate, and reach their decision. With few exceptions, they never saw the dossier until the prisoner appeared before them. And the time devoted to each case was very brief. Although variations did exist, surviving board minutes and investigators' observations show clearly that whether the board was full-time or part-time, the typical interview and subsequent discussion lasted only a few minutes.

In New York, the part-time board which functioned before 1930 met one day each month in each state prison in order to resolve 50 to 100 or more applications; the full-time board, created after 1930, worked a similar schedule, resolving 80 to 160 cases a day. The Pennsylvania board, according to Clair Wilcox's report, convened its monthly meeting at two in the afternoon and adjourned somewhere between four and six o'clock, devoting, on the average, six minutes to each inmate. "Its members are busy men. . . . The business is rapidly dispatched." In Washington, the warden of the state prison actually kept a stop-watch record of the board (with its permission) at one of its monthly meetings in 1935. The board disposed of almost two-thirds of each of its 38 cases in three minutes or less; only 18 percent took longer than five minutes. In Idaho, one investigator arranged for a stenographic record of the hearings of the parole board; no case took more than two minutes to resolve. Little wonder, then, that inmates complained of excessively brief encounters with their parole boards, or that the Attorney General's survey concluded: "Individual consideration cannot usually be given to each case."[8]

Despite all the variations that might be expected among boards, the hearings were remarkably consistent not only in tone and content, but in the principles that guided decision making. Most states, including New York, Pennsylvania, New Jersey, Ohio, Illinois, Michigan, and California, provided by statute for a parole hearing when an offender's minimum sentence expired.[9] At this time, the inmate came before the board, alone, without a lawyer or spokesman, and wearing prison garb. He sat down without any introductions. (The prison grapevine, of course, not only spread the identity of the board members, but their peculiar characteristics. So in Washington Bunge was supposedly "tough," and Dally was a "stooge for Bunge," and Waters was "easy and sleepy like an owl"). The members, more often at the start of the day than at its close, allowed him an opening statement:

Q. You have something you would like to say?
A. I would like to say that I got enough. I would like to get out.

Immediately, the meeting moved to its first important item of business: reviewing the crime for which the inmate was incarcerated, in effect retrying, in capsule fashion, the original offense.

The style of questioning of the Oregon parole board exemplifies the process. Take the case of James Clark, sentenced to the state prison for a year and a half for the crime, as the DA's rap sheet described it, of arson:

> Wanted a woman to marry him after supplying her with money for a car. She laughed at him. Followed her to a friend's house, slashed her automobile tires and set fire to the house where she was visiting. Fire extinguished before much damage done.

The parole examination opened with these questions and answers:

> Q. Did you have a jury trial?
> A. Yes, jury trial.
> Q. Tell us about the case.
> A. Well — I was drunk at the time and I don't remember much — but I was taken out there and I came to and I asked a man if he knew me and he said no and he asked me if I knew him and I said no but they found my footprints and I couldn't give a clear account of my time when it happened.
> Q. Did you have a row with this girl?
> A. Well — no, I hadn't seen her.[10]

Or, follow the board's consideration of the case of Charles Hughes, given a three-year maximum for breaking into a gravel plant, stealing machine belts, and selling them:

> Q. How about the trouble in Yakima?
> A. I just sold some belts and machinery for some people that asked me to do them a favor of selling it to the junk man for them.
> Q. Oh — it was just a favor — you didn't actually take the things?

A. No sir — they asked me if I would do them a favor and I said I would if I could — I always do a favor for anybody if I can. So I just took the things and sold them.

Q. How much money did you get from the articles sold?

A. I think it was around $6.00 but I only got $1.00.

Q. Did you admit taking the things?

A. No.

Q. But the case history says you pleaded guilty.

A. I don't remember pleading guilty.

Q. Do you think you got a fair sentence on this charge?

A. Yes.

Q. You were tried by a jury and pled guilty?

A. I don't remember pleading guilty.

Q. So you claim you were innocent of stealing those things?

A. Yes sir I do — I just sold them.

Q. You didn't have any knowledge that they were stolen property?

A. No sir.

Q. But here in the case the Judge, District Attorney and Sheriff all state positively that you broke in and stole the things — these facts must all have been established at your trial. You can hardly expect us to believe you innocent can you?

A. I'm just telling the truth as I told it then.[11]

This line of questioning pervaded all parole hearings.[12] The transcripts of the Idaho proceedings are replete with such board queries as: "What were you accused of stealing?" "Who was the prosecuting attorney?" "You had a trial did you?" "Did you have a lawyer?" "You pled guilty?" One investigator who sat in on parole hearings noted how basic the matter of the initial offense was to the board's considerations: "The prisoner was almost always asked if he committed the crime and why. . . . It is, of course, to be expected that the prisoner would make replies which would either be a denial that he committed the crime or if he did, he would give the most plausible excuses, all of which had been brought out in his trial and were not material to determine the question of whether or not he was fit for parole." Clair Wilcox, too, discovered just how heavily the boards focused on the circumstances of the original crime. "Although these boards invariably assert that they will not retry the prisoner's case when he appears for parole, it is almost inevitable that they will frequently do so."[13]

The second major concern in the board interviews was the inmate's prior record: was he a first offender or recidivist, did he have a juvenile record or an adult one? The docket contained this information and it was the one item that members looked at closely. It often sparked rhetorical questions, and even more often, comments once the prisoner left the hearing and the members were discussing their decision. The Idaho board was notably frank about the significance of the "priors":[14]

> Q. You have a previous record?
> A. Yes.
> Q. I can say this, we don't look with very much favor upon you fellows that have previous records.
> A. I know you don't.[15]

Some parole boards gave such weight to prior criminality that they went beyond the official court record.[16] In New York, for example, as one member explained to the State Crime Commission, "we . . . pay a great deal of attention to his previous history. For instance, he might be there under an indeterminate sentence, not having been [before] convicted, and may have committed misdemeanors. We write to the court then and ask the court if he knows that this fellow has so many convictions." More, "we check up before the applicant comes up for parole, and there are often convictions that the courts knew nothing about or as to which the applicant made misrepresentations to the court. If he fooled the court, we hold him for his maximum."[17]

Finally, the boards usually inquired about an inmate's future plans, asking explicit questions on employment prospects and seeking verbal assurances that he would now go straight, give up whatever vices he had, and live a law-abiding life. Thus, the Oregon board terminated its interview with James Clark, the disappointed suitor turned arsonist, by asking:

Q. What would you do if released, James?
A. I'd go back to Namath Falls, it is my home and I'm pretty well acquainted there and never had trouble getting work there.
Q. What is your trade?
A. I'm a cook by trade and still belong to the union.
Q. Are you through with drinking?
A. Yes, I think I am.
Q. Well, are you sure or do you just think you are sure?
A. I'm absolutely sure.
Q. Where is this woman now?
A. I don't know where she is. The sheriff said he couldn't find her at the time of the trial.
Q. What would you do if you were to see her again? Would you cause her any trouble?
A. No — no, I wouldn't cause her any trouble of any kind.
Q. Do you feel any malice against her?
A. No, no — I'm perfectly willing to just forget all about her. I haven't any grievance against her at all.
Q. Of course, you realize, James, that leaving liquor entirely alone would be one of the conditions of your parole. Do you think you could live up to that?
A. Yes, yes, I'm sure I could.[18]

Whatever doubts one might have about the reliability or the significance of such professions, the Oregon board diligently cross-examined inmates until getting the answers it wanted to hear, as in the following dialogue with Roy Bingham, guilty of assault with a dangerous weapon in what was essentially a drunken brawl:

Q. What would you do if released? Have you any
definite work?
A. I have some kids in Christie Home and I want to
take them back to their own mother in California.
Q. Do you think you could leave liquor alone if re-
leased?
A. I think I could as I don't want more of this.
Q. Answer direct.
A. Sure I can leave it alone.
Q. *Will* you leave it alone?
A. Yes, I will.[19]

With one or more of these three topics completed, the inmate
left the room and the board turned to making its decision.[20] The
statutory guidelines generally instructed them to make certain
that a released inmate had a job awaiting him; they also laid
down vague criteria to the effect that an inmate's release "will not
be incompatible with the welfare of society" (Ohio); or that he
"has shown a disposition to reform; that in the future he will
probably obey the law and lead a correct life; that the interests of
society will not be impaired thereby" (Rhode Island); or that he
"is likely to lead an orderly life" (Massachusetts); or that there is
"reasonable probability" of his not violating the law (Pennsylvania, New York, Washington). In short, the boards were to
make a guess as to which inmates would stay out of trouble,
based on probabilities.[21]

Given the background of most board members, the brevity of
their discussions, and the ill-defined nature of the guidelines,
parole cases were often resolved for capricious or foolish reasons.
The Idaho board discussion (in the presence of an investigator
from the Attorney General's office and with a stenographer taking
down every word) on whether to parole an inmate serving time
for theft, included such observations as:

No. One: I vote yes.
No. Two: Yes. That man has a good face.
No. One: I think so.

Or, in the case of another inmate:

No. Three: I vote yes. He isn't a bad looking fellow. He is a kind of slob, but I think he is all right.[22]

A particularly flagrant instance of arbitrary decision making was the following dialogue, which took place with the inmate present throughout:

No. One: Where do you live?
Prisoner: North Dakota.
No. One: Where were you in this state when you were accused of burglary?
Prisoner: Shelley.
No. One: What did you try to steal?
Prisoner: Adding machine.
No. Two: You were sentenced by Judge Stevens?
Prisoner: Yes.
No. Two: You didn't get anything out of the adding machine?
Prisoner: No.
            (Letter from Judge Stevens read)
No. One: This is a nice looking boy.
No. Three: I wish I had his physique. With my combative mind and his physique I would go to prize fighting.
No. Two: Your trouble in North Dakota was checks?
Prisoner: I run out of funds at the bank one time. That was all taken care of. My brother wants me to come to California. He has a place for me. My brother runs a little farm there.
No. One: All right we will vote. I vote yes.
No. Two: Yes, when he has served his minimum.
No. Three: I will pass him. He has a beautiful body.
No. One: All right. The next one.[23]

Despite the all too common character of such occurrences, parole outcomes were not invariably devoid of reason. Decision making was, at least some of the time, more than just a lottery in which the handsome body won. The boards' attention to an inmate's crime and prior record was relevant to their determinations.

First, board members did reach their own estimates of the seriousness of the offense and set parole dates accordingly. For crimes they considered minor, they would grant release more quickly; for those considered major, they would withhold it. The rapid-fire retrying of the case represented the boards' attempt to make this calculation: the docket said arson, but it turned out that the matter was really a drunkard's way of seeking a lover's revenge, and so parole was granted at the minimum; the docket read armed assault, but the prisoner had only been driving the car, so again parole was granted at the minimum. The Idaho board, for example, when learning that a twenty-one-year-old inmate had received a term of seven to fifteen years for stealing $250 worth of jewelry, was outraged at the disparity between the length of the sentence and the seriousness of the offense. And since this particular board also had the power to grant conditional pardons, the young man went out after serving less than a year and a half.[24]

Second, and more important, boards were usually harder on the recidivist than on the first offender. They were not at all eager to release those with a long criminal record, and the Idaho board's decisions reflected this judgment:

> Deputy Warden: He has worked every day and been faithful. . . . He has been a top hand, and has done his time.
> No. One: Call the roll — I vote yes.
> No. Two: I vote no — too long a criminal record — three times up.
> No. Three: No.

Parole declined. Or:

> No. Three: He has a long record.
> No. One: He does look rather hopeless. I think it will work out all right, however, I vote yes.

No. Two: I vote no, too long a criminal record.
No. Three: No — too much of a criminal record, and
undoubtedly a confirmed criminal.
No. Two: Who is next?[25]

The Wilcox report on parole in Pennsylvania also pointed to
the significant role of prior criminal record in determining board
actions. Only one-quarter of the 249 inmates released on parole at
the minimum in 1925 from the Eastern State Penitentiary were
recidivists. Of the 59 prisoners forced to serve out their maximum,
a little over one-third had committed serious offenses (assault to
kill, robbery); the rest had all been incarcerated two or more
times before. Similarly, in the state of Washington, as one observer noted, "the general practice is to double the sentence for
every previous felony. A first offender may get 18 months, for his
second offense, 36 months, for his third offense, 60 months, for his
fourth offense, 90 months, and for his fifth offense, 120 months. A
study of the average length of sentence imposed by the Board of
Prison Terms and Paroles . . . shows that the Board unquestionably punishes the recidivist. There is no escaping this fact." Thus,
one of the few considerations that the Attorney General's survey
found linked consistently to parole outcome was the inmate's
criminal history. In almost all institutions, "persons having a
record of three or more incarcerations had less chance of being
paroled than first or second offenders."[26]
   Despite the fact that some elements of uniformity can be found
in board interviews and decisions, parole was at its core arbitrary
and capricious. Board members were predisposed to link the seriousness of the crime to the severity of the punishment; but no
board, in any jurisdiction, attempted to define what constituted a
serious crime or to reach a consensus on crime rankings that
would guide them and inform inmates. Instead, each member
made his own decision. The judgments were personal and therefore not subject to debate or reconsideration. One man might
decide to grant an inmate parole, but if his colleague declared,
"No; he committed a rather serious crime," that ended the dialogue. There was nothing left to do except tally the votes.

Under these circumstances, individual board members would become well known for their particular biases about what constituted a serious crime. Tom Waters of the Washington board had the reputation of being tough on males who committed sex crimes, and "in the main disagrees with other members of the Board whom he considers too lenient in such cases." Entire state boards, too, would gain their reputations. The Massachusetts board was especially harsh on those guilty of rape, arson, armed robbery, and drunken driving; in Kansas, they penalized bank robbers; and so on. Hence, when the Attorney General's survey attempted to correlate the offense committed with the likelihood of parole, no significant trends emerged. "Although persons convicted of robbery apparently had a better chance for parole in 12 institutions, they appear to have had a significantly worse chance for parole in 8 institutions. . . . Sex offenders had a better chance of being paroled from 10 institutions and less chance in only five. . . . No uniform tendency to consider the offense committed as a determinant of parole selection is disclosed." In sum, one man's nightmare case did not necessarily frighten another.[27]

Further, the boards' inclination to punish recidivists severely had too limited an applicability to make the system coherent. Not that many three-time losers appeared on parole dockets. Indeed, the very willingness of the boards to add on time for the multiple offenders points to an even more fundamental problem in the administration of parole: by legislative mandate, members were to try to predict future conduct, to decide which offenders could safely be returned to society. Yet neither they, nor anyone else, had sound criteria upon which to base such a decision. In the 1930's, some criminologists like Sheldon and Eleanor Glueck did attempt to identify factors determining parole outcome, but such efforts at prediction did not move beyond a primitive stage. In the meanwhile, parole boards were making and would continue to make decisions.

Under such discouraging conditions, board members adopted various stratagems. A few admitted to the difficulty of it all. "I listened to twenty-five hundred convicts one at a time," noted Henry Broderick, a wealthy Seattle banker, real estate operator, and member of the Washington board. "I studied their faces closely, weighed their words, observed their ways, and in short did everything that a sociologist, penologist, criminologist, or all three rolled into one would do — and after four years of it, I confess little headway in the art of telling a 'bad man' from a 'straight-lace.'" Others simply followed their hunches: since he has a good face or body we will trust that he will not return to his evil ways. Still others assumed that three-time losers were more likely to become four-time losers than first offenders were to become second offenders. But there was no evidence to support this assumption, nor did boards attempt to analyze the results of their actions. Rather, faced with an impossible situation, they looked to the face and to the past record — and the one was no less arbitrary than the other.[28]

It is not, then, surprising that boards cross-examined the inmate until he promised to go straight. However absurd it was to take such declarations seriously, the boards were seeking their own comfort, trying to get some support, however flimsy, for reaching their decisions. Tell us, they were in effect saying to the inmate, that you will not drink, that you will leave the girl alone, so that for a moment at least we can decide to parole you with a more or less good conscience. Are you absolutely sure you are through with drinking? Declare it unequivocally so we can think to ourselves that we know what we are doing.

Some boards adopted still another tactic: to release (or to refuse to release) more or less automatically the inmates who appeared before them. In states like New York, Pennsylvania, Maine, New Jersey, and Indiana, boards were prone to grant parole to prisoners at the expiration of their minimum sentence. On the other side, in states like Illinois, California, Maryland, Minnesota, and Kansas, boards generally declined parole to the majority of inmates at their minimum. In part, such practices reflected the boards' eagerness to process their cases as quickly as possible; but in part they revealed some glimmer of a sense that since future behavior could not be predicted, boards might just as well decide cases on a wholesale basis — which is precisely what reformers did not want them to do.[29]

In the end, none of these tactics made parole into anything other than a game of chance. The odds on some cases for release were better than others: a first-time offender who had not committed a major crime was more likely to be paroled at the minimum in New York; a recidivist guilty of a major crime was probably not going to win parole at the minimum in Illinois. Nevertheless, parole decisions remained arbitrary. No inmate could be confident that he would not fall in that group of cases not paroled in New York; on the other hand, each inmate could be hopeful that he would end up among the cases that gained parole early in Illinois. For the boards never announced in advance or formulated among themselves guidelines that would limit their discretion or rules under which they would operate. Parole rhetoric remained committed to giving individual consideration to every case, to responding to the particular character of each inmate rather than to his offense. In practice, the boards did focus far more on the offense, and on past criminal records, but they would never admit openly to such practices; and, more important, they would never issue regulations that gave their unspoken criteria any binding force. Thus, the boards were both bureaucratic enough to get through their dockets and unpredictable enough to keep everyone guessing as to the outcome of specific cases.

The frustrations of reaching an initial decision on whether to parole an inmate were all the more acute because parole supervision was not merely unsatisfactory but grossly inadequate. In effect, parole boards understood that to release an inmate on parole was to grant him unconditional freedom, and accordingly, they were even more cautious about their decisions. The credo of the Oregon board was not idiosyncratic: "It is obvious that adequate supervision is impossible, and therefore the Board had determined to take no chances in recommending paroles."[30]

In the Progressives' design, parole, like probation and incarceration, was to assist the ex-offender, perhaps by finding him employment or by providing him with psychological counseling. At the same time, it was to protect society by closely observing the

parolee and recommitting him whenever he was about to lapse
into crime. Parole, too, was to mix therapy with control, social
work with police work. Thus, the Illinois parole department insisted that its officers take a "lively interest in the subject of this
parole. They will counsel and advise him as he may need, and
will assist him in any reasonable way to reestablish himself in
society." But it added immediately: "They will vigorously follow
and re-arrest him in the event that he wilfully violates the conditions of his parole, sparing neither time nor expense in doing so."
In the same spirit, the Michigan manual for parole agents instructed them to be the ex-inmate's "first friend. . . . He must be
convinced of your unselfish concern in his welfare only." Yet it
went on to say, quite openly: "There is a mailed fist cleverly
concealed in the relationship but it need not be brought into play
without adequate cause. You will remember parole is provided
for the protection of the people and it is not founded upon any
sympathetic appeal."[31] In the case of the prison, as we have seen,
the balance never held and incarceration became exclusively police work to the end of incapacitation. With parole, the balance
also failed, but here the program fulfilled neither purpose. The
former inmate received little or no assistance and the society,
little or no protection.

That reformers' hopes for parole were disappointed can hardly
be surprising to anyone familiar with the fate of other contemporary criminal justice programs. The inability to deliver rehabilitative service through parole was at one with the inability to
deliver it through probation or in prisons. Injunctions to be the ex-
inmate's best friend and to readjust him to his environment came
up against deficiencies in techniques; the lack of well-formulated
and effective treatment procedures undercut so ambitious a goal.
Indeed, the same litany of complaints that ran through reformers'
other tracts was echoed here. Parole officers, like probation and
prison staffs, were badly trained, rarely approximating the educational or social work qualifications that reformers established.
Thus, the advisory committee to the Wickersham Commission
protested bitterly about the "appointment of incompetent and
untrained parole officers. We have already pictured the situation

concerning probation officers and the somewhat tragic lack of adequate training for their difficult and responsible work. If possible, the situation is worse with respect to parole officers. Almost anybody is considered good enough to be a parole officer."[32]

. What is more unexpected, the exercise of parole's policing function was feeble and ineffectual. The parole boards, after all, did have jurisdiction over ex-inmates for several years at least; moreover, parole officers generally came from the ranks of law enforcement officials, so that one might at least have anticipated that they would watch the ex-inmate. The chief parole officer of the state of Washington took the post after twenty-five years as a policeman and sheriff. His field supervisor was a former police officer and one of his two parole officers was the son of the chief detective of Spokane who believed "he was selected by the Board because of his training as an officer on the city of Spokane police force." Washington also relied upon a network of unpaid "sponsors" to supervise parolees, of whom "A great majority . . . are law enforcement officers such as sheriffs, chiefs of police and occasionally a prosecuting attorney or a justice of the peace." And these types of appointments were not at all unusual. In Illinois, too, the field agents were former sheriffs and deputies.[33]

Nevertheless, parole supervision remained a paper program, in both a literal and a figurative sense. Fourteen states released inmates on parole without so much as appointing an agent to exercise surveillance; another thirteen states appointed one agent only, and usually put his office in the state prison. Hence, more than one-half of the states administering parole made no efforts whatsoever to police, let alone to assist their charges. In Oregon, one investigator revealed, "there is no reformation work. . . . There is no supervision of parolees of any kind. Parole Officer Duffy has over 200 (probably 400) cases on parole covering territory of 92,000 square miles. No assistants. Spends 75 percent of his time back of penitentiary bars." In Idaho, "supervision of the parolee became a joke. . . . The parole officer can play no part in the supervision . . . as he has no car, no expenses, and no time or authority to go into the field." Another six states appointed two to four parole officers, but their case loads were so heavy that effective supervision was impossible. In Washington, for example, three field agents had responsibility for some 1730 cases, and obviously a ratio of 1:570 precluded careful oversight.[34]

As a result, each parolee left the institution with two forms in hand: one a list of his parole conditions, the other a questionnaire to be completed and mailed to his parole officer monthly. As with probation, the conditions repeated broad injunctions and admonitions. From the state of Washington:

> The parolee shall avoid evil associates and not frequent improper places of amusement, nor loiter upon the streets at night, and shall respect and obey the law and at all times conduct themselves as good citizens.

From Pennsylvania:

> Lead a life of honesty and sobriety, obey the law, avoid all evil associates and keep steadily employed.

Nearly every state, in fact, required parolees to avoid bad companions, the "vicious, lewd or unworthy," to stay away from "improper places of amusement," pool halls, dance halls, and saloons. Without the permission of the officer, parolees could not purchase an automobile (or, in some places, drive one), or borrow money, or buy on the installment plan, or marry, or change residence, or switch jobs. And, again, many states added their own favorite item, whether to remain at home after working hours, to save a certain percentage of earnings, to pay for room and board in advance, or to waive extradition rights if apprehended out of state.[35]

The monthly forms required the parolee to report the number of days worked and the wages earned, to explain any idleness, to describe his use of spare time, to admit whether he drank, and to note any difficulty with local authorities. A few jurisdictions did require employers to countersign the forms, but the parole officer could not check on the reliability of the information or the authenticity of the signature. From the standpoint of supervision, the whole process was not worth the price of the postage.

Some of the larger states attempted to administer a more elaborate program, appointing full-time salaried parole agents to carry out supervision. Indeed, when reformers in smaller states were disturbed by inadequacies in their own parole organization, they would cite Minnesota, California, Pennsylvania, Ohio, Illinois, and New York as the models to emulate. Yet the gross weakness of supervision in these ostensibly exemplary jurisdictions is altogether apparent. A larger staff did not in itself make supervision more intense. By 1934, the Minnesota Crime Commission had persuaded the legislature to appoint eight parole officers, but since their duties also included pre-release investigations, probation work, and such assorted tasks as investigating the dependents of those incarcerated in penal institutions, little time was left for supervision. Field work was a hit-or-miss affair, as an observer who accompanied one officer in Minneapolis–St. Paul discovered:

> Went into the field and called on parolees with Agent Kersey. One fellow named Matthew Neilson had skipped out. Kersey got wind of a girlfriend of Neilson's in Luck, Wisconsin, and hopes to be able to trace Neilson through her.

> Called on Lanny Wheelock, house prowler . . . had been picked up by police night before for questioning; screwy looking household.

> Called on Mrs. Ott, trying to get her to take her son home; he boarding out with young couple . . . unsatisfactory; Mrs. Ott sickly, two other grown children. Apparent much prior discord in family.

> Called on Robert Johns, his foster-mother had called that he didn't get in until midnight the night before.

The parole officer would try to locate a parolee here, check up on another there, but he provided little surveillance or assistance.[36]

Conditions were no different in Illinois, another "model" state. Eight agents had responsibility for field work, but four of them had only a handful of cases (either because of other administrative tasks or because of the enormous geographical distance that separated one parolee from another), which left the other four with combined responsibility for over five hundred. These officers, reported Professors Bruce, Burgess, and Harno, "carry a load beyond any hope of efficient work; in fact, the load itself is indicative of the mere formal nature of the supervision." So too, according to the 1927 report of the Pennsylvania Parole Commission, "at the Western State Penitentiary, one-fifth of the time of one employee is devoted to the actual supervision of six hundred parolees. . . . No more than a sixth of the time of three men is devoted to the personal supervision of the six hundred prisoners who are on parole from the Eastern Penitentiary." The commissioner of parole in Massachusetts complained that thirteen parole officers could do little with two thousand men, while his counterpart in California was not more satisfied with fifteen officers for twelve hundred men.[37]

Of all states, New York undoubtedly made the most dogged efforts to translate parole theory into practice. Yet it fared no better than others. Throughout the 1920's, complaints of inadequate supervision were pervasive. The blue-ribbon panel headed by Alfred Lewisohn, appointed by Governor Franklin Roosevelt in 1930 to investigate the "parole problem," issued a damning report. "An examination of the files . . . justify the repeated complaints which have been made against parole for many years. It is evident that after-care of men released on parole is not a sustained and helpful service." Only twelve full-time agents, together with an assortment of volunteers from private, religious, or social organizations, supervised some two thousand parolees. In fact, they kept such poor records, and the confusion between private and public officers was so rampant, that no one could be certain of exactly who was on parole or who was responsible for a given case. The Lewisohn Committee recommended a total reorganization: a state agency should oversee a professional corps of workers who would each supervise no more than seventy-five persons. The legislature acted, but again performance fell short. A New York grand jury examination in 1934 found that the changes in parole laws "not only increased the number of men eligible for parole, but increased the number of pre-parole investigations . . . so that today, approximately the same number of parole officers as there were in 1930, are attempting to supervise approximately four times the number of men under parole supervision." The next year, a special committee appointed by Governor Herbert Lehman was no less critical of parole administration.[38]

The final indicator of the inadequacies in parole surveillance emerges from revocation practices. Parole officers, like probation officers, were supposed to spot signs of relapse and recommit a parolee in advance of a new offense. In fact, parole officers were usually in no position to make such judgments. An agent with a few hundred cases and a responsibility for a host of other administrative duties could not keep close track of any one parolee's activities. Even under optimal conditions, with a case load of seventy-five, it is very doubtful whether an officer could have known if the parolee was associating with other criminals, visiting dance halls, or even committing crimes; but as matters stood, a parolee had merely to falsify his monthly written reports or to move to another section, another city, or another state, and his parole officer was almost helpless.

Under such circumstances, revocation rates for parole, as for probation, were low, generally under 20 percent; and the majority of revocations occurred after the parolee had been arrested on a new charge. Thus, in Illinois, the Bruce Committee learned that those returned to prison for parole violations had almost always been apprehended by the police for another offense. In New York, where the ratio of parole officers to parolees was unusually high, new arrests still made up the majority of the roughly 10 percent of cases recommitted to the penitentiaries. In Pennsylvania, the Wilcox Committee report concluded that "parolees are practically never reincarcerated because of their behavior on parole unless they are arrested for the commission of further crime. . . . Many of those returned to the institution as parole violators have been regularly reporting up to the time of their arrest and are listed in the books of the institution as parole successes." Whatever administrative purposes parole revocation was fulfilling, the program was not satisfying the original design.[39]

Nevertheless, the system persisted, and without basic changes. For all the public clamor and widespread dissatisfaction, parole survived relatively unscathed. How could failure and unpopularity have had so little impact on the continuity and structure of policy? The answer is to be found, first, in the functions that the program did fulfill for several types of officials within criminal justice. The day-to-day advantages that they gained from administering the system far outweighed (for them) its apparent defects.

The most vigorous champions of parole, those who gained the most from its operation, were the prison wardens. Their support was critical to the survival of the system and it was unwavering, despite some gradual diminution of their authority over parole decisions. Before 1925, wardens dominated the parole boards. They usually served as one of the three members; the meetings were held on their grounds, at the prison; and at least at the start, the inmate's record of institutional conduct probably counted for most, if for no other reason than as a carry-over from the time when parole was defined as a reward for the good inmate. After the mid-1920's, however, the parole system built up its own bureaucracy. It became more independent of the department of corrections and moved away from the warden's direct control. He no longer served on the committee, the final decisions were more frequently made in the state capital, and institutional behavior ranked well behind an inmate's prior record in importance as a release consideration. As Warden Lewis Lawes of Sing-Sing told a New York investigatory committee: "I have never attended a meeting of the Parole Board. I have never been requested to. . . . I did attempt at first to make a good warden's report and recommendation; but when I found they didn't read it or pay any attention to it I will admit my efforts became very perfunctory." The Wilcox study in Pennsylvania found that "good conduct in prison does not inevitably lead to parole, nor do minor disciplinary infringements always prevent release. Eighty percent of those paroled at the minimum had perfect prison records. But it is also noteworthy that 80 percent of those refused parole had maintained good conduct in prison." And the Attorney General's survey cautioned that "Parole should not be used as a device for solving some of the problems of prison administrators. Prison administrators . . . are liable to employ it as a good time regulation or reward rather than as a correctional device."[40]

Nevertheless, wardens had good reasons to continue to support the program and to resolve in their national meetings that parole was "an essential element in protective penology." Some of them did manage to keep the boards under their sway: in such states as New Hampshire, Connecticut, and New Jersey, the warden still had the most to say about who went out on parole. In many cases, too, a warden could persuade a board to take into account his own prejudices in any one particular instance. Hence, the following dialogue in the Montana parole board meeting:

> Case of Fred Albo, a Mexican, was considered.
> The Clerk read the history.
> Governor: Hold him I think.
> Secretary of State: Go to it.
> Attorney General: It makes no difference if he is a Mexican.
> Clerk: The Warden hates Mexicans and recommends him. He must be a good man.
> Governor: All right, don't hold him.[41]

(One cannot be certain, of course, whether the warden was very impressed by this inmate or whether he simply wanted to get rid of a noxious Mexican.)

More important, whatever the board's assumptions about the significance of the prior record, the warden could thwart the opportunity for release for any especially troublesome inmate. Boards would not pay attention to minor infractions or necessarily release someone who minded his own business inside. However, the inmate who was far out of line would suffer, and wardens as well as convicts understood this. Wardens, or their principal keepers, were very often present throughout board deliberations; but at any rate it was they who made up the dockets and so they had ample opportunity to tell the board about the bad cases. In Pennsylvania, for instance, the inmate who "carried coffee from the mess hall, cursed an officer, refused to enter his cell, and stole and drank shellac," did not win release at the minimum. In effect, wardens had a veto power, and their ability to blackball was sufficient to serve their own disciplinary ends well. "Complex and difficult as is prison management under the best conditions," insisted one Indiana official, "it would be immediately more difficult without the parole law. The prisoner looks upon the parole as the reward for good conduct and steady industry and does his best to earn it." Or, as Pennsylvania's Wilcox concluded: "The power possessed by the state under parole laws . . . provides penal administrators with a club which is even more effective than the old 'good time' laws in inducing internal discipline. Prison managers generally favor parole for this reason."[42]

Moreover, wardens found themselves locked into the system once it was in operation. They were compelled to favor its perpetuation for the critical reason that any talk of a diminution in the availability of parole (let alone its outright abolition) provoked substantial inmate hostility — and wardens did not enjoy suppressing riots. Under indeterminate sentences, any effort to restrict parole had to mean significant increases in time served. Almost invariably, then, wardens were eager to see more and more paroles granted to keep peace among the inmates. Joseph Moore, chairman of the New York State Board of Parole, complained that wardens were directing inmates' anger at parole boards and away from themselves. "The Parole Board finds it advisable to hold a large percentage of prisoners beyond their eligibility for release and we have abundant evidence that prison officials disapprove of this. Unfortunately, this feeling whether purposely or not is conveyed to the prisoners and it is permitted to be a general idea among them that so far as the prisons are concerned they would be glad to release them but the hardboiled Parole Board holds them up."[43]

In much the same way, the warden of the penitentiary in Washington State kept up a running battle with parole board members. Because they were (in his view) too strict about release, his own job of preserving good order was more difficult. In fact, the warden "usually placed about five or ten men on the Docket who had served a long time, but who had no present chance for release. Why? Because when a 'con' has put in a lot of time and is denied any chance for a hearing before the Board, resentment occurs, and if there is enough of that, trouble occurs inside." That same warden resisted all efforts to abolish parole for three-time losers: "Such prisoners could not be controlled . . . [and] prison administration would be impossible." The warden of the Illinois State Penitentiary at Stateville, to choose one case from many, knew the truth of that argument first-hand: in 1937, responding to a newspaper crusade, the parole board cut back on releases (granting only 3 from 274 applications), and in short order the warden had to contend with a hunger strike. Or, to turn the point around, the warden at Charlestown, Massachusetts, consistently recommended parole "because he expected it to improve discipline. He proved correct in his anticipation as there has not been a riot or outbreak in State Prison since parole went into effect." In sum, the wardens were parole's warmest friends. They supported the system and were eager to keep the numbers granted parole as high as possible — always excepting that difficult case which had to be made into an object lesson.[44]

Legislative committees investigating parole found the wardens' conclusions not only well-taken but almost unanswerable. No matter how critical they were of one or another part of the system, they were reluctant to restrict release procedures for fear of undercutting prison officials' power. The New York Crime Commission, a tough group with little good to say for parole, moved very cautiously for fear of disturbing the wardens' authority. Not only the wardens but representatives of the state parole board took pains to inform the Commission just how critical parole was to discipline. "It is your opinion," Senator Caleb Baumes, the chairman of the Commission, asked the head of the parole board, "that you create and maintain a better morale, if you please, amongst the prisoners generally, if they know that system is in vogue?" To which the chairman replied: "Absolutely." The Commission accepted the argument, and as eager as some of its members were to abrogate the board's right to release inmates immediately at the minimum, they did not dare do so. "If you tell 3,000 men in the prison," concluded one of the most law-and-order-minded members of the Commission, "that they are likely to be held from months to five or six years more, you will make a hell on earth of every prison in the State. . . . 3000 men expect . . . from all the years of practice by the Parole Board . . . that they will be released at the end of the minimum, and if you tell them that now it is likely or probable that their time will be extended beyond the minimum . . . they are going to insurge and feel vicious, and you can not blame them, no matter how heinous was their original offense." His conclusion was clear: "If we are to go ahead on any rough and ready method of extending sentences and taking that definite hope away from them, the consequences will be extreme." True, public opinion (and his own instincts as well) would prefer to "make them serve indefinitely." But "we cannot do it without smashing prison discipline." It was this kind of reasoning that helped to preserve parole, no matter how poor its reputation or inadequate its practices.[45]

State investigatory committees and legislators were also reluctant to tamper with parole because of an idea that the boards served as safety valves against the pressure of prison overcrowding. It is surprisingly difficult to gauge the accuracy of this belief. The exact degree of prison overcrowding during these years remains unclear. Every observer of the system agreed that American prisons were overcrowded; yet the census returns on prison capacity and population through these years do not seem to bear this out. Much of the problem of course, was one of definition. To measure overcrowding required agreement on what constituted an institution's proper capacity — and this judgment was left to each warden. For some administrators, two men to a cell was a bit tight, but not overcrowded; to others, converting a school-room into a dormitory justified reporting a reduction in over-crowding. Still others counted each cell as appropriate for one man, then calculated any excess of population as overcrowding. Given these discrepancies, the returns themselves, not unexpectedly, showed that overcrowding varied widely. Southern and western states generally reported the greatest amount, eastern states the least.[46]

The only safe conclusion from the data is that everyone assumed that prisons were overcrowded; and that assumption itself became an important fact in the way everyone responded to parole. Just as wardens feared that restrictions on parole would breed inmate unrest, so legislators worried that cutbacks in parole would increase the number of inmates, generate more overcrowding, and thereby (most important) increase the pressure on them to appropriate funds for new prison construction. Professors Bruce, Burgess, and Harno informed the Illinois legislature that the state's three institutions were already "overcrowded to such an extent that their proper management is greatly interfered with and the proper training of their inmates is practically impossible." More, some three thousand new convicts would have to be admitted annually (and the number was certain to swell over time), so at least this many inmates would have to be released annually "or new institutions must be built to provide for the increase." The conclusion was inevitable: "One advantage of the parole system is that . . . the prisoner . . . is not required to be confined in the penitentiary." Or, as the chairman of the Illinois Parole Board argued more dramatically: "The members of the Legislature . . . were confronted with the choice of either appropriating for and making efficient the system of indeterminate sentence and of parole or of expending nearly forty million of dollars during the next ten years in the erection and maintenance of penitentiaries and reformatories." Here was a trade-off legislators had to reckon with. Newspaper attacks were one thing; to raise the taxes for the forty million quite another. Parole could be curtailed only at a staggering cost.[47]

The Minnesota Crime Commission, well aware of all parole's faults, encouraged great caution in abolishing or curtailing the procedure for many of the same reasons. "We must pause to point out," it reported, "the prison capacity that would be necessary if terms of imprisonment were lengthened or the maximum required in all cases. . . . All three institutions are now full. . . . A statistician has advised the Commission that an increase in one year in the term of all prisoners would necessitate another institution of the capacity of the prison at once." On this basis, the Commission concluded, "it is easy to calculate what would be necessary if the maximum were required."[48]

Did parole boards actually release inmates in response to overcrowding? The answer remains obscure: parole boards never had to account for particular decisions and surviving transcripts do not contain any candid admissions that crowded conditions were affecting outcomes. Still, some evidence suggests that overcrowding was a consideration. "Without doubt," reported the Attorney General's survey, "some parole boards are sometimes greatly influenced by the fact that their prisons are overcrowded and room needs to be made for the newcomers. Some parole board members . . . pointed out that the only alternatives were larger prisons or more dangerously congested prison conditions." And some boards, like the one in Oregon, also admitted "that practically no paroles are revoked unless the parolee is again convicted of a felony . . . because of the overcrowded condition in the penitentiary." In all events, state legislators were caught in a difficult position. If the prisons were not overcrowded, they were told to credit parole procedures; if the prisons were overcrowded, they were told not to dare to cut back on parole. So no matter what the reality, it seemed the better part of wisdom to keep hands off the system.[49]

A few groups, particularly judges and police chiefs, did press for a fundamental revamping of parole. Unlike the diffused public opposition, which rarely came directly before the legislature, they testified in opposition to release practices. Some judges were especially vocal, letting the New York Crime Commission, for example, know of their objections. "When it was started," declared one magistrate, "I felt that it had much of excellence." But now, "the power of these people of the Boards of Parole has increased, and the powers of judges trying criminal cases have decreased. . . . It is from this source, the Board of Parole itself, that these modifications come, modifications in the power of the judge until he is bereft of power and made almost a laughing stock." A judge sentenced an offender to a maximum term of life, but then "met him on the street in four years. . . . It was a joke, a perfect joke."[50]

In truth, the complaint was only slightly exaggerated. Because of parole, judges had lost power to the boards, and they could do little to win it back. One of their favorite stratagems to recapture control over sentencing was to pass minimums that were almost identical to the maximums, to give a sentence of nine-and-one-half to ten years. But that tactic was soon outlawed; New York, for example, prohibited judges from setting a minimum that was greater than one-half the maximum. Moreover, judges were not very persuasive in front of the legislature. One reason was that they lobbied poorly. "The Board of Parole," noted one magistrate, "are at Albany. They are in a position to be in touch with the making of laws. The judges are not indifferent to the means, but they are out of touch . . . unconscious of what is being passed in that way in the Legislature." Besides, parole board members had a convincing retort to judicial protests: "It is the unequal sentences that we have to contend with all the time," and the point was well-taken. Their counter-story to the lifer who went free after four years was that of three men, each guilty of the same crime (sending a girl out to solicit), who received respectively "5 to 10, 9 to 18, 3 to 6 — for the same crime." George Kirchwey, Dean of the Columbia School of Social Work and one of the leading advocates of parole, amused the New York Crime Commission with a variant of this tale. His friend, a new judge, was unsure of how to set a particular sentence. He turned first to the chief judge who told him "it is clearly a ten-year case." He then heard from a colleague that "the Chief is way off. You should not give a man like that more than a year. . . . You might give him a suspended sentence."[51]

Then too, judges had to concede that parole served a vital

disciplinary function within the prison, a concession that weakened their case. "I know the length of time in prison," one of them admitted, and "that for the discipline of the prison itself and for the discipline of the prisoner himself it is necessary . . . to allow him some reward for his being a good prisoner." Finally, judges were often no more comfortable with some of the legislative remedies for parole abuse, such as the passage of "habitual offender" laws that forced judges to sentence three- or four-time felons to life terms. Here was a cure that was worse than the disease. So judges grumbled and complained, but they had neither the power nor the arguments to bring about fundamental changes in parole.[52]

The hostility of the police chiefs to parole was only slightly more effective. Although they did complain about coddling the criminal (parole "let out the dangerous type of criminal too early") their major argument was that the boards did not inform them of the whereabouts of released inmates. New York City Police Chief Lewis Valentine wanted "a complete history and photograph of every parolee sent to the Police Department of the City from whence he came immediately upon his release," including his place of residence and employment. "Remember," he told one conference on crime, "Dillinger was a parolee." The parole boards, for their part, insisted that compliance would lead to harrassment. "Somebody in charge of a division or precinct might line up all the parolees and bring them in. . . . It is the fear that the parolees will be given the run-around and dogged." Valentine had his response well prepared to that kind of argument: "That, ladies and gentlemen is pure unadulterated 'bunk.' 'Hounding' of parolees by police, is much like the 'alarming third degree;' it exists chiefly in the minds of those who have least knowledge of the subject." And besides, "I wonder how many of those who fear we will institute this 'hounding' have ever knelt at the bedside of a policeman, mercilessly and cowardly shot down by a man released on parole. I wonder how many of them have looked into the tear-filled eyes of a policeman's widow, or into the faces of a policeman's children." Not surprisingly, this rhetoric often carried in the legislatures, and the police chiefs received names and addresses; crime control took precedence over civil liberties. Still, insofar as the totality of parole was concerned, this was a minor concession.[53]

Finally, district attorneys on the whole remained cautiously in favor of the system. Their instincts for law and order tempted them to join in the chorus condemning the release procedures, but no matter how keenly they may have wished to endorse a get-tough-with-the-criminal position, to lengthen sentences and to curtail parole, their self-interest precluded it. The district attorneys, as we have noted, wanted to facilitate plea bargaining; and reducing parole board prerogatives or allowing judges to set minimums that were just short of maximums would complicate the process. So too, longer sentences might discourage those charged with crimes from striking a bargain; if the difference in time to be served between robbery, first degree and robbery, second degree was not substantial, or if the penalty remained severe, they might choose a jury trial over the plea bargaining alternative. Parole offered the prosecutors another critical advantage — any released inmate could be returned to the penitentiary without the formality of a trial. A parolee apprehended for a new crime or suspected of one could be revoked without going through an elaborate judicial process. And to the district attorneys, who always had one eye trained on the court docket, this was no small advantage.

The prosecutors (like the judges) were also aware that alternatives to parole might well be worse than parole itself. They were, for example, very uneasy about the suggestion (already heard in the 1930's) of establishing sentencing councils; the greater the number of judges who had to pass on the results of plea bargaining, the more burdensome the situation. They were also ambivalent about habitual offender laws. Any offender who faced a life term if convicted of a fourth felony was certainly not going to cop a plea that kept him in the felony ranks; on the other hand, such an offender would willingly bargain to have his charge reduced to a misdemeanor — which is precisely how prosecutors subverted habitual offender laws. But in all, the district attorneys found it convenient to work within the bounds of parole. They were certainly not going to lead a crusade that might produce legislation substantially reducing their own maneuverability.[54]

One last feature of the administration of parole deeply affected the attitudes of criminal justice administrators. For all the public insistence that parole was a grant of leniency, they had good reason to believe otherwise. The indeterminate sentence and parole release may well have served to extend, not to curtail, state control over the offender. District attorneys and wardens did not have to choose between satisfying their operational needs and maintaining a strict system. Reformers also unembarrassedly insisted that rehabilitation was not in conflict with protection of society. Parole, they maintained, was not only helpful but tougher on the offender. One did not have to choose between making sanctions rigorous and doing good.

It is easy to understand why lay observers believed that parole coddled the criminal. They focused exclusively on the disparity between the maximum sentence that the judge imposed and the time that an inmate actually served. The average sentence in the mid-1920's was eight and a half years; the average time served was a little over two years. More particularly, the average maximum for homicide was eighteen years, but the average male offender served "only" five and a half; the average maximum for robbery was thirteen years while the average time served was three years and three months. Small wonder, then, that the press and private citizens were irate. If not for parole, murderers would ostensibly serve eighteen years and robbers thirteen.[55]

But the situation was far more complicated than such a simple judgment would suggest. The public juxtaposed the time inmates actually served against the maximums of indeterminate sentences — not against the time that they would have served under traditional definite sentences. In effect, critics were comparing the indeterminate sentence against itself, not against what had been typical practice. Hence, administrators and reformers rebutted these criticisms by contrasting the new program with the old. For one, parole (ostensibly, anyway) provided a measure of supervision for the offender after his release. "Parole is not leniency," argued the Wickersham Commission. "On the contrary, parole really increases the State's period of control. It adds to the period of imprisonment a further period involving months or even years of supervision." The Wilcox analysis of parole in Pennsylvania also noted that as a result of "a period of conditional liberation . . . the state's control of the criminal is extended rather than restricted. *Parole is thus a supplement to imprisonment rather than a substitute for it.*"[56]

More important, proponents insisted that indeterminate sentences actually confined inmates for longer periods of time than determinate sentences did. Far from coddling the criminal, parole brought more incapacitation. It is exceptionally difficult to weigh the merits of this argument. Almost all of the studies from the 1920's and 1930's that buttressed this conclusion were self-serving; that is, they were conducted by advocates of parole who were eager to demonstrate that time served had increased. And to approach the seemingly straightforward question of whether parole did change the actual duration of confinement raises troubling methodological considerations. It will not do, for example, to compare length of time served in the 1920's and 1930's in states which used determinate sentences against states which used indeterminate sentences, for in effect, one is comparing rural states with urban states, or southern states with eastern and western ones; the differences may well reflect general attitudes toward punishment, not the effects of a system of sentencing. Nor is it altogether satisfactory to compare time served in a single jurisdiction before the introduction of the indeterminate sentence with time served after it — for changes between the 1890's and the 1920's may well reflect general shifts in social attitudes toward punishment. If time served did increase in the 1920's, a "crime wave" mentality, rather than an alteration in sentencing procedures, may have been the critical cause. Had determinate sentencing been in effect, confinement might also have increased.

Yet despite these problems, the burden of evidence does suggest, to phrase it cautiously, that the new system certainly did not represent a way of shortening prison sentences. Indeed, it is probably true that in many, although not in all instances, the introduction of the indeterminate sentence and parole encouraged and promoted an increase in time served.

It is clear that the maximums established under indeterminate sentences were generally longer than the fixed time that judges dispensed under determinate sentences. "The more extensive use of the indeterminate sentence," calculated the federal prison census, "tends to increase the *potential* length of imprisonment, by setting higher limits to the terms of imprisonment than are, in general fixed under the definite-sentence term." In other words, when judges passed a sentence that they knew would be served, they were more sparing with time than when they set a maximum, which they knew in most cases would never be served. So although this change did not necessarily increase actual time served (even if parole proponents, eager to strike a point, often misinterpreted it in just this way), the indeterminate sentences did inflate the measurement of time within criminal justice. It has never been an easy matter to equate seriousness of crime with years to be served. How is one to calibrate the right and fair amount of time that a robber owes to society — is it five years, or ten, or one? But the indeterminate sentence, which announced that it was legitimate for some robbers to serve as much as fifteen years, probably introduced a bias in favor of longer sentences. The lengthy maximums probably encouraged judges and parole boards to ask themselves how much less than fifteen years did this particular robber deserve? Their inclination, then, was to look at a given case from the top down, to set particular sentences by a standard that found fifteen years acceptable. In short, the elasticity of time within an indeterminate sentence expanded prevailing judgments on how much time society should exact from an offender.[57]

There is also some evidence that inmates spent more time in prisons under indeterminate sentences. The Bruce Committee, comparing the times served in the Illinois penitentiaries by those released in 1897 (under determinate sentences) with time served by those released in 1927 (under indeterminate sentences), reported that "the actual time served by the criminal . . . is longer under sentences fixed by the Parole Board than when flat sentences were fixed by the courts." The average term in Joliet for those discharged in 1897 was 1.9 years, in 1927, 2.6; in Menard, time increased from 2.0 to 2.4 years, and in Pontiac, from 1.5 to 2.1. The Committee also contended that the rise probably reflected the parole board's tougher treatment of recidivists. Unlike the judges, it was far more prepared to penalize the offender with a past record (a finding that does fit well with the board's style of questioning and the dockets themselves). Hence, at Pontiac, first offenders under a sentence of one to five years served on the average eighteen months; "occasional offenders" served twenty-two months, and habitual offenders, twenty-four.[58]

Similarly, the parole board in the state of Washington exacted considerably more time from inmates than had the courts. Beginning in 1935, Washington's judges were allowed only to establish the maximum terms for an offender; the parole board set the minimum, and it was a real minimum in the sense that no inmate was released before its expiration. One researcher, calculating the average term in 4,445 cases between 1920 and 1934 (when judges were in control), as compared with 555 cases between 1935 and 1937 (when the parole board held the critical authority), found that the board was confining inmates for twice as long as the judges had. And in Washington, as in Illinois, the board's punitive attitude toward the recidivist seemed to account for much of the difference. "The contrast in sentencing as between sentencing judges and sentencing boards," he concluded, "is . . . that for each additional crime the sentence of the Board is uniformly higher. . . . In many instances sentencing judges were more lenient after the second offense and sometimes even after the third. . . . The Board unquestionably punishes the recidivists."[59]

Other investigations reported very similar results. One member of the California parole board insisted that his committee was "holding men for longer terms within walls before parole or discharge than ever before in the history of California." Indeed, this board member conceded that the practices of the parole boards were responsible for the overcrowding at San Quentin and Folsom, with "prisoners jammed into every attic, basement, and cell."[60]

In Massachusetts, as Sanford Bates, head of the federal prison system, reported, sentence time under parole board authority also went up. The 186 prisoners released in 1895 (the last year of the determinate sentence) served on the average, 4.65 years; the 200 inmates released in 1925 (under the indeterminate sentence) served on the average, 4.95 years. Thus, Hastings Hart, one of the most active prison reformers, was able to testify to the New York Crime Commission in 1928 that on the basis of most existing studies, "the average stay of the prisoner under an indeterminate sentence was actually longer than the average stay of prisoners on a time sentence."[61]

To be sure, occasional investigation yielded contrary results. In Utah, a comparison of the terms of 748 prisoners released between 1908 and 1913 (under determinate sentences) with those of 701 inmates released between 1913 and 1926 (under indeterminate sentences) revealed that "time served in prison for all offense classes decreased, except assault with a deadly weapon, assault to rape, and indecent assault, all three involving few prisoners." Still, when investigators added time under parole supervision to time served in prison, those released under indeterminate sentences spent about 12 percent more time in punishment than those under determinate sentences. They concluded that "the dominant purpose of a parole system . . . is to lengthen the period of state control and supervision of the prisoner." The federal prison census of the mid-1920's also reported varied effects of indeterminate as against determinate sentences: longer periods of confinement for homicide and assault, shorter for robbery, burglary, and forgery, about the same for larceny and related offenses. Nevertheless, the bulk of the data does justify the conclusion that parole was not a matter of leniency. Administrators and reformers had grounds for believing that the network of state control had not been curtailed; if anything, it had spread still further.[62]

Finally, any legislature that wished to respond to public dissatisfaction with parole and yet not impinge on administrators' needs or reformers' ambitions, had several options. Most simply, with the least controversy and the least real significance, a legislature could extend the maximum penalties for particular offenses;

here was a perfect way to score points with constituents without provoking opposition. The New York legislature, in response to the get-tough attitude of Senator Caleb Baumes and his Crime Commission, raised the maximum penalty for first-degree robbery from twenty years to life, for second-degree burglary from ten to fifteen years, for third-degree, from five to ten years. More, it could single out particular offenses that warranted more severe punishments and raise both the minimum and maximum terms. Armed robbery became one favorite target: between 1923 and 1929, nine states substantially increased the penalties for this crime.[63]

Second, legislatures prohibited parole altogether for certain classes of offenders, generally the multiple recidivist. While some states had enacted "habitual offender" laws even before 1900, such provisions were generally disregarded. During the 1920's, however, these older statutes were strengthened or new statutes were enacted, so as to reduce the discretionary authority of the parole board. Under Baumes's leadership, New York provided that all fourth-time felony offenders should be committed for life — and if a judge, at the time of sentencing, was not aware of the criminal's record, the inmate could be brought back from prison to be resentenced whenever his true history became known.[64]

Last, to take care of the nightmare case, several states enacted special codes for "defective delinquents," the criminal offenders who were found to be mentally retarded. New York and Massachusetts led the way, allowing lifetime maximums for this class of offenders, regardless of the seriousness of the offense. Indeed, New York established a separate institution for defective delinquents at Napanoch. To open the prison door for some offenders via parole did not mean that all offenders would have to be turned loose.[65]

None of these responses produced particular opposition. To lengthen the maximum terms for the heinous offender bothered no one; the prosecutors had their eyes on the minimum — indeed, a high maximum could facilitate plea bargaining. And reformers who were often committed to genuine indeterminate sentences, who were comfortable with one-day-to-life terms, certainly had little to say about extending the limits of confinement for robbers and burglars by five or more years.

Habitual offender laws were only slightly more problematic. The district attorneys, as we have seen, were uneasy with any effort to decrease discretionary authority. But it did not take very long for them to undercut the system altogether, so that soon enough habitual offender laws were actually facilitating plea bargaining. To the disgust of some members of the Crime Commission, but as ample testimony to the skills of the district attorneys, it turned out that again and again those charged with a fourth felony were allowed to plead guilty to a misdemeanor or to plead guilty to a felony "as a first offender." So the dockets in New York regularly reported:

> Glen Whitman, seventh felony (four 3rd degree burglaries, two robberies). Pleaded guilty to attempted burglary, 3rd degree, as first offender. Sentence — 2 years, 6 months.

> James O'Hara, sixth felony, two misdemeanor convictions. Pleaded guilty to robbery in 3rd degree, as first offender. Sentence — four years.

Under the Baumes law, each would have received a life sentence as a fourth offender.[66]

By the same token, reformers were not in a position to protest effectively against habitual offender laws. As the first report of the New York Crime Commission declared, such statutes were "merely carrying into effect what criminologists, social workers, students of public affairs, jurists and members of the Bar have been urging for some years, namely, that our laws and our punishments should be made to suit the criminal, not the crime. That is just what this law does." Indeed, Hastings Hart, with excellent reformist credentials, on several occasions professed: "It is a mystery to me why people are so easy about sentencing insane persons for life, when they think it is a horrible thing to send up convicted people for life.... If we can do that with insane people why can not we do it with convicted criminals that have shown themselves to be established criminals?"[67]

Nor were reformers at all uneasy with institutions like Napanoch, which could hold offenders for life terms. It is no accident that when Napanoch opened in 1922, a doctor, Walter Thayer, became its superintendent. Thayer did not doubt his ability to identify the criminal who was a social menace, or society's right to confine him for life. "We have so much reverence," he complained, "for . . . the rights of the individual, and so little care of the rights of society." Napanoch would help to shift the balance. "We should avail ourselves to every bit of information that we can before we turn that man loose," and clearly, anyone diagnosed as defective did not have to be released from confinement.[68]

The defective delinquents were not the only group that warranted permanent commitment, either. Psychiatrists during the 1920's and 1930's frequently discussed the menace of the criminal psychopath. Not that any of them could easily or rigorously define that category. "I have lived with the criminal for 24 years," one of New York's leading institutional psychiatrists told the Crime Commission, "and I know there is the psychopathic individual, but I cannot just describe him." He was not insane or defective, "but he is abnormal and decidedly abnormal"; this type ostensibly composed 15 to 25 percent of the entire prison population, and a still higher percentage of recidivists. Dean George Kirchwey was no more explicit about the category, but no less eager to recommend extended confinement. "I asked our friend Dr. [Thomas] Salmon once," he testified, "what is a psychopath? He said, 'It is hard to express to a lay mind like yours.' I said 'try to explain it'. . . . He said 'Any one who is a queer guy, the fellow that does not fit, he is a psychopath.' I said 'I have seen quite a number of esteemable characters who did not fit, a man named Socrates.' He said 'Yes, he was a psychopath, obviously, and the people of Athens put him out of the way.' "[69]

Kirchwey, not especially disturbed by this dialogue, then explained that the psychopath was someone "whose experiences have been such or whose emotional tendencies are such that under strain he breaks and commits a criminal offense. . . . We ought to have a State institution for the Psychopath . . . in which these psychopaths could be kept in permanent custodial care and treated and looked after and studied." Or, as still another psychiatrist put it: "We would quarantine a man with smallpox; we do not wait until he has spread infection." Why then turn the psychopath loose? Psychiatrists, he insisted, were unfairly criticized as too prone to coddle the criminal. "Psychiatry has nothing to do with soft and sickly sentimentality affecting the criminal or crime. If the psychiatrist had his way, the criminal would be detained much longer than under present day conditions."[70]

Under these circumstances, legislators were able to make their peace with parole. They could perpetuate the system with good conscience and without particular political cost. They could keep administrators and reformers happy, and at the same time demonstrate to their constituents their commitment to rigorous punishment and the full protection of society. Thus, despite rank failures to deliver on its promises, parole persisted. In the 1920's and 1930's, and indeed on through the 1950's, the indeterminate sentence and parole board discretion remained at the heart of criminal justice.

III

The World of Juvenile Justice

CHAPTER SIX

The Invention of the Juvenile Court

IN THE FIELD of juvenile justice, the character of Progressive innovations emerges in clear and stark fashion. Between 1900 and 1920, reformers revolutionized social policy toward the delinquent and created a new mechanism, the juvenile court, that would dominate both the administration of justice and all right-minded thinking on the subject for at least the first half of this century. Even by Progressive standards, the champions of the juvenile court acted with exceptional audacity; and of all the reform measures, this one remains the most controversial. It was the first Progressive program in criminal justice to be successfully challenged by a new wave of activists in the post-1960's as arbitrary and counterproductive in its exercise of discretionary authority (witness their victory in the Supreme Court Gault decision). Yet even today the program continues to attract dedicated support and remains surprisingly invulnerable to fundamental change. All of which, of course, constitutes an open invitation to historical inquiry. To understand the origins and consequences of the juvenile court movement is to examine Progressivism at its most aggressive and influential.

It is not surprising that such aggressiveness should have involved procedures for juveniles, for Progressive programs were to a remarkable degree child-oriented. From child labor legislation to compulsory schooling laws, from kindergartens to playgrounds, from widows' pension provisions to municipal bureaus of child health and hygiene, Progressives sought to insure the proper physical, mental, and moral development of the child. Inevitably, this orientation encouraged Progressives to reexamine the fundamentals of juvenile justice, to see how this system too could be made more responsive to the best interests of the child.

In part, the child-centeredness of Progressives reflected their response to the hordes of immigrants who were crowding into American cities. However unsettling it was for native-born Americans to confront strange ghettos where oddly dressed newcomers spoke in a babble of tongues, it was still more disturbing, or at least challenging, to watch their countless children (and they seemed countless to those limiting their family size to two or three children) continue to follow Old World ways. Admittedly, reformers' ability to affect the life style or life chances of the first-generation immigrant was circumscribed — but surely they could influence the second generation. There was both ample opportunity and ample reason to make the child of the immigrant understand and then fulfill the promise of American life, to win his allegiance to the American way by letting him reap its rewards.

Each of the Progressive child welfare measures looked to this goal. The kindergartens and settlement clubs would inculcate the right attitudes in children, thereby promoting their chances for success and, perforce, their love of country. They would teach the newcomers such mottoes as "The clock helps us to be good," and "patriotic songs and stories of the great men who have made America what she is." The municipal clinics had their important contribution: to impart the rules of preventive medicine so that sickly and puny children would become sturdy youth and thus take full advantage of American opportunities. Since this aim

seemed so realizable and significant, Progressives were not afraid
to introduce the coercive force of law. Immigrant parents did not
understand that removing their children from the classroom and
putting them to work as common laborers doomed them to a
permanent place in the factory and subjected them to grave risks
of injury. Therefore, reformers moved to ban children from the
labor force and to compel them to attend schools — which would
increase the likelihood of their becoming healthy, vigorous, and
upwardly mobile adults.[1]

However important these considerations, the Progressives' orientation toward the child had a second source of inspiration. Not
only their view of American society but their concept of the
intrinsic nature of childhood inspired their programs. Probably
the best starting point is with the work of G. Stanley Hall, the
psychologist at Clark University who made the first systematic
studies of child development in the United States. Hall's influence
was large, not only within the academy (where he trained a host
of students in child study) but among the general public. Hall
introduced and popularized an idea of childhood as composed of
a series of distinct stages: the child moved from level to level in
his growth, and each level demanded a particular kind of response. In the early years, a child should be trained to habits:
"Never again will there be such susceptibility to drill and discipline." Then, in adolescence (a stage to which Hall ascribed particular significance), "individuality must have a longer tether." To
treat the adolescent as a ten-year-old was to invite disaster. Hall
went on to instruct mothers (not fathers; we are still in 1900) to
learn about childhood and, more, to observe their children closely
— for in no other way would they be able to react appropriately
to each stage. Childhood, in other words, was a vastly more complicated phenomenon than had heretofore been imagined. Maternal instinct was not enough — now one needed insight.[2]

Hall's contribution helped to change the way a generation of
women thought about motherhood and the way a generation of
Americans thought about child care. Mothers were to be trained
to their responsibilities, to learn the intricate lessons necessary for
guiding proper child development. Taking up this theme, the

presidents of women's colleges assigned a new importance to female education. As M. Carey Thomas of Bryn Mawr informed her students: "Women cannot conceivably be given an education too broad, too high, or too deep to fit them to become the educated mothers of the future race." Or, as her counterpart at Wellesley, Alice Freeman Palmer, phrased it: "Little children under five years of age die in needless thousands because of the dull, unimaginative women on whom they depend. Such women have been satisfied with just getting along, instead of packing everything they do with brains, instead of studying the best possible way of doing everything."

On a more popular level, no organization took Hall's teachings more seriously or spread them more energetically than the National Congress of Mothers (the forerunner of the Parent Teacher Association). Organized in 1897 by 2,000 delegates, within twenty years the Congress attracted 190,000 members in thirty-six state chapters. Its purpose was "to recognize the supreme importance of the child" — which meant to equip mothers to respond appropriately to this complex creature. The Congress advocated courses for women students in domestic science and promoted university chairs in child study to extend Hall's work and influence.

These views reshaped attitudes not only toward middle-class children but toward children at risk as well. The concepts of educated motherhood sparked changes in public and private programs for the dependent and delinquent child. The National Congress of Mothers became a major lobbying force for Progressive child welfare measures, supporting, for example, kindergarten, playground, and compulsory school legislation. The Congress, together with practically every major settlement house leader, urged the passage of public pensions for widows with children. This innovative and altogether Progressive proposal looked to substitute family care for asylum care. Convinced that the resources of the private charities were inadequate to meet the needs of widowed mothers and that public officials all too often dispatched the widow to the almshouse and her children to the orphan asylum, Progressives urged municipalities to keep the family together at home. The point was not only that the causes of dependency were essentially economic (as Robert Hunter had explained in *Poverty*) so that the widow deserved support, but that asylum care was too uniform and mechanical to satisfy the child's diverse needs.[3]

At the 1909 White House Conference which reformers organized to endorse widows' pensions, speaker after speaker condemned asylum care in these very terms. "Childhood is too sacred," declared Rabbi Emil Hirsch, President of the National Conference of Jewish Charities, "to be handled on the ready-made plan." Even "the best of institutions . . . must neglect individual differences. . . . Discipline of military rigor is absolutely indispensable where hundreds and hundreds of children are herded together in one asylum. No account may be taken of individual needs and no patience can be shown individual idiosyncrasies. The inmates are trimmed and turned into automatons." Visitors to asylums in the Jacksonian era had marveled at a superintendent's ability to train children to march into a chapel and then to drop to their knees in unison at the sound of a whistle; but their Progressive successors were acutely disturbed that inmates "have to eat together, to hold their spoons sometimes at the same angle, to pray at the same moment . . . and to go to bed at the hour indicated." Such routines, concluded Hirsch, "always make for the elimination of individuality. . . . The result is the institutional type . . . marked by repression if not atrophy of the impulse to act independently."[4]

These anti-institutional sentiments were so widespread that a good number of asylum superintendents expressed their disapproval of traditional routines. Rudolph Reeder of the New York Orphanage complained of "the stupefying monotony of institutions. . . . The life of the child in most of these institutions is so dreary, soul-shriveling, and void of happy interests, the daily routine of marching and eating and singing and lining up . . . so stupefying as to inhibit the child's normal development." His colleague at the Minnesota State Institution for Dependent Children agreed that inevitably, "institutions make for repression, and repression hinders growth." With this judgment constituting almost a cliche of the period for dependent children, clearly juvenile justice was ready for change.[5]

G. Stanley Hall himself extended his perspective to delinquency. No one, he explained, could understand the juvenile offender without appreciating individual differences. "Criminaloid youth is more sharply individualized than the common good child. . . . Virtue is more uniform and monotonous than sin. There is one right but there are many wrong ways, hence they need to be individually studied." Traditional procedures, Hall insisted, violated these precepts. "Those smitten with the institution craze or with any extreme correctionalist views will never solve the problem of criminal youths." If Hall and his followers complained that the public schools had "too much uniformity, mechanism, and routine," imagine how acute their distress with the reformatory.[6]

Hall next identified several causes of delinquency. That they were mostly environmental points to his close fit with the new social sciences — in part he reflected and in part he promoted this kind of outlook. The causes ranged from "heredity, bad antenatal conditions, bad homes, unhealthful infancy and childhood," to "overcrowded slums with their promiscuity and squalor, which are always near the border of lawlessness, and perhaps are the chief cause of crime." In fact, Hall returned frequently to environmental considerations. "There is much reason to suspect," he declared, "that the extremes of wealth and poverty are more productive of crime than ignorance, or even intemperance." Hall's roster of causes was practically a checklist for Progressive action: the health bureaus were to combat maternal and child diseases, and innumerable other measures were to alleviate poverty.[7]

From these premises, Hall strongly advocated a juvenile court system. Obviously the program "must have marked reformatory elements." That end was as old as the house of refuge and no one debated it. Rather, the novelty lay in Hall's means. First, juveniles had to be treated completely apart from adults. "The problems of criminology for youth cannot be based on the principles now recognized for adults"; and here Hall was referring to the Jacksonian asylum's traditional principles of fixity, uniformity, and the like. "The greatest need of the penologist and criminologist," Hall contended, "is the further study, by expert methods, of individual cases and their relations to the social environment. We must fathom and explore the deeper strata of the soul, personal and collective, to make our knowledge really preventive, and recognize the function of the psychologist, pedagogue, and the physician." Once again, an individual (and expert) approach presupposed wide discretion; and since the object of treatment was a youth, Hall was ready to expand this discretion well past recognizable adult standards: "We must pass beyond the clumsy apparatus of a term sentence or the devices of a jury, clumsier yet, for this purpose." With this statement, we are at the heart of the juvenile court ideal.[8]

Hall's views helped to define the Progressive goals for juvenile justice. At points he inspired reformers, making them aware of the complexity of childhood. At points he confirmed their views, emphasizing, too, the significance of environmental considerations. And at points he laid the groundwork for new departures in child psychology and psychiatry. But rather than stress the contribution of any one figure to the Progressive mentality, it is appropriate to point out just how well these various components fit together. Whether one came to a concern about delinquency from child study or from the settlement house or from psychiatric training, whether one had a sociological interest in social problems or a psychological orientation to patients, clearly the delinquent had to be treated case by case, with exclusive attention, in Hall's terms, to his "soul, personal and collective."

Breckinridge and Abbott reached this same conclusion through their examination of immigrant ghetto life (as reported in *The Delinquent Child*). It was also the finding of William Healy in *The Individual Delinquent* (and it is hard to imagine a more Progressive title). And these two types of analysis attracted most professional and lay reformers. Richard Tuthill, one of the most indefatigable supporters of the juvenile court, was persuaded that the delinquent's "faults are due not to hereditary taint, but to bad environment." For his part, Adolf Meyer, the outstanding figure in the mental hygiene movement, was convinced, along with Hall and Healy, that the nineteenth-century insistence on breaking the child's will and compelling his blind obedience to commands was giving way to the notion that children and adolescents should be "ever more encouraged to develop confidence in their own nature." Accordingly, the response to the delinquent had to demonstrate "more emphasis on the inner needs of the individual and less on the necessity of merely conforming to traditional authority-determined patterns."[9]

That such a policy would enlarge the state's discretionary authority seemed altogether appropriate to reformers. Indeed, nowhere did such a practice appear to make better sense than in juvenile justice. Not only were the stakes high and the prospects for success great, but the child, as a minor, was already subject to almost unlimited parental power. Thus reformers did not have to justify the exercise of authority, merely (and for them it was "merely") to substantiate the state's right to act as parent. Noting that "no child has liberty in the sense that we understand the term," proponents cited a history even older than the Bill of Rights as proof of the right, indeed the duty, of the state to act in the best interest of the child. "We know," declared Chicago juvenile court judge Julian Mack, "that for over two centuries the Court of Chancery in England has exercised jurisdiction for the protection of the unfortunate child" — and that its proceedings were not hemmed in by due process requirements. American legislatures and courts had also followed in this tradition. Colonial education statutes, after all, had permitted the state to remove a child from a family which neglected his training; and nineteenth-century commitments to houses of refuge had generally taken place without formal adult criminal trials. Thus, reformers had at hand the most respectable precedent of *parens patriae*, the state as parent to the child, to justify enlarging the scope and style of their program. Certainly if the pre-modern state could intervene freely on behalf of the child, so could — in all senses of the term — a Progressive state.[10]

The design for the juvenile court set out to realize these precepts. The court was to represent a wholly new and Progressive way of responding to the delinquent. Heretofore, reformers contended, the state had to adopt one of two equally objectionable tactics, to choose, as it were, between evils. It could move against the young offender with the full rigor of the adult criminal law: detain him in a jail, prosecute and try him with all the strictness appropriate to criminal procedure, and sentence him to a prison-like institution. In short, it could adopt a tactic that almost certainly would transform a juvenile delinquent into an adult criminal. Or, shying away from so disastrous an intervention, the state could refrain from acting, turn the delinquent loose again, and in so doing know that it had encouraged him to resume his life in crime. The brilliance of the juvenile court solution lay in its ability to follow a middle course that would substitute rehabilitation for punishment or neglect.

This course was to alter every aspect of the state's actions. A special children's court, oriented to the individual case and administered under the most flexible procedures, would, as one reformer announced, "banish entirely all thought of crime and punishment," moving beyond the "mere attempt at punishment." The delinquent, upon being apprehended, would go to a juvenile detention center, not to a jail. The court hearing would be an informal investigation that looked to the needs of the child, not to his guilt or innocence. The disposition of the case would aim for rehabilitation, not punishment, in most (though not all) instances through probationary work. Here was a program that promised to be both helpful and effective, that would satisfy the needs of the child and the welfare of the society. As one of its most active supporters, Bernard Flexner, phrased it, the great discovery of the juvenile court was that "individual welfare coincided with the well-being of the state. Humanitarian and social considerations thus recommended one and the same procedure. . . . Sympathy, justice and even the self-interest of society were all factors in bringing about the changed attitude."[11]

The innovation seemed so capable of solving the problem of delinquency without sacrificing anyone's interests that reformers did not anticipate objections. "Only ignorance of what it really is could make anyone oppose the juvenile court," one proponent declared — and, in fact, opposition was scarce.[12] As we shall see, the court plan made friends for the best of reasons and the worst of reasons: in juvenile justice, as in adult justice, reforms satisfied the most humanitarian of impulses and, at the same time, some very narrow and self-interested considerations. But here again, the proper starting point for understanding both the structure and the popularity of the court is with its doing-good quality. The groups that campaigned most enthusiastically and effectively on its behalf carried outstanding credentials as philanthropists.

The most active among them, as might be expected, were the club women, particularly the members of the National Congress of Mothers. It was not a maudlin sentimentality for childhood (as some historians have charged) that motivated them, but quite the reverse, their sense that the delinquent required very sophisticated and particular attention, in effect, the prescriptions that G. Stanley Hall was offering. Chicago's first juvenile court judge, Richard Tuthill, understood their aims and political contribution well: "The women's clubs are the parents of all children. They have taught the state how to be a parent. . . . The women got the juvenile law passed." And women carried the court idea to other states as well. In Ohio, for example, the National Congress of Mothers was so active that one court supporter pleaded "that the men not leave all the work of securing passage to the women."[13]

Other prestigious organizations and leaders testified to the benevolence and wisdom of the court idea. The first founders of schools of social work, like Henry Thurston, and their counterparts in the settlement house movement, like Jane Addams and Julia Lathrop, heartily approved the measure. Those who first administered the new system were also among its most articulate advocates. It is difficult to exaggerate the significance of the founding of the juvenile court in Chicago to the movement as a whole precisely because its judge, Richard Tuthill, and its chief administrator, Timothy Hurley, were indefatigable in popularizing the program. Hurley, in fact, from 1900 to 1910 published a monthly, the *Juvenile Court Record*, which not only reported every step in the progress of the movement but issued countless editorials and columns promoting it as well. And Tuthill and

Hurley were not the exceptions. Denver's juvenile court judge, Ben Lindsey, was a one-man traveling road show; and if most of his speeches were variations on the theme of the insights of Lindsey, still he did find time to praise the concept of the court too. Further, by 1910, psychologists and psychiatrists, with William Healy the most active among them, not only endorsed the program but were eager to assume a major role in it. With such exemplary and diverse supporters, the court seemed to represent a significant victory for humanity and progress.[14]

The speed with which states rushed to enact the appropriate legislation confirms the power of the rhetoric and the alliance. The first formally constituted juvenile court opened in Chicago in 1899. Within five years, ten states had implemented similar procedures, and by 1920 every state except three provided for a juvenile court. As one New York official aptly concluded: "Considering the slowness with which changes in judicial procedure are brought about, the rapid extension of the children's court is extraordinary and bears witness to its social need and constructive worth."[15]

The juvenile court was to concern itself first not with the specific charge facing the delinquent, but with his character and life style, his psychological strengths and weaknesses, the advantages and disadvantages of his home environment. It was not his act but, in Hall's term, his soul, that was at issue. As Chicago's juvenile court judge, Julian Mack, promised: the court intended to discover "what he is, physically, mentally, morally, and then, if he is treading the path that leads to criminality," to take charge, "not so much to punish as to reform, not to degrade but to uplift, not to crush but to develop, to make him not a criminal but a worthy citizen." So, too, it was obvious to Boston's juvenile judge Harvey Baker that "of course the court does not confine its attention to just the particular offense which brought the child to its notice." If a boy came to the court "for some trifle," like failing to wear the badge entitling him to sell newspapers, but he turned out to be a chronic truant, then the court would respond to the more serious problem. The boy arrested for playing ball in the street who turned out to be a loafer, a gambler, and a petty thief would be treated not for the stated offense but for his vicious habits.[16]

Since a court that was determined to explore the soul of the delinquent could not be bound by formal and technical rules, proponents everywhere moved to relax the style of its proceedings, to make them non-adversarial. Although judges could not banish a lawyer from the courtroom altogether, they did not consider his presence either appropriate or necessary. Minnesota juvenile court judge Grier Orr boasted that in his courtroom "the lawyers do not do very much . . . and I do not believe I can recall an instance where the same attorney came back a second time; he found that it was useless for him to appear . . . for an attorney has not very much standing when it comes to the disposition of children in the juvenile court."[17]

In a similar spirit, juvenile courts were not to follow the rules of testimony appropriate to adult trials. Not that the codes establishing juvenile courts invariably and explicitly gave judges the authority to disregard such stipulations. Rather, as Judge Orr accurately noted: "The laws of evidence are sometimes forgotten or overlooked, because the juvenile court was a court of inquiry and not of prosecution; it is to find out the good that is within the boy or the child and to point out the way to reform, not to punish." The docket entry was not "the State versus Johnny Smith," and therefore "the laws of evidence could not be referred to in a law school as being exemplary." In almost every anecdote that judges or other proponents recounted about the workings of the court, a gentle and clever judge persuaded a stubborn or recalcitrant offender to "fess up," to tell the truth. Obviously this represented not a violation of the individual's right against self-incrimination but the first step of the delinquent toward rehabilitation.[18]

Trial by jury seemed equally out of place in a juvenile court. The judge who was competent to act as lawyer and district attorney was equipped to find the facts as well. Juries were useful when a court wanted to know precisely what an offender had done. But here the act was irrelevant and the "facts" were not traditional facts; they involved the social background, the psychological make-up, and the level of maturity of the child. And judges, better than juries, could master and respond to such data.

Given the juvenile court's delicate mission, reformers looked to a specialization of function among judges. They hoped that magistrates would not rotate through the court but that one of them would take the assignment permanently and acquire all the appropriate skills. In this way, too, the judge could be selected at the outset with full regard to the empathetic qualities necessary to the task. Proponents also wanted the physical design of the courtroom to reflect its special character. Judges were to sit alongside the participants in the case, not look down upon them from an elevated and isolated bench. Reform tracts frequently included photographs of newly established courtrooms, suggesting that physical intimacy would promote sympathetic and insightful treatment. A photograph of the new Columbus, Ohio, juvenile court, for instance, depicted a simple chair set upon a low platform and carried the caption: "The conventional bench has given way to a desk or table so arranged as to permit the judge to come into a close personal touch with the children." A photograph of the Boston court showed a larger desk, with an X inserted alongside it to mark the spot where the child stood. Here "the judge can see him from top to toe and can reassure him if necessary by a friendly hand on the shoulder."[19]

Reformers preferred that the juvenile court have its own building as well. The promotional literature took great pride in reproducing the design of new juvenile facilities. It was not the stateliness of the structures that they applauded (as their Jacksonian predecessors had been prone to do), but the fact that the administration of juvenile justice would occur in totally separate and self-contained settings. That the new juvenile courthouse in Chicago was quite ordinary in architectural terms seemed unimportant. What was significant was that all the facilities for responding to the juvenile were "grouped in one modern building." The physical separation from the adult criminal courts meant first that the child would no longer be contaminated by "daily association with the older criminal . . . [whose] demoralizing effect . . . upon these youthful minds can hardly be imagined." Further, a juvenile court building demonstrated the state's recognition of the need to deliver unique services to the young, to give them their own brand of justice.[20]

The single most important component of the juvenile court program was probation. Indeed, it assumed a significance to these proceedings that was still greater than in adult criminal justice. Probation represented, in the words of Timothy Hurley, "the keystone which supports the arch of this law." In the more elaborate phrases of Judge Tuthill, it was "the cord upon which all the pearls of the juvenile court are strung. . . . Without it, the juvenile court could not exist."[21]

The first task of the probation officer was to provide the juvenile court judge with all the appropriate information for understanding the personality and condition of the child. The Illinois legislature charged probation officers "to make a personal inquiry into the facts of the case with the view to assist the court in what ought to be done. To this end, it will be necessary to record the history and the circumstances of the child as fully as possible. . . . The court will desire to ascertain the character, disposition and tendencies and school record of the child; also the character of the parents and their capability for governing and supporting the child, together with the character of the home, as to comforts, surroundings." To satisfy so far-reaching a mandate, the law gave the probation officer full latitude in making an investigation. "This information will be obtained in your own way, from the child, from the parents, neighbors, teachers, clergymen, police officials, and from the records of the poor department, the police department, and the various charitable agencies." In addition, the probation officer (or the judge himself) was to enlist the services of experts in child psychology and psychiatry to understand the peculiarities of each case. Indeed, this commitment was so much stronger for the delinquent than for the adult criminal that reformers recommended that the court itself hire a staff of psychologists or psychiatrists or have a very close working relationship with a clinic. The search for knowledge about the child had to lead everywhere.[22]

The second task of the probation officer was to supervise the young offender released into the community. Given the strong sense that juvenile institutions were too rigid or, conversely, that only a mother would respond to the complex and changing nature of the child, proponents anticipated that most court dispositions would be probation. "No two of the boys coming to a juvenile court are alike," observed child welfare advocate Homer Folks, and accordingly, "The probation system offers many and varied things for many and varied kinds of boys." Reformers did not doubt the difficulty of this assignment; since the child was in trouble, his family and social circumstances were bound to be inadequate. The probation officer would have to assume the duties of an educated mother and at the same time train other family members and even neighbors to fulfill their responsibilities. But at least no legal restrictions were to interfere with the job. "With the great right arm and force of the law," declared Judge Tuthill, "the probation officer can go into the home and demand to know the cause of the dependency or the delinquency of a child. . . . He becomes practically a member of the family and teaches them lessons of cleanliness and decency, of truth and integrity." Admittedly, Tuthill continued, "Threats may be necessary in some instances to enforce the learning of the lessons he teaches, but whether by threats or cajolery, by appealing to their fear of the law or by rousing the ambition that lies latent in each human soul, he teaches the lesson and transforms the entire family into individuals which the state need never again hesitate to own as citizens." So once again proponents confidently enlarged the scope of state action. The same latitude and discretion that characterized juvenile courtroom procedure and pre-sentence investigations belonged to probation supervision as well.[23]

Reformers were fully prepared to empower the courts to exercise still another option: to incarcerate the juvenile offender. In some cases of delinquency (and estimates of the frequency of these cases varied widely), institutionalization was a fully legitimate response, an integral part of a rehabilitative program. Yes, probation was a proper first resort. To incarcerate children, such a champion of probation as Homer Folks explained, "is to administer opiates to the community. It is to turn its mind away from its own serious problems." Nevertheless, Folks and his fellow reformers acknowledged that "juvenile probation is not proposed nor advisable for all cases of delinquency." Some boys simply would not take probation seriously and so institutionalization was an appropriate back-up sanction. Also, as Richmond, Virginia, juvenile court judge James Ricks noted, if "the child's parents are hopelessly weak or morally bad, or if he has no home, he should then be given a chance in a good institution or foster home." Moreover, the confirmed delinquent certainly belonged in an institution. Far better for him to be incarcerated in a setting, in Judge Tuthill's terms, "where he can be taught even against his own will the primary duty of obedience to authority," than to be left alone with his "vicious habits and demoralizing associates." Commitment to an institution could well be in the child's best interest and the court, therefore, could order it without tightening procedures.[24]

In fact, many juvenile court proponents were also determined to expand the types of institutional programs for the delinquent. "The information which we are slowly accumulating as a result of more scientific investigation," declared Louis Robinson, the chief probation officer in Philadelphia, "does not show us that there will be no need for institutions in the future but rather that there is great need for institutions of a new and better type." Or, as his counterpart in Milwaukee insisted: "The new law was not a protest against institutionalism, for that was not the weak point. It was a protest against a criminal system which provided nothing better than suspended sentence or jail to cut delinquency at its first stages."[25]

This sentiment was present from the start of the movement. No sooner did Richard Tuthill take his seat as Chicago's juvenile judge, than he was busily agitating for the construction of an Illinois state school for delinquents. The only existing facility, he complained in 1901, was the John Worthy School, which was, simply put, "a prison." Its administrators, Tuthill believed, were trying to do their best, but the institution was located on the grounds of the city poorhouse and workhouse, with only a wall separating the young from the depraved; the School was also "surrounded by all manner of saloons, low dives, and gangs of bad boys and worse men" who encouraged the inmates to rebel and escape. Moreover, the Worthy School, Tuthill added with no sense of irony, was so overcrowded that the boys typically remained only a few months, which was hardly enough time to allow for much rehabilitation. Tuthill proposed that the state erect an institution in the country that would not only teach basic classroom skills, but give the boys vocational, particularly agricultural, training. "To enact a juvenile court law and not to provide for such an institution," concluded Tuthill, "is as illogical as if the state should . . . provide that insane persons should be sent to a state asylum, but do nothing toward the erection of one." Tuthill quickly had his way. In December 1904, the Illinois State School at St. Charles opened and the juvenile courts now had a new option at their disposal.[26]

The institution-building role of juvenile court proponents was apparent in other cities as well. The Nashville Boys Club and Aid Society thought it logical that its support of the juvenile court should lead to agitation for a new state school. We "sincerely hope that Tennessee men and women will be aroused and awakened to the great and absolute necessity of having a State School for Boys where the unfortunate children of our state can be placed under proper care and protection, and not be sent to workhouses, jails, and penitentiaries." And the chief probation officer for St. Paul was a leader in the campaign to bring a state school to Minnesota. In sum, reformers saw nothing inconsistent in giving the construction and improvement of institutions a place in their movement.[27]

Reformers' willingness to incarcerate at least some among the delinquent was but one example of their general readiness to elevate the power of the juvenile court over the family. Indeed, to many proponents, the most notable feature of the new court law was its clear expression of this principle. "The juvenile court laws," concluded one survey, "are usually so broad that the State, in its capacity of *parens patriae* . . . will take jurisdiction over practically every significant situation where it appears it should do so in the interests of the child."[28] In part, this posture reflected Progressives' determination to rescue the immigrant child; his welfare was too important to allow the family the final say, whether the issue was the parents' right to put the child to work or to keep him out of school — or their right to discipline or fail to discipline him in their own fashion. In part too, it revealed reformers' confidence in their own program. Given the complex character of the child, the better part of wisdom was to trust to the court and its expert allies.

Whatever the motive, supporters eagerly justified the state's entitlement. The first case histories that Timothy Hurley reprinted in the *Juvenile Court Record* were frankly designed to give legitimacy to the extended reach of the state. Hurley recounted how he once "stood outside the door of a shanty and watched 'Mother Shevlin' teach a beautiful young boy to steal a handkerchief out of a coat pocket without being detected." (Hurley was a master salesman — the story was about "shanty" Irish, and the victim was a "beautiful boy," as though good looks ought to have precluded delinquency.) To be sure, Hurley continued, existing statutes would have permitted court intervention in this instance, but under the older system the boy could have been sent to an institution for only a brief time and "the rest of the family of degenerate children was, perforce, left to pursue its infamously criminal way, because there was no law on the statute books of the state of Illinois whereby they could be brought into court and cared for as they should have been." It was such cases as the Shevlin family, concluded Hurley, that led his organization (the Chicago Visitation and Aid Society) and others as well, such as the city's women's clubs and the Bar Association, to advocate a new law that would "provide a more comprehensive way . . . to bring about desired results than any that had been so far devised."[29]

Hurley's perspective was widely shared. Mrs. Martha Falconer, a Chicago probation officer, was quick to tell the 1901 meeting of the National Congress of Mothers that "the women who cannot control their boys of eight or nine years of age should not have the care of them." Fully aware that she was addressing middle-class women on the problems of lower-class children, that it was other mothers, less capable and prepared than they, who had to be censured, Falconer promoted the juvenile court's discretionary authority because "I want those boys in a reform school; I feel there is no love there in the home, and that his home is no place for that boy." And she urged her audience not to be fooled for a moment by the public protests of the parents. "Those who neglect their children most are the ones who weep and wail loudest about them in court. To those women I say, 'You will keep your children off the streets or the city of Chicago will do it for you.'" In no less unequivocal terms the police matron of St. Louis made the same point to her state legislature. She had recently asked a little girl who was sitting around the jail where her mother was, to be told that she was "down in the Holdover drunk." The police matron had been able to get this child away from her mother and thus rescue her from a disastrous upbringing, but she had accomplished it "with difficulty." "Had we a juvenile court, these many cases could be easily settled and save the lives, and also the souls, of hundreds of just such unfortunate little ones."[30]

The judges themselves were often sensitive to parents' rights. Still, they did not hesitate to defend their newly acquired powers. As Minnesota's Judge Orr told a meeting of school principals in 1906: "I believe in this kind of court. . . . It is to reach the boy and teach him to follow in the correct line . . . and if need be, to take him from an immoral and vicious and criminal environment, *even if it takes him away* from his parents, that he may be saved, even though they may be lost." Chicago judge Victor Arnold, writing for the Children's Bureau, the federal agency created to promote child welfare, about the "sufficient grounds for the removal of a child from his home," did insist that "this jurisdiction should be exercised with grave caution. The integrity of the family circle is a relation so fundamental . . . that the law . . . has clothed it with a special sanctity." Taking a child from the family had to be "a last resort. . . . Juvenile court laws are laws of mercy and not vindictiveness, and should be mercifully and sympathetically administered." Nevertheless, some cases warranted such action: "If the home is depraved by habitual drunkenness of the parents or guardian, or by habitual furious or violent quarreling,

or by habitual indecent, vulgar and profane language, then I
have no scruples about taking the children from them."[31]

Reformers had fashioned a rationale and a program whose
goals seemed to offer something to everyone, and it is small wonder that their synthesis lasted for most of this century. The juvenile court rhetoric and procedures were at once benevolent and
tough-minded, helpful and rigorous, protective of the child and
altogether mindful of the safety of the community. One might
debate endlessly, and futilely, whether reformers used benign
language to cloak a repressive innovation, whether "social control" motivations were more significant than humanitarian concerns. The critical point is that reformers saw no conflict here;
they did not believe they were in an either/or position. There was
nothing hypocritical in their approach, no covert message that
had to be sorted out, no code language that had to be cracked.
Openly and optimistically they presented a program that seemed
so very right and necessary precisely because it did not require
trade-offs. The welfare of the child was synonymous with the
welfare of society. The juvenile court, the whole program for
understanding and combating delinquency, was in the best interests of everyone.

Thus the rhetoric of helpfulness that would open a speech or
pamphlet on behalf of the juvenile court would effortlessly give
way to a rhetoric of repression and public safety. The most important organ of the movement, the *Juvenile Court Record*,
demonstrated this capacity well. Its columns asked its readers to
be "patient and forgiving: Whereas, it is often necessary to bring
the little ones to court in order that they may be taught to discriminate between right and wrong, in truth we must hold them
guiltless. . . . Would we have done better in their places?" But its
motto, prominently displayed in every issue, declared: "Every
homeless child is a menace to society and the State."[32] In just this
way Judge Franklin Hoyt, of the New York juvenile court,
opened his anecdotal account of his service with gentle phrases
addressed by the "spirit of justice" to the "spirit of youth." "You
are bruised and bewildered . . . but you need not fear. . . . Trust
in me, for I am here to help you. . . . In me you will find no fair-

weather friend, but a guide and protector who will stand by you through storm and stress." Hoyt then proceeded to fill his pages with stories of how he combated the various "isms" of the young, and to tell how he won "recruits for law and order." To Hoyt, the wisdom of the juvenile court arrangements were never better demonstrated than in a certain case when a boy came before him on a petty charge, but upon discussion revealed himself to be a Socialist. Then the judge had the chance to teach someone who thought "that our established institutions are but forms of slavery" the Progressive credo: "Kindliness, common sense, and humane justice can exist side by side with the enforcement of law and order."[33]

In juvenile justice particularly, the ease with which proponents moved from one message to another, from the promise to uplift to the threat to coerce, testified to their ultimate confidence in the moral and social superiority of the American system. There was no conflict between the helping power and the policing power because both sought to adjust the youthful deviant to an environment that provided optimal conditions for promoting his own well-being. Since the delinquent was by definition young and oftentimes immigrant, in two senses a newcomer to the scene, he was doubly blind to the American promise. Hence the rights and wrongs of the situation were easily drawn up: intemperance, vulgarity, antiquated customs, loose street life, ignorance, were on one side of the ledger; the careful nurture of the child, education, training to lawfulness, obedience, close supervision, on the other. The juvenile court was the bridge between the two. It would at once reform and correct, uplift and protect.

The rapidity with which the juvenile court won legislative approval reflected not only ideological considerations — the appeal of its rhetoric and its all-encompassing goals — but functional ones as well. A diverse group of its supporters, ranging from members of voluntary and philanthropic organizations to administrators of criminal justice, discovered that the enlargement of the powers of the court generally fit well with their own particular needs. Shifting the balance of authority from the private sec-

tor to the state furthered their own concerns and agendas. The
added reach of the court promised to enlarge their influence and
freedom of action.

Many benevolent associations, who might have defined state
action as intrusive and encroaching on their own territory (which
was often the posture of charity relief organizations), were altogether comfortable with the new court design. This was particularly true of the women's clubs, who were eager to see their
messages spread beyond the confines of convention halls and college classrooms. To them the juvenile court represented the opportunity for their precepts on child welfare to be translated into
systematic programs. As Louise Stanwood, president of the Illinois
Federation of Women's Clubs, explained, the court would move
"away from the old ideas of a mere surface charity which relieves
distress for the moment, to a deeper and more scientific interest
in doing away with the sources of poverty and crime."[34]

Other Progressive-minded organizations supported the court as
a strategy for advancing the entire child welfare movement. To
Breckinridge and Abbott, the court represented "the greatest aid
toward social justice which this generation comprehends — *the
truth made public*" — and that truth, of course, was the great
number of services that the community owed its children. The
National Child Labor Committee, too, warmly endorsed the reform because the court would promote its particular mission.
"Obviously, juvenile court employees," noted one committee-
woman, "have an unusual opportunity for cooperation in the
enforcement of laws regulating the employment of children." Not
surprisingly, many juvenile courts assumed a wide variety of
duties, from enforcing child labor laws to administering widows
pensions to supervising truant officers. In short, all Progressive
friends of state intervention placed the juvenile court high on the
roster of necessary reforms.[35]

Perhaps somewhat more surprisingly, the private child care
organizations also supported the juvenile court movement. The
private sector had protested strongly when the state, under Progressive prodding, had moved to assume responsibility for reliev-
ing needy widows. Charity, the agencies had claimed, should be a

voluntary, not a public activity. But here private charities lined up with public-minded Progressives. The difference lay in the fact that most private charity work in the pre-Progressive era did not require any coercive legal authority over the client: it was the poor who came to the agency soliciting help, and the agency could set whatever conditions it wished on the clients in return for its aid. The circumstances confronting private child care agencies, however, were very different. These organizations often wanted to intervene on behalf of a child, but the parents, vested with full legal authority, could, and did, refuse to accept their services. They could take a child's parents to court; in gross cases of abuse or neglect, they might well win custody. But when the child was not in imminent danger, the agencies were helpless. It was this situation that the private organizations wanted the juvenile court to correct. The extension of the state's authority over the child would provide them with the ability to intervene more frequently. They would alert the court to the child's unfavorable circumstances, and the court would then delegate to them the right to take all necessary action.

The role of the Chicago Visitation and Aid Society in the passage of the Illinois juvenile court act demonstrated this process at work. No one was more active than Timothy Hurley, and Hurley was in charge of this Catholic child-caring organization. "Before the law," he frankly explained, his agency "could take only such children as were voluntarily surrendered to them; if the parents would not surrender their child, no matter how distressing the case, they could do nothing. To this class belong the children of drunken fathers and drunken mothers, the lazy and licentious and those who lived off the beggings and stealings of their children." Hurley was probably exaggerating the helplessness of his organization, but still he welcomed the court because it "supplies that common authority." Now, when the court found a child "to have no home or that for some reason it must be taken from its home, the court assigns it to that society or institution willing to take it, best furnished to care for that particular child." And parents could not block the delegation of authority and, no less important, they could not later cancel it. "I have always advocated the idea that it was the duty of the State to strengthen the hands of the different Child-Saving Societies," declared Hurley. "And now . . . it is but natural that I should be a firm believer and advocate in what might be called the 'new movement.' "[36]

The juvenile court carried still another advantage, as Hurley saw it: it would strengthen the hand of established child care agencies against newcomers to the field. "Now no society or institution can take children from the court that has not been approved by the court after a full showing as to responsibility . . . and no new society can become incorporated to carry on the business of caring for children except with the approval of the state board of public charities." In essence, then, the juvenile court law was to strengthen the authority of Hurley's Society not only against parents but against weaker and less substantial agencies as well, and the Chicago Visitation and Aid Society would be able to dominate the "business" of child care that much more completely. Finally, Hurley and other leaders of religiously affiliated agencies were comfortable with the court because it promised to respect, even to advance, their sectarian concerns. In many jurisdictions, the juvenile court's enabling legislation or informal practice called for assignment of cases by religious preference: Catholic boys to Catholic societies or probation officers or institutions; Jewish boys to Jewish societies or officers or institutions, and so on. If Hurley and his colleagues were good friends to the court, they expected it to be the best friend to their agencies.[37]

Superintendents of institutions for deviant or dependent children, like the heads of private agencies, also looked to the juvenile court to define and substantiate their own authority. A fair amount of confusion had characterized the type of child that any one institution could hold. Could a state reformatory, for example, admit not only those found guilty of delinquency but dependents who were in need of supervision or suffering from neglect? Some courts said no; others said yes; still others changed their minds in midstream. Or, in the opposite case, could institutions incorporated for dependent and neglected children admit those guilty of delinquency? Here again confusion reigned. All observers recognized that in practice the distinction between the neglected and the delinquent child often depended less upon what the child had done than upon the credentials of the complaining officer. If a policeman intervened, the child came up on delinquency; if a representative of a child care agency acted, the child came up on neglect. Asylum managers hoped that since the juvenile court did not have to issue technical verdicts of guilty before making commitments, it would be able to dispatch a youngster to the type of institution it believed appropriate.[38]

A fair number of administrators from within the criminal justice system also joined the reform coalition. One state legislator in Missouri, James Blair, who painstakingly organized committee hearings to support a pending juvenile court bill, brought together an incredible array of officials: the president of the board of police commissioners, the chief of police, the chief of detectives, a police sergeant with twenty years' experience, the police matron, the city jailer, the superintendents of both the house of refuge and the city workhouse, and a criminal court judge. These speakers articulately put forth the basic principles of the movement, particularly the argument that to mix juvenile with adult offenders was to educate the young to a life in crime. But their testimony also reflected the assumption that the extended authority of the juvenile court would allow them to carry out their assignments more easily and efficiently. The police officials expected the new courts to keep delinquents off the street for longer periods of time. If incarceration reformed the offender, so much the better; at least he would be out of circulation for a few years instead of a few weeks. So too, the criminal court judge welcomed the new options for the handling of delinquents, from probation to commitment to a state training school. And the local workhouse manager, eager to be rid of nursemaid duties, seemed no less happy with the court. Even though his inmate census would go down, he would be spared the job of caring for ten- and eleven-year-olds.[39]

District attorneys also supported the juvenile court, anticipating a reduction in their workload and a more rigorous system of justice as well. As one Illinois prosecutor explained, the creation of the juvenile court spared him from presenting to the grand jury some two hundred cases of young offenders a year. And at a time when his own docket was overcrowded, this relief was welcome. Moreover, the grand juries had typically dismissed about three-quarters of the juvenile cases that he had brought before them: they preferred running the risk of not punishing juveniles to punishing them in adult fashion. The new courts would not be faced with this choice and hence would exercise much firmer control.[40]

To be sure, some opposition did emerge, particularly among officials who found their own authority circumscribed by the new court powers. The most important and consistent antagonism came from police ranks. "In the early history of the juvenile court," reported Bernard Flexner, "it has been difficult to win the cooperation of the police. The purposes of the court differed so widely from what the average police officer believes to be the function of the court, that his attitude has been either one of open hostility or amusement." Yet the police groups could never mount a serious attack. In Baltimore, all they managed to argue was that the court represented "an interference with established discipline," and an inconvenience as well — now police officers would have to transport juveniles from remote parts of the city to the one downtown juvenile court location. In Cincinnati they claimed that reform was unnecessary: their own concern for the young offender was sufficient. But these contentions were too narrow and flimsy to gain much respect. It was easy for reformers to counter with stories of ten-year-olds mingling with depraved adults; a few minutes of travel time were well worth spending to save a child from a lifetime of crime.[41]

The lower-level municipal judges, serving in so-called "police courts" with jurisdiction over the petty crimes that made up the bulk of delinquency cases, also complained about the transfer of their authority to the juvenile courts. In New York, for example, they defended their own record ("Proper justice has always been given to children's cases in the existing courts") and insisted that they informally separated youth from adult cases. Further, they protested that the staff of the juvenile court would be drawn from their own administrative personnel, and "with this radical reduction in their working force, the chances are good that within a short time the police courts will be hopelessly behind in their work." Once again, however, these points were ineffectual. Why not do in formal fashion what they claimed to be doing in an ad hoc way? Even the supporters of the police courts had to concede that "the idea of a children's court may be all right in theory"; only given the realities of New York politics, it would "do more harm than good." But then, as one friendly newspaper editorial admitted: "Those advocates of the Children's court who were not in politics — including a good many women of this city — might reply that practical difficulties are not the question at issue. The experiment, at any rate, is to be tried." The one comfort the editorial could offer was that the experiment would be short-lived — and what a mistaken prediction that was.[42]

A handful of legal scholars and lawyers did attack the core principles of the juvenile court, objecting to its discretionary authority for civil libertarian reasons. In 1913, Roscoe Pound, the ranking Progressive legal theorist, suggested (but did not pursue) the line of argument. "The powers of the court of star chamber," he remarked, "were a bagatelle compared with those American juvenile courts. . . . If those courts chose to act arbitrarily and oppressively they could cause a revolution quite as easily as did the former."[43] The next year Edward Lindsey, a Pennsylvania lawyer writing in the prestigious *Annals* of the American Academy of Political and Social Science, elaborated this view. The juvenile courts, he wrote, exhibited "the entire disregard as far as the statutes themselves go, of established legal principles and the absence from them of any limitation on the arbitrary powers of the court, which always involves dangerous possibilities." Lindsey had little trouble explaining this fact. The statutes "are, of course, the expression of certain theories for social betterment, rather than of social experience or practice." In the name of social betterment, the courts were surrendering their traditional allegiance to "the right of the minor to his liberty as against the state, except after conviction of crime."

To Lindsey, the justifications for abandoning this allegiance were nothing more than "evasions." Label them what you will, the court dispositions remained punitive. "In the case of commitment to an institution, there is often a very real deprivation of liberty nor is that fact changed by refusing to call it punishment or because the good of the child is stated to be the object." So far as he could see, the result of court intervention "is that the child is handed over to some organization or institution . . . which in some cases does its work well and in others badly." Moreover, "everything should not rest with the personality of the judge. While with the right man in the right place the very indefiniteness of his powers may be productive of immediate good, in the long run it will be just as unsafe as experience proved it to be in the criminal law." Lindsey's conclusion was straightforward: "All criminal questions should be dealt with by a criminal court. Every child accused of crime should be tried and subject to neither punishment nor restraint of liberty unless convicted."[44]

These same objections were the grounds for legal challenges to the constitutionality of the juvenile court. Parents eager to contest court commitments of their children to institutions mounted test cases in more than a dozen states. Their lawyers questioned the court's right to deprive a child of liberty without due process, to forego trial by jury, to deny the right to appeal, to impose unequal penalties, and to disregard provisions for the equal protection of the law. But such efforts almost without exception were to no avail.

Defendants' briefs typically cited and relied upon the Illinois court decision of 1870, the *People v. Turner*. This decision, issued when public disillusionment with institutional conditions first emerged, declared unconstitutional the Illinois 1867 law that allowed a police court judge or a justice of the peace to commit to the Chicago reform school "any boy or girl, within the ages of six or sixteen years, who he has reason to believe is a vagrant, or is destitute of proper parental care, or is growing up in mendicancy, ignorance, idleness or vice." The statute, in other words, allowed children who had not been found guilty of a crime, and who had been examined and sentenced without a jury trial, with only "slight evidence required," and under an "informal mode of procedure" to be confined to an institution against their and their parents' will. The Turner decision struck down the law, unequivocally elevating the rights of minors and parents over those of the state. It found such terms as "idleness" and "vice" excessively broad. "Vice is a very comprehensive term," declared the court. "Acts, wholly innocent in the estimation of many good men, would according to the code of ethics of others show fearful depravity. What is the standard to be? . . . What degree of virtue will save from the threatened imprisonment?" The fact that the objects of state action were children did not obviate the need for strict procedural standards. "The disability of minors does not make slaves or criminals of them. They are entitled to legal rights, and are under legal liabilities." And because the state was trying to act in a minor's best interests did not justify a sentence to a reformatory. Foreshadowing today's doctrine of "least restrictive alternative," the court in the 1870 Turner decision insisted that the state devise alternatives to incarceration. "Other means of a milder character; other influences of a more kindly nature; other laws less in restraint of liberty, would better accomplish the reformation of the depraved, and infringe less upon inalienable rights." Concluded the court: "The principle of the absorption of the child in, and its complete subjection to the despotism of, the State, is wholly inadmissible in the modern civilized world."[45]

In the Progressive period, however, the courts overrode the Turner precedent, fully accepting the reformers' prescriptions. The exercise of the state's power over the delinquent was justifiable because its purposes were to rescue and rehabilitate. The courts' decisions were frequently tautological. Of course, they noted, if the child were to be punished, then he had a right to trial by jury; if this were a criminal proceeding, obviously due process protections were necessary. But the very fact that the hearing took place without a jury and without procedural formalities demonstrated that it was not a criminal action but an attempt to do good, to benefit the child. The most noteworthy decision upholding the juvenile court, *Commonwealth of Pennsylvania v. Fisher*, argued in just this manner. The defendants maintained that juvenile court proceedings were actually criminal proceedings, and that therefore all due process protections were required. The court answered that the very absence of due process protections proved that these were not criminal proceedings and were, therefore, constitutional.

Such lapses of logic reveal how deep the appeal of the juvenile court was. The promise of reform made it simple to dismiss constitutional objections. You say the laws create different punishments for different children? Answered *Commonwealth v. Fisher*: This "overlooks the fact . . . that it is not for the punishment of offenders, but for the salvation of children" that the court acts; the state is concerned with the welfare not of a special class of children, "but all children under a certain age." You say appellant is denied a trial by jury? "Here again is the fallacy that he was tried by the Court for any offense." The juvenile court was not acting to establish the child's guilt but to effect "its salvation." You say that to incarcerate the young is to deprive them of liberty? No, the law does not contemplate "restraint upon the natural liberty of children" but merely "the wholesome restraint which a parent exercises over his child. . . . No constitutional right is violated but one of the most important duties which organized society owes to its helpless members is performed."[46]

Court after court echoed these findings. The Idaho appellate judges dismissed the claims that juvenile courts abrogated rights to trial by jury, speedy and public hearing, defense by counsel, and bail, because "this statute is clearly not a criminal or penal statute in its nature. . . . Its object is to render a benefit upon the child and the community in the way of surrounding the child with better and more elevating influences." The Utah Appeals Court would not entertain challenges based on the procedural inadequacies of the juvenile court, insisting that "it is the welfare of the child that moves the state to act, and not to inflict punishment or to mete out retributive justice." One Illinois judge, who did not find Turner a binding precedent, commented on the "great numbers of the best men and women of this state who are working . . . for the advancement and interest of the children." Although he admittedly had "started on the consideration of this case with some misgivings as to the extent of power exercised by the Juvenile Court . . . as I have looked into it, I have become satisfied [that its protective powers] . . . are almost supreme and sovereign powers." Hence, when the Kentucky appeals court ruled on the issue in 1911, it noted that supreme courts in thirteen other states had already upheld the constitutionality of the juvenile court, all "upon the theory that the proceedings are not criminal, but merely the services of the government called into play for the purpose of protecting, training and correcting a class of children who . . . are unable or unwilling to care for themselves."[47]

In sum, to the courts as to the reformers, the innovation of the juvenile court was all light — no darkness intruded. The potential for abuse or mischief did not have to be explored. Here was an effort to promote the best interest of the child and the state.

CHAPTER SEVEN

The Cult of Judicial Personality

HOWEVER STRAIGHTFORWARD the task of defining the principles that underlay the Progressive program for juvenile justice, the reality of implementation, the day-to-day working of the system, was almost bewildering in its variety. Proponents knew well what a juvenile court should do; there was little disagreement on the essential characteristics of the innovation. Yet practically no two courtrooms (let alone any two states) followed identical procedures. It is far more appropriate to think not of *the* juvenile court, but of many juvenile courts.

The differences among them were by no means minor and more often than not exerted a critical influence on the courts' operations. Many states, for example, formally designated the juvenile courts as chancery courts, enabling them to adopt informal rules of procedure. An important minority of jurisdictions, however, including Massachusetts, New York, and Washington, D.C., considered juvenile courts to be criminal courts and therefore demanded more rigorous procedures. The courts' duties also differed markedly from place to place. The St. Louis court could try all crimes committed by juveniles; its Boston counterpart could deal only with the less serious offenses, those that could not bring (even to adults) a sentence of capital punishment or life imprisonment. Most of the courts heard cases of neglect, but some among them had responsibility for widows pension, adoption, and truancy proceedings, as well as for cases of adults contributing to the delinquency of minors and the commitment of minors to state institutions for the insane or the retarded. And such statutory distinctions were only one element of the confusion. In some cities, the juvenile court was nothing more than the adult criminal court and its judge sitting in a special late-afternoon or Saturday session; in others, it was a court apart, with its own building, full-time judge, and staff. Small wonder, then, that the Children's Bureau and like-minded reform organizations periodically issued elaborate guides to state juvenile court practices and statutes. Without such charts, it was impossible to know what these courts were about.[1]

Such extensive variations did reflect the vagaries of legislatures in implementing a new program. Here a group of very tax-conscious politicians insisted upon giving the juvenile court more duties so as to make it earn its appropriation; there a corps of tough-minded, law-and-order legislators insisted on keeping serious crimes in the adult courts. But even more significant than such political differences were demographic distinctions among and within the states. In essence, the more urban the location, the more likely that the juvenile court would be "special," that is, presided over by its own particular judge, with separate facilities, a probation staff, and a commitment to gathering and somehow or other using "social information." The less urban the location, the more likely that the juvenile justice system would be ad hoc, with a rotating judge sitting in a regular courtroom and lacking an investigatory or supervisory staff. When in 1918 the Children's Bureau investigated some twenty-four hundred juvenile courts (to discover how the movement had fared, twenty years after its founding in Illinois), it learned that in cities with over 100,000 inhabitants, all the juvenile courts were "special"; in medium size cities, 71 percent were "special"; in smaller cities, 16 percent; and in rural areas, 4 percent. Put another way, every juvenile court in a city of over 100,000 inhabitants had a probation service, but only 25 percent of the courts in rural areas did. The juvenile court, like so many other Progressive social reforms, had taken root most firmly in the cities.[2]

The most important variations among juvenile courts, however, went still deeper and had a more fundamental cause, one which brings us back to the reform ideal. Diversity was built into the design itself. Since the court intended to rehabilitate the individual delinquent, and not primarily to exact the just measure of the law, the judge's hands could not be tied with procedural requirements. But translated into practice, this grant of authority meant that juvenile courts would be as different from each other as judges were different from each other. Indeed, the various structures that the Progressives expected to direct if not fetter judicial discretion were never able to take hold. The result was a system that made the personality of the judge, his likes and dislikes, attitudes and prejudices, consistencies and caprices, the decisive element in shaping the character of his courtroom.

Let it be clear that every judge does enjoy a degree of autonomy. We all recognize (and lawyers plot strategy accordingly) that some judges are more lenient, some more harsh; there are some whose manner is loose and relaxed, others whose style is more formal. In adult criminal courts, however, the great number of procedural rules restrain the personality of the judge and impose a marked uniformity. Should a judge prejudice the jury in his summary instructions or violate canons on admissibility of evidence, the parties have the recourse of appeal. Adult defendants do have a measure of protection against a hard-line judge or a judge who is simply having a bad day. These restraints, however, weaken or disappear when one analyzes the Progressive juvenile courts. Without set rules of evidence, without fixed guidelines, and, in many cases, without the prospect of appeal, the court quite literally had the delinquent at its mercy. The person of the judge himself assumed an altogether novel significance.

One indicator of this fact is the remarkable prominence of a number of juvenile court judges in the Progressive period. They were in a real sense "personalities," very well known, not for their legal doctrines (as with Supreme Court judges), or because of their work for investigatory commissions, but specifically as juvenile court judges. Ben Lindsey of the Denver juvenile court was only the most notable example. To Progressives, the names of Charles Hoffman (Cincinnati), or Harvey Baker (Massachusetts), or Julian Mack and Merritt Pinckney (Chicago), or Franklin Hoyt (New York) were outstanding ones. The judge and his court, the man and the program, were almost inseparable.

Accordingly, contemporary investigators of the juvenile courts devoted extraordinary attention to the presiding judges. Although this was not their exclusive focus — the nature of the probation staff, the clinic facilities, and institutional commitment patterns were important too — still, any attempt to analyze the workings of a given court demanded a lengthy evaluation of its judge. To choose but one example, the noted sociologist and child guidance advocate, William I. Thomas, reported on the workings of the Cincinnati Juvenile Court for the Rockefeller Foundation's Bureau of Social Hygiene. After describing the duties of the court, Thomas immediately turned to "Judge Hoffman and the Policy of the Juvenile Court." (Pause with this phrase and reckon with how odd it would be to address Judge X and the *Policy* of a Criminal Court.) As his account made clear, Thomas neither liked nor respected Hoffman; he considered him "a clever, smooth politician," albeit someone who was "approachable," had a "pleasant personality," and had built up "great personal loyalty among his immediate associates and a considerable public following." (Again, the cult of personality.) What disturbed Thomas most was Hoffman's ignorance of the principles of psychology and development; the court, after all, was to be deciding the fate of the delinquent on the basis of his treatability, and here the presiding judge really knew very little or nothing about the matter. Hoffman had all the respect in the world for psychology — indeed, too much respect. "He believes," declared Thomas, "in the infallibility of 'science,' especially as embodied in the psychiatrist. . . . He has read widely, and talks of 'Psychologies of 1925' and 'gestalt' quite glibly. The prestige of psychology rather than the fact of behavior have influenced him, however." Ultimately, Hoffman's "policy is one of 'common sense' rather than scientific procedure." Of course, common sense to one judge need not be common sense to another, and so Thomas went on to clarify Hoffman's style of conduct. *"The judge is exceedingly impulsive* — as he himself admits, and as watching him operate . . . amply demonstrated. *He is likely at any moment to depart from his policies to 'make an example' of someone. He has marked sympathies — which often switch with bewildering rapidity."* He was surrounded by "yes men," so that "the judge is constantly asking his [chief probationer officer's] advice and getting confirmation of his previously expressed opinion." With it all, neither the juveniles nor their families had recourse from Hoffman's verdicts: "There is no appeal from the decision of the court." In sum, the Cincinnati Juvenile Court was Judge Hoffman's court. The man was the system.[3]

The most notorious example of a judge whose flamboyant personality dominated, indeed monopolized, juvenile court proceedings was undoubtedly Denver's Ben Lindsey. Lindsey's courtroom was his stage, with the youngsters as bit players whose role was to set off Lindsey's charm, his intuitive grasp of human nature, and his ingenious solutions to the problems of delinquency. So when 250 boys on probation crowded into his courtroom, Lindsey opened the session with a speech filled with homilies. He quoted Teddy Roosevelt to the effect that "You can help a fellow along, but you can't carry him." He next recounted some anecdotes — about how he had trusted two boys to travel to the reform school on their own and they didn't let him down; about "a boy who was wanted by the sheriff's office, but who came to the judge for advice." One favorite Lindsey tale involved a boy known in the press as the "worst boy in Denver." Because of his repeated truancy, everyone recommended commitment to a training school. Lindsey, however, "took him into chambers alone and after discussing the situation with him — much as I would with a man — I said, 'Now, Charlie, these people all say I will make a great mistake if I do not "send you up;" and should I let you go a third time and you again become incorrigible, you see you would be getting both of us into trouble.'" Well, Charlie said that he would protect Lindsey's reputation, Lindsey struck the bargain ("I am going to trust my reputation as a wise judge to your keeping"), and the boy soon became an outstanding student. The anecdote clearly has more to do with Lindsey's reputation than with rehabilitation. It was Lindsey who was saved, not the boy.[4]

With a judge like Lindsey presiding, the Denver court inevitably assumed an arbitrary quality. When two boys appeared before him for fighting, Lindsey summarily dismissed the case with the line: "He could not waste his valuable time as umpire of ordinary 'kid' fights." In other instances, the results were quite different. Lindsey sent many of his probationers to the local farmers to work at thinning and spacing beets. Known appropriately to the farmers as "Judge Lindsey's boys," they were, in effect, contract laborers, living in barracks under an officer's charge. "Obedience is the first law of the camp," noted one admirer of the system. "Officer Withers is a believer in military discipline." The boys rose at five in the morning, were at work soon after, had an hour's rest with lunch, then worked until six. The pay was not much, but "when these boys report to Judge Lindsey . . . all will probably be dismissed from the juvenile court because of their good record made in the beet fields."[5]

The particular preferences of other judges set the tone for their juvenile courts. As one researcher into child welfare practices in Pennsylvania discovered, every county had a different type of judge who followed a different method. While the counties that she visited were dissimilar in economic and demographic terms (they included a poor mountain county, a more prosperous dairy county, a coal-mining county, and so on), the distinctive style of each court was altogether idiosyncratic, reflecting not the wealth of the community but the personal style of the judge. The judge in the mountain county preferred to hold meetings privately in his chambers, to discourage the presence of attorneys, and to question everyone informally. His colleague in the dairy section "preferred hearings in a court room rather than in his office because he thought such hearings more dignified and more impressive for the child." He did not prohibit outsiders from attending or limit newspaper publicity. The judge in the coal county (a former probation officer who had once been in the tombstone business and therefore "had become well acquainted in the county") sometimes held hearings in his office, sometimes in the law library, and sometimes in the courtroom, which seated four hundred. The district attorney presented the cases; occasionally the delinquents were sworn, occasionally they were not. The hearings, it seemed, were not perfunctory but the judge paid little attention to his probation staff's recommendations. In a commercial county, the judge squeezed the juvenile court cases into his regular docket "whenever the judge felt he could give the time to them." He had no patience for Lindsey-like sermons and no inclination "to win the boy's confidence." Observers were permitted, but "testimony was usually given in such low tones that it was difficult, if not impossible, for spectators to hear." The judge in a farm county considered the juvenile court sessions "an unimportant part of his work." The hearings, held on Saturday mornings after other business had been completed, adhered to adult criminal procedures: "The child was put on the stand, sworn, and cross-examined," and so were all witnesses. Unless one noted the age of the defendant, it would have been impossible to know whether the criminal court or the juvenile court was sitting.[6]

The Progressives, it is true, had not intended to build up a cult of judicial personalities. They did insist that an individual response to individual need made the imposition of uniform rules, particularly of the due process sort, inadvisable and inappropriate. But they did not anticipate that to champion discretion would be to generate gross disparities in juvenile court proceedings. Rather, reformers believed that the entirety of the juvenile court program would provide a relatively tight framework in which judges would operate. Specifically, a highly trained and diligent probation staff was to guide judges in their decision making; the principles of psychology and social work would thus give court decisions an underlying consistency. By the same token, mental hygiene clinics would cooperate with the courts, and their staffs' knowledge of human development would bear so directly on the cases that judicial decisions would assume a uniformity of logic and purpose. Of course, there would be differences in dispositions among delinquents who had committed the same act — but these differences would reflect the special qualities of the case, not the idiosyncracies of the judge.

Once again, however, reformers' expectations and the realities of implementation markedly diverged. Many courts lacked the supporting services of trained probation officers; and the probation staffs that were on hand were generally so ill-prepared for their assignments that the only issue was whose common sense would rule, the officer's or the judge's. In either instance, instinct was not enough to bring consistency to any one court, let alone to hundreds of courts. So too, many courts did not have clinic services available and, further, judges often proved unwilling to defer to the experts in ways that Progressives had hoped.

All the failings of juvenile probation need not be rehearsed. Suffice it to say that conditions were substantially the same as in adult probation, and a few illustrations can substantiate the point. As we have noted, little probation work went on in more rural areas, so that fully one-third of the juvenile courts operating in communities of between 5,000 and 25,000 lacked all probation services. And small town as well as rural probation officers tended to be part-time or jack-of-all-welfare-trades types of workers. Thus, in one Illinois county the relief agent was also the truant officer and the adult and juvenile probation officer; another county had its public health nurse do duty as a probation officer; still others relied upon policemen or school teachers. As one survey of probation throughout the state concluded: "In different instances the duties of the probation officers were found to be combined with those of sheriff, police officer, lawyer, state's attorney, salesman, village clerk, janitor, school superintendent, railroad clerk and minister." Moreover, the diversity of officers' tasks was matched by the inadequacy of their training. "Among the probation officers now serving," reported a New Jersey investigation, "were found those who had had the following occupations previous to their probation work: Undertaker, Electrician,

Draftsman, Detective, Tax Collector, Cleaning Woman, Mail Worker, Bookkeeper, Store Manager, Fire Insurance Agent and Mail Clerk."[7]

More important, not even the metropolitan centers managed to administer satisfactory juvenile probation programs. No city was able to fit all the pieces together to make up an efficient system; a fatal flâw always crept in. Philadelphia appointed a large number of probation officers and gave them manageable case loads — but the appointments were altogether political. The ward bosses told the judges whom to appoint, and the judges agreed. After all, those same ward bosses had given them their seats on the bench; besides, as one judge complaisantly noted: "The ward leaders would not recommend any 'dead ones.'" In Rochester, on the other hand, the juvenile court probation staff staggered under a burden that made investigation impossible: two people had to handle 430 juvenile cases. In Westchester the case loads were lighter — but then the probation officers had to assume so many different tasks that little time was left to do anything well. Cincinnati did manage to appoint a handful of well-trained college graduates with social work training in the girls' division, but the boys' division, as William Thomas reported, had "two very inferior men [who] look like political job holders of the Chicago type." Soon enough the case loads mounted in both divisions so that Thomas concluded: "For the most part, the probation work is done by the secretaries. . . . Probation is a farce."[8]

National surveys inevitably confirmed these failures. When in the mid-1920's two of the most active Progressive reformers, Katharine Lenroot and Emma Lundberg, investigated ten major urban juvenile court systems (including Boston, St. Louis, Denver, and San Francisco), they gave a grim accounting of the status of probation. Not one of the jurisdictions "specified the qualification that probation officers should have," and thus the staff "had little preparation for their work through education or previous experience." In seven of the ten courts, the majority of the officers "had no previous experience in occupations allied with probation." Worse yet, only four of the courts kept the case loads below seventy-five, and each of these four piled a variety of duties on their staffs. Everywhere, then, the pre-sentence investigation was superficial and so was supervision. Thomas's conclusions for Cincinnati applied to practically every other city as well: probation was a farce.[9]

These glaring weaknesses obviously prevented probation work from bringing coherence or consistency to court decisions. Judges like Lindsey and Hoffman turned their probation officers into "yes men." Others, too busy to be involved with juvenile proceedings, delegated responsibility to their probation staff and rubber stamped their decisions. In either instance, an amateurish and overworked group of officers could do nothing to lend structure to discretionary justice.

Perhaps the most dramatic indicator of how ineffective Progressive innovations were in directing court procedures, is the fate of the psychiatric clinics associated with the juvenile courts. That these clinics existed in only the largest cities is not surprising; the availability of psychiatrists as well as the courts' affinity for such an approach made this outcome logical. But what is more curious, the clinics did not exert much influence on the courts. Judges were all too often unwilling or unable to follow clinic recommendations. The clinics, for their part, only diagnosed the client; they did not provide treatment and the labels they attached carried little practical import. Taken together, these considerations generally rendered the clinic's role in juvenile justice inconsequential.[10]

No court clinic enjoyed a greater reputation in the 1920's than Boston's Judge Baker Foundation (JBF). Organized in 1917 and named after the first presiding judge of Boston's juvenile court, the clinic was under the administration of William Healy and Augusta Bronner, two of the most dedicated psychiatrists working with delinquents. And yet, as Sheldon and Eleanor Glueck discovered when they meticulously examined the records of one thousand juvenile cases referred to the JBF, both the quality of its work and its impact on court decisions were very limited.

For one, the judge, here Frederick Cabot, and not the clinic staff, determined which delinquents would undergo examination and testing. Only when Judge Cabot believed psychiatric intervention to be necessary were the clinic facilities used; and even Cabot, who was probably more sophisticated than most of his fellow judges, turned to the clinic "only when he felt really puzzled or saw that the juvenile before him obviously had some physical or mental handicap." Over the years, he usually referred children with prior records of delinquency or who appeared to be retarded or suffering from a disabling disease or impairment. "But even this policy," observed the Gluecks, "was not always and uniformly followed." In effect, the clinic staff was very much the handmaiden to the judge. It did not so much direct judicial discretion (by explaining that a given case was "different" or appropriate for examination), as respond to judicial requests.[11]

The clinic examination had its own arbitrary quality. In 80 percent of the cases that the Gluecks investigated the clinic saw the youngster only once; as they appropriately noted: "It is obviously not possible, in most cases, to delve deeply into the personality difficulties." Further, the superficial character of the JBF examinations was at one with the superficial quality of the diagnoses. The problem may have been caused partly by a shortage of time. Even more, it reflected the weaknesses of Healy's approach, the limitations of an effort to substitute a case-by-case study for a more general theory of deviant behavior. The Gluecks had little intellectual patience with assertions in the JBF case records that poverty or a father's drunkenness or a mother's need to work were the "causes" of delinquency. "The mere presence of such factors in a situation should not be taken as necessarily indicating their etiologic significance. There are many boys who come of poor families and/or whose parents are drunkards . . . who, nevertheless, do somehow not become delinquent." Not that the Gluecks could offer more compelling explanations. But at least they did recognize the "limited knowledge of human nature" that characterized all the disciplines: "Despite many years of research and experiment, scientifically valid knowledge of human mentality and motivation is as yet decidedly meager." To declare, as William Thomas did, that "personality formation in its normal and abnormal aspects is a very complex matter, bound up with the whole environing social situation," was merely to put the obvious into bad language.[12]

None of this, of course, prevented the JBF from issuing treatment recommendations. It did not itself carry out treatment, but it was ready to tell the judge how best to proceed. As a rule, it instructed the court to follow one of four placement options: to use probation, to resort to foster care or military service, to incarcerate in a state training school (ostensibly for educational purposes), or to incarcerate in a state reformatory (ostensibly for correctional purposes). To its general recommendation, the JBF often added a series of more limited ones (improve his use of leisure time, upgrade his vocational education, and the like). What use did the court make of this advice? Not very much. The Gluecks found that "one-fifth of the place-of-living recommendations . . . were not followed at all by the court; in another fifth they were in effect for a period so short as to be of questionable value." The record was still worse for the related recommendations. Only 14 percent were followed in full, the rest partially or not at all.[13]

Although Cabot never indicated why he failed to carry out clinic recommendations, it sometimes appeared that he lacked the appropriate authority. One institution for the retarded that the clinic suggested had closed admissions because of overcrowding; in another case the parents balked at getting their son to enlist in the army. In other instances, the appropriate welfare agencies refused to assist the court. As one of them frankly conceded, delinquents were simply too tough to handle. "Our organization aims to use its money . . . in behalf of those children where there is at least a reasonable prospect of accomplishing *permanent* results." Then, as now, the voluntary agencies preferred to "cream" their cases, accepting the more manageable and rejecting the hard core, whether the field was delinquency or foster care or retardation.[14]

But the problem was even more basic. As the Gluecks noted, many of the clinic's recommendations were terribly vague. It was one thing to declare that the boy "must be cured of his sex habits" or must be helped to get over his enuresis, but it was quite another to specify *how* this should be done, and the clinic rarely took this second step. What the judge received was goals without means — again, not surprising in light of existing knowledge, but still not very helpful. And because the clinic diagnoses of causation repeated the obvious ("lack of parental control very marked," "excessive street life," "love of adventure very marked"), and the recommendations were, at best, commonsensical (move to a less poverty-stricken environment, avoid bad companions, study more, find outlet for adventure), the judge was not reluctant to substitute his own view of things. In sending the case to the clinic he had paid obeisance to expertise and now he could go about doing what *he* wanted to do, perhaps recognizing that the professionals were of only marginal assistance, or perhaps ready to pit his own common sense against somebody else's. Whatever the motivations, Cabot and his colleagues took little instruction from the clinic. Reformers' expectation that psychiatric counseling would guide juvenile court decisions went unrealized.[15]

More than a little caution is appropriate as the historian approaches the decision making of the juvenile courts. Their procedures and decisions were diverse and major methodological difficulties bar conclusive answers (although not informed speculation) to some basic questions, such as whether the juvenile courts were more or less harsh in their dispositions than earlier courts. And this warning must be issued quickly because the very difficulties that confront the historian of the court point to the problems that contemporaries had in trying to understand the courts and render them accountable. In this sense, the historian and the objects of court action are very much in the same position. What remains obscure about juvenile justice in retrospect was obscure at the time.

The ways in which juvenile court judges exercised their open-ended authority illuminate the second critical characteristic of Progressive juvenile justice: the new courts were far more interventionist and extensive in their reach than traditional courts had ever been. The discretion that judges enjoyed in procedural terms was matched by the latitude that they enjoyed in substantive terms, in the types of cases they considered and the sentences they passed down. Taken together, these two features gave the administration of juvenile justice an awesome quality. Judicial authority had both a novel autonomy and an enlarged scope — which, in effect, meant that that system was at once powerful and unpredictable. Put another way, the distance between a discretionary system and an arbitrary system was not very great.

One procedure that extended the reach of the juvenile court (and not coincidentally complicates attempts at evaluation) was the practice of treating a substantial number of cases as "unofficial." Many courts (in the 1929 Children's Bureau *Survey*, sixty-four of ninety-three, including Los Angeles and Denver, but excluding New York and Boston) conducted these informal sessions; petitions were not filed, transcripts were not made, lawyers were not present; indeed, the interviews usually took place away from the judges' courtrooms or chambers. The San Francisco juvenile court handled 22 percent of its cases in this manner; the Westchester juvenile court, 40 percent; the Philadelphia juvenile court, 47 percent. Moreover, the courts conducted these informal sessions in very different ways. Some judges (as in Los Angeles) appointed a special referee to hear them; others (as in St. Louis) gave them over to the chief probation officer. This surrogate would be the one to visit the home and try to resolve the matter himself, bringing before the judge only those serious cases which might require a commitment order to a welfare agency or institution. In other instances, the judge conducted the informal hearings (as Ben Lindsey did in Denver), again reserving for formal session any case that demanded more sustained intervention.[16]

To some degree, the use of an "unofficial" docket was an efficiency measure. By relying upon a referee or probation officer to handle the minor cases, the judge left himself only the complicated ones. And in part, too, the use of unofficial proceedings reflected the personal preference of some judges for sessions that were altogether relaxed, even by the lenient standards of regular juvenile court hearings. But there was another side to this practice: an unofficial docket meant that the court was encouraging parties to bring before it the most minor transgressions, the most petty infractions and arguments. The very ease of avoiding anything as formal (or time-consuming or "legal" or mysterious) as filing a petition or even appearing in an actual courtroom effectively reduced the distance (both physical and psychological) between the community and the court. Here was an invitation to police, parents, and neighbors to make the juvenile court a place of first resort, a court that would have a say in even the most ordinary and commonplace aspects of daily living.

As the records of the District of Columbia Juvenile Court convincingly demonstrate, the invitation was often accepted. The preponderance of cases brought before this court for "unofficial" adjudication were trivial. Over the five-year period 1917–1922, the court handled some 5,100 cases informally. Most of them involved "disorderly conduct" and petty property theft and damage; that is, quite literally, noise making, apple swiping, and window breaking. The roster of informal complaints also included ball playing in the streets, nude bathing, soliciting baggage and roomers, and shooting craps. Through the 1920's the cases remained very much the same, with the exception that traffic violations became more common ("fast riding, motor cycle"). And every year at least some cases of an incredibly trivial sort came before the court: sleigh riding, throwing papers in sewers, and riding bicycles on the sidewalk.[17]

Taken by itself, the long reach of the court in these instances was not especially mischievous. In the great majority of cases, the judge did restrict himself to issuing warnings and dispensing advice. On the average, very few cases moved from the informal to the formal docket; the court did not typically use the occasion of a trifling matter to take custody or to arrange for psychological testing. Indeed, a portion of these cases (it is impossible to know precisely how many) would earlier have come before the local police sergeant in the precinct house. A neighbor might have complained to the policeman on the beat; or the policeman on his own might have brought the youngsters into the precinct house to deliver a talking-to or a warning. And perhaps it was preferable that a probation officer or a judge should now take over this task—there was less chance that either of them would try to teach the youngster a lesson through physical punishment.

Nevertheless, all this being granted, several critical points do remain. For one, probation officers by training were not so different from policemen; to substitute the one for the other was not to guarantee a more helpful response. For another, the scope of intervention in a few instances did create a dragnet effect, so that some petty offenders ended up on the formal court docket (imagine that youngster who shot craps then talking tough and not showing contrition), with the possibility of more serious consequences. For still another, some juvenile courts organized a system of "voluntary" probation to go along with informal cases—which meant that the delinquent had to report on a regular basis and that another infraction might make him appear to be a troublesome case. He was, in effect, beginning to build a record. And no one should take designations of "voluntary" or "informal" too seriously, for the youngsters and their families all knew full well that at the judge's discretion, an "informal" case could become "formal"; that to refuse a "suggestion" of the court might precipitate a "verdict" of the court.[18]

In this way the substitution of a more bureaucratic mechanism of control (which the court at its most informal still represented) for the control of the policeman on the beat (let alone for the discipline of neighbor upon neighbor) did carry special consequences. The potential for serious abuse was always present. The courts could track and coerce in ways that a policeman or a neighbor could not; their reach was greater, the stakes were higher, and they had a much more powerful and legitimate rationale for their actions. No less important, the existence of informal proceedings helped to define the courts' style. It makes us, as it made contemporaries, keenly aware of just how much the thrust of the juvenile courts was outward, just how prepared they were to preside over a broad range of behavior, to enlarge the dimensions of their jurisdiction. These characteristics were realized in still more dramatic and less ambiguous ways in the courts' formal operations.

All juvenile courts, in their official as well as their unofficial capacity, had authority over a wide range of behavior. The legislation that established their jurisdiction was notably open-ended, even by the standards that might prevail in a lax adult criminal code. Juveniles were peculiarly liable not only for "status offenses," that is, for behavior that had it been committed by an adult would not have been considered a crime, but also for behavior that was never defined with any precision. Thus, almost 30 percent of the boys appearing before juvenile courts were charged with "acts of carelessness or mischief." In some places (like Hartford, Connecticut, and Dutchess County, New York) this catch-all offense accounted for almost half of the docket. So too, another 10 percent came to court for being "ungovernable," or "beyond parental control," but not guilty of any more specific infraction than that. Such nebulous complaints were even more commonplace in the case of girls; they were liable for acts of "mischief" or being "ungovernable." And exactly what constituted one of the most popular charges leveled against girls (but not boys), "sex offense," was rarely spelled out; it might include anything from dating a young man whom parents disliked to outright prostitution. When one adds to these "status offenses" the innumerable local code violations that could also occasion court intervention — from profane language to late hours to forms of conduct that constituted "stepping stones to more serious delinquency" — it is altogether apparent just how extensive the court's reach was.[19]

Since the court was inescapably a part of the criminal justice system these broad powers were, not surprisingly, exercised more regularly over the lower-class and immigrant populations than over middle-class and native-born groups. A good majority of court cases did originate with the police (on the average 55 to 60 percent), and all the biases that are known to affect arrest patterns among adults reappear among juveniles. By the same token, parents and relatives (who brought in some 10 percent of the cases) were, if middle-class, far less likely to take their problems to court than if lower-class; the poorer family was more apt to come under the pressures of a social welfare agency or school officials, or simply to have no other way of coping with its difficulties. So too, school officials (who brought in another 10 percent of the court's docket) were less prone to report a middle-class truant than a lower-class one — and anyway, since the pressure to earn money (sometimes self-imposed but often generated by parents) was one major cause of truancy, middle-class children confronted the problem that much less often. And neighbors (responsible for initiating 15 percent of the docket) were also less likely to turn to the courts if the youngsters to be disciplined were middle-class. To choose just one example, the cases that came before the New York City juvenile court in 1925 were composed disproportionately of lower-class and second-generation immigrants. The economic profile of the delinquent cases closely resembled the profile of the neglected cases (where poverty was the determining element); and of all the youngsters arraigned before the New York juvenile court in 1925, fully 71 percent had foreign-born parents. In sum, the judges' authority came to bear most heavily on the bottom sectors of society.[20]

That such a bias would characterize the courts' dockets was perfectly predictable. For one thing, it is a consistent feature of almost all aspects of criminal justice (not unique to the juvenile court or to the period 1900–1940). For another, the Progressives, altogether candidly, intended the juvenile court to affect the lower classes most deeply; after all, the innovation was a humanitarian advance to benefit those in trouble as well as to preserve the stability of society. But this bias does make even more serious the question of whether the court actually delivered beneficial services. Could the court fulfill both humanitarian and correctional aims? Could it punish and treat, hurt and help? Could it satisfy the needs of the middle classes and the lower classes simultaneously?

Any attempt to define with precision the outcomes of juvenile court proceedings is treacherous. To compare juvenile courts in different cities or in different regions, or to contrast traditional police courts with the new juvenile courts, is to confront a series of considerations that muddy the data. Some court records, for example, did not distinguish the formal from the informal docket — so they give the impression that the courts treated a large number of cases leniently, letting off a sizable proportion of the youngsters with nothing more than a warning. Other courts restricted their record entries to formal actions, so that they appear to have been harsh in their sentencing patterns, with a sizable number of delinquents receiving the sanction of incarceration. In a place where police or neighbors were prone to settle matters among themselves, the court received only the most serious cases, and therefore its sentences appear to be harsh; in a place where the police preferred to let the court handle more or less everything, the court appears to be lenient. Hence, the annual statistics on juvenile court dispositions, like so many other records in the field of criminal justice, are of limited value. Most conclusions about juvenile court dispositions must be delivered in a whisper.

With such warnings to mind, one may also note some clues and hints that encourage informed speculation. According to practically every observer, the first recourse of the juvenile court, the preferred sentence, was probation. In fact, a great number, oftentimes a majority, of those brought up on formal proceedings did receive probation. Yet, not surprisingly, with juveniles as with adults, an untrained probation staff with heavy case loads could not provide significant assistance or even surveillance. All the inadequacies that characterized the pre-sentence reports of probation officers reappeared in their post-sentence supervision. Boys filed past a judge or probation officer and flashed a school or work report, or they sat and heard a lecture on good behavior, and by no one's definition could such rituals constitute friendly assistance or social work. Indeed, in many jurisdictions, probationers merely had to mail in a monthly postcard — a practice which had neither treatment nor policing benefits. No less important, in juvenile proceedings even more clearly than in adult, probation was probably not used primarily as an alternative to incarceration, a way of sparing youngsters the corruptions of a jail or the discipline of a reformatory. Rather, it was a substitute for dismissing a case, for the judge lecturing the youngster and letting him go. In brief, juvenile courts may well have used probation instead of a milder sentence, not a harsher one.

This pattern is hinted at in the Children's Bureau's annual com-

pilation of juvenile court sentences in different cities. Recognizing
that many considerations could affect these figures, still it appears
that the courts that depended heavily upon probation were less
likely to dismiss a large percentage of their cases; in cities like
Columbus and Indianapolis, dismissal was a rare occurrence (7
and 14 percent) and probation was frequent (67 and 51 percent). On the other hand, in courts where dismissals were high,
recourse to probation was low. Buffalo and San Francisco dismissed over half their case loads and put less than one-quarter on
probation. Among all of these courts, commitments to institutions
did not substantially vary, remaining at about the national average, between 10 and 20 percent.[21]

A comparison between juvenile court dispositions of formal
cases in Philadelphia and Chicago suggests this same point. Philadelphia dismissed 11 percent of its cases and placed two-thirds
on probation; Chicago dismissed one-third and put another third
on probation. To be sure, rates of incarceration were lower in
Philadelphia than in Chicago (20 percent compared to 32 percent
of the docket). But the greatest difference remained that in Philadelphia the reach of the court was more extensive; in Chicago
many more juveniles went out on their own. Here too, then, the
significant link was between probation and dismissal, not probation and incarceration.[22]

Still more intriguing is the comparison between the sentences
in the specifically juvenile courts and those in the ordinary municipal courts which continued to hear cases involving minors.
These ordinary courts were, in effect, carry-overs from an earlier
period — the juvenile reform program had not spread to their
districts — and so they suggest (though no more than that) ways
in which the old system and the new system differed. Again, the
core of the distinction involved verdicts of dismissal as against
probation. An extensive investigation of child welfare conditions
in Pennsylvania in the early 1920's revealed that numerous
counties were still relying upon police or aldermanic courts to
handle juvenile offenders. The report carefully tallied the dispositions in juvenile courts and regular courts and demonstrated that
the extent and duration of state oversight was the distinguishing

element. The regular courts in the overwhelming majority of instances (71 percent) dismissed their cases or imposed a fine; probation was rare and so was incarceration (both at 12 percent). By contrast, the juvenile courts dismissed only one-third of their cases, and never levied fines. Instead, they placed delinquents on probation (28 percent), or resorted to institutionalization (28 percent). In brief, the regular courts moved in and out of their cases quickly, while juvenile courts exercised more supervision and retained longer jurisdiction.[23]

Practices in other states conformed to this general rule. In Georgia, where the Progressive innovation made only modest advances, a comparison of dispositions in juvenile delinquency cases demonstrates that regular courts most frequently fined or dismissed (61 percent). Only 1 percent of cases went on probation, and another 20 percent were incarcerated. The juvenile courts, for their part, dismissed or fined much less frequently (30 percent), relying instead upon probation (28 percent) and institutionalization (33 percent). Reviewing this record, juvenile court proponents were disturbed that Georgia's regular courts failed to provide delinquents with probation, with (in their terms) "help in overcoming the difficulties that had brought them into conflict with the law." A proper juvenile court would intervene in the lives of minors in much greater depth.

Similar kinds of complaints came from juvenile court advocates in Maine. The absence of a formally constituted juvenile court system, they noted, prompted the police to treat many cases of delinquency themselves. As a result, "the largest number of children dealt with unofficially were released—sometimes with a warning, a reprimand or a threat, but seldom with any constructive action having been taken." This same conclusion emerged in South Dakota — where one chief of police reasoned: "He had learned from experience that the judge would dismiss the cases and that he himself could do that as well as the judge." Accordingly, when one twelve-year-old was arrested for stealing coal from a freight car, the chief "had 'scared him up,' ordered him to pay for the coal, and released him." In light of the family's poverty, the officer had neither the illusion that the boy would pay nor the intention of enforcing the order. Since the regular judges simply turned most cases loose, he would too.[24]

Thus, the novel feature of the juvenile court was its use of probation to keep contact with the delinquent. Reformers' nightmarish stories about the harshness and corruptions of nineteenth-century practices were, on the whole, misleading: the mix of children and adults in local courts probably had not meant that children were punished with the full rigor of the adult law but, to the contrary, that typically they were let off with nothing more than an admonition. The severity of what would have constituted the punishment encouraged leniency. Such a dynamic is surely one of the oldest in the field of criminal justice, being simply a variation on the theme of jurors unwilling to vote for conviction when many crimes called for capital punishment. But juvenile court judges, unlike their predecessors, were not in so tight a bind. Probation provided them with an alternative — and one that did not so much moderate as extend the power of the court over the delinquent.

To carry this argument one step forward, juvenile court reform did not significantly reduce rates of juvenile incarceration. It is unlikely that the number of commitments to training schools or reformatories diminished substantially as a result of the creation of the court. The tentative quality of this statement must be immediately underscored. Given the nature of the data, one cannot talk confidently in terms of either percentages or absolute number of commitments. Where the dockets of traditional police courts reveal a higher percentage of commitments to institutions than juvenile courts, the only proper conclusion may be that only the very worst cases made it on to the police docket; the rest were dismissed informally. Nor are absolute numbers, rates of juvenile incarceration per 100,000, any more satisfying. One reason is that no accurate census exists on the size of training school populations over time. Worse yet, the confusion between commitments for dependents and for delinquents was so rampant, indeed, the confusion between which institutions were for the delinquent and which for the dependent was so total, that it is hopeless to try to sort out the effects of the juvenile courts by counting the institutional population. Nevertheless, shreds of evidence, often more qualitative than quantitative, do indicate that the juvenile court did not spark a major movement away from incarceration.

On a common sense level, there is really nothing at all surprising about such a conclusion. Clearly juvenile courts did not put reformatories or state training schools out of business either in rhetoric or in reality. To the contrary, census statistics on juvenile institutions, however limited their value, do point very much in the other direction. Between 1923 and 1933 (a period when the data were collected in relatively consistent fashion), the public juvenile reformatory population rose (from 25,251 to 30,496, or from 22.8 to 24.4 per 100,000 of the population); the number of annual juvenile court commitments also increased (from 17,296 to 25,329, or from 15.5 to 20.2 per 100,000). As one would expect, wide variations existed among the states, but differences were not related to the progress of the juvenile court movement. In Massachusetts, the population of the training schools and the rates of court commitments actually declined over this decade, as they did in Illinois, Ohio, and California. The trend, however, went the other way in New York, Pennsylvania, New Jersey, the District of Columbia, and Missouri. Moreover, new institutions for delinquents continued to be built, and even a quick glance at the populations of the older institutions makes clear that they had not fallen on hard times.[25]

What may require explanation is why anyone thought that the juvenile court would, or did, reduce institutional populations. In part, the rhetoric of some court proponents encouraged this view. Their frequent attacks on the machine-like discipline of the institutions, and their contention that confinement ought to be a last resort, could promote such an impression. The juvenile court judges, too, frequently declared their unwillingness to turn first to incarceration; when asked about sentencing practices, they generally expressed a reluctance to institutionalize anyone who had not already failed on probation. But to ignore the other side — to forget how often both reformers and judges admitted that some percentage of delinquents would require institutional care, how often they used probation as an alternative to dismissal, and as we shall soon see, how often they attempted to reform the reform school into a "truly rehabilitative" system — is to omit a critical part of the story.[26]

The percentage of delinquents that the juvenile courts incarcerated also appeared to be low: some 15 percent of their cases, on the average. (Again, variation was great. In one of the most frequently cited Children's Bureau tables, the figures ranged from 5 percent in Boston to 9 percent in the District of Columbia to 17 percent in Philadelphia to 41 percent in New Orleans and 42 percent in Minneapolis.)[27] Were the figures considered out of context, some courts at least would appear to be eschewing institutional commitments. This conclusion, however, would be unwarranted. The wider the net that the court spread and the greater the number of trivial cases that it heard, the smaller the percentage of incarceration would be. The hard-core cases were still committed — as they had always been. In fact, the juvenile court system did regularly confine certain types of delinquents. Recidivists headed the list — making up a little over one-half of all those committed to institutions — but did not complete it. Among boys, those found guilty of theft or of being in one way or another uncontrollable (truants, runaways, and ungovernables) were more likely to be committed than those convicted of drunkenness or carelessness. Among girls, those guilty of sexual offenses were more often incarcerated than those guilty of theft or truancy. In brief, the more serious offender, especially with a prior record, was a prime candidate for institutionalization, and so was an ungovernable boy and a sexually active girl. The institutions had ample categories of eligible populations.

Thus, last resort or not, the juvenile courts consistently relied upon the juvenile facilities and accorded them legitimacy. As more than one appellate opinion declared, the very fact that juvenile courts sent youngsters to the training schools meant that these were places of treatment, not punishment. But were they? Any final judgment on the court must confront this issue. Did the routine of the training school differ substantially from that of the prison? Did the reformatories deserve the approbation of the juvenile courts? Or to frame the question at its most significant: did the quality of the institutions justify or render dubious the almost unlimited grant of power to the juvenile court judge? Were they so treatment-oriented as to give purpose to his discretionary authority? Or, to the contrary, were they so punitive as to make procedural protections for defendants a clear necessity?

CHAPTER EIGHT

When Is a School
Not a School?

THROUGHOUT THE OPENING DECADES of the twentieth century, the administrators of juvenile institutions were especially uneasy and defensive about their operations. The facts of ample court commitments and a steady inmate population aside, they constantly had to justify themselves against charges that conditions in juvenile asylums were mechanical, abnormal, and guaranteed to warp the personalities of children. Being the last resort was an unenviable position. When talking among themselves, superintendents gave vent frequently to their irritation and displeasure. "How often at charity conferences do we hear it glibly stated," declared one official, "that the worst of homes is better than the best of institutions. It, therefore, required great hardihood for a poor, discredited institution head to venture a word in defense of his calling." What constituted this defense? That the typical critic was "a young lady graduate of a six week's course of a summer school of philanthropy" who had never even bothered to visit an institution; and that by the time she began to "get things at least partly in focus" she was "lost to social work . . . [being] young and attractive and marriageable." Indeed, considering "the large number of homes where the moral atmosphere is poisoned with dishonesty, dissipation, immorality, lack of care, it is apparent the statement that most any home is better than an institution for a child is a gross slander on the large number of faithful, conscientious, high-minded employees who care for the children."[1]

At the annual meetings of the National Conference of Juvenile Agencies, superintendents frequently debated such questions as "Is the Reformatory such a bad place as the public thinks it is?" They relished the story of a Massachusetts judge who had boasted of never sending a boy to the reformatory — until he went out to visit one, and then the very next week committed seven. More than one superintendent demanded to know why it was expected that reformatories would rehabilitate all their charges when every other community organization had failed. And managers regularly blamed the newspapers for sensationalism in their stories about mistreatment; the state legislatures for miserliness in their appropriations; and the public for not visiting to learn first-hand about the institutions' good work.[2] The major function of the annual Conference, it would appear, was to give institutional directors the opportunity to confirm for each other the unfairness of the burdens that they carried.

However comforting such sessions, juvenile institutions had to respond in more direct and practical fashion to the Progressive viewpoint. Clearly, they, like the prisons, had to abandon all the essential features of the Jacksonian style of incarceration. But it was not enough for them to give up uniforms and rules of silence, or to liberalize parole regulations. They had to administer, all ironies and confusion intended, non-institutional institutions. Their routines had to be not only normal — that is, approximating life in the outside community — but intimate — re-creating the close ties of the family. More broadly put, the juvenile institutions had to deliver on the promise of rehabilitation more promptly and consistently than any of the other institutions. After all, they were working with the most plastic and impressionable group and, given Progressive attitudes, also the most precious. It was one thing to try to cure the hard-core adult offender or the chronically mentally ill patient but, seemingly, quite another to rehabilitate the delinquent who might not even have been guilty of a real crime. Here the burden of performance was on the superintendent, no matter how he might wish to avoid it.

In fact, the reform agenda, at least in terms of rhetoric and design, was more acceptable to the superintendents than might have been expected. Well before the Progressive period, the juvenile institutions had begun to shift away from the Jacksonian model. They were quick to introduce grading and classification schemes, to leave cellular arrangements for dormitories and, more notably, cottages. They were also the first to introduce some amenities behind the wall: before 1900, the commissary, the band, and the freedom of the yard appeared in one or another juvenile institution. Hence, the Progressive rhetoric was by no means alien to reformatory superintendents. Despite their defensive tone, they were prepared to move their institutions further in this direction, to restyle their routines to satisfy the new prescriptions.

One symbolic indication of the impact of Progressive ideology and the superintendents' receptivity to it was the widespread change in the names of juvenile institutions. What had been "houses of refuge" in the 1830's and "reformatories" in the 1880's now became almost everywhere the "training school" or the "industrial school" or the "boys' school." The Vermont Reform School became the Vermont Industrial School; Connecticut's Reform School became the School for Boys. Already in the 1880's and 1890's, institutions had begun to adopt the "industrial school" title. But by the end of the Progressive period, the "reformatory" label had almost completely disappeared; and behind this shift lay an attempt, more representational than real as we shall see, to abandon the remnants of a rigid and fixed style of institutional routine. "Reformatory" suggested a military model: marching, uniforms, rigid rules of conduct, a barracks-like quality. "Training school" suggested a campus-like atmosphere, an organization no different from others in the community. Moreover, the reformatory concept presupposed that the roots of delinquency were found primarily in the realm of morality, so that a heavy-handed discipline (with shades of breaking the will, or beating out the devil) would be appropriate. The idea of a training school carried very different associations: an environmental cause of crime (no training for an occupation); a parental failure (in G. Stanley Hall's terms, inadequate habit training, or in the later terminology inspired by John Watson, a failure to "train the child to happiness").

A reformatory, in other words, was old-fashioned, crude, and primitive. A training school was modern, sophisticated, in accord with the latest developments. As the Children's Bureau summarized it: "The original purpose of institutional care of delinquents was to protect society by confining those who endangered its security. . . . The newer purpose of the institution is to deal with the child on the basis of careful, scientific, and understanding training and education and to prepare him to return to the community as soon as there is assurance that he can fit into community life again."[3]

The training school designation points directly to the reformers' educational ideals for juvenile institutions. Although the notion that inmates should be educated was anything but novel, Progressives believed that a well-planned school program would assure rehabilitation. In good Deweyite fashion, the curriculum was to include a School of Letters, providing academic instruction, and still more important, a School of Vocational Training, in which "highly qualified experts in their several lines" would fit inmates "to the industrial trades, and to farming and gardening, according to their desires, ability and probable future." As one proponent explained: "Education will concern itself first and foremost with the vocational training of John so that he may be able to earn a living which will also yield him some emotional satisfaction." No one could doubt, declared the 1932 White House Conference report on the Delinquent Child, that "vocational training is of great value to the older boys and girls who, almost without exception, must face earning a livelihood on leaving the institution." Not altogether unaware of pitfalls that had defeated past programs, reformers often tried to distinguish between institutional maintenance and vocational education. "Insist that the child be given a full public school day," urged one Progressive-minded woman superintendent, "and protest persistently against . . . permitting a so-called state supported institution to prop itself on the labor of the child as a crutch." There should be "a minimum of scrubbing and a maximum of schooling." More, scrubbing should never be confused with schooling — which was all too easy to do in a vocational program.[4]

The model institution had a second characteristic: living arrangements were to follow a cottage, not a cell block or even dormitory design. The plan was not new, dating back to the 1880's, but again, the Progressives added their own special interpretation. Earlier, the great advantage of the cottage had lain in its promise to deliver a family-like affection to institutional inmates. To the Progressives, however, affection was not enough. The new cottage plan, echoing the essential themes of child-rearing tracts, had a more varied and extensive agenda to fulfill. It was to provide the setting in which highly trained and insightful surrogate parents would shape the development of the child, always meeting his individual needs.

This notion pervaded the Progressive design for juvenile institutions. The cottage, declared Carrie Smith, superintendent at the Texas State Training School for Girls, had to be "under a woman possessed of the highest education, culture, and practical Christianity," and the ordering testifies to her Progressivism. And from Wisconsin came the complaint that "too often an institution is a shelter for the worn out teacher, the failure in the business world, or the unattached housekeeper." If inmates were to gain "self-control, a better angle on life and adjustment to meet the world . . . it takes the finest type of matron and the best trained teachers."[5]

The cottage plan would also promote the individuality of the resident — and no goal was more popular among Progressives. Children should have their own rooms and a place for their possessions, insisted Carrie Smith. Without this, "we give *humane* treatment, as we do with our dogs and cats, the while they are yearning for *human* treatment. Eliminate the 'e' from humane and you have helped to eliminate the reformatory." Other superintendents linked this principle to dress and abolished the uniform. The family model meant not only bringing good order and affection to the institution, but recognizing the particularity of each child.[6]

The cottage arrangement was designed to help realize still another Progressive aim: to make the institution over into a normal community. "The entire atmosphere of the institution," declared the White House Conference, "should be one of cheerfulness and inspiration. Every effort is made by the well organized institution to provide situations such as are met in well rounded community life, in the home, in school, at group activities such as competitive games, and clubs." In this way, the "compelled conformity" of a military-type institution would give way to "the useful citizenship of a community-like institution." A "real home, as distinguished from the cold, hard discipline of a military unit," promised another proponent, would encourage "the warm, friendly co-operative spirit." In sum, the new asylum, in spirit akin to the settlement house, would insure that the boy who became "adjusted to institution life" would be "able to make adjustment to community life with a similar degree of success."[7]

This precept received its most unusual expression in the George Junior Republic. Organized in 1895 by William George, a onetime charity worker, and located at Freeville, New York, the Republic was an effort to recreate in miniature an American community. Intending to be more of a school than a reformatory and serving children who were more often dependent than delinquent, it was the most consistent and noteworthy effort to duplicate normal life within an institutional setting. The Republic adopted a town meeting form of government — the boys and girls voted and held office — and it even tried to introduce a kind of capitalist economy — "Nothing Without Labor" was its motto. The complications that ensued can easily be imagined and by 1920 internal dissension and external political wrangling killed off the enterprise. For a moment, however, the Republic captured reformers' enthusiasm. Teddy Roosevelt marveled at it: "The place is a manufactory of citizens." Thomas Osborne, who would carry the scheme over into adult prisons, called it "a laboratory experiment in democracy." To be sure, observers recognized its flaws. "Big Daddy" George was too much the benevolent despot; and did a Republic like this really need its own jail? And there were few efforts to re-create the operation; it remained an idiosyncratic venture. Still, for a time, it seemed to confirm the possibility of bringing a social environment to an institution.[8]

By 1920, and still more clearly by 1930, the training school had discovered the relevance of still another model. Not only would its organization duplicate those of the school, the family, and the community, but it would assume the attributes of the hospital and guidance clinic. As with the prisons, the relationship of one design to the other was never sorted out. The question of whether a facility could at once serve as family, school, and clinic (and as jail too) was not confronted. Rather, observers and administrators took comfort from the diversity of approaches. The greater the variety, the greater the likelihood that something might work.

To psychiatrists and their allies in social work and psychology, the clinic model seemed especially appropriate to the juvenile institutions. In these settings, they would diagnose the causes of deviant behavior and prescribe the antidotes. "The institution," as one New York psychiatrist declared, "is looked upon as a great laboratory where the maladjusted boy may be thoroughly studied, more or less socialized and brought to understand the mechanisms back of his behavior." Or, in the words of a social worker, "this kind of institution will not be the dumping ground of the community's failures . . . [but] . . . a sanitarium for sick personality; a definite and constructive link in what should be an endless chain of service to maladjusted childhood."[9]

Ideally, this chain of service began the moment the juvenile arrived at the institution. He would be assigned to a "diagnostic cottage for observation extending over a period of a month at least. Here he will be studied with minute and painstaking care by a trained and competent case worker, physician, psychologist and psychiatrist." They would interview and examine him, and also conduct "an extensive inquiry into [his] early history, home surroundings, school, court and detention room experience." Then, at the monthly staff conference, "which will include at least ten of the extra-mural social workers who have probably known [him] before . . . this child's past, present and future will be discussed in terms of diagnosis, prognosis and plan." The results would compose a "detailed case record to which will be added a continuous history of [his] stay in the institution." The youngster would then be assigned to the "cottage corresponding to his classification" (under the care of a trained case worker), and to the appropriate school and vocational programs. Periodic conferences would mark his progress and when he was finally ready to leave the institution, "careful placement and careful supervision by a case worker" would make certain that his "good habits, means of earning a living, considerable self-mastery and stability and a happy eager and hopeful outlook upon life" were all turned to good use in the community. In sum, psychiatry would make institutions genuinely rehabilitative, and altogether legitimate.[10]

The descent from the rhetoric to the reality of juvenile institutions is precipitous. The ideals that justified incarceration had little relevance to actual circumstances. No matter how frequently juvenile court judges insisted that their sentences of confinement were for treatment and not punishment, no matter how vehemently superintendents declared that their institutions were rehabilitative and not correctional, conditions at training schools belied these claims. To be sure, practices did vary from place to place. "There are now in existence state institutions for delinquents," noted the White House Conference report, "which represent almost every stage in the development of principles and methods of treatment." Some private institutions were able "to provide more specialized training and apply progressive principles of treatment in advance of institutions that rely entirely on public appropriations." And here and there a particularly devoted superintendent administered a less custodial routine than his counterparts. But these cases were exceptional. The closer the scrutiny of juvenile confinement, the more inadequate and, indeed, punitive, the programs turned out to be.[11]

"When is a school not a school?" asked one reformatory superintendent. "When it is a school for delinquents. Because the child has shown by her anti-social attitudes how much she is in need of more education, she is put in a training school where she will get less." National surveys, investigations of particular institutions, and institutional reports themselves all confirmed this answer. The failure was obvious in the formal academic programs; the institutions were incapable of administering a grade school or high school curriculum. Perhaps this was because not many superintendents came to their positions through career lines in education: in terms of personnel recruitment and advancement, training schools were more typically a part of the prison system than of the school system. Or perhaps it was because the institutions could not often recruit trained teachers or teachers in sufficient numbers — they paid too badly or gave too much of the salary in room and board or were too isolated. "I went to the local teachers' agency," reported the superintendent of the Rhode Island School for Boys, "and asked what they had to offer and they told me they had nobody who would consider what I had," that is, a salary of $50 to $65 a month at a time when Providence paid its teachers between $150 and $165 a month. What staff there were faced impossible conditions. The eight licensed teachers at the Indiana Boys' School had to instruct 554 inmates — and the added fact that the older boys often were removed from class to do farm work did not simplify the task.[12]

Still more glaring was the failure to provide vocational training. The programs were not merely inadequate but involved a fundamental deception: just as some had feared, institutional maintenance masqueraded as vocational education. The training that inmates received was in how to keep their institutions operating. As child welfare researcher William Slingerland reported: "Many superintendents admit that vocational training in their Schools is merely elementary, and some confess that for practical results their efforts are unmitigated failures." Slingerland had no trouble in identifying the root of the problem. "Most of the large institutions have what they call trades departments, and use them mainly for repair and construction work about the plants. The inmates become the unskilled helpers of the carpenters, painters

. . . farmers, and dairymen. A majority of the tailor shops are devoted to the mending of worn garments; most of the shoe shops are used for the cobbling of impaired shoes. This gives a small amount of instruction while utilizing the labor of the inmates in reducing the expenses of the institutions." Numerous other investigators confirmed his findings. One national survey of the training school experiences of 751 boys discovered that almost one-third of them were not enrolled in any kind of vocational training course. The rest spent six months to a year "learning" to do farm work (although only a handful of them came from or would return to rural communities), or to mend inmates' clothing or to do the institution's wash or to print its stationery and annual reports — all "convincing testimony to the fact that . . . major emphasis was placed on maintenance and production for the institution."[13]

The records at the Boys' Industrial School at Lancaster, Ohio, reputedly one of the more satisfactory institutions, also verify the prevalence of these conditions. Of the 900 inmates in vocational training, 5 learned automobile mechanics, 5 learned electrical work, 2 learned about telephones, while 48 took their "training" by playing in the musical band, 116 carried out farming duties, 135 were educated to "housework," and another 185 were enrolled as part of the "general force." The educational program (so-called) at the New Jersey State Home for Boys was no different; again, "the work to be done, rather than the needs of the boys, was rated as of primary importance." At the Illinois Training School for Girls at Geneva, "it is still assumed that all these girls are capable of carrying on the one occupation of domestic service, and that all of them are suited for it and that they can be given an adequate preparation for this vocation by cooking institution food," or by laundering and ironing. That not so much sexism as institutional needs were operating here is apparent from a comparison to the boys' training school at St. Charles. The great majority of its inmates, too, were "busy with cleaning, serving tables, paring vegetables, and general labor about the institution." The verdict at St. Charles can stand for the system everywhere: "Trade training of a quality which fits boys for self-maintenance is non-existent."[14]

To paraphrase the reformatory superintendent's earlier question: When is a home not a home? When it is a cottage for delinquents. The dismal truth of this statement was apparent in the conditions at St. Charles. The number of inmates per cottage was itself a problem: "Fourteen large cottages house from 35 to 64 boys each," noted one visitor to the school. "Since these cottages were designed for no more than forty, the degree of overcrowding is marked." To expect that life in a dormitory of forty would re-create family-like intimacy and promote family-like cooperation was absurd. But not numbers alone belied the cottage ideal. The personnel at St. Charles were incompetent to provide guidance or instruction. "While there are many fine-spirited and capable persons on the staff," noted one investigator, "the number who are entirely unfit to handle youths . . . is so great that little improvement in the students can be expected." Working conditions were dismal, the staff patently overworked and poorly paid. Besides, the "staff are themselves institutionalized, and have dealt so exclusively with delinquents under institutional conditions that they cannot understand a boy's problems in normal life." Finally, the routine of daily living at St. Charles bore no resemblance to that of a household. "In all too many cases, silence and arbitrary conformity to mechanical routine rob the boys of any chance to develop initiative, group spirit or self control." Whatever else, St. Charles did not replicate a normal family or community.[15]

The same conditions prevailed in most other training schools. The average cottage housed between forty and sixty inmates, but still larger numbers were common. In the Oregon training school, sixty to eighty-five boys lived to a cottage; in Lancaster, Ohio, forty to ninety. Accordingly, a dormitory, not single rooms, became the common sleeping arrangement — not only for reasons of limited physical space, but because it was easier for a single night watchman to supervise.[16]

Under these circumstances, some institutions had great difficulty in sustaining household language. At the Kansas Boys'

Industrial School, where as many as eighty inmates lived to a cottage, the superintendent reported:

> Immediately after entering the school each boy is assigned to his 'home.' . . . By accepted usage the name 'Company' now designates the particular family to which the boy belongs. . . . Each home building includes living quarters for the company officer. . . . It has been our goal to set up a situation approximating as nearly as possible the family.[17]

This superintendent's inability to keep his terminology straight, his shuffle between military and household terms, reveals just how far the institution was from a normal family.

So too, staffs everywhere were inadequate to the task of instruction or counseling. A juvenile institution job was a last resort, so, as in the case of prison guards, some men took a position and left it quickly; others, usually the majority, stayed on and on, unable or unwilling to do anything else. At Ohio's Lancaster Industrial School, for example, 98 of the 138 employees had served the institution for over five years, and 17 for less than two years. As would be expected, their credentials were meager. Practically none of them had more than a grammar school education (otherwise they would not have accepted, let alone remained in, these posts). They had been employed in other institutions (training schools, state hospitals, and prisons) or had held jobs as unskilled laborers. Once again, the school was so distant from the town that staff members were as incarcerated as the inmates.[18]

A number of institutional rules also belied reform rhetoric. Training schools typically allowed inmates to write only one letter a month and to receive only one visit a month — so much for bridging the distance between the institution and the outside world. And it was all too easy to give a cottage living room a prison atmosphere. At the Illinois State Training School for Girls, "The typical cottage has on the first floor a day room, which is fairly large and with a sufficient number of windows, but with a distinctly institutional air. All the chairs, for instance, are placed in straight rows, and there are most unhomelike lockers along one side of the room." The girls had their own bedrooms, but "the single window is barred and the doors of all rooms are locked when the girls go to bed, usually about 8:30." Also, "each [cottage] 'family' has its own uniform . . . in different shades of blues and pinks." Perhaps most institutional of all: "Although it was a very beautiful day and quite warm when we visited the institution, not a single child was outside." The matron quickly explained the fact: "There are not enough people to look after the girls, and they would simply run away."[19]

Just how completely a cottage could become a prison was amply confirmed at the Wisconsin School for Girls. "The first impression on entering the institution," commented a superintendent from a neighboring state, "was one of extreme suppression and abnormality. . . . Glass in many of the [cottage] windows was painted so girls could not look out. . . . The girls were not allowed to sit within two feet of the window in their rooms. . . . There was very little chance to get outdoors even for exercise — in one of the houses the officers were afraid to take the girls outside of the building. Some of the girls were spending twelve of their fourteen waking hours in the same room." The Girls' Industrial School at Beloit, Kansas, was no different. "This seems to be," reported one investigative committee, "an institutional home — penal in nature and purpose. . . . The Committee was impressed by the apparent fear on the part of the management and the staff that every irregular move of the girls was a designing move toward escape. The spirit of the institution was altogether one of unnecessary distrust and suspicion." Rules of silence prevailed and domestic chores were the most important institutional activity: "The whole institution is kept spotlessly clean — the girls are constantly on their hands and knees scrubbing and polishing floors."[20]

The style of life at most training schools for boys was no less rigid. Disregarding the Progressive rhetoric, many superintendents could not resist incorporating military routines into their institutions. Perhaps it was because they often had prior army careers. Probably more important, the drill and the march vividly represented the goal of the transformation of unruly boys into obedient and disciplined men. The idea seemed to be that to learn to keep in step and obey a command instantly on the exercise field would lead to conformity and lawfulness in the community. (And, after all, even settlement houses included cadet corps and drill team clubs for young boys.) At the Lancaster institution, each cottage drilled separately and then, with a marching band, the whole school drilled together. ("The older boys drilled with old Army Springfield rifles from which the firing pins had been filed off. The younger boys carried wooden rifles.") Dress parade took place every Saturday evening and once a year there was a public exercise and contest. One speaker at just such an event at the Philadelphia House of Refuge captured its purposes well: "Let me compliment you on the splendid appearance you make. If, when an order were given to 'file, right,' one went this way, and another that way, and some didn't go at all, do you suppose visitors would ever come out to see you? . . . There must be discipline and there must be order, and this military drill that you have given . . . is in part the very thing that this school was established for and is maintained for, to inculcate the knowledge that this is a world of law and order." The Colorado State Industrial School was no less convinced of the value of the drill. "If a boy is compelled to hold his head up and have his shoulders squared while in line and learns the necessity of each remaining in his place and filling it well, and then gauges his conduct, when he becomes a unit in the development of his country, by the same standard, he becomes a man who may mingle with his fellow men . . . a desirable citizen." Accordingly, the school set the boys to work in the trade department making the wooden guns with which to drill.[21]

Under these conditions, psychiatric diagnosis and treatment obviously had little relevance to the training school. There were token appointments and affiliations. A number of schools made consulting arrangements with a nearby mental hygiene facility and included a psychologist on their staffs. Some even went so far as to appoint a psychiatrist. But the impact of these steps was in the realm more of public relations than of service delivery. As it worked out, the most important service that psychologists or psychiatrists performed was mental testing; the IQ test became a standard item in the schools' month-long "reception process." But aside from becoming an entry in the case record and occasionally allowing a superintendent to transfer a severely retarded inmate to another facility, the IQ test score hardly mattered. The institutions did not have the academic or vocational programs to make use of the results.

In fact, this was the rub insofar as all psychiatric services were concerned. It was not only that one psychiatrist or psychologist could accomplish very little with three hundred or five hundred inmates. Even had the staff been larger, the contributions would have remained minimal. Psychiatrists might provide an elaborate case history and, perhaps, a recommendation for treatment. The institution, however, had no way to respond. Classification was an absurdity when cottages were overcrowded and grouped inmates by age and size. Should a boy have an aptitude for a particular kind of training, his real choice remained between kitchen work and farm work. Even in New York's Industrial School at Rochester, which by the standards of the time was exceptionally well staffed (including two full-time and two part-time psychiatrist and psychologists as well as a social worker), all that professionals could claim for treatment was that one boy was transferred from one classroom to another because of a "personality clash" with his teacher.[22] Hence, the frequent and accurate answer to the question, "What good has psychiatry been in an Institution for Delinquents?" was: "To start surveys; give us technical diagnosis and work out more and more elaborate records which no one uses."[23]

However disturbing the institutions' sins of omission were, their sins of commission were still worse. The institutions not only failed to do good, they frequently did harm. It was never easy even for contemporary investigators to uncover institutional abuses; inmate complaints might be self-serving, a staff member who reported ill treatment might be disgruntled, and a reporter's exposés might be inaccurate. The problem is still more acute for the historian. Institutional records cannot be trusted for many punishments were administered without being recorded. And yet, there is enough consistency in surviving materials to indicate that the discipline of the training schools, like so much else about them, was prison-like.

There is little doubt that inmates regularly abused each other, that in the training school as in the penitentiaries homosexual rape was not an unusual occurrence. Occasionally an ex-inmate described in authentic tones such episodes:

> After my promotion to chief clerk I became wise to the worst racket in any institution and one that flourishes in all institutions. Anyone who reads this will readily understand what I mean when I say sexual pervert. These unfortunates are referred to in prison as 'punks' . . . a great many of them are forced to submit to these practices because they haven't the courage to fight back. . . . While acting in the capacity of chief clerk I was in a position to admit men to ward x of the hospital and keep them there. . . . I can truthfully say I have gotten 'punks' into the hospital to be used by other inmates when my whole being revolted at the idea of young kids that couldn't staff the gaff, yellow, just without friends and willing to do anything to keep from getting beat up.

But then why did he go along? Because he was a member of a prison gang that "did a lot of favors for me, were back of me when I needed help and — 'once in a mob, never out.'" Besides, "If I would have refused, the condition of my body with shiv marks. . . ."[24]

Some superintendents openly admitted how widespread these abuses were. The head of the Indiana Boys' School, for example, while not ready to admit that all juvenile institutions were total failures, did concede that among the evils "that seems to pervade these institutions is the horrible and revolting practice of sodomy. . . . This crime has become so common as to be lightly regarded by the administration. . . . So long as this attitude is held by those who should protect the inmates . . . so long as they proceed on the theory that it is a necessary evil, the boys' schools are damned." Why was the practice pervasive? "Pack boys into a dormitory like sardines . . . leave them without a wakeful guard or officer, consider . . . the prior evil habits of at least a few in the dormitory, and it will be an easy matter to find one source of trouble."[25]

Any remaining question as to the pervasiveness of these practices disappears when one examines the lists of infractions for which inmates were punished: sexual offenses were invariably among the leading three or four causes of disciplinary action. But if superintendents did not necessarily treat the matter lightly, they were incapable of halting it. Year after year the punishment went on, and year after year administrators were unable to make the training school safe for its inmates.[26]

Not only the inmates but the staff itself introduced a significant degree of brutality into the institutions. Punishments pervaded the training school routine and it was the rare inmate who escaped correction. A national survey of 751 boys discharged from training schools revealed that only 55 of them had records that were free of disciplinary action. In fact, the great majority of the boys had been punished at least three times, and more than one-sixth had been punished ten or more times during their incarceration. One need only read the rules of most institutions to understand how simple it was to violate a regulation. At the Kansas Industrial School, the girls were punished for "Writing notes, lying, stealing, impudence, disobedience, negligence, talking in dormitory, talking on line, communicating between cottages, running away, fighting, mutilating property, carving initials on themselves."[27]

The style as well as the frequency of discipline made the training schools essentially punitive. Almost all of them did follow a merit and demerit system — dispensing points and promotions in grade until the inmate became eligible for parole. But the marks were only a part, and not the most important part, of the system. The amount of confinement time that these superintendents controlled was even less than prison wardens, either because inmates had to be released upon reaching their majority, or because judges were more sparing with time for juvenile offenders, or because overcrowding put a premium on rapid turnover. In all events, demerits seemed inadequate for handling major violations. All superintendents had stronger penalties available, from "standing on the line" (at attention for so many hours at a time), to the segregation cottage, the training school's variation on prison solitary and the hole.

The model for these disciplinary or segregation cottages was, frankly, the prison. At California's Preston School of Industry, the segregation cottage was made up of thirty-five cells, indistinguishable from those at the penitentiary. (Ostensibly, the boys appreciated its rehabilitative qualities; according to the superintendent, they called it the "Thinkatory.") At the Illinois State Training School for Girls, the segregation cottage windows not only had bars and were locked from the outside, but the door panels were lined with galvanized iron so that inmates could not break them down. A sentence to the disciplinary cottage not only cost the inmate all privileges (such as the weekly movie or exercise period) and set him back in grade, but carried, as at the Rochester Institution, the obligation to perform the "roughest and most unpopular forms of manual labor . . . usually working about 7 hours a day." At Whittier, California, these inmates did "the heavy work around the school," such as road work and digging trenches; at the other state school at Preston, they manufactured bricks or did "other heavy labor work." At Lancaster, Ohio, not only did the cottage boys "do the hardest and most unpleasant manual labor around the institution," but they were also forced, as one observer reported, to maintain complete silence in the cottage and to sit "in rigid positions on straight chairs. . . . The monitors for the cottage, two physically powerful boys, walked back and forth . . . apparently watching for any relaxation in attitude or any movement."[28]

Even these punishments had back-up sanctions. Many institutions gave those guilty of repeated infractions or of trying to escape extended periods of confinement in the segregation cottage, so that some inmates remained there for over a year. Other institutions withheld food, still others required grueling exercises.

The New Jersey State Home for Boys took its hard-core offenders off the work detail: "Instead they were required to spend the entire working day going through disciplinary routine exercises ... old style calisthenics for 5 minutes, a rest period for 5 minutes, and repeat." And some institutions, emulating a prison model completely, included in their disciplinary cottage a solitary, hole-like cell, dark and unfurnished: the jail had its own jail. At Preston, California, the most troublesome boys were confined to solitary, as the superintendent conceded, for seven to ten days, and "not often" for more than ten days. They received "usually one square meal each day; but in bad cases, we give them bread and milk twice a day, and one square meal every three days."[29]

Nor was this treatment reserved for boys. The Illinois State Training School for Girls put its inmates in solitary under the charge of a matron who boasted to one visitor "that she had had excellent training for this difficult work, having been 'on the two worst wards in Lincoln [State School for the Feeble-Minded], the wards for the great big epileptics.'" At the Kansas Industrial School, "there are two places where the girls are put in solitary confinement. One is a small dark room in the cottage. The window is painted to make the room dark and a mattress is laid on the floor for a bed, and the culprit is fed bread and milk. The other is a cell-like place located in a dairy room. The walls and floor are of cement and the only piece of furniture is a small iron bed. One wall is covered with iron bars." No coddling of the girls here.[30]

Finally, the institutions had recourse to corporal punishment. A good number of superintendents forswore its use, but others frankly endorsed it — and even where it was officially prohibited, it may well have flourished in fact. The girls at the Kansas Institution, one state investigator discovered, were punished with "huge doses of castor oil, shaving the eyebrows off (this, when a girl is caught plucking her eyebrows), and cutting the hair in various lengths, whippings and a preponderance of slapping." (Needless to say, it was against the rules for girls to write home about punishments.) At Lancaster, Ohio, disobedient inmates received six to fifteen strokes with the paddle, "a flexible piece of leather shaped like a regular paddle about 6 or 8 inches wide and 12 to 15 inches long, with a stiffened leather handle at one end."[31]

Thus it was no easy matter to distinguish a training school from a prison — and this was precisely the verdict that Austin Mac-Cormick, one of the most knowledgeable reformers, reached after investigating conditions at Michigan's Boys' Vocational School in the mid-1930's. By reputation, the School was one of the better ones; "a very definite impression was gained," two Children's Bureau researchers had reported, "that discipline was thoroughly individualized. . . . No corporal punishment of any kind for any reason was permitted." And certainly the institution's rhetoric was Progressive: "The school itself exists to prepare boys for life at home and in the community. Successful adjustment depends largely upon the boy's success in learning social living at the Boys' Vocational School. . . . Boys . . . find their cottage parents, teachers, shop instructors, and other school officers, to be friendly, cheerful, consistent and impartial." But as MacCormick discovered, reality was very different. MacCormick was no soft sentimentalist: "Nothing in this . . . report," he noted in his preface, "should be taken to indicate that he does not believe that strict discipline is needed for boys . . . in this School. They need discipline . . . a certain amount of routine and regimentation." Nevertheless, the school's routine was so unbending and abusive as to warrant unqualified condemnation.[32]

In the cottages MacCormick found "an emphasis on repression and regimentation, enforcement of silence rules more rigid than those prevailing in most prisons . . . which effectively destroy any home-like atmosphere . . . and serve only to teach conformity to a mode of life that will not be found anywhere in the free world." Moreover, "what relationship marching in single file with folded arms from the living room to the basement or dormitory bears to the offense of stealing automobiles is also difficult to see." When he suggested to the cottage managers that boys be allowed to talk together "in a natural tone of voice, and that they thus be taught how to live and play with other boys," the response was: "If you permitted the boys to talk, bedlam would be the result."[33]

The disciplinary procedures were even worse. Boys in the ordinary cottages were regularly subjected to punishment from "almost everyone on the institution staff." Neither a supervisory committee nor the superintendent exercised oversight; not even a "record is kept of the ordinary day-by-day punishments." The school permitted inmates to police inmates (their own "trusty" system) and these monitors could order boys to stand "on the line" and lose privileges. Hence when MacCormick entered one cottage and found four to six boys "on the line" the cottage parent had no idea who had put them there, or for what reason.[34]

Those confined to the disciplinary cottage wore a thin khaki coverall (with no underwear) and lived under a rule of total silence. "When they are not engaged in calisthenics, or in the process of cleaning up the basement . . . they are required to sit on the backless benches against the wall, without speaking to each other, and with no diversion except perhaps looking at a tattered magazine or comic supplement under the dim lights." When night came, the boys "undress in the basement . . . leave their clothes there for the night, and walk naked in single file, with folded arms, up the two flights of stairs to the dormitory," where a light bulb shone all night long. Were all this not disheartening enough, MacCormick was convinced that the use of physical force was commonplace. Those caught trying to escape not only went to the disciplinary cottage but stood "on the line" all day and evening for two weeks. And MacCormick found one boy who in the course of an afternoon and the following morning did three thousand knee bends. Moreover, the boys' accounts of being beaten and kicked and struck with chairs were so consistent that MacCormick brought the facts before the superintendent. Eventually one of the offending cottage managers was dismissed. But the story had a more revealing ending. The discharged official protested to the State Civil Service Commission, which upheld him both on the grounds that "he had received no order against corporal punishment from the Superintendent," and, to clinch his case, "that such punishment as he had inflicted on the boys was common practice in other cottages."[35]

So lengthy and unrelieved a recitation of the inadequacies of the administration of juvenile justice, so unambiguous a failure on the part of the juvenile court and the juvenile institutions to approximate the designs outlined in their rhetoric or to protect their charges from injury, raises the two recurring and troubling questions: why did such dismal conditions come to exist, and why did they continue to exist? How explain both the defects of the programs and their perpetuation?

Some of the causes of the system's inadequacies are obvious; with such notable failures, there is no shortage of places to heap blame. The legislatures deserve a share. The courts and the training schools never had sufficiently large budgets to hire an adequate staff. Because the state or the county did not appropriate enough funds, probation case loads were ridiculously heavy, the cottages were overcrowded, the case workers and cottage parents were untrained, and inmates had to perform maintenance work. A paucity of knowledge was also detrimental. The art of rehabilitation had not progressed to the point where intervention could be constructive. Even if the case loads had been limited and the staffs more professional, the medical model would still have been undermined. The doctors had no potent medicines to prescribe.

All this granted, the causes are more complex, for not only the sins of omission but those of commission must be explained. Once again we return to the incompatibility of custody and rehabilitation, of guarding and helping. A few observers, more often than not from the world of psychiatry, did perceive how custody precluded treatment. As one investigator of the St. Charles School reported to the National Committee for Mental Hygiene: "The psychiatric and medical problems which abound in this institution receive only the barest attention, however, because of the subordination of this work to custodial functions." In the same vein, Dr. Max Windsor, surveying the results of psychiatric work in institutions, concluded: "There is usually no treatment that we would recognize as such. There is no thought out concept of training. The big drive in the ordinary institution is to keep inmates from escaping and to keep them in a state where discipline may be maintained."[36]

Why was it that the cottages were anything but home-like? Because the inmates had to be kept under firm control, because the fear of disorder and escape was the nightmare that dominated the institution. The rules of silence, the dormitory with the light on, the generally rigid tone of daily life, were not just random preferences on the part of the staff, but a way of keeping guard, of insuring control, of fulfilling the ultimate requirement of the training school, that is, to confine its charges securely.

In fact, this consideration crowded out all others. Perhaps it always must; certainly, in historical perspective, it did. So if the school and vocational training programs were grossly inadequate, if the staff was uneducated, no matter: the critical point was to keep the inmates confined. Why did visitors find that no girls were outside the cottages in the beautiful weather, why were they prohibited from sitting within two feet of the windows? Because of that "apparent fear on the part of the management and the staff that every irregular move of the girls was a designing move toward escape."[37]

The point is still more obvious when one reviews the disciplinary procedures. Every sanction had to have its back-up sanction (until punishment degenerated into cruelty), because institutional order had to be maintained, because one more threat always had to be available for the inmate who insisted on challenging institutional boundaries. Accordingly, the worst punishments went to those who tried to escape; for them, weeks of solitary with calisthenics and corporal punishment were appropriate, both to deter them (and other inmates) from such attempts and to incapacitate them in a setting which made escapes far more difficult. In essence, the rhetoric of treatment provided only the external trappings. Inside, incapacitation and deterrence ruled, as befit a holding operation.

Still the question remains: why did no one issue a more fundamental challenge to juvenile courts and institutions? Why were not their glaring inadequacies the starting point for a sustained and systematic critique? Clearly, such a confrontation would not come from within the system. That judges did not condemn the programs by ruling that commitments to these institutions constituted deprivation of liberty and not treatment; that training school superintendents did not publicize the failures of their programs by clamoring for remedies; that neither group sparked a search for alternatives, can be quickly understood. The judges were fully content with their discretionary authority. They could give probation to whomever they wished and they really had no quarrel with incarceration, since they could reserve it for the hard-core case. The superintendents, for their part, were not likely to lead a crusade against their own institutions. They had, perhaps, the best of both possible worlds, the justification that a treatment rhetoric provided and innumerable excuses for not delivering it.

The child care agencies, too, were well contented. The public training schools took over the very cases that they wished to avoid; the institutions were their back-up sanction and protection as well. As for the court, it generally respected their sectarian concerns. To be sure, conflicts did break out over who had ultimate authority over the child, the judge or the benevolent society. The agencies claimed that "the matter of the care, training and nurture of children . . . is an administrative matter, for the just and wise carrying on of which court experience is of no particular value; whereas the experience of members of the boards of managers and agencies and institutions which care for children is of the very highest value, and should not be subjected to interference by the inexpert court." On the other hand, to the court and its defenders, such as Julia Lathrop, no private organization should supersede a public body in authority. "I have no confidence," declared Lathrop, "in a theory of law which reposes greater responsibility in the agents of large unsalaried boards than in the bench." But the issue never cut so deeply that the private agencies attacked the conceptual basis of the juvenile court. In the major urban areas, in fact, the courts continued to rely on the agencies for the delivery of services. Court-appointed probation officers and court-sponsored clinics cooperated with the community's voluntary societies and depended upon them to carry out programs. In short, the agencies had far too great a stake in the court ever to lead an opposition movement.[38]

Even tough-minded officials, whether in the legislature or in the prosecutor's office, had no basic quarrels with the court, and even less with the training school. One reason was that legislation in many states permitted juvenile court judges to transfer any given case to an adult court, an allowance that they occasionally took advantage of when the charge was especially serious. The Cook County juvenile court, for example, asked grand juries to weigh the merits of a regular indictment in about fifteen cases a year — a figure which represented no more than one percent of its cases but did include the most notorious. Typically these boys were older (sixteen, not twelve) and were arrested for "deeds of violence, daring holdups, carrying guns, thefts of considerable amounts, and rape." These transfers probably muted criticism of the courts for coddling the criminal.[39]

Moreover, law-and-order-minded administrators may have recognized that juveniles tried for the less serious offenses in adult courts were likely to win sympathy votes and acquittals. The choice, in effect, was between no punishment through adult proceedings or some punishment through juvenile ones. To be sure, when in the late 1930's a state like New York considered raising the age limit for juvenile court jurisdiction from sixteen to eighteen, law enforcement groups protested and did block the move. Their testimony presented two contrasting images: the twelve-year-old who swiped apples and the seventeen- or eighteen-year-old who robbed banks. And if these fantasies prevented the juvenile court from enlarging its domain, they may also have spared it from being attacked for generating the latest crime wave.[40]

But what of the posture of those outside the system? If officials with day-to-day responsibilities found the juvenile justice system too convenient to denounce, why were the designers of the programs, the child welfare reformers, unwilling to strip juvenile courts and institutions of their legitimacy? Although they did criticize one or another practice, the gross failures in implementation never led them to reexamine first principles.

They certainly were aware of the many deficiencies. From their ranks came the most telling exposures, both in descriptions of wretched circumstances and in quantitative measurements of disappointing outcomes. Sheldon and Eleanor Glueck's investigation of the fate of *One Thousand Juvenile Delinquents* (1934) was read and reported upon so widely that no activist could have been ignorant of its findings. And what disturbing findings they were: "It is seen that *88.2 percent of our juveniles recidivated and 11.8 percent were non-delinquent during the five year post-treatment period.*" Perhaps even more discouraging, the Gluecks compared cases in which the recommendations of the Judge Baker Foundation psychiatric clinic were put into practice and cases in which they were not and concluded that implementation did not much matter. "The length of the treatment period bears a low and erratic association to the post-treatment conduct of our young delinquents. The nature of the clinical recommendation regarding the place of residence of the offenders [the most important recommendation] . . . has only a very slight association with post-treatment conduct. . . . The number of contacts which the J.B.F. clinic had with our delinquent boys after the initial examination is not significant as bearing on post-treatment conduct." So even when carried out, treatment was markedly ineffective.[41]

Other studies confirmed the Gluecks' conclusions. Alida Bowler and Ruth Bloodgood studied a random group of 632 ex-training school inmates five years after release. The findings, circulated by the Children's Bureau, were "not a record with which any institution could be satisfied." Fully 58 percent of them already had a subsequent criminal conviction. "Evaluating outcomes on a broader basis led to the conclusion that 220 (35 percent) of the 623 boys seemed to have failed entirely to make the hoped-for adjustment to community life. An additional 203 (33 percent) had achieved adjustment of such doubtful character as to make it very uncertain whether the community could count on having no further difficulty with them." So too, William Healy and Augusta

Bronner reported in *Delinquents and Criminals* on "the huge percentages of failure to check delinquent careers by treatment under the law."[42]

However widespread and acute the failures, reformers could not let go of their favorite prescriptions. Confronting the ineffectiveness of their proposals, they recited the same propositions over again. The Gluecks' response to the marginal performance of the courts and the clinics was to locate a shred of hope in the fact that "the carrying out of *all* the clinical recommendations by the Boston Juvenile Court in an individual case bears a consistent, but low, relationship to subsequent conduct." Accordingly, they recommended that the ties between the court and the clinic be tightened, that intervention occur still earlier in the delinquent's career: perhaps a larger dose of medicine delivered quicker would produce better results. At the same time, the Gluecks' study so stunned a group of Massachusetts citizens that they made it the focus of a task force investigation. The ensuing report called for establishing a "treatment board" to assist the court in carrying out the recommendations of the clinics. Also, the committee "by no means discards the institution but . . . would bring the institution back to its original idea of education and training on a consistent plan." Again, the thought was that more of the same would work where less had not.[43]

In this spirit, Bowler and Bloodgood interpreted their negative findings to "indicate the necessity to individualize treatment plans and to adapt them to the requirements of each boy as discovered through study by properly qualified persons." The institutions should upgrade educational programs, emphasize "training aspects" in vocational work, conduct "an intensive study of . . . disciplinary features," and redesign the cottage program to teach lessons "that might carry over into life after release." And although no single organization more consistently described the failures of the juvenile justice system than the Children's Bureau, when it came time to publicize "Facts about Juvenile Delinquency" the Bureau concluded that institutions had a vital role to play. They should "provide an environment in which the child may lead a regular, fully occupied, wholesome life" and "give each child special study and assistance in meeting his own personal and social problems." Repeat the maxims enough times and perhaps they would be realized. Finally, the White House Conference report on the Delinquent Child concluded that the juvenile courts "are concerned to remedy the underlying conditions and set the child free for responsible living" — as though the courts could do this job. The report took several pages to describe the duties of probation officers — as though they really had the time to visit the family, the teacher, and the employer, or had the conceptual ability to analyze the data and evolve a treatment program. At the institutions, "the cottage father and mother, the teacher in the classroom, the leader on the playground and the instructor in charge of the work squad form the keystone of the institutional arch" — as though they had the credentials or even the inclination to rehabilitate the inmate.[44] In sum, one searches in vain for any thorough reappraisal of the Progressive ideology or any coherent effort to review reform postulates in light of their marginal relationship to actual practices.

It is difficult to trace this record without some impatience and disappointment. Our predecessors should have known better. But rather than second-guess them, it is appropriate to analyze why they remained so dedicated to their principles, so unwilling to entertain self-doubt. In part, it may be inevitable that reformers become partisans, unable to examine the outcome of their efforts. In part, child welfare advocates (like criminal justice reformers) were frightened that the obvious alternatives to their design would generate even worse abuses. However inadequate the juvenile institutions, the prisons were worse.

The past was so bleak and so lacking in humanitarian spirit, that to undermine the Progressive program would be to return to barbarism. When William and Dorothy Thomas described the many inadequacies of juvenile institutions in the 1920's, they proceeded to quote a 1642 Connecticut statute that called for capital punishment for children who would "curse or smite their natural Father or Mother," for any girl over fourteen convicted of incest, and for any boy over fifteen convicted of sodomy. The Thomases' conclusion seemed to them irrefutable:

"In comparison with these historical situations even the institutions to which we have just referred seem very advanced." In similar tones, Miriam Van Waters, an ardent proponent of the juvenile court system, was also prepared to argue that either our "society will continue to 'try out' humanitarian theories . . . or else medieval darkness will again sweep our courts and institutions." This special reading of history was a major barrier to social experimentation.[45]

Reformers did have one last defense: how could anyone condemn their principles or search for alternatives when their recommendations had never been truly implemented? Failures reflected not faulty conceptualization but inadequate funding. Hence it was appropriate to call for more clinics, better probation officers, smaller cottages, and better trained house parents. "Juvenile probation in Illinois has never been given a fair chance," noted one proponent. Or, as a committee chaired by John D. Rockefeller III concluded, if only the size of institutions were reduced, then treatment would become effective. For her part, Miriam Van Waters was certain that "knowledge far outruns practice. There is no longer reasonable doubt that delinquency could be checked, practically eliminated from the normal population, if a sufficient number of social workers would dedicate their lives to application of scientific knowledge of behavior we now possess." Put knowledge into practice and the Progressive ideals would be accomplished.[46]

All of these contentions had a point. Given the many flaws in implementation, there was no shortage of corrective measures that might be adopted, and then perhaps rehabilitation would occur. And Progressives were entitled to believe that only an ethic of rehabilitation could dampen the spirit of retribution. The points certainly were fair — but they did not reach to the heart of the problem, to the tension between punishment and treatment. How condemn a court's casual indifference to the child when it claimed to be helping him? How condemn the severity of an institution when it purported to be acting in the child's best interest? But these were issues that could not be raised on the Progressive agenda.

IV

The World of Mental Health

CHAPTER NINE

Civic Medicine

THE TRANSFORMING QUALITY of Progressive ideology brought a new orientation and design to the field of mental health. Just as reformers altered traditional views and policies toward the criminal and the delinquent, so they revised inherited definitions of the etiology of insanity and programs to combat it. Indeed, the new orientations were so much a part of Progressivism that psychiatrists themselves, as well as their lay supporters who championed these innovations, are best understood within the context of the movement. To be sure, they were graduates of medical schools instead of social science departments, they were trained in hospitals instead of settlement houses, and they used scientific jargon instead of sociological jargon. But these differences should not blur the crucial character of the underlying similarities in outlook and goals. The crusading psychiatrists were as much Progressives as they were doctors.

Well into the 1890's, the asylum continued to dominate, really monopolize, the system. The medical superintendents had charge of the top floors of the institution, giving their time over to questions of management, to determining the optimal ways to provide custodial care to the chronic patients. The neurologists, at best, had charge of a few basement laboratories, devoting their energies to questions of pathology, to analyzing the lesions uncovered in examination of tissues. But whether locked behind laboratory doors or confined behind asylum walls, the study and the care of the insane went on in isolation. Only a handful of doctors were concerned with mental illness and their administration and research had a narrow and exclusive quality about it. Then, beginning in the first two decades of the twentieth century, a profound reaction occurred. Psychiatric reformers set out to explore the causes of insanity through the individual history of the patient and his development within the family and community. At the same time, they designed new facilities, the outpatient clinic (for periodic consultations) and the psychopathic hospital (for intensive, short-term treatment). Finally, they looked to educate the general public to the principles of mental hygiene, aiming not only to cure but to prevent mental illness.

In mental health, as in crime and delinquency, Progressives shared a grand sense of mission. Unlike their post–Civil War counterparts, they were not content with custodial care for the chronic patient. Their goals were much more ambitious: to effect a massive reduction in insanity. Many psychiatrists now stood ready to extend their reach into the community, to go out from the asylum into the society.

The first impetus for this program came from the continuing decline of the reputation of institutions for the insane. Whatever glimmer of hope for cures superintendents had been able to offer in the 1870's and 1880's had almost disappeared in the 1890's. To make matters worse, other physicians and concerned citizens were beginning to look at the asylum with the model of the general hospital in mind; if one group of doctors was making notable progress with the physically ill, why could not another group make progress with the mentally ill? The contrast between hospital and asylum did not serve the superintendents well, and by the close of the nineteenth century, a substantial number of critics were impatient with the institutions' monopoly over the care of the insane.

No one better expressed this position than S. Weir Mitchell in his lecture to the medical superintendents at their 50th annual meeting in 1894. That the superintendents invited him to address them on so notable an anniversary indicated the extent of their own unease. Mitchell, trained as a neurologist, was on record as a critic of asylum conditions. To the degree that his audience had almost requested a jeremiad, it was not disappointed. Mitchell's attack was as devastating as it was accurate. And lest anyone think his view idiosyncratic, he bolstered his position with thirty letters from colleagues.

From Mitchell's perspective, the asylum had lost all purpose. It was inadequate as a custodial setting, a total failure as a rehabilitative institution, and altogether dismal as a teaching or training place. It lacked, in short, any basis of justification. Asylum superintendents, like so many other institution heads, had shuffled between claims of custody and rehabilitation; between claims of restraining the dangerous and caring for the senile on the one hand, and curing the insane on the other. To Mitchell, both claims were sham. Custody simply would not suffice; doctors could not rest content with such a function, and medical superintendents did, after all, claim to be doctors. Providing nothing more than custodial care inevitably meant that the discipline could not make scientific progress. "Compared with the splendid advance in surgery," noted Mitchell, "the alienist had won in proportion little." Superintendents had charge of 91,000 patients, but had taught the profession nothing. "Where," Mitchell demanded of them, "are your annual reports of scientific study, of the psychology and pathology of your patients? . . . Want of competent original work is to my mind the worst symptom of torpor the asylums now present." And the superintendents had only themselves to blame. The problem was not a shortage of funds, but a shortage of nerve and imagination. "You quietly submit to having hospitals called asylums; you are labelled as medical superintendents, and some of you allow your managers to think you can be farmers, stewards, caterers, treasurers, business managers and physicians." How absurd: "You should urge in every report the stupid folly of this." So long as "you shall conduct a huge boarding house — what has been called a monastery of the mad," you will be unable "to move with the growth of medicine, and to study your cases, or add anything of value to our store of knowledge." Doctors had to be something more than superintendents.[1]

Mitchell went on to suggest that they had not even done a good job at providing custodial care. Asylums were by no means superior to almshouses. "Your too constantly locked doors and barred windows," he charged, are "but reminder relics of that dismal system. . . . I presume that you have, through habit, lost the sense of jail and jailor which troubles me when I walk behind one of you and he unlocks door after door. Do you think it is not felt by some of your patients?" Further, the asylums still relied upon restraints, perhaps reluctantly, but nevertheless frequently. And boards of managers charged to oversee institutions were useless. "I have seen hospitals," declared Mitchell, "that smelled and looked like second-class lodging houses, and have found their managers serenely contented."

The prospect of achieving cure under such conditions was totally illusory. Mitchell would not allow asylum keepers to hide behind the notion that the routine or environment of an institution could be rehabilitative. It was nothing more than a "superstition" that "an asylum is in itself curative." "You have for too long maintained the fiction," Mitchell told his audience "that there is some mysterious therapeutic influence to be found behind your walls and locked doors. We hold the reverse opinion and think your hospitals are never to be used save as a last resort. . . . Upon my word, I think asylum life is deadly to the insane."

Mitchell blamed the isolation of the asylum for this grim state of affairs. "You were the first of specialists and you have never come back into line," he argued. "You soon began to live apart, and you still do so." In effect, superintendents had cut themselves off from the medical profession. "Your hospitals are not our hospitals; your ways are not our ways." In what was perhaps the cruelest remark in a speech filled with hostility, Mitchell asked the asylum heads to get out of the asylum, to seek the "fresh air of the outer world," for they had become more like their patients than their colleagues: "I cannot see how with the lives you lead, it is possible for you to retain the wholesome balance of the mental and moral faculties."[2]

Yet Mitchell, like the neurologists of the 1870's and 1880's, had little to substitute for the asylum beyond a general charge to superintendents to behave like doctors. He closed his speech with a sketch of his "ideal hospital" which was not very different in organization and structure from the designs that medical superintendents themselves had been offering for fifty years: "It is near to a city . . . vine covered . . . [has] farm and vegetable garden." Mitchell did want more research, more teaching, more reports, more visits from neurologists, and better trained nurses. But something other than shortage of time forced him to declare: "Of treatment I say no word."[3] In effect, Mitchell was brilliantly capable of tearing down every prop that medical superintendents could construct for the perpetuation of their institutions. But he did not have much to offer in substance of his own. The day of the traditional asylum may have been passing, but it was unclear what would come in its place.

A number of medical superintendents did attempt to counter the attack, but invariably their responses were weak and, from Mitchell's perspective, totally predictable. Some claimed to have made these same points themselves, as if such a concession in any way reduced the weight of the charges. Others defended the custodial function, taking refuge in the role of caretaker to the chronic. "How best and cheapest to provide for the wants of the insane in State institutions," insisted superintendent Walter Channing, "is still the first question." Waving what was the bloody shirt of the psychiatrists, the miserable state of the insane in almshouses, Channing argued that "the medical superintendent, whatever he may wish to be, is essentially an executive officer. . . . His real specialty is insane-hospital management . . . giving rest and succor to as many of a wretched and neglected class as a niggardly and ignorant public will allow." The insane were "his helpless children," for whom he would provide "a good, clean bed to sleep in; good, nourishing food to eat; clean clothing to wear; a neat place to stay in day and night." Concluded Channing: "Scientific men, put in charge of institutions, are apt to be failures. . . . Custodial care is both delicate and exacting."[4]

Other asylum keepers described the insane as exceptionally violent, justifying themselves in the role of policemen. Mitchell might ask for pretty flower beds at the entrance to his ideal institution, but "a violent and destructive maniac" was certain to be "tearing to pieces his flower-beds, shattering his painted vases, breaking his bicycles, and using the croquet balls and mallets to . . . molest the peace and endanger the personal safety of fellow patients." Mitchell's visions were utopian. In the real world, mechanical restraints like "neat canvas muffs" were necessary to asylum care; experienced asylum superintendents knew that moral suasion was too weak to keep order. The insane "tend to deeds of violence, homicide, or suicide. . . . An insane being can no more resist an inclination to destroy flower vases . . . or keep from striking an attendant . . . than he can control . . . or stop the spasms of strychnine poison."[5]

Finally, medical superintendents argued that ultimately no one could cure the insane because no one knew how. Neither neurologists nor physicians could effect rehabilitation; like it or not, one had to "preclude the possibility of basing our therapeutics upon a highly scientific rationale." The best advice a superintendent could follow was to "make haste slowly."[6]

A still more dramatic outcry against the asylum appeared in 1907 in the autobiography of Clifford Beers, *A Mind That Found Itself*. An expose of institutional conditions by an ex-inmate was not in itself original; from the 1850's on, personal accounts of being forcibly committed to an insane asylum by greedy relatives, and suffering horrible indignities, appeared almost regularly. But Beers's book was different; both the public and the academic community paid it special attention. No less a figure than William James encouraged Beers to publish the manuscript and then endorsed it; the book sold well, going through four editions within ten years. "You have handled a difficult theme with great skill," declared James in a letter that served as an introduction, "and produced a narrative of absorbing interest to scientist as well as layman. It reads like fiction, but it is not fiction; and this I state emphatically."[7]

The warm reception accorded Beers's book did reflect the widespread popularity of muckraking accounts in the Progressive era. Here was one more instance of hidden evils that deserved publicity; the shame of the institutions matched the shame of the cities. The book was also exceptionally well written, lacking any shrillness of tone. Beers did not deny that he was ill or that he needed treatment. In fact, the power of his analysis rested precisely in his candid admission that he was sick but that the asylum did nothing to help him. With sensitivity and insight, Beers was able to explain why this was so.

Taking his own case history as evidence, Beers skillfully described how the behavior of the insane followed an internal logic. Seemingly bizarre or unpredictable responses were part of a system, delusional to be sure, but nevertheless consistent. Beers recalled, for instance, that he would not swallow a medicated sugar tablet because "that innocuous sugar disc to me seemed saturated with the blood of loved ones." The asylum staff, however, rather than understanding his fears, interpreted the refusal "as deliberate disobedience," deserving punishment. Indeed, the ward staff were the obvious villains in Beers's story. He would often hear "the dull thud of blows" on an inmate, "the cries for mercy until there was no breath left the man with which he could beg even for his life." Anyone vaguely familiar with asylums recognized the accuracy of Beers's comment that "the attendants seemed to think their whole duty to their closely confined charges consisted in delivering three meals a day. Between meals he was a rash patient who interfered with their leisure." However, it took an insider's knowledge to observe: "When attendants' ears become as nicely attuned to the suppliant cries of neglected patients as they now are to the summoning sound of breaking glass, many of the abuses of which I complain will cease forever to be heard of."[8]

Beers explained that the patient who was quiet, passive, and self-sufficient did not suffer the worst evils of the asylum. "My observations convinced me of an anomaly; namely, that the only patients in a hospital for the insane who are not likely to be subjected to abuse are the very ones least in need of care and treatment." Let the inmate be infirm or require assistance, then the problems began; he was "frequently abused because of that very helplessness which makes it necessary for the attendants to wait upon him." Even more reprehensible, let the inmate be violent, noisy, or troublesome, and he would end up in padded cells that left him half-frozen for days on end, or on the violent wards where the noises and the smells would constitute an "exquisite torture."[9]

Beers went on to insist that the medical superintendents were "largely responsible for the perpetuation of the dread of institutions wherein the insane are confined." As he argued: "Brutal attendants are arrant cowards. They would fear to lose their positions . . . if they were made to realize that the slightest infraction of the rules will *insure* immediate dismissal. The trouble to-day is that superintendents, generally, do not enforce rules to the point of dismissal." Moreover, "Hospital managements deliberately, wilfully, and selfishly suppress evidence which . . . would lead to the conviction of guilty attendants, and eventually to their almost complete elimination from asylums." Intent on running holding operations, they were more frightened of adverse publicity than eager to correct abuses. "Evasion of fact has become with them an unconscious art."[10]

Beers's reform agenda in *The Mind That Found Itself* reflected precisely his personal experience. Familiar with the horrors of asylum care, he wanted to upgrade asylum conditions. Certainly, he was not ready to abandon institutionalization. "Most insane persons," he contended, "are better off in an institution than out of one." The problem was how to upgrade the asylums; specifically, "The central problem in the care of the insane is the elimination of actual physical abuse." Accordingly, Beers urged better pay and better living conditions for attendants, hoping to attract a better class of persons to the job. He urged that patients have complete rights of correspondence, expecting publicity to help eliminate abuses. He admonished hospital officials and trustees to demonstrate an "honest desire" to ferret out abuses. And his single favorite solution was to abolish all reliance upon restraints, from mechanical devices to padded cells.[11]

Beers did assimilate and repeat some Progressive postulates. "Collective treatment is now the rule," he wrote. "But not until individual treatment prevails will the ratio of recoveries . . . progress." For the insane, as for the dependent and delinquent, "a uniform mode of living . . . is not at all conducive to their well-being. In many instances this machine-like existence has been the death of patients." And Beers, too, relied upon a medical model to validate his point. "Does any one believe that twenty patients, ill with typhoid fever, should, for an indefinite period, be given the same kind of medicine and the same kind of food at the same hour each day?" He also advocated better provision of care for the insane upon their discharge into the community. He applauded the early efforts of Louisa Schuyler in New York to provide after-care services to ex-inmates, believing that many patients were forced to remain incarcerated because of the indifference or hostility of their relatives. He even called for a change in public attitudes so as not to restrict employment opportunities for ex-inmates. But all in all, Beers's focus in 1907 was still very much on improving conditions in the asylum, on making institutions for the insane more comfortable and less brutal places. He urged the formation of national and local societies to work to this goal, and was optimistic about its realization. "I have criticized with a considerable, yet merited, severity, our State Hospitals for the Insane," he concluded. "Nevertheless, these two hundred and odd hospitals, erected at a cost to the Nation of over one hundred millions of dollars, constitute the nucleus of what will, in time — if rightly managed — become the most perfect hospital system in the world."[12]

Thus a keen dissatisfaction with institutional conditions might well stimulate reform, but not necessarily of a sort that would move away from asylum walls. Beers's response was not atypical: for all his unhappiness with the lack of humane and rehabilitative treatment within the asylum he could not, at least at the outset, conceive of another system. Rather, it took a second, and very

different impulse, to channel reform energies in a new direction.
Both in the context of Beers's career and in the history of the
movement as a whole, it was Adolf Meyer who led the turn
"away from mere reform of psychiatric hospitals and mainly official legislative investigation" to a new program, that of mental
hygiene.

Adolf Meyer not only coined the term "mental hygiene" but,
more than any other single figure, defined and popularized its
principles. Although his own upbringing and training was certainly by American standards highly idiosyncratic, still his route
to the mental hygiene movement was far more common among
psychiatrists than one might at first imagine. The son of a Swiss
Zwinglian minister and the nephew of a practicing physician,
Meyer early decided on a medical career; he studied first in
Switzerland, later in France and England, then migrated to the
United States in 1903 to head up the Kankakee, Illinois, asylum.
Upon arrival there, Meyer still considered himself more a neurologist than a psychiatrist; but "sooner than expected" his interest
shifted. Meyer, like many other American psychiatrists, became
impatient with the narrow, materialistic, purely physiological
orientation of neurologists toward insanity. The examination of
tissues did not seem a promising enough method for exploring
mental disorder. Meyer, comfortable with traditional philosophical categories, faulted neurologists for being too Cartesian, too
committed to a dualism between mind and body, which in their
case meant neglect of the mind for the body. He, on the other
hand, was determined to strike a balance, to investigate the
"interaction" of mind and body. "We sense," declared Meyer, "a
complete person with flesh and blood, a product of growth,
cerebrally and functionally integrated." One had to adopt a
pluralistic attitude toward the individual, not simply the "aggres-
sively agnostic materialism" of the neurologist, but what Meyer
called a "psychobiological" approach.[13]
In his eagerness to give mind a place where only tissue had
reigned, Meyer focused more on the role of psychology than
biology in the etiology of mental disease. "If too much dissection

into sensations and neurons gets the facts too far from life, why not turn to the events that *are* life, a specific kind of order of meaningful function that will make experience telling and effective?" He certainly did not deny the importance of biological considerations, but in the end, he came down far more emphatically on the side of the mind.

Meyer's efforts to distinguish himself from the neurologists still left him with the problem of taking on two other schools, the one traditional, the other pathbreaking. First, if he wished to explore the mind, wherein would his methods differ from the customary analyses of medical superintendents, who had insisted all along that social causes were more important than lesions in accounting for insanity? Second, and this question became more and more pressing over the first decades of the twentieth century, if he wished to explore the mind, would he follow the new Freudian model and investigate the role of the unconscious? Meyer answered with an attempt to construct his own system. He would be more scientific than either of these two camps. Where they were either overgeneral or hypothetical, he would be faithful to rigorous and precise observations.

Like so many other Progressives, Meyer sought to discover the roots of deviant behavior in the intensive analysis of "the facts of the case." The first duty for the psychiatrist (as for the probation officer and the juvenile court judge) was to examine each individual closely so as to let the facts emerge, to allow the particularities of each history to assume a logical structure. Meyer's approach did amount to a belief that the facts would speak for themselves, and he was not insensitive to charges of intellectual naivete. Nevertheless, he insisted that alternative methods were worse. "Unsystematized information," he conceded, "is useless, and the question arises whether it is not necessary to take the students [of psychiatry] very much further into detailed studies à la Freud and others." His response was a firm no. For one thing, this was not the way he liked to investigate phenomena. "I personally prefer to remain on the ground of those facts with which I am likely to be forced to work"; delving into the unconscious was far too mysterious and abstract an exercise for him.

For another, the Freudian approach to the unconscious and the neurological focus on lesions both put construct before data, hypothesis before evidence, and therefore forced the material of each case into a prearranged formula. "If we are imbued with the idea that there necessarily must be something inherently wrong in taking facts *as* we find them, or at least *can* find them at *work*, and that we must speak of some manoeuvres of a reality-shy 'unconscious' or some hypothetical lesion or chemical findings, in order to give them respectability, we may consider the working with the facts of the case futile." But if psychiatrists were not reality-shy, they would be able to expose the "natural" links among facts, and thus understand the causes of insanity. "If we allow the facts to appear in their natural connections," insisted Meyer, "we shall much more definitely keep on a ground of actualities representing the facts rather than on the ground of a hypothetical tune or incantation habitually sung to satisfy appearances of a diagnostic and prognostic skill." Briefly put, other investigators either were too sloppy (the medical superintendents) or hid behind intimidating but artificial constructs (the Freudians or the neurologists). He, Meyer, would ultimately be able to discover more than any of them.[14]

As befits a man who incessantly presented facts as objective in and of themselves and the links among them as natural, Meyer unabashedly labeled his approach commonsensical. Others might call it crude and unscientific. But Meyer doggedly insisted that "the first step in a course of psychology for medical students is to restore in them the course of common sense." Rather than introduce them to psychiatry through the unconscious, it was best to teach them to compose "what I call the life chart." The chart would help them to evaluate the individual's psychological assets, to analyze the conditions under which they would fail, and to devise ways to strengthen them. "You can readily see," Meyer declared, "that we are dealing with absolutely objective and positive facts," that "we keep on the ground of common sense."[15]

With much pride, Meyer presented a sample life chart. On its left border was the year; on the right border, the patient's age, and between them were the facts of the case. The life chart of a case of invalidism reported that in 1891, when the patient was six years old, her headaches began. At age seven she started private school; at age eleven she had typhoid, and at age twelve repeated the fifth grade. At age thirteen, she had headaches, "partly menstrual, partly reactive." She married at age eighteen; at nineteen, she lost her first child. At twenty she suffered "complications of sex life," at twenty-three, the "indifference of husband;" she also complained about her heart and feelings of depression and exhaustion. At age twenty-four, the chart noted, "Growing invalidism. Need of sympathy." At age twenty-seven, "Invalidism; mostly in bed"; operation for an appendectomy; at twenty-eight, removal of ovaries and "exhaustion; pressure in head; marked fatigability . . . numbness on left side . . . poor sleep." At thirty, with "menstrual headaches," she entered an asylum. To Meyer, the construction of this record was not merely the first step, the case history preceding an examination, but the crucial step. Here was "the objective practical procedure of modern psychopathological studies," demonstrating "how simply, controllably, and suggestively the facts can be brought into a record."[16]

Much of Meyer's confidence in the value of a fact-oriented approach, as well as his readiness to differentiate his method from others, reflected his definition of the cause of insanity (most typically, although not exclusively) as "maladaptation." He calculated that 10 percent of asylum admissions resulted from general paralysis following venereal disease; another 20 percent were a consequence either of alcoholism or "disorders with a plainly bacterial or toxic non-mental factor as the exciting link." But "at least thirty percent of the admissions seem to make up a group of disorders of the more *personal*, instinctive adjustments involving a miscarriage of instincts through lack of balance." This 30 percent were the schizophrenics, victims of a disease that was "peculiarly liable to lead to permanent collapse." To Meyer, the majority of these cases were "the inevitable and natural development from a deterioration of habits . . . [due] in part, at least, to the clashing of instincts and to progressively faulty modes of meeting difficulties. The patient . . . comes to react to the difficulties of life in ways which are bound to vitiate the life of the

brain." Hence, the psychiatrist had to study the patient's particular responses, his adaptive and maladaptive reactions. In this
way, "psychiatry is no longer limited to being our brother's
keeper, but it has its definite work with each patient — and that
not merely in the form of hospital routine . . . but in the thorough
study of all the integrating factors of each individual patient's
health and problem of adjustment." Now, psychiatry could move
from custody to diagnosis and treatment. Psychiatric treatment
would become "experiments of nature," designed to offer "adequate differentiations of the disease pictures, formulate the conditions under which they occur, the essential factors at work,
and the preventive and therapeutic modifiability of both the
conditions or causes." The case study made psychiatry into a
science and a promising one too.[17]

All of these ingredients led Meyer to his novel effort to transform institutional psychiatry into "civic medicine." He was among
the first to insist that for the purposes of both diagnosis and
treatment psychiatry had to go out from behind the asylum walls.
Jacksonian medical superintendents, it is true, had agreed in the
1830's that the ultimate causes of insanity were to be found in the
environment; they too had shared a commitment to social reform.
But their critique was overarching, faulting the open-ended and
fluid organization of American society. Even more important,
their reform strategy was to teach by example, to build a model
community behind asylum walls. By the 1890's, not only had the
critique itself lost all relevance but the asylum was not a model
for anything. What Meyer did was to revive the crusading spirit
of psychiatry and point it in a new direction. "Psychiatry," he
concluded, "is a field for action."[18]

Meyer justified this expansive view in terms of the best interest
of the patient and of the wider society. The relevant facts of the
individual case had in the first instance to do with the patient's
behavior in the community, his ability or inability to cope with
daily demands. To keep the patient isolated, either in a conceptual or physical sense, was diagnostically futile and prescrip-
tively self-defeating. But the problems did not rest exclusively
with the patient. Psychiatrists had to become "concerned with

conditions at large where the mental disorders are bred." Not only was that dictum pervasive among Progressive reformers in settlement houses but among medical specialists as well. "Just as bacteriology studies the water supply and the air and food of communities, schools and homes," noted Meyer, "so we psycho-pathologists have to study more effectively the atmosphere of the community and must devise safeguards in the localities from which the patients come, and to which they are to return." Convinced that mental illness was more easily prevented than cured, Meyer wished to intervene in advance of disease, to root out the elements damaging to mental health. And such preventive measures were socially invaluable. "Much of what we need for the prevention of relapses and of new outbreaks of nervous and mental disorders is exactly what we need to make normal life tolerable and effective."[19]

Meyer's formulations helped to define the Progressive outlook. Indeed, the thrust of his message was almost indistinguishable from those of G. Stanley Hall and William Healy or for that matter of Robert Hunter and Sophonisba Breckinridge. The essential point, however, is not to draw hard and fast lines of influence (who was reading whom), but to understand how consistent the new viewpoint was, whether one applied it to poverty or crime or delinquency or mental illness. Progressives united on a case-by-case, individual approach. More, they were all devoted to the concept of civic medicine, to use Meyer's apt phrase. Tenement house reform was one aspect, municipal bureaus of health another, clinics for juvenile courts still another.

The links were so tight that a child welfare reformer like Homer Folks also composed a pamphlet for popular distribution on the subject, "Why Should Anyone Go Insane?" Folks set out to denounce sexual license and intemperance not so much for being evil, but for being unhealthy. He carefully explained that what was commonly referred to as "softening of the brain" was scientifically known as paresis, that it was an incurable disease whose source was syphilitic infection. "Every man and boy should know that by yielding to the temptation to go with immoral women he is exposing himself to the probability of getting this disease, which may result, years after, in incurable insanity. Over the door of every immoral resort might truthfully be written: 'Incurable insanity may be contracted here.'" Folks moved next to the damage inflicted by "alcohol and other poisons." "This is not a temperance tract," he insisted. "We are dealing only with scientific facts. ... Not only is the highest mental development impossible in the presence of the continued use of alcohol, but impairment of the mental faculties is likely to follow." So too, "opium, morphine, and cocaine . . . often weaken the mental powers and produce insanity." It was not virtue that was at stake but the scientific prevention of disease.[20]

No less fundamental to the popularity of Meyer's position, in terms of the number of psychiatrists who were themselves reaching similar conclusions and quoting Meyer's writings enthusiastically (such as Frederick Peterson, William Russell, Vernon Briggs, and Warren Stearns), was the fact that he had responded to the major crisis affecting the professional care of the insane. Many physicians were equally impatient with the narrowly custodial functioning of the state asylums and the lack of progress in pathology laboratories. The caretaking approach of the medical superintendents and the materialistic stance of the neurologists both seemed at a dead end, provoking an almost desperate search for new approaches to insanity. As a 1902 editorial of the *Boston Medical and Surgical Journal* said in praise of Meyer's work: "The microscope has as yet accomplished little in the solution of the fundamental questions, and the pathological laboratory, of which so much was hoped a few years ago, has not justified expectations. This is not in the least surprising; the laboratory is an essential adjunct of any hospital, but the problems to be solved do not emanate from the laboratory, but rather from the patients, for whom the laboratory exists." Meyer's ideas were welcome among professionals precisely because they gave psychiatry a way to escape from the asylum and the laboratory.[21]

Thus Progressives, be they lay or medical, with the clear urgings of Meyer translated the idea of civic medicine into a program of outreach. Novel institutions and procedures would bring psychiatric care to a larger number of people at an earlier stage in their illness; at the same time, psychiatrists would assume responsibility for elevating the mental health of the entire community. Once again, Progressive reform would promote the individual welfare and the common welfare.

In the world of mental health, the innovation that would best realize this promise was the psychopathic hospital. In Meyer's terms, it was to be "the center of the mental health work." The psychopathic hospital would administer an outpatient clinic, treating those who heretofore could have received assistance only within an asylum. Since the new clinic would be convenient to attend (patients could come for treatment during the day and then return to their homes or jobs), and without stigma (the shame of the asylum would not attach to it), more people would seek help, and seek it earlier. As a result the clinic would be able to serve the person, as Meyer put it, "that might by no means necessarily be willing to consider himself, or would not be considered by others, as sufficiently disturbed mentally to require removal to a state hospital." The new clinic also would have a higher rate of cure, because patients would enter treatment in an acute, as opposed to a chronic, state. As Meyer's fellow psychiatrist, Frederick Peterson, noted, to this "dispensary . . . will come not inconsiderable numbers of patients on the borderline of insanity for still earlier treatment." Hence, a community facility would not only alleviate lesser problems but prevent them from becoming major disabilities.[22]

The psychopathic hospital would also provide inpatient care. Some individuals required short-term confinement, perhaps because of the distress that their illness caused or because they needed a few weeks' or months' respite from a troubling environment, or because they could profit from the opportunity to begin to form new habits in a more structured setting. Accordingly, the outpatient clinic would first examine the patient and then, where appropriate, make the referral to the inpatient facility. "Early diagnosis and speedy removal to a special hospital for the insane are of paramount importance in nearly all acute psychoses," explained Peterson. "This object can be attained only through the establishment of psychiatric clinics in all our larger cities." And, of course, the psychopathic hospital would have to scrutinize admissions carefully, not accepting the chronic insane or those for whom nothing could be done. "If the clinic [psychopathic hospital] is not forced to serve mainly as another crowded reception hospital," declared Meyer, "watching helplessly the endless procession of victims without time for thorough study, our clinic will, of course, be most serviceable." He was, to be sure, somewhat uncomfortable with excluding the chronic, preferring to distinguish not so much between the "recoverable" and the "chronic" as between "those for whom something can be done (even if it is not a recovery) and those who belong to the organized boarding house." Still, however he phrased it, the psychopathic hospital was an effort to establish a dual system of care, with one place for the curable, another for the incurable.[23]

Supporters marshaled still more justifications for the program. The psychopathic hospital would serve as an excellent training and teaching center. Precisely because its clientele would be limited to "those for whom something could be done," medical students there would learn how best to effect cures. It would also broaden the knowledge of psychiatry among general practitioners. The clinic staff would teach physicians to identify the initial symptoms of mental illness so as to refer patients immediately. Further, the clinic would sponsor and carry out significant research. Its location in the community and the movement of its patients between the facility and the community would allow it to conduct what Meyer called "experiments of nature." Here was the perfect opportunity to explore both the individual and the social role in the etiology of mental illness. The clinic staff would be able to see on a daily basis what elements contributed to the recovery of patients and what elements exacerbated disease. Accordingly, Meyer and his colleagues insisted that the clinic confine its work to "well circumscribed districts in the neighborhood" in order to fulfill both its sociological and its medical mission.[24]

Should any question remain whether the aims of the psychopathic hospital justified the exclusion of the chronic insane, proponents added that the facility would lessen the shame of all forms of mental illness. It would help, pledged Meyer, "to do away with the widely spread notion of the stigma of insanity . . . by showing that any kind of mental disorder receives very intense and well-directed work." And were all this not enough, the routine of the psychopathic hospital would become a model for the state hospital. The system of care and treatment worked out in the smaller and more experimental setting would be incorporated into the larger institution.[25]

Finally, the outpatient clinic would serve as a diagnostic and referral center for many community organizations. As Dr. Douglas Thom, head of the clinic at the Boston Psychopathic Hospital, contended, it was at "the hub of the wheel." The juvenile court would properly turn to the clinic to evaluate the delinquent; school officers would rely upon its findings on the persistently truant. Welfare agencies, too, would use it for the dependent. By the time proponents had finished making their case, it was difficult to think of any social welfare organization that would not benefit from the clinic's skills.[26]

The appeal of the psychopathic hospital was without question broadly based. Settlement house workers did identify with its mission and the ties between G. Stanley Hall's child study clinics and Meyer's outpatient clinics were also close. The bonds between William Healy and Adolf Meyer were still closer. The two men met frequently at one notable gathering place for Progressive reformers, the Chicago home of Edith Dummer, a wealthy patron of social welfare programs. They shared a nearly identical orientation in their respective fields, both eschewing theory for a devotion to the facts of the case, both insisting that only an intricate analysis of the individual situation could promote understanding and treatment. As their ties indicated, changes in the field of juvenile delinquency were at one with changes in the field of mental illness.

At the same time, as Meyer himself noted, the psychopathic hospital received support from "several conflicting interests." General practitioners, he explained, welcomed the innovation for self-serving reasons: they "were glad to be rid of the neurotic," to be able to refer their troublesome cases to an outpatient clinic. The program was also attractive to psychiatrists and professors in medical schools. The clinics broke the near monopoly of medical superintendents over the care of the mentally ill. Now a new group of physicians could enter the field, bringing the practice of psychiatry in line with the practice of medicine. Both disciplines would conduct scientific research; both would work within the community. "We should never dream," declared Frederick Peterson, "of placing a general hospital for acute disorders in some remote region of the country. Why deal differently with acute disorders of the brain?" In sum, for a variety of reasons, from good conscience to convenience, from professional interest to scientific concern, the idea of the psychopathic hospital attracted staunch supporters.[27]

The second major program that recast the practice of psychiatry and the treatment of the mentally ill looked to post-institutional programs. Although a concern about the discharge and after-care of asylum inmates preceded the Progressive era, the first efforts were of such a limited character as to make clear just how novel the Progressive innovations were.

Toward the end of the nineteenth century, the idea of extra-institutional care for the insane appeared in the form of boarding-out. The aim was to provide inexpensive but decent care for the chronic and harmless insane, to move them from the asylum to local families as boarders. The practice looked back to the eighteenth century, to the way communities had usually cared for the insane before the rise of the asylum. At the same time, there was something fresh about the proposal, pointing to a disillusionment with the quality of institutional life. In 1887 the *Boston Medical and Surgical Journal* congratulated the Massachusetts Board of Lunacy for its pioneer effort to place "cases of chronic insanity, under official supervision in families." The *Journal* was confident that respectable families would assume the task, thus allaying fears of abuse and neglect. Over the next two decades, boarding-out continued to win modest support for its limited purpose. Julia Lathrop, for example, hoped that it might bring a ray of hope into otherwise bleak lives. The faces of the insane placed within a family setting, she conceded, still expressed "that melancholy with which we are familiar in every asylum." But at least "there is a placidity . . . not so often seen behind locked doors." Surely, Lathrop concluded, "the garden is a better guarantee of contentment than the jangling keys of the institution."[28]

The aims of the new Progressive after-care movement were much more ambitious. After-care looked not to the chronic but to the curable patient, not to custody but to adjustment, not to continued dependence but to independence. The movement itself went through two distinct stages. From the late 1890's until about 1910, proponents made their case mostly in terms of financial support. After 1910, they typically cast their arguments in terms of psychological support.

The initial idea of providing the discharged mental patient with assistance, in the form of a small stipend or help in locating a job, not only had an obvious logic to it but fit neatly with early Progressive concerns for the underprivileged. Most of the insane released from state institutions were indigent; worse yet, their own efforts to become self-supporting often came up against employers' reluctance to hire them. Many observers were concerned that the strain of poverty was certain to provoke relapses of insanity; and accordingly a number of doctors, like neurologists Henry Stedman and the medical superintendent Richard Dewey, together with such Progressives as Jane Addams, set out to provide financial relief.

The most notable effort, indeed the model program, was organized by the New York State Charities Aid Association. In 1906 the Association established a subcommittee on the After Care of the Insane and appointed Louisa Schuyler to head it. Schuyler had long been concerned with the dependent; she had begun her notable career in philanthropy in the 1850's as a friendly visitor for the Children's Aid Society, and over the years had worked to improve the welfare of the sick as well as the epileptic. The first after-care program of the Association followed in the tradition of the friendly visitor. It hired an agent, "trained and experienced

in work among the poor in their homes," and made the economic
well-being of the ex-patient the primary task. The Association
pledged to maintain contact with ex-patients "until they are
absorbed into the community as self-supporting, self-respecting
men and women." Relapses would be avoided not through psychiatric intervention but rather "owing to the freedom from
anxiety afforded the convalescent of knowing that upon leaving
the asylum he will be befriended, cared for and started anew
after an interval of rest."[29]

In practical terms, from 1906 to 1909, the Association and its
agent operated an employment agency. It obtained situations as
domestics for most of its women clients, obtained clerkships for
some of the men, and provided younger ex-patients with a sea-
shore holiday and a membership in a social club at a settlement
house. The Association did occasionally discuss the need for preventive work in the community, but it still conceived of such
work as providing periods of respite for those on the brink of
illness.

The turning point for the Association in particular and the after-
care movement in general came in 1909. That year the Association invited Adolf Meyer to address its annual meeting; it then
proceeded to alter its definition of purpose along his lines. The
Committee on After Care became the Committee on Prevention
and After Care; the friendly visitor began to give way to the
trained professional social worker. In phrases that echoed Meyer's
formulations precisely, the Association began to concern itself less
with economic assistance and more with psychological adjustment: "Diseases of the brain and nervous system are more closely
related to social conditions and more likely to be directly caused
by unfavorable elements in a person's environment. . . . In connection with no other disease is an understanding on the part of
the physician of the patient's previous manner of life more essential to intelligent treatment, and in no class of homes could a
social worker undertake more preventive and ameliorative work."
It went on to urge state hospitals to establish outpatient clinics,
and to encourage psychiatrists to leave asylum wards and enter
the community in order to provide after-care. Finally, and in the

best Progressive style, the Association urged that the state, not the private charities, assume primary responsibility for these tasks. The services were too essential to be left to the private sector.[30]

The transformation of the goals of the New York Association was typical of the changes in after-care across the country. These changes were so significant and widespread as to encourage the emergence of a new profession, that of social work. As soon as attention focused more on the psychological well-being than on the economic status of the ex-patient, a trained and sophisticated social worker seemed much more appropriate for after-care work than a friendly visitor or even a settlement house worker.

The social worker's responsibility made her, in design at least, an important adjunct to the psychiatrist. The social worker would monitor the ex-inmate's progress in the community, helping him to adjust to his environment and making certain that he followed the psychiatrist's prescriptions. "The doctor," explained one practitioner, "cannot treat the patient's environment itself. This is where the social service worker steps in, supplementing, extending and following up the doctor's treatment beyond the dispensary or hospital into the patient's home." This effort might well prevent the recurrence of illness; but should another crisis occur, the social worker would arrange a quick, and therefore more successful, psychiatric reintervention.[31]

The social worker was also supposed to alter the setting in which the patient took sick, thereby facilitating the patient's eventual return to the community. The social worker would make certain not only that he was "supplied with the ordinary needs of life" (that a friendly visitor could do), but that "the irritating elements which may have existed in the home prior to the mental breakdown . . . are either removed or properly modified," or that he went elsewhere. And the social worker's assignment quickly extended beyond after-care to fulfilling other needs of psychiatrists. It became the social worker's task to make certain that no relevant item in the patient's case history escaped the psychiatrist's attention. Although his own interviews would probably uncover the most critical details, still, given the importance of the facts of the case, it was crucial for the social worker to interview family and neighbors.[32]

The after-care program thus fit well into the Progressive reform movement. All the groups that promoted the psychopathic hospital and the outpatient clinic defined the goal of after-care and the means of social work as vital. So too, the similarities to probation and parole were obvious. There was a terminological resemblance; one talked of the "parole" of patients from the asylum. More, the case history that the social worker compiled resembled the pre-sentence report of the probation officer; the supervision of the ex-patient in the community was at one with the work of the probation and parole officers in "watching over" the offender. Indeed, the social work model, as we have noted, soon took hold for probation and parole.

At the same time, after-care helped to create its own most enthusiastic supporters, the social workers themselves. The psychiatric definition of tasks for social work met the needs of an emerging profession to establish its credentials. Here was a mandate that allowed the new social worker to distinguish herself from friendly visitors and gave her the edge over settlement house workers. While the old-fashioned visitor offered moralistic advice, the new worker treated mental as well as social problems and dispensed psychiatric counsel. Anyone of good heart and sentiment could serve as a settlement house worker; only someone who had received special training would know how to record a case history. Friendly visitors had no offices; settlers worked in brownstones; but social workers were located in prestigious clinics and hospitals. In sum, after-care, like the psychopathic hospital and the outpatient clinic, attracted support from a wide group of professionals and would-be professionals.

The new principles that underlay the psychopathic hospital and after-care also promoted a third program, the expansion of psychiatry's educative role. Eagerly and confidently Progressive psychiatrists set out to publicize the rules for mental health, to bring those rules to bear on personal behavior and institutional procedures. No organization better fulfilled this task than the National Committee for Mental Hygiene (NCMH). Its founding in 1909, appropriately enough, grew out of the first encounter between Clifford Beers and Adolf Meyer.

Having heard that Meyer "was the one man of all others in his special field whose support should, if possible be secured," Beers sent him the page proofs of *A Mind that Found Itself*. The two met soon after, and Meyer immediately, and successfully, set out to broaden Beers's reformist impulse to include "not only the amelioration of conditions among the insane but also the idea of prevention of mental disorder." Meyer had some trouble in coming up with a phrase that could capture the ambitious quality of his program, but after a few days he suggested to Beers the term "mental hygiene." Beers himself testified generously to the impact of Meyer's views: "If I took the initiative in the founding of the National Committee for Mental Hygiene, it was Dr. Meyer who, because of his profound knowledge of the scientific, medical and social problems involved, helped more than anyone else to place the work on a sound basis."

The sound basis was actually a careful blending of agendas, incorporating Beers's concern with institutions and Meyer's more wide-ranging interests. One of the first tasks that the NCMH performed was to conduct detailed and elaborate surveys on institutional conditions in a number of states and to present the findings and recommendations to citizens' committees and state legislatures. At the same time, the NCMH promoted the establishment of outpatient clinics and after-care programs. The "Needs of the Insane," it noted, were for "a psychopathic hospital in each of the 50 American cities of more than 100,000 population . . . [and] more careful supervision of patients after they have been discharged."[33]

The NCMH also dedicated itself to the "general dissemination of knowledge regarding the basis of mental activity and the causes and prevention of mental disorders." In New York, the Committee distributed pamphlets such as Folks's "Why Should Anyone Go Insane?" giving out some 600,000 copies within two years. It supplied local newspapers with stories about mental disorders and sent circular letters to physicians, teachers, social workers, and clergymen. And it organized public lectures, with speakers using stereopticon slides to convey their message on mental health all the more vividly.

The NCMH particularly delighted in mounting exhibits for public education. It arranged programs in Connecticut, New York, and Illinois, around the motto: "A Nation's Greatness Depends on the Efficiency of its Citizens." Posters and printed material explained that the origins of mental illness were found in "disorders of adjustment" (again Meyer's influence was obvious) and "bad mental habits." Some of these habits were hereditary in nature, stemming from "faulty mechanisms to begin with"; but others were social, emanating from "mechanisms made faulty by the bad environmental influences." Visitors learned that they should follow such "methods of prevention" as "cultivation of frank emotional attitude in general," avoidance of malnutrition and overwork, and a reduction in the "stress and strain of life." They were also encouraged to launch "a crusade" against alcoholism and syphilis.[34]

It was not only the message but the medium that made the NCMH so typically a Progressive organization. Its exhibits were very similar to those mounted, for example, by the National Child Labor Committee. Instead of Lewis Hine photographs of frail children alongside oversized machines, the NCMH presented drawings of the normal brain juxtaposed to one diseased by syphilis, and photographs of the insane dressed in rags, confined in bare, cage-like rooms, supervised by attendants who obviously resembled policemen more than physicians. Instead of charts on the number of children working and the rate of tuberculosis in their families, the NCMH supplied tables on the number of insane in institutions and the frightful cost of keeping them there. The NCMH noted that a typical state spent $32 million a year to incarcerate its insane, precisely the cost per year for the ten years that it took to build the Panama Canal. So if Americans could cut through the Isthmus, then surely . . . , which was the

1910 version of if Americans could send a man to the moon, then surely....

Only one group could consider their own interests and welfare threatened by the new doctrines, and that was, of course, the medical superintendents. Those in charge of the large state asylums certainly did bear the brunt of attack from Meyer and his supporters. Meyer considered the state institutions to be obsolete and anachronistic in organization and routine. "Any one who tries to follow the work of the hospital," insisted Meyer, "will see . . . there is no branch of medicine so little prepared to make use of all the new methods of investigation as psychiatry." And he had little difficulty in making his charges specific. Diagnosis and treatment were impossible to carry out inside the asylum. Staff turnover was too high: "A body of attendants which in some hospitals changes over four times a year is too far from utopia to even deserve the unqualified title nursing-force." Overcrowding had reached scandalous proportions, making even the most rudimentary form of patient classification impossible. Staff doctors raced through their rounds at a gallop, eager to be done with the chore. "They turned their work into mere routine," contended Meyer. Under such circumstances abuses were inevitable, and Meyer reported seeing in an asylum "one of three women in permanent isolation on one ward, in a blanket smeared with faeces with a pool of urine under the bed." And yet board investigations of asylum conditions were invariably useless. Asylum trustees identified far more closely with staff than with patients, ignoring any sign of inadequacy or abuse.[35]

For all the keen dissatisfaction with these conditions, neither Meyer nor Beers, nor any other leader in the mental hygiene movement, wanted to close down the institutions. Asylums were to be upgraded, not eliminated. In effect, they offered the medical superintendents two options. They could transform the state asylums into psychopathic hospitals, joining the mental hygiene movement as full partners; or they could administer institutions which were back-up places for the new program, offering custody to those beyond treatment.

In sloganeering terms, mental hygiene proponents like Dr. August Hoch of Bloomingdale urged medical superintendents to administer "hospitals and not mere asylums." As Meyer put it, they ought "to create a remedial rather than a merely custodial environment for the patient." State hospitals should become "centers of the mental health work of the community," administering outpatient clinics and after-care programs as well as dispensing individual treatment on the wards. Rather than remain a last resort "for cases with whom nobody likes to be associated," hospital care should become "something desirable and a privilege." Here, in other words, was an invitation from the new professionals to the medical superintendents to join with them in creating modern treatment centers.[36]

At the same time, reformers kept open the option of custodial care. For all their urging of treatment-oriented programs, they were not about to disallow the more traditional caretaker functions that state asylums were performing. After all, psychopathic hospitals could not cure all patients; advanced cases of alcoholism or paresis, for example, would not respond to treatment. There would also remain those who, despite every effort, would not come for help until their disease was too far advanced to be cured. For them, care should be provided in suburban or country settings, perhaps in large hospitals, perhaps in small colonies. Further, mental hygiene advocates foresaw the need for custodial treatment to serve eugenic purposes. Society had to confine some among the insane so as to make certain that their defects were not passed on to future generations.[37]

Probably most important, Meyer and his allies believed that the psychopathic hospital and the state hospital could coexist — more, that the work of the psychopathic hospital would be facilitated by the state hospital. Since the new facility would treat acute cases and patients who would not have entered the asylum, a back-up facility serving the chronic was necessary. The relationship between the psychopathic hospital and the asylum was to be symbiotic, not competitive. As we shall soon see, Meyer was wrong, fatefully wrong; his innovation would not be independent of the state hospital but subservient to it. But to remain for the moment in the world of reformers' rhetoric, the expectation was for coexistence and cooperation.

For that reason, the message that psychiatric reformers delivered did not disturb medical superintendents. When, in 1916, the mental hygiene advocate Owen Copp, Superintendent of the Pennsylvania Hospital for the Insane, addressed the convention of medical superintendents on the subject of "The Psychiatric Needs of a Large Community," his reception was, if anything, too generous. Copp carefully spelled out the implications of the mental hygiene movement. He spoke first about prevention of mental illness (by combating alcoholism and syphilitic infection, by early education, and by the segregation of defectives); he then moved to promote community outpatient care and after-care as representing "the psychiatric hospital idea." Copp next outlined "other aims of institutional provision," shifting from notions of cure to those of custody. Some among the insane would be "long residence patients," who should be made "happy and useful within their limitations" by placing them in colonies under medical supervision. Meanwhile "the infirm and other patients with dangerous and degenerate tendencies" were to be cared for in large state hospitals located "at some distance in the country." Finally, institutions would have to carry out "segregation as a protection of the mentally affected who are weak and neglected and as a defense of the public against present danger in the community and future menace by reproduction of their kind."[38]

This presentation was in every respect ordinary, representing nothing more than a brief outline of the principles of the new movement. Yet the medical superintendents rushed to congratulate Copp with an enthusiasm that is inexplicable unless one recognizes that Copp in particular, and mental hygiene rhetoric in general, provided medical superintendents with the very rationales for their institutions that they so desperately needed. The superintendent of the Iowa state hospital, Dr. G. H. Hill, opened the discussion by declaring: "This is the very best paper I ever heard in my life and I am old enough to have heard a great many." Hill only wanted Copp to come visit Iowa to aid in "perfecting our system of caring for the insane in state institutions."

Others echoed Hill's sentiments, with the superintendent from North Dakota resolving that Copp's paper receive the official endorsement of the association.[39]

Some superintendents committed themselves, at least in rhetorical terms, to the goal of treatment. One Indiana psychiatrist insisted: "We must make our institutions psychiatric centers which reach out into the community and by advice and treatment prevent many mental upsets and the necessity of many commitments to the institutions." Dr. James May, head of Boston State, repeated these sentiments: "The purely custodial care of mental diseases has led to a dread of asylums on the part of the public. There are unfortunately too many hospitals that are asylums in everything but name." He urged that state institutions transform themselves into psychopathic hospitals and psychiatric clinics: "The institutions must be such that they will be looked upon by the community not merely as a place to which the insane may be sent for final disposition, but as hospitals where the development of mental diseases may be prevented and where recoveries may be reasonably expected. . . . This should be the principal object of the state hospital of the future."[40]

Other medical superintendents were more comfortable with the idea of a custodial function, with responsibility for long-term institutional care. This was, let it be clear, not an unrespectable choice. The National Committee for Mental Hygiene itself linked a concern for the mental health and efficiency of the community directly to the diagnosis and segregation of the constitutionally inferior. The NCMH exhibits included charts on the numbers of mental defectives in the United States (33,000 retarded were in institutions and 166,000 others were not), to the point that more confinement of the retarded was in the national interest. In fact, in 1917 and 1918, under a grant from the Rockefeller Foundation, the Committee undertook special studies in several states to detect the extent of retardation. The results of such surveys were intended "to lead people in the community to provide the best kind of continuous institutional care for the feeble-minded and to see to it that they are given such care." And NCMH leaders even promoted the outpatient clinics by contending that the facilities would be especially useful for diagnosing cases of feeble-mindedness and locating what otherwise might remain a hidden menace.[41]

If such attitudes permeated the most Progressive of mental health organizations, the NCMH, it is apparent just how easily mental hospital superintendents could adopt a custodial rationale. Confinement of the hard-core case was as sufficient a program for the mental hospital as for the prison. Just as wardens could claim that the minor offenders were on probation and the rehabilitated inmates on parole, leaving them only with the dangerous, so medical superintendents could now insist that the treatable were in the clinics or in the psychopathic hospitals, and that they were left with the back-ward, chronic, essentially untreatable cases. Hence, superintendents in good conscience could pledge to house the hopelessly insane and defective, without distinguishing very carefully between the two. Apparently, reformers and superintendents each had their respective domains. The problem, however, was that in practice coexistence did not operate so neatly. Institutional needs were in conflict with the new programs — and institutional needs invariably won out.

CHAPTER TEN

The Enduring Asylum

NOWHERE WAS THE GAP between Progressive ambitions and day-to-day realities greater than in the field of mental health. When one looks to accomplishments, the record is meager even by standards of criminal and juvenile justice. In probation, parole, and juvenile courts, the critical question is why the letter of the law survived without the spirit. In mental health the question moves back one step: why were proposals for change so rarely put into effect? The issue is not so much the distortion of aims as the failure even to establish the new programs. In the years 1900–1940, neither the insane nor their doctors returned to the community.

This blunt statement carries not only a descriptive but an analytic import. To understand the minimal success of outpatient clinics or psychopathic hospitals or after-care measures, one must confront the asylum and its residents, the chronic insane. Mental hygiene proponents were eager not to abolish asylums but to restrict them to a back-up and secondary role. The major concern of the mental health system was to be the treatment of acute cases within the new community facilities. Reality, however, did not fulfill their expectations. The asylum never lost its centrality and its needs shaped the outcome of all reform ventures.

The fate of the psychopathic hospital at once reveals the priorities that ruled in public policy. More than any single innovation in mental health, the psychopathic hospital carried the burden of reform; and yet only a handful of these hospitals came into existence. The first one opened at Ann Arbor (affiliated with the University of Michigan) in 1909; soon, psychopathic hospitals appeared in Boston, Chicago, New York, Denver, and Baltimore. But at no time before World War II were there over a dozen such places. Even more critical, the psychopathic hospitals became the handmaidens of the asylums. Rather than fulfill the ambitious programs of mental hygiene, they satisfied the narrow aims of the state institutions.

The course of events at Boston Psychopathic is an apt and not atypical case in point. In 1911, the Massachusetts State Board of Insanity, persuaded by Adolf Meyer's arguments, successfully urged on the legislature the creation of such a facility. The first function of the psychopathic hospital, the Board explained, was to "receive all classes of mental patients for first care, examination and observation." Its inpatient service would then "provide short, intensive treatment of incipient, acute and curable insanity. Its capacity would be small, not exceeding such requirement." In contrast to the asylum, it would be a hospital ranking with "the best general and special hospitals . . . in any field of medical science." Moreover, the new institution would provide clinical instruction to medical students ("who would thus be taught to recognize and treat mental disease in its earliest stages, where curative measures avail most"). It would also conduct an outpatient clinic (giving "free consultation to the poor and such advice and medical treatment as would . . . promote the home care of mental patients"). Finally, it would promote research through "the clinical study of patients on the wards and scientific investigation in well-equipped laboratories." Boston Psychopathic, in other words, would have nothing to do with custodial care — it was to be advancing "cure and prevention."[1]

Nevertheless, from its moment of creation as a ward within the Boston State Hospital (1912), through its subsequent development as a separate institution (after 1921), the facility could not carry out this mandate. The inpatient department, to begin with this aspect, did not provide systematic, let alone effective treatment of the acute insane. It was not that Boston Psychopathic became one more storehouse for the chronic insane, indistinguishable from the state institutions. Rather it turned into a "diagnostic center," or more accurately put, a first stop on the road to the state hospital. Boston Psychopathic examined patients and offered a recommendation — it did not make a sustained effort to treat or to cure. In this sense, it was much less like a hospital than like a prison reception center.

In part, this development reflected the prevailing strengths and weaknesses of psychiatric knowledge — or lack of knowledge. As we shall see later in more detail, the available treatments for insanity were crude, at best capable of calming a patient, but unable to attack the disease itself. Under such circumstances, even the best-trained psychiatrists, like those at Boston Psychopathic, were, predictably, more willing to attach labels than to try to conduct therapy. They were more eager to make referrals than to deliver treatment.

But in part, too, the issue transcended the skills of psychiatry and involved broader social considerations: specifically, the ways in which families, judges, and legislators preferred to handle cases of insanity. The fate of Boston Psychopathic was tied to the operation of commitment laws, the mechanisms by which someone suspected of being insane was confined, against his will if need be, to a state institution. Ever since the 1870's, commitment laws had posed difficult and complicated policy problems. In the pre–Civil War period, the widespread belief in the ability of the asylum to cure the insane made the issue of commitment procedures appear simple; the promise of effective treatment seemed to obviate the need for procedural protections. Then, as superintendents in the post–Civil War decades reduced their claims of cures and as horror stories about institutional conditions grew more prevalent, many jurisdictions began to impose more stringent requirements. Massachusetts, for example, demanded that a certificate of insanity be signed by two doctors and that a court hearing take place, with a judicial finding that the individual was insane. Some states, like Illinois, even insisted upon a jury trial before allowing involuntary commitment.[2]

The Progressive reformers, sharing the optimism of their Jacksonian predecessors, also shared their impatience with procedural barriers to quick and simple commitment. From their perspective, there was no reason why a doctor who wished to treat a mentally ill patient should have to satisfy numerous legal stipulations that his colleague who wished to treat a physically ill patient did not. To equate commitment with deprivation of liberty for the insane seemed to make as little sense as equating hospitalization with deprivation of liberty for the tubercular. The entire thrust of the mental hygiene movement, after all, was to make insanity into a disease like all others, to make asylums into hospitals and psychiatrists into doctors — and hence it seemed unfair, punitive, and retrogressive to single out mental illness for special restrictions.[3]

Under the press of these arguments, the Massachusetts legislature, like many others, enacted a series of laws designed to simplify the commitment process. The legislature could not abandon all procedural requirements; the stigma that the insane asylum continued to bear was too powerful to permit that. But it could and did establish alternate modes of commitment that substantially eased the placement of a patient in a mental hospital. In 1909 the legislature enacted a "temporary commitment" statute, so that someone believed to be mentally ill could be confined for observation and treatment for seven days (in 1911, it became ten days) without a court finding of actual insanity; a guardian or a police officer or a member of the Board of Health could obtain this temporary commitment order from a judge by submitting a certificate signed by one physician. At the expiration of the period, the hospital would either release the patient or go through regular court channels to obtain a formal and permanent commitment. The Massachusetts State Board of Insanity was proud of its role in winning this new legislation. "A total of 1,705 persons," it boasted in 1915, "secured the benefits of treatment in our public or private hospitals for the insane without the formality of a procedure before a judge, which would have been attended with delays, legal exactions, semi-publicity and the stigma of having been pronounced insane, all of which was thus obviated, to the comfort and satisfaction of the patients and friends."[4]

Commitment laws, it turns out, follow Gresham's law. Just as soft currency will drive out hard currency, so simple procedures will drive out more complex ones. Temporary commitment quickly became the preferred route into the mental hospital, so much preferred that it soon affected the entire operation of Boston Psychopathic. The founders of that institution were enthusiastic about the temporary commitment statute, believing it fit perfectly with their desire to carry out "short, intensive treatment." What they did not anticipate, however, was that the temporary commitment order would become the most attractive and convenient method of committing all insane, chronic as well as acute, to the state's mental hospitals. The State Board of Insanity had expressly defined the first purpose of Boston Psychopathic as the examination and observation of "all classes" of patients; but the Board, according to the institution's first director, had not really meant "all," but rather, all "except to that class of patients which can and should be committed under the regular law." In other words, the psychopathic hospital was not to admit the chronic and obvious cases of mental illness; those could go directly to the state hospital. It was to examine and treat the borderline case or the acute case, where the diagnosis was difficult or the disease was not so crippling as to require long-term confinement in a mental hospital. Boston Psychopathic, in short, was designed for the curable insane, not the incurable.[5]

The widespread use of the temporary commitment statute for all types of mental illness undercut that original mission of the Boston Psychopathic. Families and physicians found it especially convenient to bring their patients to the institution under this order, regardless of the state or prognosis of the illness. The facility was located in the city, not the countryside; its image as a hospital reduced, at least somewhat, the stigma of confinement; patients may well have objected less to a temporary initial commitment to such a place. In all, the first step to permanent hospitalization could be accomplished with a minimum of fuss and trouble. As the director of the Boston institution well appreciated: "The special role of a psychopathic hospital, its close affiliation with the general hospital, the absence of the large accumulation of chronic patients, make it easier for a patient to accept the suggestion of admission to a psychopathic hospital than . . . to a large hospital for mental disorders." Moreover, "to send the patient to a large state hospital at an early stage of a mental disorder often seems to the family a rather drastic step. The family accepts more readily admission to a psychopathic hospital; should the patient have to go later to a state hospital for continued treatment, the relatives feel that the step has been taken after due consideration and a thorough diagnosis."[6]

The sympathetic tone of these remarks makes it evident that the administrators would do little to interfere with this process. Although they had the statutory authority to refuse admission to any patient whom they considered inappropriate, they rarely exercised it. They did complain periodically about "the employment of our hospital as a mere vestibule to the custodial institutions, a tendency somewhat easy for physicians to slide into under the operation of Chapter 395" (the new temporary commitment law); and they did occasionally send circulars to physicians requesting them to commit the chronic patients directly to state hospitals. But these efforts were without effect. The director conceded that "it has not been easy to put a stop to the practice of sending obviously commitable cases into the State institutions by this [temporary commitment to Boston Psychopathic] route." In fact, the members of "the medical profession and of the community in general, accept this as the main role of the hospital."[7]

Confronted with this distortion of their purpose, the administrators of Boston Psychopathic would not take a tough stand on admissions policy. They would not restrict themselves to accepting only the non-chronic cases so as to make the facility into something other than the most convenient route into custodial care. There were ample explanations for their reluctance, and by no means were the explanations without merit. One official noted: "If any insane patient is brought to the admitting office, it is not easy to deny him admission on the ground of his not needing 'temporary' care, simply because he needs permanent or prolonged care."[8] Or, "Theoretically, cases of alcoholic intoxication and of delirium tremens are not admitted to the hospital," since they were obviously chronic conditions. Nevertheless, "practically, the danger of overlooking some serious physical or mental condition that is masked by the intoxication or delirium is so great that any such case brought to the hospital is admitted in order that a satisfactory diagnosis be made." In other words, the admissions officer would not say no — for humanitarian as well as for medical reasons.[9]

The price that Boston Psychopathic paid for this decision was heavy, at least if its performance is judged by its original purposes. Designed to bring a new dedication and effectiveness to treatment, it became instead a processing mill for some two thousand patients a year. They came, spent their ten days, and then left, going back to their families or on to the state hospital. The institution could make few claims for recovery; in one year, for example, it reported that 6 of its discharged patients had recovered; 640 had improved; and 1,086 were unimproved. Clearly, treatment had little relevance in the daily routine. As one superintendent declared, treatment "is a complicated activity"; and "with the limited number of beds at the hospital [under one hundred] and its large admission rate [over two thousand], it is obvious that only in a small proportion of the cases admitted can psychotherapeutic treatment be carried to a termination in the hospital itself."[10]

Occasionally the directors took refuge in the argument that the institutional milieu, quite apart from therapeutic programs, had a remedial value. "Students are apt to think," one of them noted, "that there is little treatment being carried on in the wards because the familiar apparatus for treatment of medical and surgical cases is comparatively little in evidence." But they should not be misled. "They may not at first realize . . . how important for the treatment of the individual case are not only removal from the ordinary social and economic responsibility of the everyday environment and adaptation to the hospital routine, but also the repeated interviews with the physician, the contacts with the nurses, the atmosphere of the department of occupational therapy." But the bankruptcy of that position was altogether evident. By focusing on the patient's removal from the community as valuable in and of itself, on "interviews" whose purpose was to gather data not provide therapy, on "contacts" not intimate encounters, and on the "atmosphere" of a program not its substance, Boston Psychopathic was offering rationales that were not very different from what superintendents of frankly custodial state institutions had been saying for a very long time.[11]

Other psychopathic hospitals did no better in fulfilling the mental hygiene design. The majority followed the Boston model, whose procedures were, as one director accurately noted, "more or less applicable to psychopathic hospitals in general." Thus, the Syracuse State Psychopathic Hospital, a sixty-bed institution affiliated with Syracuse University, admitted the great majority of its six hundred patients under a thirty-day observation order; it then devoted practically all of its energies to diagnosis. Its routine appeared so imbalanced — spending thirty days in making a diagnosis and then releasing the patient immediately thereafter — that a very defensive tone entered the director's reports. "It has been our policy," he explained, "to carefully examine . . . and to make a thorough social study of every case possible regardless of the length of time we may expect to have the patient under treatment. Although many cases remain with us for only a brief period and then go on to another hospital, we feel . . . that the patients' interests are best served by this painstaking and thorough method although at times it would seem a great deal of work is being done without adequate return." The result was that somewhere between 40 and 50 percent of Syracuse Psychopathic's patients moved on to a state hospital. The institution intended to revitalize the system had itself become an adjunct to the system.[12]

Michigan's Psychopathic Hospital, affiliated with the state university at Ann Arbor, recapitulated this experience. By the end of its first year of operation in 1908, its directors were complaining about the high number of custodial cases that not only created overcrowding but also thwarted a program of treatment. The patients were "suffering from widely contrasting conditions of mental disease. Some are noisy and violent, some are depressed and apprehensive, and some bedridden from serious diseases of the nervous condition." Hence, administrators were forced to concede time and again that "it has been found impossible to restrict the admissions to conditions which were peculiarly suitable for treatment in a strictly psychopathic hospital. A large number of patients who are admitted are suffering from incurable conditions."[13]

No one had any difficulty in accounting for this turn of events. At Michigan, just as at Boston and Syracuse, the commitment process was at the core of the problem. "There is a hesitancy on the part of the general practitioner," reported Michigan's director, "to recommend the State Hospital, especially if he is not certain of the diagnosis or if the family objects. An observation order for the Psychopathic Hospital is frequently used as a simple way out of the difficulty because it not only relieves him of the responsibility for a correct diagnosis, but also shifts the family's disfavor." The hospital complained that "this is not always a wise disposition of the case, as many of them have old psychoses and are distinctly custodial types. They could be committed directly to Pontiac [the state hospital] and save unnecessary expense and extra time . . . thus leaving the Psychopathic Hospital for those cases with borderline conditions or psychoses of more recent onset." But here, as elsewhere, the institution did little to put this preference into action. Instead, the initial promise to provide treatment faded. Such concessions as "This institution in common with the State Asylums must meet the discouragements of treatment which are inherent in the very nature of mental diseases" became commonplace. The numbers of patients reported as "unimproved" made up half the discharges; and a substantial proportion, not less than one-quarter, went on to the state hospital. The primary aim of Michigan Psychopathic became "to develop to the utmost the diagnostic side of the hospital's activities. The institution has thus assumed to a considerable degree the functions of a clearinghouse for mental disorders and has . . . developed its medical routine to best serve this purpose." Once again, the state hospital remained at the center and the psychopathic hospital moved to its periphery.[14]

Two other extremes marked developments in the psychopathic hospitals: one extreme, as at the Cook County institution, was of conditions so primitive that even diagnosis was not carried out; the other, as in New York City's Psychiatric Institute, of conditions so special as to have practically no impact at all on the wider community. To take up the crude side first: in 1918, the National Committee for Mental Hygiene investigated the Cook County Psychopathic Hospital and concluded that "except for the fact that it is located in the city of Chicago, it is on the whole less desirable than the state hospital service." The director had no experience in treating mental illness; the bulk of the attending physicians were part-time; the younger doctors received no training. The hospital lacked a library or adequate laboratory facilities; it frequently applied restraining mechanisms to patients. Doctors on rounds appeared more intent on disciplining the nursing staff (which was notably untrained) than on "giving professional service to the individual patients." Here was a case, then, of the psychopathic hospital not as an adjunct to the state hospital, but as practically indistinguishable from it.[15]

At the opposite end of the spectrum was Psychiatric Institute in New York. Initially a separate unit of the Manhattan State Hospital at Ward's Island and under the direction of Adolf Meyer himself, the Institute moved in 1930 to its own building at the Columbia University Presbyterian Medical Center. There it administered a highly exclusive program — in several senses. First, it was one of those rare facilities in which the number of patients (usually some 170) was less than the capacity (200). Second, almost all the patients were voluntary admissions. This sign-in procedure was an innovation of the mental hygiene reformers; it was designed to facilitate hospital admission by reducing legal barriers to quick treatment. The great majority of state institutions had very few voluntary admissions, but Psychiatric Institute had practically nothing else. Moreover, its patients were exceptionally young (some 70 percent were below the age of thirty) and, generally, paying patients, with a substantial number being middle-class. What this profile reflected was a rigorous screening procedure by which Psychiatric Institute admitted only those cases that it chose to; in effect, it took in the patients that either demonstrated the greatest probability of cure or fit into a particular research program. Only an exceptional institution could note, as Psychiatric Institute did in 1937, that an unusual press of would-be patients was actually benefiting the program. "There have been so many demands for hospitalization," reported the director, "that it has been impossible for the Institute to provide facilities for all of these requests. In a way, this has been an advantage for a better selection of cases can be made, and those of special interest can be admitted."[16]

Psychiatric Institute actually did administer treatment. The ratio of medical staff to patients was low: 17 doctors, 79 ward attendants, and 139 supporting staff for some 170 patients. The length of stay was typically short, most often under twelve months; and reported rates of recovery and improvement were substantial, generally about one-half of those discharged. Psychiatric Institute rarely transferred a patient to a state hospital — not more than 3 to 4 percent of its clients were sent to such facilities. Yet, as these figures indicate, Psychiatric Institute's treatment program had little general relevance. It practiced individual psychotherapy, which may well have been appropriate for carefully selected cases of young, articulate, and mildly disturbed patients in a setting filled with staff, but obviously had no bearing on the numbers and variety of the mentally ill in the state hospitals, to say nothing of the available number of psychiatrists. To be sure, the Institute did conduct some research in schizophrenia (and it would be absurd to fault it for not coming up with a cure); still, its work was not particularly innovative. When the state hospitals began to experiment with insulin and electric shock treatments in the 1930's, so did Psychiatric Institute. It was by no means a leader in the field. In sum, the Institute defined its primary mission not as confronting the public health problem of insanity, but as treating a limited number of special cases. It worked to its own agenda.[17]

By one route or another, then, the psychopathic hospitals failed to realize the goals of their founders. Most of them became diagnostic centers, processing patients rapidly; a handful, like Psychiatric Institute, went the route of administering psychotherapy. But none of them became the central institutions for the care of the mentally ill, even the acute and treatable mentally ill. The ultimate function of the psychopathic hospital, in fact, may well have been to legitimate the state hospital, to endow it with a propriety that was as necessary as it was important. The message put out by a Boston Psychopathic or a New York Psychiatric Institute was that those committed to a state hospital belonged in a state hospital. In the one instance the judgment was explicit (based upon a diagnosis); in the other it was implicit (reflecting the patient's unsuitability for psychotherapy). How the state hospitals fulfilled this mandate we shall now see.

Beginning in the 1890's and continuing right through the pre–World War II decades, some state institutions for the insane did attempt to associate themselves in one way or another with the model of a treatment hospital. To this end, the "asylum" of the nineteenth century became the "hospital" of the twentieth, with the change in name intended to signal a change in operation. In 1900, the superintendent of the New Hampshire Asylum for the Insane successfully requested an alteration in "corporate title." "The name 'asylum'," he argued, "is identified with the care of the chronic and incurably insane." Since the institution's "chief primary present and future mission has been and always will be the care and treatment of the curable insane," since it was "a hospital in the true sense of the word," and since "in nearly all other states the word asylum has ceased to be applied to institutions that are remedial in character," it was appropriate that "the title should be changed from asylum to hospital." By the same token, institutional attendants became nurses, State Boards of Lunacy (as in Massachusetts before 1899) became State Boards of Insanity (1899),

THE WORLD OF MENTAL HEALTH

then Commissions on Mental Diseases (1916). So too, the Rhode Island Asylum for the Pauper Incurable Insane (1869) became the State Hospital for the Insane (1897) and then the State Hospital for Mental Diseases (by 1922). Indeed, many states, sensitive to the stigma of insanity, preferred not to designate at all the type of disease that these hospitals were treating. So whenever one noted the signpost "state hospital," and in ignorance asked, "hospital for what?" the correct answer, of course, was mental illness.[18]

The contrast between "asylum" and "hospital" became the point of departure for a host of speeches and newspaper articles anticipating improvement in the care and treatment of the mentally ill. "What every asylum requires in order to become a curative institution," declared one doctor, "is a hospital for the treatment of recent and acute cases. . . . Although in certain particulars this might require special arrangements, it need not differ very materially from the general arrangements of a fever hospital." Or, as a journalist noted, "We are making a beginning when we throw over the 'retreat' idea and call our institutions for the insane 'hospitals' — which is what they should be, in fact as well as in name."[19]

But, to encapsulate in one phrase the history of the mental hospital in the period 1900–1940, "fact" and "name" bore practically no relationship. With a candor that was rare, one superintendent asked: "Is it not a confession of weakness to commit an act of grand larceny by assuming a name which we have not earned and thus take a short cut to popular favor? There is nothing to gain by masquerading in borrowed plumage. . . . Unless a name has behind it the merit of good works . . . it will be but a term of reproach."[20]

Grand larceny was not too strong a charge. To be sure, mitigating facts must be mentioned: Progressive penal institutions did the same thing; the Norwich, Connecticut, asylum superintendent who in 1908 wanted his "Hospital for the Insane" to be known as "The Norwich State Hospital" properly noted that "Prisons are becoming known as reformatories and correctional institutions as schools."[21] The insane were entitled as much courtesy as the criminal. Moreover, name changes to reduce stigma were certainly not confined to the Progressive years. In 1978, a special act of the New York legislature altered the designation of the Willowbrook Developmental Center (itself an updated term for an institution for the retarded that even earlier had been known as an institution for the feeble-minded), to make it the Staten Island Developmental Center. "Willowbrook" simply conjured up too many horror stories. But the grand larceny indictment stands. Label asylums hospitals, claim to be as concerned with and capable of cures as doctors are, refer to attendants as nurses; and yet, in the end, the state hospital was not very different from the post–Civil War asylum. Both were custodial institutions.

The state hospital, like the asylum, was caught in a cycle from which it could not escape. The routine, almost without exception, amounted to custodial care for the chronic patient, which meant that for the most part, the institution received chronic patients, which in turn meant that the routine had to be designed for the chronic patient, and the cycle commenced all over again. Under these circumstances, to sort out cause from effect, to weigh the impact of overcrowding as against the state of psychiatric knowledge as against the quality of the staff, is not only difficult but relatively unimportant. The critical consideration is that every influence that bore on the functioning of the state hospital promoted and reinforced a holding operation.

Let us turn first to the treatments offered in the state hospitals. What was it that an institution could and did do for its patients? To judge by the procedures at the Northampton, Massachusetts, State Hospital, one of the better state facilities, the answer was, first, compile a relatively detailed intake record. The one- or two-page document of 1900 became the ten- to fifteen-page document of 1920. It now included several pages on the family history, sibling history, and personal history and then several more pages on the personality, habits, interests, and illnesses of the patient. But in the hospital as in the probation department and the juvenile court, the case record was descriptive, filled with biographical facts but with practically no interpretation. The doctors and social workers had absorbed the lessons of Adolf Meyer and William Healy and diligently set out to draw up a life chart. They did so, however, aimlessly, piling detail upon detail. In effect, the record led nowhere. Its very inability to discriminate among data meant that it could not translate the patient's history into recommendations for treatment. So, not surprisingly, the staff, having first proceeded to compile the dossier, then proceeded to ignore it almost altogether. The diagnostic work-up was irrelevant to how the institution actually responded to the patient.[22]

What was relevant, what did determine the responses of the Northampton State Hospital was the patient's behavior that very day, then and there, in the institution. For the first two to three weeks after admission, the staff members paid relatively close attention to the inmate. As standard procedure, they interviewed him daily, noted his reactions and his condition, and established the course for "treatment" on the basis of these observations. The newcomer who was aggressive or violent was literally put to bed, that is, forcibly confined in tightly wrapped sheets, or given hydrotherapy, kept for hours in a hot bath. Those who arrived depressed or suicidal spent several hours a day in "packs," wrapped tightly between wet sheets.[23]

The hospital routine is illustrated well by the case of one patient admitted on May 19, 1928, who "says he is worthless. . . . 'I have a lack of courage and no backbone. I have never thought of suicide. I have not the courage to attempt anything like that.'" The first entry was two days later:

> May 21: Patient is cared for in bed. . . . There has been little change in his condition since his admission. . . . He is retarded and depressed. His response to questions are very slow and he does not smile.
>
> May 23: Patient is still being cared for in bed. Today packs were ordered for him as he has been complaining that he is unable to sleep. 'I am afraid of everything. . . .' He never smiles.
>
> May 24: Patient is . . . going to the hydrotherapy room twice daily for packs. There is very little change

in his condition. . . . Today he is feeling very emotional, and controlled his tears with difficulty.

May 28: Patient is receiving packs daily. . . . This morning he was very emotional and quite depressed.

June 1: Patient . . . is going to the pack room daily. He is extremely emotional.

June 2: Patient has had several attacks of marked depression in the course of the last two or three days. He is frequently found crying and saying: 'What's going to become of me?'

June 4: Patient . . . spends the day in the treatment room where he is receiving packs. . . . 'I am worthless . . . I am impossible.'

June 8: Patient . . . is spending the day in the treatment room, where he is receiving packs. He is still very uncomfortable mentally. 'What is going to become of me? Life is a burden.'

June 11: Patient is being given routine packs twice daily. He seems rather depressed.

June 22: Patient is . . . being packed twice daily. There has been no improvement in his mental condition. . . . He is very emotional, weeps frequently when he is talking with the physicians.

June 30: Patient is very disturbed mentally. He groans and grunts. . . . He is sure that there is no prospect of recovery.

July 6: This morning patient said: 'Do you suppose that I will ever get well?' . . . The patient has been taken . . . to the hydrotherapy room for treatment twice every day. He has been brought down shortly after one o'clock today and was sitting in the sun-room while the attendants were packing a disturbed patient. Another patient was sitting side of him. He said that John jumped up . . . went out into the next corridor, and he followed him. Said that when he got to him John was on the floor. . . . He called the attendant. The

attendants found him at the foot of the stairs unconscious. There are seven stairs which lead upward. . . .
The patient was not considered suicidal, and it is
thought that he had slipped while he was going up-
stairs and fell down. Dr. Brown . . . thought it was
improbable that the patient had jumped from the first
landing.[24]

Suicidal or not, the patient died and this case record is revealing on several accounts. It confirms that the new patient was
closely watched (there were twelve entries in less than two
months) and often interviewed; the institution staff knew his feelings and did try to alleviate his symptoms. At the same time, his
daily behavior, and not the details of his case history, set the
course for treatment; however rich his dossier, it bore no relationship to the hospital's response. Moreover, the treatment once prescribed remained constant; and the arsenal of weapons in the hospital's stock was very limited. Finally, without belaboring the
point, the hospital did attempt to avoid responsibility for failure,
to make the death of an obviously suicidal patient seem like an
accident.

If improvement and discharge did not take place within a few
months, as was all too true for the great majority of cases, the
hospital routine moved into a second and very different phase.
Now the patient received a ward assignment, determined almost
exclusively by his behavior in the institution. The quiet and orderly patient went to one ward, the noisy to another, the violent
to still another. The classification was not by illness or by prescribed treatment, but by manageability of conduct. Once again
the intake record was irrelevant and the etiology of the illness of
no interest; all that mattered was how easy or how difficult it was
to control the patient. In this way, classifications in a state mental
institution were much closer to those of a prison than those of a
hospital: both of them placed inmates according to custodial, not
treatment, criteria. In fact, the resemblance between cell block
assignment and ward assignment was even closer, for the state

hospital would often reward or punish a patient by placing him on a better or worse ward.

In this spirit, the Northampton State Hospital reserved its Upper floors for the more violent and disturbed patients (Upper Third and Upper Fourth were the snake pit); it gave the Middle floors over to the more cooperative patients, and the Lower ones, which were unlocked, to the best patients. So the sixty-four-year-old woman (admitted August 21, 1935) who was somewhat troublesome began her stay on Upper Second, moved to Upper Third when she was "disturbed," came back to Upper Second when she was "more comfortable," and then went back to Upper Third with the following notation: "Patient is an extremely disagreeable old lady, who shouts at the patients and calls them names and they resent this very much. She was moved to U-3" (May 25, 1938). In the case of a twenty-seven-year-old single girl (admitted December 15, 1931), her essentially quiet demeanor ("She much prefers sitting around daydreaming. . . . She is very solitary in habits. . . . Apparently she has not the slightest desire to leave the hospital") brought an assignment to Middle One, a good ward. As her condition deteriorated, she was moved to S-I-4 (a less comfortable setting but still better than Upper Third) "because she seemed decidedly confused and was hiding around off the ward."[25]

For a difficult forty-one-year-old woman (admitted April 26, 1930), the initial placement was to Upper Third. As the record explained, "The patient is very troublesome on the ward and making many requests for an interview with the physician. When the physician is interviewing another patient, Miss H. will frequently interfere. . . . The patient . . . complains that she is not receiving any treatments." Her complaints did bring her "two wet sheet packs daily," and she became more manageable; as a result "The patient is now on M-1. . . . This morning when asked to do some work it was suggested that she try the laundry. She is very pleasant and has adapted herself to the ward routine very well." Perhaps the progress testified to the benefits of the wet-packs — or perhaps Miss H. had come to understand the system, for soon after her transfer to Middle One "her aunt wrote that the patient was afraid for fear that she was to be transferred to the other ward where she was before."[26] Finally, one male patient was "transferred to U-2 . . . after it was reported that he was making advances to one of the female employees working in the cafeteria." After two months of this punishment, he went to Middle Three "where he is reported to be quiet and cooperative," and eventually he became compliant enough to stay on Lower Two.[27]

With what we might call ward therapy as its most potent weapon (the sheets and the baths were more intensive and short-run responses), the Northampton State Hospital paid less and less attention to patients the longer they remained. After the first several months of a stay, entries in the case file trailed off to one every six months, then to one a year, and ultimately to one every two or three years. A patient's impending death would set off a flurry of brief notes about his physical condition, preparing the record for the final certificate. The rhythm of these charts, even apart from their content, makes vivid just how custodial this institution was.

Northampton's efforts at treatment represented the state of the art. Reports of investigations at other state institutions very quickly become repetitious. In 1909, William James urged John D. Rockefeller to support mental hospital reform because "everywhere routine and safety are the first consideration and prevention and cure take the second place." The Utica, New York, Asylum in 1901, like the Northampton Hospital in the 1920's and 1930's, had explained in its "Treatment of Cases" that "Acute patients have been confined to bed . . . the length of time being determined by the amount of improvement in each case . . . ; the restless patient has been soothed, the noisy quieted, the feeble in body strengthened. . . . Baths and packs have played an important part in the treatment."[28] A generation later, when two psychiatrists at the Worcester State Hospital in the 1930's set out to devise a new method for treating schizophrenia, they rediscovered the 1854 prison grading system of Sir Walter Crofton and introduced it into the institution. As the ward posters explained:

THIS WAY OUT.

All patients on the RESEARCH WARDS are graded according to their progress. As they improve they are promoted. They are sent home ONLY from GRADE B. If you want to go home, improve your grade.

GRADE A — AT HOME.

Able to act like normal people.
Able and willing to work.
Able to get along with family and friends.

GRADE B — GOING HOME.

Working well.
New interests and new ideas.
Old ideas controlled or understood.
Rebuilding mental strength to stay well.

Toward the bottom end on the ranking was GRADE E:

Working and playing poorly.
Lazy and shiftless.
Too proud of own ideas.
Not very cooperative.
Careless of clothing.

Followed by GRADE F:

Mute, resistive.
Silent or too talkative.
Excitable and disturbed.
Not cooperating.
Not working or playing.

Without much revision at all, the poster could have been used to explain the parole system at the state penitentiary.[29]

A few more examples of what passed for treatment should suffice. At Rhode Island's Hospital for Mental Diseases in the 1920's, the list of "Special Features of Treatment" that an investigation for the State Mental Hygiene Committee compiled was very brief, amounting to Hydrotherapy ("considerable use has been made of this apparatus"), Physiotherapy, and Occupational Therapy. Classification consisted of four wards for the aged and infirm, another four for the suicidal, and nine for disturbed patients. "Some of these wards," the Committee noted, "lack cheerfulness." Dr. Samuel Hamilton and three other researchers for the U.S. Department of Health, surveying public mental hospitals in 1937 and 1938, reported a common reliance on occupational therapy; perhaps because the list of treatments seemed so short, or perhaps because anything that an institution did could qualify as a program, they took note of "music therapy." "The band, the orchestra, even the rhythm orchestra, contribute happiness to the participants and others." But even then, conscious of staff shortages and cost constraints, they quickly added that "a certain amount of individual instruction in music may be desirable, but in a public institution more useful results are obtained from group work." They also had kind words for "bibliotherapy": "The use of books has been organized of late years in so definite and extensive a fashion as to justify the term."[30]

A good many institutions did experiment with prescribing one sort of drug or another, without very much in the way of either discrimination or success. As the Norwich State Hospital reported in 1930: "Homeopathic, endocrine, sedative and hypnotic medications are included in our armamentarium," the very mixture testifying to the ignorance and uncertainty that generally prevailed.[31]

The most popular and prevalent form of hospital "treatment" throughout these years remained occupational therapy. It is no easy matter to sort out what this program involved. Practically every institution reported using it (Dr. Hamilton's survey noted that 155 of 166 state hospitals had "special therapeutic procedures of occupational therapy"), and many considered it the essence of their treatment. To some superintendents, its import lay in preventing the mentally ill from succumbing to the vices of idleness. Like poor relief officials who feared that outright support for the poor would be corrupting, they worried that "lack of employment

. . . is extremely prejudicial to mental health and tends to foster vicious habits and to induce both mental and physical decay." To others, like Adolf Meyer, mental illness frequently reflected a "disorganization of habits," and hence "occupation . . . is at the bottom of the success of the treatment of a large number of the insane."[32] To still others, occupational therapy represented an antidote to the fact that "patients come to the mental hospital with a feeling of unreality"; accordingly, "work, and especially work in making something beautiful, seems real and is therefore . . . one of the most useful means of combating some of the effects of the mental disorder." There were superintendents who praised work for taking the patient's mind off his illness: "The mind necessarily becomes more or less occupied with the work in hand, and . . . the long, dreary, tedious day passes with less monotony, and the patient does not have time to nurse his afflictions and exaggerate them." And there were yet others who thought of occupational therapy as akin to practicing a craft; ostensibly the patient would return to a more simple time when "the ring of the anvil was the best of music," and events followed a "just order." Whatever the explanation, all physicians agreed: "The therapeutic value of occupation for the insane is axiomatic and is based upon sound psychological laws."[33]

What did the institutions do to implement this therapy? In some instances, the program attempted to reach the schizophrenic inmate who otherwise might remain lifeless on the ward bench, staring into space. The staff would bring such a patient to a weaving or basket-making group. E.W., for example, "was invited into the basketry class. . . . She was idle, apathetic and untidy, sat idly with the raffia in her hand, giving it no heed. After about one week, however, she was induced to sort waste raffia and tie it in small bundles. . . . Gradually improving . . . she has begun to talk to the other patients and actually accomplishes creative work, which still is of the simplest sort, she merely makes raffia rope." The routine could yield modest gains, even if it was not a particularly potent treatment. Similarly, for W.T. an attendant would put "the handle of a heavy floor polisher . . . in his hands and he was made to walk up and down the ward, accompanied by an attendant. In the course of a few days he would drag the polisher from one end of the ward to the other without being attended but would not turn around. . . . An attendant at either end of the ward would turn him around and start him toward the other end." This mastered, W.T. then joined the "wheelbarrow brigade . . . which is just a little more complex," requiring him to load and unload the dirt on his wheelbarrow. Under this regimen "he improved rapidly," went on to work in the storehouse, and seemingly confirmed the superintendent's judgment that "occupation as a treatment is a powerful remedial measure."[34]

Occupational therapy, however, was more than an occasional patient weaving or joining the wheelbarrow brigade. As in correctional institutions, it affected the very existence of the mental hospital, for inmate labor was essential to day-to-day maintenance of the facility. And there was no disputing this fact. Superintendents' reports frankly conceded that without patients working, costs would have been dramatically higher, perhaps even so high as to discourage public reliance upon institutional care. Thus, for most inmates, occupational therapy involved daily assignments to endless chores, chores as meaningless to their lives as they were important to the survival of the institution.

The manager of New York's Willard State Hospital (accurately noting that "what I shall say of Willard will apply in greater or less measure to all the other State hospitals") calculated that because of patient labor "the entire work of the boot and shoe industry at Willard, providing for the needs of nearly 2,500 patients year after year, is supervised by two employees only, with no provision for a detail of substitute employees. . . . Yet, under these conditions, the hospital has not purchased in 25 years or longer any . . . boots, shoes and slippers . . . nor any of the thousands of mattresses used during all these years." Also, the "men patients employed in the agricultural operations . . . [were] producing all the fresh milk requirements of the hospital . . . most of the fresh vegetables," as well as all the fruits and breads. Were this not enough, patients were making "thousands of kitchen and bath towels, pillowcases and sheets. . . . In addition . . . thousands of boots, shoes, suits and dresses are repaired over and over again." Thus, in New York state, patient labor meant the "annual saving in . . . many thousands of dollars. . . . The total of manufactured articles will exceed a million annually."[35]

The managers of other hospitals drew up similar accounts. Just as in the early nineteenth century institutions had rivaled one another in claiming high rates of cures, so in the early twentieth they matched each other in claiming high rates of production. The trustees of one Massachusetts hospital boasted that "the extent of development of occupational therapy is strikingly exhibited in the statistical changes of laundry personnel. Six years ago, 42 employees were required to operate the laundry in addition to patient labor. Today only 12 employees are necessary for a business of greater volume. The difference is due to co-operation by patients." Another Massachusetts hospital took great pride in its "various industries and kinds of employment. First, there is the daily routine work of the hospital, the farm, kitchen, laundry, stable, engineer's department, domestic work of all kinds, etc., in all of which patients take an active part." Since labor should be carried out "in the manner must natural to the doer, it is natural for men to go to the field and shop" and for women to "do their work . . . at home." Thus, on the farm, the men produced "milk, pork, eggs, small fruits and vegetables . . . and considerable hay and fodder," and in the shops they made and repaired "all our boots, shoes, slippers, moccasins, all men's clothes . . . all our mattresses and pillows, and . . . repair, renovate and upholster furniture." Meanwhile, on the wards, the women "make and repair all clothing for women except knit underwear and stockings, all table linen, bed linen, and the thousand and one articles used about a large institution." The annual output was considerable, including the manufacture of 10,031 towels, 4,027 pillow slips, 3,589 sheets, 1,104 hair mattresses, 987 skirts, 682 shirts, and 571 pairs of pants, and the repair of 7,176 socks, 7,265 pants, 4,990 coats, and 3,372 vests.[36]

Everywhere one turned, the same reliance upon inmate labor appeared. "The greater part of the routine work," announced the medical superintendent of the Hudson (New York) State Hos-

pital, "is done by the chronic patients. . . . Few patients are so
deteriorated that they can not be taught to do some form of work
if efforts are persistently kept up by attendants." The Elgin (Illinois) State Hospital inmates not only made clothing in the sewing room but manufactured cement blocks. "These have been
used for the construction of stone buildings, erected by patients
and employees."[37]

It remains very doubtful that inmate labor was more a mode of
therapy than of institutional peonage, more a matter of treatment
than of exploitation. Superintendents certainly insisted that however important the fiscal aspects of the patients' work, occupation
was therapy. What was good for the patient was only incidentally
good for the institution. "There is of course," noted one New York
hospital physician, "an economic as well as a therapeutic aspect
to this work," but that was no cause for worry. "While taken in
the aggregate, the economic side is of great importance, yet that
will care for itself, if the therapeutic standpoint be sufficiently
emphasized." His counterpart in Massachusetts found the same
congruence: patients' labor was "beneficial to themselves in the
highest degree and advantageous to the hospital in producing
household goods, clothing and food." And the managers of Virginia's Western State Hospital agreed: "In hospital economy employment establishes the blessed circle; work is good for the patient and the patient is good for work."[38]

Despite these assurances, the jobs were obviously chosen not
for their therapeutic value but because they fit institutional needs.
There was no effort to match case history to work assignment, no
attempt to train inmates for post-institutional employment. Tasks
had to be performed on the farm, in the laundry, in the kitchen,
in the sewing room; and the inmates had to perform them. The
ease with which directors and superintendents presented maintenance work as therapy, their ability to cloak the making of
cement blocks or towels as treatment, points to their essentially
managerial roles, to the fact that they remained first and foremost
overseers, not physicians. The self-serving phrases came too easily; self-delusion was too rampant; all of which indicates that they
were thoroughly comfortable with running holding operations.

Seen another way, the very ability to confuse menial labor with therapy indicates just how crude the state of treatment was. In brief, the custodial character of the mental hospital is clear in the activities that constituted treatment in general and occupational therapy in particular.

The very weaknesses of the hospitals' therapeutic techniques made it most likely that mainly the hopeless cases would seek admission, which in turn meant that the prospects for delivering intensive care, or for attracting the less hopeless cases, were reduced still further. Call a facility a hospital, use the rhetoric of the mental hygiene movement, but ultimately know that the institution was in the asylum business.

Thus, as the national census figures on patients in mental institutions confirmed, the mental hospital retained much of the character of the almshouse and the old age home. Throughout the pre–World War II period, approximately 40 percent of the patients on the wards were fifty years old and over. In fact, to judge by average age of admission between 1922 and 1939, the reform rhetoric had little impact on the demography of the institution, for the percentage of elderly kept rising. The diagnostic classification of the patients further confirmed that the hospitals were essentially holding operations, that the prospects for cure were minimal. During 1922, over half of first admissions to the mental hospitals consisted of cases of the senile (16 percent), the syphilitic (11 percent), the alcoholic (4 percent), the retarded (3 percent), and the schizophrenic (23 percent) — and by all accounts, the overwhelming majority of these types of patients were incurable. The physical deterioration that accompanied senility, alcoholism, and syphilis was irreversible. The likelihood of recovery among the schizophrenics was no greater; superintendents estimating it as less than 2 percent. Predictably, then, the majority of inmates in the state hospital on a given day (here January 1, 1923, but the figures were almost identical for January 1, 1939) were the chronic: the senile, syphilitic, and alcoholic patients made up 13 percent of the wards; the schizophrenic, 45 percent. Finally, statistics on the length of time that patients on the wards on a given day had been in the hospital revealed that only 17 percent had been confined for under a year, and another 9 percent for under two years; fully 54 percent had remained in the institution for five or more years — and a little over one-third of the patients were resident for over ten years. A commitment to a state hospital meant a stay of a very long time.[39]

The national averages did not mask significant fluctuations among the institutions. In Massachusetts (in 1939) 53 percent of the patients admitted were fifty years old or more, and by diagnosis, one-quarter of the cases were schizophrenic. The pattern was similar in New York (1923–1925): only a little over one-third of the entering patients were fifty or older, but fully 10 percent of admissions were over seventy. Again, the classifications did not make cures likely: 12 percent syphilitic, 5 percent alcoholic, and 27 percent schizophrenic. And the institutions' figures on rates of recovery confirmed the limited expectations; less than 20 percent of those admitted were eventually discharged as "recovered." In Illinois, too, the senile, syphilitic, alcoholic, and schizophrenic made up an overwhelmingly chronic hospital population.[40]

It was also a population that, to judge by its economic status, had few other options. A disproportionate number of foreign-born were on the state hospital wards. As the Bureau of the Census calculated in 1920, 14.5 percent of the nation's population was foreign-born, but patients in mental institutions were 30 percent foreign-born. This difference probably reflected the greater amount of economic dependency among the newcomers that forced them in time of illness or trouble to turn to the state hospital, no matter how inadequate it might be. Moreover, the records of the institutions did, albeit crudely, divide patients into "dependent," "marginal," and "comfortable" economic categories — and everywhere the overwhelming majority of patients were dependent or marginal. In New York, for example, the "Economic condition of first admissions, 1925" was: 11 percent dependent, 79 percent marginal, and 9.5 percent comfortable. In Massachusetts, the comparable figures for 1939 were 21 percent, 70 percent, and 4 percent. Finally, the institutions' data on patients' prior occupations confirmed their lower-class status. The great majority of inmates were laborers. Rarely was anyone from a professional or white collar occupation to be found in a state hospital.[41]

This combination of ineffective treatment with a chronic and lower-class population was bound to create institutional over-crowding — which in turn reduced still further the prospects for giving patients adequate attention and care, and reinforced the hospital's reputation as a place of last resort. To administer a custodial operation almost inevitably meant too many patients for too few beds, a condition that was endemic to mental hospitals in the decades 1900–1940. "Each succeeding year," reported the Census Bureau in 1939, "there is a greater number of resident patients in State hospitals. There is a constantly increasing number of beds provided to care for them, but at no time has the number . . . been sufficient to furnish adequate facilities for all patients. . . . There is almost always a certain amount of over-crowding in practically all State hospitals."[42]

The problem was of several dimensions. The number of patients seeking admission to the state hospitals increased annually; the institutions were unable to discharge patients quickly enough to make room for newcomers; and hospital construction never kept pace with increased burdens of responsibility. Nationally, between 1922 and 1939, the number of state hospital admissions per year rose from 64,000 to 108,000, while the number of patients resident on a given day climbed even more precipitously from 230,000 to 440,000, and facilities could not expand to meet numbers. As a result, the institutions, on the average, held 7 to 12 percent more patients than their "rated capacity" — an index which itself may well have been inflated.[43]

To illustrate the effects of this general condition on several state systems, in New York between 1903 and 1925 the annual rate of hospital admissions swelled by some 4,300 patients (from 5,110 to 9,436), or from 65 to 84.5 per 100,000 of the population; at the same time, the daily institutional population climbed by 19,400 (from 24,187 to 43,601). But the construction of facilities lagged: rated institutional capacity increased by only 9,676 places (from 22,002 to 31,678). Hence, New York's mental hospital population was 9 percent in excess of capacity in 1903, and 27 percent in excess in 1925. Under these circumstances, to choose the most obvious indicator, hospital specialization was impossible. Institutions which were to serve the chronic only (as at Willard) were housing the chronic and the acute; hospitals intended for the acute (as at Hudson in Poughkeepsie) were also filled with the chronic. In 1903, the State Commission had complained that "the present hospitals are so enormous and so overcrowded that proper classification is not possible." Some twenty years later, the situation was even worse.[44]

Massachusetts faced similar circumstances. In 1905, the rated capacity matched the number of patients in the institutions: 8,552. Then, year by year, the degree of overcrowding increased. In 1910 there were 10,364 patients for 9,627 places (8 percent overcrowding); by 1925, 15,156 patients for 13,343 places (14 percent overcrowding); by 1939, 20,623 patients for 17,538 places (18 percent overcrowding). The only state facility that managed to avoid this condition was Boston Psychopathic. Because of its ten-day turnovers or, better put, because of its sending patients on to the already overcrowded state hospitals, it had in 1939 a daily population of 75 for its 109 beds.[45]

One can open almost any series of annual hospital reports to find recurrent descriptions of overcrowding.[46] In Connecticut, for just one sample:

> 1928: The resident census was . . . 2,882, which represents an . . . overcrowding of 545 or 23 percent. . . . This institution is now so overcrowded that there remains practically no day-room space in some of the buildings, except a dark corridor. In other buildings the beds are so close together that one can hardly pass between them.

> 1934: There has been *no construction to increase the bed capacity for patients for the past thirty-nine years.* From the very beginning of the institution, the superintendents have stressed the condition of overcrowding.[47]

What the superintendents did or did not do about the problem will be addressed shortly. Here the point is that overcrowding was part of the complex circle that confined the state hospital to a custodial routine.

The staffing of the institutions also reinforced this outcome. The ratio of physicians to patients was absurdly low — that is, if one took the notion of treatment seriously. The standard that the American Psychiatric Association (APA) set in 1926, of one doctor for every 150 patients, was itself inadequate to insure the provision of treatment. (Assuming that a physician could explore the nature of the illness and counsel as many as ten patients a day, a case load of 150 meant that he would see each patient once every three weeks.) No one, however, will be astonished to learn that this figure was beyond the accomplishment of practically every state institution. Between 1900 and 1940, the average physician-to-patient ratio stood at about 1:250. The Depression did not make things that much worse; in 1938, the national figure was 1:248, with New York at 1:189, Massachusetts at 1:197, Illinois 1:224, and California 1:340, ratios that would have allowed for a single meeting between physician and patient every five or six weeks. Confronting such case loads, many physicians did not remain with an institution for very long; about 25 to 30 percent of the two hundred doctors in New York's mental hospitals turned over each year. It is clear, too, why a newly admitted patient was given only a few months to make progress or else be consigned to the therapy of ward changes and institutional maintenance. The small number of professionals could do nothing more than watch over the new patients and maintain the custody of everyone else.[48]

The quality of the ward staff, those with "hands on" responsibility for patient care, was appropriate only to a holding operation. First, personnel shortages were endemic; while patient rolls overflowed, the employee rolls generally had vacancies. Images of a day room filled with many patients milling about aimlessly under the nominal supervision of one attendant were altogether accurate. Moreover, the rhetorical commitment to employing a trained ward staff, to making attendants into nurses, amounted to very little in reality. No man with anything of an education would take the job; and women, despite major limitations on their employment opportunities, were not much more eager. As of 1938, only 4,000 graduate nurses were employed in the state hospitals, and a little more than a third of them served in New York.[49]

To make matters worse, turnover among attendants was astonishingly high, much greater in mental hospitals than in prisons or reformatories. In New York's institutions, a ward staff of 4,175 (as of July 1, 1925) turned over almost completely in the course of a year: 3,432 resigned, 3,777 were appointed, and there were still another 241 vacancies left to be filled. In Massachusetts, the average tenure of ward staff members was four to five months, with women toward the higher end and men toward the lower. The State Board reports repeatedly complained that "many employees hardly begin their training before they give place to their successors." As a result, superintendents had to fill each attendant slot three times a year and, not surprisingly, they were often unable to do so; at any given moment, between 10 and 25 percent of the positions were vacant. These shortages did have one unintended consequence: hospitals became places of employment for ex-patients unable to obtain work in the community. "We commend," declared one board of trustees in Massachusetts, "the practice of giving employment to worthy patients who are discharged from the hospital. . . . An average monthly number of 50 men on the pay rolls of the Foxborough and Norfolk State hospitals were formerly patients. These men have been employed for periods ranging from one to four years. . . . For the greater part these employees have discharged their work conscientiously." Indeed, the Board went on to praise the "continued cooperation of the probation officers of the State, who have shown their appreciation by sending to the hospital men under probation or under suspended sentence." Such practices were reminiscent of nineteenth-century almshouse and jail inmates coming over to care for the asylum inmates.[50]

No one familiar with working conditions within the institutions had the slightest difficulty in accounting for the high turnover and poor credentials among attendants. As one superintendent frankly noted: "The fault was with the institution rather than the employee." Wages were low, generally under $1,000 a year, and the "benefit" of free room and board really exacerbated the situation. "The hospital employee," one student of Illinois institutions remarked, "was faced by the prospect of a drab, routine employment, with little color, recognition or reward to offset the routine features. Institutional life at best is almost inevitably routinized; in the large mental hospital . . . the routine may become unbearable." Living conditions reinforced the drabness. Some state hospitals provided separate staff cottages but they were sex-segregated and often overcrowded; other institutions compelled attendants to sleep in rooms off the wards, which were not only without privacy but very noisy. Moreover, until the 1920's, most institutions used only two shifts, so that attendants worked twelve to fourteen hours a day, with three days' leave every four weeks and a two-week vacation; even after the 1920's, only the larger industrial states adopted a three-shift schedule. Add to this, "scant opportunity for recreation, with but little promise for the future," and the conclusion of the superintendent of the Manhattan State Hospital seems incontrovertible:

> No other line of occupation demands so much for such small return. The result is that those offering themselves for employment consist largely of three classes:
>
> (1) Those who have been unsuccessful in other fields of work and at last turn to the institution for employment. The percentage of this class is quite large and requires constant weeding out.
> (2) Those who are out of employment and take the institution position merely to tide them over until they can find more attractive and remunerative employment. . . .
> (3) A class which takes to institution work . . . but in common with every superintendent, I find it increasingly difficult to retain a sufficient number of these to carry on the work satisfactorily.[51]

The failure to "carry on the work satisfactorily," as directors and superintendents were painfully aware, occasioned not only the institution's inability to do good, to care for its patients, but a propensity to do harm, to injure its patients. In ways that recall the prison situation (but in frequency and intensity do not match it), the hospitals' custodial operation was all too often physically abusive. Given the primitive techniques available to physicians, it is not clear how and where one draws the line between good faith (albeit crude) treatment and outright punishment. Were hours in restraint, whether in a bed or a wet-sheet or a very hot tub, abusive? What of the frequent use of seclusion rooms or transfers to violent wards or even "occupational therapy"? These procedures probably served the institution more than they benefited the patient, and may have been actually injurious. And yet there would be something unfair about criticizing the institutions for not having more effective treaments available. (Of course, the hospitals might have admitted their weaknesses with more candor, but that is another matter.) So, rather than pursue the harshness of what was ostensibly treatment, let us talk in simpler terms about outright physical abuse that could not possibly pass for treatment.

Even this narrower question must be addressed cautiously, for the amount and degree of cruelty was, and remains, obscure. It was too easy to claim that a patient with fractured ribs had tripped or that the injuries he suffered came from an attendant acting in self-defense. Nevertheless, from innuendoes and from some direct evidence as well, it appears that hospitals could not protect their patients from harm. The superintendents themselves occasionally clarified some of the elements that led attendants to mistreat inmates. "Is it to be wondered," asked one Connecticut hospital director, "that the nurse, who has been on duty for fourteen hours and has no place for amusement or relaxation . . . whose room is so situated that she may be kept awake the greater part of the night by the clamor of some disturbed patient, should arise in the morning not feeling a keen interest in her work or in the welfare of the patients under charge?" By the same token, low wages, as the student of Illinois' institutions noted, led attendants not only to steal institutional supplies, but to exploit patient labor for personal advantage. Superintendents also conceded that staff shortages regularly produced "more restraint and seclusion" and were "a material factor in increasing accidents, injuries and escapes." Just how much neglect attendants were guilty of because they saw their jobs as temporary can only be surmised. And just how much abuse attendants committed because they could claim that patients were imagining things also remains uncertain. At the Willard State Hospital, for example, Mrs. H. "made various complaints regarding the food. . . . She also stated that the nurses had ill-treated the patients. A very careful investigation of these allegations was made by the Board and it was found that they were the result of delusions of persecution from which the patient is suffering. . . . The patient is a case of paranoia, and similar complaints had been made by her while an inmate of the Kings Park State Hospital."[52]

Yet, despite the ease with which such findings could be reached, it was apparent that patients were not always imagining things. However short-handed superintendents were, they still dismissed several attendants every month, usually for drunkenness or for abusing patients. In New York's institutions the figure was around eight per month, a low percentage of employees but substantial enough to suggest how common maltreatment was. And some superintendents were well aware that the causes of patients' injuries were frequently the result of something other than attendants acting in self-defense. Yes, inmates were at times violent and staff members might have to protect themselves — but attendants could also intentionally prod a patient into an attack. "When the pitiless attendant," noted one superintendent, "is cautious enough to fear detection, and possibly discharge, if it becomes known that he assaulted an insane man, he can usually irritate and provoke the patient into . . . resisting or striking . . . and when the patient has actually struck the first blow his fate is sealed. Under the plea of self-defense the attendant can, until satisfied, safely pommel the innocent victim." Yes, patients were old, their bones fragile, the floors hard, and mishaps did occur — but a verdict of "accident" was often a way of whitewashing a nasty incident. "In the findings," this superintendent continued, "the sad results of such 'hospital accidents' are always regretted, but are deemed unavoidable. . . . Such official investigations are almost always superficial, and the verdict serves little purpose beyond softening the process of closing the incident."[53]

All of this makes apparent that in official accounts of hospital incidents (these taken from the New York records) the narrative and the conclusion may bear little relation:

> WM, a disturbed patient . . . complained of soreness in the left chest. Examination disclosed a fracture of the left seventh rib. Investigation showed that because of the patient's restlessness, he had required close attention for about a week. There was no evidence of any improper treatment. It is probable that the fracture was caused by the patient striking himself against the edge of the bed.[54]

But just what did "close attention" mean on what was probably an overcrowded ward? And what did "restlessness" imply? Difficult to manage? Abusive to the attendants? Rib fractures were probably the most common injury reported in the state hospitals, often being discovered when the patient was examined for pneumonia. The findings, however, were generally the same and not persuasive: no evidence of mistreatment.

> Patient PM attempted to throw a stone; was prevented by the attendant and in the struggle they fell to the ground, the patient sustaining a fracture of the left eighth rib. This patient is very excitable and irritable.

> AM fell while in the hall of Ward 13 and sustained a fracture of the left arm bone. She was being escorted by two nurses. . . . This patient is at times very assaultive and being of large size and strength, her efforts in this direction are usually successful. While turning into the cross hall . . . the patient . . . suddenly turned and fell to the floor together with the nurse who had hold of her left arm.[55]

Did the reports protest too much? After all, inmates ought not to throw stones or attack attendants; why then note that the patients were, by reputation, prone to assault, except as a gesture at explaining inappropriate injuries?

> WB, a disturbed patient, attacked attendant McPharland and in the scuffle that followed the patient received several severe contusions. While the attendant did not intentionally injure the patient it is apparent that the latter had some rough handling. Under the conditions the attendant was permitted to resign.[56]

But who was being protected, the attendant or the institution? If guilty, the attendant ought to have been prosecuted, and if innocent, kept on the staff. Further, to calculate the extent of institutional brutality, some number of unexplained resignations must be added to dismissals for abuse.

> On July 3 JS barricaded himself in his room and began smashing out the panels of the door, so that it became necessary for two attendants to force the door. While this was being done, the patient placed himself in the corner between the door and the wall in such a way that when the door was forced open he was squeezed between the door and the wall. . . . It was found that he had been injured internally. The patient died the next morning. The Coroner . . . returned a verdict of accidental death. . . . The District Attorney . . . decided that no action by him was necessary.[57]

Once again, the findings do not ring true; the logistics of the situation are thoroughly implausible. Rather, what we discover is that attendants were ready to assault patients who destroyed property, undoubtedly confident that they would be exonerated from any charges.

The institutions' failure to protect patients against harm involved not only attendant:patient abuse, but patient:patient abuse and patient self-abuse. A "Casualty Table" that the Massachusetts State Board of Mental Diseases compiled in 1939 estimated that about 5 percent of the hospital population suffered accidents, most of the injuries being self-inflicted or the results of the "asocial acts of another patient." The New York hospital records were also filled with accounts of patients taking an overdose of morphine or a suicidal leap from a stairwell or attacking one another. "AN was pushed down by another patient (EF) and sustained a fracture"; GS, "while working in the kitchen was stabbed in the chest by patient B with a kitchen knife. . . . No blame could be attached to anyone." But this judgment is suspect. How many such incidents could have been prevented in a closely supervised setting? Undoubtedly, not all of them, but less overcrowding and a more diligent staff, for example, might have made a significant difference. To be sure, the fact that the institutions took note of these incidents and even attempted to construct and publicize a "casualty table" bespeaks a concern for the welfare of the patient that was qualitatively different from the prison's concern for the welfare of the convict. Attendants were more frequently dismissed than guards. Nevertheless, in the hospitals as in the prisons, a holding operation was all too often a brutal operation. The air of hopelessness that pervaded the state hospitals, together with their difficult patients, short-handed and badly trained staff, overcrowded wards, and ineffective treatments, meant that institutional life would be in a very real way, dangerous. This kind of care, however well-intentioned, generated abuse.[58]

The custodial quality of the state institutions not only undercut the mental hygiene design for the hospitals but also thwarted the effort to extend the reach of treatment and the principles of prevention into the community. Reformers had looked to promote alternative procedures, from outpatient clinics to after-care, which would cure and prevent mental illness. Their goals, however, were not to be realized. The traditional needs of the state hospital shaped, and finally distorted, the implementation of the mental hygiene agenda.

The fate of family care, or boarding-out as it was also known, is a useful first case in point. Although mental hygiene proponents did not so much promote the idea (that some among the chronic could be better cared for in community homes) as use it as a starting point for a much more novel approach (that acute and curable cases should be treated in clinics), still the disappointing history of the program begins to clarify the barriers to change. One might have anticipated a broad popularity for family care. After all, the institutions were perpetually overcrowded and offered little to the back-ward chronic patient. And in the 1920's and 1930's, some psychiatrists and social workers did contend that family care had therapeutic effects. "The boarding home," one of them declared, "becomes, not a permanent residence, but a step-ping stone to mental health, independence, and self-support." Nevertheless, only three states, Massachusetts, New York, and Ohio, even experimented with the procedure; and none of them went very far with it. Massachusetts, the pioneer in the field, had a total of 124 patients in family care in 1900, 255 in 1919, 164 in 1925, and 311 in 1935. In 1939, only a mere 1,300 patients were in family care throughout the nation, about 3 percent of the total institutional population.[59]

Why did family care make so little progress? One reason, as Massachusetts' officials explained, was that patients were often reluctant to leave the institution. "They dislike leaving the com-forts of the hospital for unknown conditions. . . . They think they will be less comfortable or will have to work hard or will miss the companionships formed at the hospital." Moreover, relatives fre-quently objected to family placement for fear that "they them-selves will be subjected to criticism for not taking the patients home instead of allowing strangers to care for them." Then too, community protest interfered. "Our assistant," reported the direc-tor of the Northampton State Hospital, "has noticed at times an opposition by the citizens of some of the smaller towns to the placing out of State dependents." Although the legislature au-thorized placing out only for non-dangerous and non-troublesome patients, some towns did not want any type of ex-inmates in their midst. Superintendents also complained of the difficulty of finding responsible families to take in the inmates, families that could meet the needs of chronic patients and at the same time not exploit them for whatever labor they could perform.[60]

But however pertinent all these considerations, the major stumbling block to family care remained the hospitals' own needs. It was not in their best interest to board out patients. First, the inmate who was most suitable for family care — who was most likely to find a family ready to take him in — was the steady working inmate whose labor was critical to the institution's functioning. Why should some family benefit from his work when the hospital desperately required it? The Massachusetts State Board noted frankly that "the lack of proper development of this [family care] department" reflected "the want of interest on the part of hospital authorities, their objection to losing the workers (which means increasing the maintenance cost)." And superintendents conceded the validity of the point. "It seemed," one of them admitted, "as if every good worker among the insane in that whole institution was, if he or she was quiet (and most good workers are quiet and manageable), turned over . . . to be boarded out, so that the institution was absolutely stripped of all the good workers it had developed." With production figures and institutional maintenance to mind, superintendents were not eager to discharge their best laborers.[61]

Second, direct financial considerations worked against hospitals' boarding out patients. Legislatures had no intention of supporting family care in ways that would increase the total amount of state expenditures; the program would have to operate within the same annual allotment of funds. (Legislators were probably short-sighted here; boarding-out might well have saved them later capital construction costs as institutions swelled beyond a point which even they could ignore. But such a saving would not turn up on an annual budget sheet, and their focus tended to be limited to the two-year periods from election to election.) What this constraint meant to the institutions was that any increased staff time for administering outpatient care would have to come out of existing positions; a hospital staff already overburdened would have to assume new obligations, to arrange for placements and visit the patients at least on an annual basis; and superintendents, again understandably, were unwilling to do this. "The principal reason why my interest has not taken more practical effect," explained one of them, "is the fact that there was no one person in the hospital, no one officer, whom we could take off for that work because their duties were already so arduous."[62]

Moreover, since the legislature would not add new funds for family care, expenditures had to come, directly or indirectly, from the institutions' budgets. For the hospital to subtract from its funds the $3.50 to $4.50 weekly per capita stipend to give to community caretakers was almost unthinkable. Not only was the patient's labor being lost, but since the costs of supervising him were lower than the costs of supervising the troublesome cases, an important margin of income disappeared. Further, superintendents were eager to keep their own enrollments high, either because state reimbursement came on a per capita basis or because a large number of patients was the most powerful argument for appropriations, or both. Again, an occasional superintendent candidly made these points: "The cost of boarding out patients," the Northampton Hospital director explained, "will keep the number small so long as the expense must be met from our maintenance appropriation. Patients who are suitable to be boarded out are of the quiet class, who need but little supervision. Removal from the hospital of 10 or 20 of their class will not noticeably reduce our expenses . . . but to board out 10 patients will reduce by about $1,500 our maintenance appropriation." In sum, economic incentives ran counter to family care and promoted keeping chronic but steady working patients within the institution.[63]

In much the same way, the state hospitals frustrated reformers' hopes for an extensive network of outpatient facilities. Mental hygiene proponents had anticipated that patients near to recovery would be paroled from institutions and would receive subsequent support in after-care clinics; these clinics would also serve the wider community, thereby reducing the number of hospitalizations. But again, the state facilities paid minimal attention to the program. Neither the legislatures, nor the hospital boards, nor the trustees, nor the superintendents ever devoted major energies to concerns or activities that went beyond institutional boundaries. To be sure, the mental hygiene movement did enjoy some success in the private sector; philanthropic agencies in the 1920's began to establish clinics and, especially, to administer child guidance programs. In the public realm, however, state dollars and state policy continued to buttress the state hospitals.

If ever a procedure seemed tailored to fit the needs of the mental hospital, it was the parole of patients. Given the overcrowded condition of the facilities, the hospitals ought to have been eager to arrange for parole. In fact, the first use of parole antedated the mental hygiene movement. It was initially designed to solve a special problem: sometimes patients left the institution to visit with relatives; they would initially adjust well and remain for a few weeks, when suddenly things would take a turn for the worse and the relatives would bring them back to the institution. The difficulty was that by law the several weeks' absence constituted an automatic discharge, and so the entire commitment procedure had to be repeated. To avoid this legal requirement, the institutions in the 1880's and 1890's secured legislation allowing patients to remain on visit — on furlough or parole — for thirty days, with the right to return at will. This initial period was soon increased to sixty days — and then, with the support of mental hygiene proponents, to one or two years.[64]

Nevertheless, parole did not become standard practice. Patients on parole did increase, from a few thousand in 1910 to 23,000 (8 percent of all patients) in 1923, to 49,250 (11 percent of patients) in 1939. In Massachusetts the number rose from 539 in 1910, to 1,675 in 1925, to 2,555 in 1939; and in New York, from 196 in 1906, to 3,362 in 1925, to 6,809 in 1939. But the percentages, particularly in the states with the greatest institutional populations, rarely exceeded one in ten; as of 1939, Massachusetts and Pennsylvania had only 10 percent of their hospital inmates on parole, New York had 9 percent and Illinois, 4 percent. And even these figures were somewhat inflated because institutions often included escaped patients in the parole category, which (as we will see) is very revealing about the quality of outpatient care.[65]

The constraints that hindered the implementation of parole resemble the considerations that restricted family care. Once again, relatives' reluctance, together with community opposition, discouraged release: "We often cannot obtain the co-operation of relatives in the parole," declared a New York superintendent. He also went on to note that because of a recent upstate murder of a physician "by an insane man (so far as I know, never a State hospital patient) . . . there was an active opposition to the parole of patients from the hospital, and had any patients been paroled . . . they would have encountered an absolutely antagonistic environment." Yet, with parole as with family care, the institution itself erected major barriers to release. Not only did it fail to prepare the inmates (thereby making them fearful about release), but more important, it placed the maintenance needs of the institution above the discharge of the patients. As two close students of New York staff practices discovered: "Active opposition to the point even of threats of resigning is apt to be met with when patients are about to be removed who have been familiarized with some important part of the routine work and trained to perform it automatically and without supervision. Such patients are to be found in almost every ward and working department of every hospital." The superintendents criticized the ward attendants for this opposition. Still, in light of personnel shortages, administrators were quite prepared to give the staff its way. After all, it was the superintendent who was ultimately responsible for operating within the hospital budget.[66]

One unusual investigation of parole practices at the Chicago State Hospital in the early 1930's confirmed this generalization. Under the auspices of Edith Abbott, dean of the social work school at the University of Chicago, physicians and social workers examined 290 patients on the "improved" wards to analyze why they had not been released. In some cases, there were no relatives to provide care; in others, no jobs were available. For almost three-quarters of the male patients, however, the failure to release reflected "the policy of not encouraging the parole of patients who were useful workers. . . . When threatened with the loss of this 'staff,' the institution interposed to block their parole." Just how powerful this interposition was should be clear from the fact that even after this policy was exposed, only 21 patients from the group went onto parole. Publicity did not affect practice.[67]

Even if investigations were to little avail, the findings did produce some scathing observations. "Here are patients," declared Stuart Jaffary, dean of Toronto's school of social work, "mentally ill and committed to a public institution for treatment. On improvement or recovery, they are not discharged but retained in the institution indefinitely to perform menial labor for the state. Here is an abuse of civil liberties which deserves much more thorough investigation. Thorough because the abuse is a widespread one, and committed under the guise of caring for helpless dependent persons." Concluded Jaffary: "A sharp question is raised as to the line between mental institutions and prisons."[68]

The hospitals were also unwilling or unable to support the staff or the facilities essential to a parole system. The demands of such a program were even greater than those for family care. By design at least, a psychiatric and social work staff were to screen the appropriate cases for release, investigate the family circumstances, make the various arrangements, and then be responsible for providing after-care in community outpatient clinics. All of this took personnel and funds — and the hospitals begrudged them both. Reformers may have agreed that "back of this whole system of trial visit is social service," but the numbers of social workers employed in the state hospitals remained very low. As late as 1938–39, there were no social workers at all in one-third of the state hospitals, and even where they were in greatest supply, they were far too few in number to deliver much assistance. In New England, the ratio was one social worker for every 833 patients; in the mid-Atlantic states it was 1:775; elsewhere the figure was 1:1,600. In only seven of the nation's institutions was the ratio better than 1:400. Under these circumstances, few of the prescriptions for pre-release or post-release practices could be satisfied. What could five social workers do for the 2,285 inmates of the Boston State Hospital? What could four of them do for the 2,403 at Worcester? "The social worker in the state hospital," noted two leading practitioners in the field, "has, for the most part, had to limit her work to the most obvious and pressing needs of the institution. . . . It is obvious that she cannot easily keep up with even these demands and in her comparative isolation . . . she may easily lose her sense of perspective and either settle down to routine work or become discouraged with the whole situation."[69]

Given the central significance of outpatient clinics in the theories of the mental hygiene proponents, the failure to implement this part of the program was perhaps the most disappointing result of all. Through the 1920's and 1930's, the clinics remained few in number and severely limited in operation. As late as 1937, almost one-third of state hospitals had not organized any outpatient facility; and those institutions that did administer clinics operated on a small and indifferent basis. A 1935 national survey of mental hygiene facilities revealed that 62 of 127 state hospitals were administering outpatient clinics; and while it is true that most of the clinics were located off the institution's grounds, in a local hospital or school building, still they met only intermittently. Almost 60 percent were open only once a month or less, and a mere 6 percent met twice a week or more. So too, three-quarters of the sponsoring state hospitals were unwilling to allocate significant staff time to the clinics; they assigned less than half the time of one psychiatrist to outpatient work. The survey concluded that only five institutions took the mandate seriously. "From neither the community nor the hospital point of view, then, does it appear that most of the state hospitals were devoting much time to preventive work." There was no disputing this finding. "The mental hospital," conceded Worcester's Dr. William Bryan, "has not been an outstanding factor in mental hygiene programs."[70]

The clinics themselves established only very superficial contact with clients. A few exceptions aside, intensive treatment was not to be found. In New York, which actually invested more heavily in outpatient care than most states, a Committee on Mental Hygiene reported that "the state hospital clinics gave insufficient time to individual examinations and had inadequate provision for following up their recommendations." The great majority of the clinics' clients were on parole (making 70 percent of the total of 23,447 visits in 1928) — the rest were discharged patients (3 percent) or community residents seeking help (27 percent). But few of them received sustained attention. There was little continuity among clinic psychiatrists: "Upon consulting with the superintendent," one social worker reported, "I learned that one physician could not be spared regularly from the service to attend the clinic"; doctors took their turns as institutional schedules permitted. To compound the problem, clinic records were so inadequate that each physician had to start each case from scratch: "The doctor was of necessity forced to ask such general questions as, Are you eating and sleeping well? Are you working? Where? How long? Do you have any difficulty in doing your work? Do you hear voices?" The case loads that clinic social workers carried were also too heavy to allow frequent contact. "With an average of 284 patients on parole," one of them admitted, "this number is entirely too great . . . to see many of these more than once [over a six-month period]. Little has been done for them in most cases beyond noting their condition and at the expiration of the parole they have automatically ceased to be her concern." Similarly, to explain "the difficulty we have in supervising our paroled patients," one superintendent calculated that "our hospital district comprises 9,125 square miles, or one-fifth of the State of New York. In order for our social worker to visit all of our paroles would require twenty-eight continuous days and much expense," and that, it seemed, was not feasible.[71]

The similarities between the care of patients on parole and the oversight of prisoners on parole appeared in Illinois as well. The State Board in 1925 admitted that "on account of the crowded condition of the hospital many patients are paroled when they do not promise to be a menace outside." Supervision was necessary ("conditions are not always what they seem") but impossible to achieve. "There are quite a number of single patients scattered about who are too far away or in out of the way communities, where the workers cannot go except in emergencies because of the time and expense entailed." Accordingly, "the hospital must depend for these on letters written by the relatives or friends every two weeks, but a very small number respond and the letters give very little insight into the patient's condition." Clearly, the parole officer in criminal justice learned as much from letters about the daily habits of his ex-prisoner as the psychiatrist learned about his ex-patient.[72]

The Northampton State Hospital administered a clinic in nearby Springfield, but again, the links between staff and client were tenuous. The case record entries were almost exclusively descriptive, reporting on the present state of the patient and nothing else. Thus for client D.C. the entries typically read:

> December 18, 1929: Patient is in good health. . . . Patient has been working regularly since his return home. Evidently he is a good workman.
> March 24, 1930: Patient has had no illness since the last report. . . . Patient was pleased at the visit and showed a very friendly attitude toward the hospital. . . . His conversation showed no evidence of confusion.

Or in the instance of client L.A.:

> March 2, 1933: Patient reported at the clinic today. She is living at home. . . . She assists with the housework, makes the beds, washes the dishes, and occasionally goes to a show or party with her sisters. There have been no disturbed periods since she left the hospital.

The social worker made no effort to delve beneath the surface — in light of her case load and other responsibilities, how could she? Hence, when both of these clients eventually suffered reversals, she was unable to understand the problems or respond to them. The social worker was as likely to prevent recurring illness as the parole officer was to prevent recurring crime.[73]

The psychopathic hospitals administered outpatient clinics whose style of operation mirrored that of their inpatient facilities. New York's Psychiatric Institute kept its outreach work as exclusive as its residential care. Only those who demonstrated a high likelihood of recovery or fit into an already existing research project were treated, a group that amounted to about one-half of the applicants. In 1937, the outpatient clinic reported accepting "Young adults, of at least average intelligence, whose mental condition was of recent origin, and could cooperate with various research programs." Boston Psychopathic, for its part, ran a clinic that was as diagnostically oriented as its hospital, and no more capable of delivering treatment. In 1921 the clinic calculated that it was serving 1,439 patients in 1,500 clinic hours. It disposed of 660 of the cases with one meeting each: "To a very large extent this group is made up of the frankly psychotic cases which are referred to the Boston Psychopathic Hospital or a State hospital." These patients took up a total of 450 hours. Accordingly, "we find that we are left with one thousand and fifty hours with which to examine and treat 779 patients, which allows us about one hour and twenty minutes to each patient per year. That such a limited amount of time for each individual patient makes adequate treatment difficult is obvious."[74]

As in the case of family care and parole, a lack of community cooperation hindered the outpatient program. But in this instance, it was not so much the general public as the local physicians and county medical societies who blocked reform goals. Some of them were fearful of state intrusions into health care. To them, outreach meant encroachment, and so just as they did battle with the clinics established with federal funds to deliver maternal and child health care (eventually succeeding in cutting off appropriations), so they opposed public clinics to deliver psychiatric care. In Illinois, one researcher noted "the opposition of county medical societies to extra-mural work by the hospitals . . . [because] the state was infringing on the field of the private practitioners." As he explained, "This was ground sacred to the feet of the private physician. If he wished, he might call in the hospital physician in consultation; that was his professional privilege. But should the hospital attempt to reach out into the community in furthering the cause of mental health, the whole foundations of medical practice were immediately endangered! Hence there was strong and continuous opposition to the parole clinics." Other doctors simply showed a fatal indifference. As one national survey discovered: "The attitude of local physicians to state hospital clinics was . . . neutral, uninterested or uninformed rather than either antagonistic or definitely favorable. The effect of such an attitude on the work of the clinics seemed to be reflected chiefly in the scarcity of referrals from private medical sources."[75]

Yet these considerations were not nearly as critical as the apathy or hostility of the medical superintendents. The notion that an institutional staff would be willing to conduct an outpatient program was altogether fanciful. To superintendents, the clinics did not even offer the modest conveniences of boarding-out or parole. From their consistently narrow perspective, after-care or community clinics were not part of what they were budgeted to do; outpatient care was a distraction and one that would siphon off their already slim resources. A superintendent explained to Helen Witmer of the National Committee for Mental Hygiene that "in his judgment, a hospital's first duty was to its inpatients and that an extensive community program was not warranted unless a staff specially equipped for such work was provided [read: on someone else's budget line]. He deplored the tendency to 'oversell' mental hygiene and said he believed that clinic work carried on by a staff of ward psychiatrists not only handicapped the hospital's normal work but was of little value to the outpatients as well." In other words, superintendents' vision was so completely bounded by institutional walls that they were not about to give attention to the outside community. They would not release their inmates, their staff, or their funds to alternative programs.[76]

The consequences of this perspective to the mental hygiene movement were fatal. The superintendents' attitudes meant that with a handful of exceptions, public expenditures in mental health would be devoted primarily, almost exclusively, to institutional care. In the 1920's and still more clearly in the 1930's, the needs of the state hospitals dominated the agenda of the state departments of mental hygiene, and by extension, controlled the budgets of governors and legislators. Between 1930 and 1937, only twelve state departments of mental hygiene made any attempt to organize and to fund outpatient work apart from the control of the state hospitals, and these occasional efforts were typically short-lived and sporadic. Only three state departments, New York, Massachusetts, and Pennsylvania, were able to establish something of a network of outpatient clinics — and even there, the facilities were devoted not to adults or to patients on parole (where alternatives to institutionalization were most at stake), but to children.[77]

Moreover, the outcomes in two of these same states demonstrated just how powerful institutional interests were. Pennsylvania's Bureau of Mental Hygiene actually hoped to work with the state hospitals, to coordinate their clinic effort, and to give independent funding only to clinics in rural areas that were distant from the institutions. But cooperation proved impossible. The dominant figure in each clinic was supposed to be a psychiatrist on loan from the nearest mental hospital. But as the Pennsylvania Bureau learned: "Having for the most part, responsible positions on the staffs of hospitals, the consultant's time is very limited." Moreover, "difficulties centering around state supervision developed in two hospitals"; superintendents were not eager to come under direct state agency control and certainly not to come under control by an agency looking to outpatient care. Finally, the Depression killed off what personnel shortages and discord did not. By 1939, the Pennsylvania Bureau abandoned outpatient work altogether: "The provision of clinics has been left largely to the state hospitals," which was, in effect, their death sentence.[78]

In much the same way, the Massachusetts Division of Mental Hygiene did manage for a time to administer a network of clinics within Boston. But it was not able to move out into the rest of the state and even half of the Boston clinics soon disappeared. Officials believed that part of the problem might have been the reluctance of first- and second-generation immigrants to use the clinics. But more, "for years the Division consistently viewed its clinic program as temporary, its aim being to stimulate the state hospitals to offer comprehensive mental health services to the districts in which they were located." The plan, however, could not succeed. As the Commissioner of Mental Diseases explained in 1936: "It has been demonstrated beyond all doubt that we cannot expect the state hospitals to operate these clinics with the by-products of their hospital staff." If clinic services were to be offered, "it is absolutely necessary that each institution be provided with funds with which to secure adequately trained psychiatrists, psychologists, and social workers and that the clinic personnel should not have duties connected with the institution."[79] But such advice merely demonstrated the extraordinary difficulties that the Massachusetts Division, indeed the entire mental hygiene movement, confronted. Reformers thought in terms of cooperation and a division of labor, but such a hope was doomed to disappointment. Perhaps it was because the funding was too limited so that the institutions, wanting to guard their every penny, blocked attempts to support alternate programs. Perhaps it was because superintendents were determined to preserve their monopoly over the care of the insane. No matter, the outcome was the same: the institutions undercut the effort to promote outpatient care.

What few successes the mental hygiene movement enjoyed came in the private sector. Some of the leading urban social welfare agencies did organize outpatient clinics, particularly for children, and by the close of the 1930's, about a hundred of them were in operation. Individual psychiatrists and social workers, too, began to affiliate with these agencies, preferring to work with clients in the community than with inmates in the asylums. But the private sector did not have adequate resources to transform the system of care for the mentally ill. Public funding was necessary for that — but the institutions, at least through the World War II period, controlled the sources of funding, the state budgets. Eventually, federal interventions would alter the balance — but even then, the contest between the institution and community care would not be easily or quickly resolved.[80]

It may well be, with all the advantages that hindsight allows, that reformers made a fateful mistake in helping to justify a custodial role for the state hospitals. The institutions consistently and successfully used this rationale to their best advantage. Superintendents were often prepared to describe their function as taking care of the "social waste," the senile, the alcoholic, the syphilitic, and the schizophrenic. It may be difficult to imagine a less inviting task, a more troublesome or unrewarding mandate, but its very grimness gave the state hospitals a powerful warrant for survival.

And survive they did. In 1950 the Council of State Governments examined "The Mental Health Programs of the 48 States" and reported that while the general population had increased 2.6 times between 1880 and 1940, the mental hospital population had increased 12.6 times. In 1903, the resident population of the state hospitals was 159 per 100,000 of general population; in 1948 the figure was 322 per 100,000. And every indicator confirmed the chronicity of the patients. The number of insane in county and city almshouses decreased over these years as custodial care became the more exclusive province of the state hospitals; during the same period private mental hospitals witnessed very little growth in number, precisely because the chronic were not filling their wards. And the diagnostic classifications of entering state hospital patients in 1946 repeated the familiar pattern: 6 percent syphilitic, 4 percent alcoholic, 28 percent senile, 19 percent schizophrenic. (The private hospitals, by contrast, admitted only 1 percent syphilitic, 9 percent senile, 2.5 percent alcoholic, and 14 percent schizophrenic.) The resident institutional population was even more pronounced in its chronicity: schizophrenics, for example, made up one-fifth of admissions but more than half of hospital inmates. Duration of hospitalization pointed in the same custodial direction. In a state like New York only 16 percent of patients resident on April 1, 1947, had been confined for less than one year; one-third had been confined five to fourteen years, and a staggering 27 percent, fifteen years or more.[81]

These figures gave superintendents their final retorts to would-be critics. First, they could point to the long list of custodial problems (overcrowding, staff shortages, chronic patients, and the like) and argue that *if only* they had more doctors or more beds or a better trained nursing staff or a better class of patients, *then* recoveries would increase, treatment would go on, research would take place, and the institution would become a hospital. If that was not sufficient, they had a last-ditch defense, as useful in the twentieth century as it had been in the nineteenth: if not us, who? Surely it was better to care for the mentally ill in state hospitals than in county almshouses or in poor farms or in household attics or in unsupervised boarding homes or in families looking to exploit patients for their labor. But in retrospect, such arguments had more to do with convenience than with conscience. As the performance of the state hospitals over these decades makes amply clear, institutional survival, and not patient welfare, was the ultimate consideration.

V

Dreams Die Hard

CHAPTER ELEVEN

The Diary of an Institution

IT IS COMMONPLACE for individuals, particularly those occupying the high places of politics and culture, to keep a diary of their activities and ideas. But it is extraordinary for an institution to do so: to maintain a running account of its ambitions and goals, its successes and failures over a period of years. By a series of odd circumstances just such a diary was created at the Norfolk, Massachusetts, penitentiary, seven hundred single-spaced typewritten pages that cover the two most critical years in its history, 1932 and 1933. It is nothing less than a text that explores, intimately and explicitly as diaries are prone to do, just what happened when the hopes of a generation of reformers were translated into practice.

If diary keepers are not usually the ordinary men of their times, Norfolk was certainly not the typical institution of its time. It represented a grand effort to implement the Progressive reform program for the deviant. Indeed, as with the nineteenth-century penitentiaries and asylums, the list of notables who visited Norfolk or were consultants to the project was long and impressive, including Sheldon Glueck, Thorsten Sellin, Miriam Van Waters, Elton Mayo, Edwin Sutherland, and William Thomas. Norfolk was to be nothing less than the model institution that realized the most advanced and scientific system of incarceration.

The novelty of the Norfolk *Diary* lay not merely in its form but in its content. The document is as clear and specific a statement of the Progressive program for incarceration as can be found, revealing the internal strengths and weaknesses of the reform design. More important, the *Diary* pages move rapidly back and forth between rhetoric and reality, between principles and practices. They expose more vividly than any other single source the dynamics that operated as reformers attempted to create a therapeutic institution. To be sure, Norfolk is clearly a unique case in many ways. The idiosyncratic elements that shaped its story are not inconsiderable. Howard Gill, in charge of the program, had his own special strengths (an optimism and a confidence) and weaknesses (an ability to delude himself and an inability to delegate authority) that helped to determine the outcome of events. Nevertheless, the *Diary* affords an unusual opportunity to explore what Progressives were attempting to do, to what degree they could succeed, and, most important here, the elements that impeded or promoted their attempt to reform the asylum.

The founding of the Norfolk Prison Colony, as it was officially designated, was no different than that of any other state prison. Agitation for a new institution in Massachusetts started in the early 1920's as state legislators and philanthropic groups, particularly the women's clubs, complained of the antiquated facilities at Charlestown — and no wonder, since that structure dated from 1805 and was severely overcrowded, with inmates confined two to a tiny cell or sleeping in schoolrooms made over into dormitories. The legislature responded in 1927, appropriating $100,000 to begin the construction of a wall for a prison that could either serve as a colony to Charlestown, holding its overflow, or perhaps come to replace it altogether. The site itself was a piece of state land some twenty-three miles from Boston which had first held an inebriate hospital, and later, after it failed to cure its charges, had become a rehabilitation camp for sick and wounded World War I soldiers. The appointment to superintendent went to Howard Gill. An efficiency expert who had graduated from Harvard College and Harvard Business School, who had worked for Herbert Hoover in the Commerce Department, and who had recently completed a survey on prison industries for the Justice Department, Gill seemed the perfect choice to oversee the construction of the new prison and its administration. In all ways, then, Norfolk had a rather unremarkable beginning.[1]

In short order, however, the institution assumed a special character, at once the result of fortuitous circumstances and the logical outcome of Progressive policies. By chance, a new state commissioner of corrections, Warren Stearns, took office in Massachusetts in 1928; but it was no accident that he was a psychiatrist. In the 1920's and 1930's, psychiatrists were proving themselves as ready to treat one class of deviants as another, and Stearns was understandably eager to import his techniques for treatment into the prison. His first report to the legislature noted that while the existing system appeared "in general to be well managed," his "most serious criticism [was] the lack of work with the individual inmate according to his needs. . . . Unless all the available data concerning individuals is accumulated and made readily accessible, we cannot hope to handle these individuals to the best advantage."[2]

At the same time, Howard Gill was undergoing something of a personal transformation at Norfolk itself. For purely financial reasons, convict laborers were building the prison wall; some one hundred inmates from Charlestown were living in the Oval, as the old hospital buildings were called, and spending almost two years erecting the barriers and the buildings that would eventually imprison them. The construction and the course of daily living went well at Norfolk, really very well; perhaps the inmates were carefully selected, or perhaps steady work did boost their morale, or perhaps Gill was an especially effective leader. In all events, Gill was soon ready to generalize a prison routine from this experience. It was not merely that the wall was being built on schedule; rather, the inmates seemed dependable — they could be given responsibility without abusing it, they could be put on their honor and trusted. Gill was learning that convicts were human beings and more, he was becoming convinced that his type of program could be rehabilitative.

These notions, as we have seen, underlay all Progressive thinking. But it was one thing to read about them and quite another to experience them directly. Exuberantly Gill told the legislature in 1928: "We are trying not only to build a wall, but to build men." And a few years later, when recounting to a visiting architect the origins of the Norfolk experiment, he declared: "We did not come here with a plan all worked out as many people imagined. The original idea was to build a bastille, but during the two years we lived down here with 150 inmates, clearing the land and building the wall, we began to get the idea of a Prison Colony."[3] Indeed, in later days, when Norfolk was having its troubles, the staff looked back to the building time with all the nostalgia that second-generation Puritan ministers reserved in their jeremiads for the building time in the Massachusetts Bay Colony. "The era of the best spirit in the Oval," recalled one official, "came to a close when the wall was put into operation, and life became as a consequence more institutionalized."[4]

But disappointments were still in the future. At the outset, Gill was certain, really cocksure, that he could organize a rehabilitative prison and build new men as he was building new walls. What the components of the plan should be, in all their detail, he was less sure of, but somehow or other the early experience at the Oval had to become a basis for a reformatory routine. And so had some sort of social work — and this not merely because Stearns was the commissioner but because of the centrality of a case work approach to all Progressive thinking. Around these principles Gill and Stearns entered into an easy partnership to make Norfolk an exemplary institution.[5]

To Gill's credit, he avoided the all too common reformer tactic of promoting the likelihood of his own venture's success by denigrating the motives of his predecessors. "These prisons of 1830," he frankly admitted, "were the reform institutions of the world." By the same token, he was fully aware of reform's bad track record; he not only had a general sense of the inadequacy of most institutional programs (through his work for the Justice Department), but like many of his colleagues, was particularly dismayed at the high rates of recidivism that Sheldon and Eleanor Glueck reported in their study of inmates released from the Concord, Massachusetts, Reformatory. Gill, however, did take comfort in the thought that prisons were a relatively new invention. "We are not so old that the prison system has developed any sacred traditions that cannot be examined to see if they are effective, and this is very helpful."[6]

The first result of these considerations was Gill's application in January, 1930, to the Bureau of Social Hygiene (BSH) of the Rockefeller Foundation for a grant. After six months of negotiations, chiefly with University of Chicago criminologist Edwin Sutherland and Bureau staff member Leonard Dunham, he had it. The Bureau, as Sutherland successfully proposed to the Board, allotted $55,000 "to defray the extraordinary expenses of a five year experiment." The state "would continue to meet the ordinary expenses of the care of the prisoners." The BSH funds would be used "to keep a complete record of the experiment and of its results, and to assist in carrying the experiment to its logical limits." More particularly, $10,000 a year would pay the salaries of persons to investigate "the antecedent records of the prisoners" (Stearns's part), to keep a record of "activities in the Colony" (Gill's part), and to check on "the behavior of prisoners after release" (Sutherland's part but never carried out). Sutherland was never especially precise in describing the nature of the experiment but he did convey Gill's sense that the work at the Oval was to be the prototype for the conduct of the prison. "Several new methods of handling the prisoners are being tested," and "extraordinarily careful studies are made of the prisoners and extraordinary efforts made to develop their interests and abilities and solve their personal problems." Sutherland went on, "The experiment is, therefore, of interest in penology everywhere and it is important that a careful record be kept of what is done in the experiment and what results are produced by it." And he concluded with a line that by itself would have won Gill the grant:

"This Colony is in many ways the most interesting and promising piece of pioneer work in penology that is being carried on in America."[7]

As soon as the grant was awarded, Dunham dispatched the foremost criminologist of his generation, Thorsten Sellin, to report on Norfolk's progress. Sellin, on the whole, liked what he saw and over the next several years served as Dunham's major evaluator of the project. In March, 1931, halfway into the first year of the grant, he judged Norfolk to be a splendid piece of administrative work, giving Gill full credit for it. But Sellin was unhappy that Norfolk lacked a serious research component. Sellin and Dunham persuaded Gill to hire a Minnesota criminologist, George Vold, to take over the research; but Gill, in what would prove to be typical fashion, would not allow anyone to operate independently on his territory. Sellin then told Dunham to stay in touch with Gill, to help him as he could, and to await the report.[8]

But so passive a posture did not content Dunham or Sellin for long. The Bureau's man wanted to be certain that something tangible resulted from the Norfolk grant; like so many other program officers, he had to show his board a product for its funds. And Sellin, whose own work was, and continues to be, acutely sensitive to the historical forces that shape the criminal justice system, did not want the Norfolk experiment to disappear without leaving any traces. It was Sellin who came up with the suggestion that pleased everyone. "I had a long talk with Mr. Gill," he told Dunham in December, 1931:

> I pointed out again that in an institution such as Norfolk, which is constantly changing aspect, many things occur from day to day, many issues are met and decisions made . . . and yet are lost sight of in the course of time. . . . If the reports on Norfolk were to be of any help to administrators . . . these transient elements must be seized and embodied in some kind of permanent record. . . . I suggested that Mr. Gill engage a competent secretary who would day by day make the rounds of the important departments, talk to the heads

and particularly to Mr. Gill himself and his deputy, ask them what significant events had occurred during the day . . . and then ask them to dictate for a few minutes on the points raised.[9]

Gill quickly agreed, immediately putting the program as Sellin outlined it into effect. Now Dunham had his monthly reports, Gill had satisfied the Bureau and kept control over research, and Sellin had served the needs of future researchers marvelously well.

Despite the tentative quality of what was to constitute the Norfolk plan, the critical assumptions that composed its program represented the essentials of Progressive thinking. To be sure, shifts in policy were not infrequent at Norfolk, even over the two-year period that the experiment lasted; Gill had a distinct aversion to being pinned down too quickly or consistently to a single plan of action. ("It has been necessary," he often claimed in the *Diary*, "to feel our way before setting out on any too definite a schedule.") And his staff recognized well his determination to avoid what he called "too rapid crystallization." Gill had what some of them called an unrivaled "ability to pass the buck," to brood over a decision for weeks without coming to a resolution. Nevertheless, Norfolk's design followed the ideas that all right-thinking persons advanced for prison reform.[10]

The *Official Manual of the State Prison Colony*, compiled in December, 1932, opened with a "Statement of Fundamental Policies":

> Norfolk seeks not only to guard securely the men committed to its safekeeping, but as a fundamental policy to assume its responsibility for returning them to society . . . as better men capable of leading useful, law abiding lives.

These first lines embodied that most significant and ultimately most problematic Progressive assumption: that the prison could perform both a custodial and a rehabilitative function, that there was no inherent conflict between guarding men securely and

making them better men, between incapacitation and reformation. "The basis of our whole social philosophy here," declared
Gill, "must be that the staff and the inmates will cooperate for the
good of all. I cannot see even a small wedge driven between the
two if we are to build and educate men in the right social attitude."[11]

The *Manual* next defined the characteristics of Norfolk's population and its own style of rehabilitation.

> It accepts its charges as delinquent, socially malad-
> justed human beings . . . who need help, understand-
> ing and guidance in rebuilding their lives and charac-
> ters. Each man is looked upon as an individual with
> individual needs and problems.[12]

In these brief phrases, Norfolk declared its allegiance to the
Progressives' interpretation of the etiology of crime and to their
prescriptions for cure. The inmate was a "delinquent," a term
that signaled a commitment to explore the "state of mind" of the
deviant rather than his "act." Then to label the inmate "socially
maladjusted" was to confirm the point: the roots of deviant behavior did not reflect inherited physical characteristics or moral
failings, but, to use William Healy's phrase, "bad habits of mind."
The Norfolk inmates, therefore, required "guidance" so that they
could "rebuild" their lives. (Gill never had difficulty in grafting
his favorite construction metaphors onto the language of psychology.) Finally, of course, the *Manual* pledged to treat each
inmate as an "individual," to pattern its response to the needs of
each case.

To Norfolk, these phrases meant that the institution should
resemble a hospital and dispense case work as its medicine.
"Sometimes I liken a prison," Gill remarked, "to a great social
hospital in which there are men with all manner of diseases — the
seriously sick, the men with minor ailments, the men who . . . will
get well in a short time, the men who will never get well." The
trouble was that, "1. In the average prison nobody knows what is
the matter with the people there. 2. Nobody is doing anything
about it." Gill delighted in extending the hospital comparison.

Should a man fall down on the street, the hospital was not interested in the fact that he fell, but in why he fell. "Supposing on the other hand that the Doctor simply asked him what he did for a living before he fell down and he told him that he was a cook, so the man is placed in the kitchen and told to come back to the office six months later as cured. We should consider this attitude ridiculous, and yet this is just what we are doing in prison." Gill then concluded: "We are the last field to apply casework to problems that deal with human beings. The things which the hospital considers elementary we look upon as revolutionary."[13]

There was a third and no less critical premise that underlay the Norfolk experiment, one whose exact fit with a medical model always remained ambiguous. Prison organization, Progressives insisted, should re-create the organization of a normal community. Such an orientation fit ever so well with Gill's own experience during the "building time." The ideal of a prison emulating society had a personal meaning and immediacy for him. Thus, the final principle of the *Manual's* "Statement of Fundamental Purposes" declared:

> The administrative organization and living conditions within the institution are made to approximate as nearly as can be in a prison the atmosphere and spirit of a normal community. . . . Community life within the institution is a common undertaking, based upon the principle of joint responsibility shared by administration and inmates.

Thus, one of the staff, in summarizing the Norfolk plan, declared: "It is a prison *Community*." And Gill returned again and again to this notion. Norfolk had to be "a replica of a normal community, with its industries, jail, farm, etc. . . . We should develop in men respect rather than docility." The test that had to be applied to every prison routine was: "Is that thing normal in community living, will it tend to make men normal?"[14]

Neither Gill nor any of his contemporaries perceived a conflict between the model of the hospital and the model of the community, and they moved easily between one kind of image and the other. Whatever differences there were would disappear when, in Gill's words, prisons "abandon the idea of uniformity . . . to get down to casework, and the individualization and socialization of the criminal."[15] But the matter could not be disposed of so easily. In a hospital model, the doctor rules and (recent rights movements aside) rules quite arbitrarily; he diagnoses and prescribes, and the patient accepts and swallows. In a democratic community model, on the other hand, authority is to be shared, responsibility divided, and autocracy prohibited — the goal is partnership, not docile obedience. In other words, in a hospital model the patient is sick and needs a cure to be imposed upon him; in a community model, the person is more of a misfit or a non-conformist who must learn new habits and behavior. Further, suppose the medicine to be prescribed is bitter: how far can one go in violating the precepts of "normal living" in order to administer it? Pain for the sake of cure is commonplace in a hospital (just think of surgery); but is it just as appropriate within a community — can there be no such thing as cruel and unusual rehabilitation? Or what if the patient says "No, thank you"? Under a community model can his wishes be disregarded and his compliance coerced?

And all these questions are intrinsic to the models. What if one steps back to ask prior questions? Were doctors or case workers able to understand the "illness" from which criminals suffered; or, even more important, did they have the medicines with which to treat them? Was the state of criminology at all equivalent to the state of medicine? And could one ever really expect to re-create a normal society behind walls? But now we are shifting, appropriately, from assumptions to programs, from principles to implementation, so let us move directly to consider how Norfolk translated its ideology into a prison routine.

Since at Norfolk form was inextricably linked to content we must look first to the institution's physical design. The dominant architectural feature, visually and structurally, was the wall that enclosed some thirty-five acres. It was true that the decision to erect it had preceded Gill's appointment. But Gill not only supervised its construction and completed its design, he staunchly defended its appropriateness. The wall was in every respect a prison wall, rising nineteen feet above ground; going four to eighteen feet below ground; equipped with floodlights and searchlights; and topped, this at Gill's suggestion, with four strands of barbed wire that carried 2,300 volts of electricity. Five towers with bullet-proof glass jutted out, each holding (again to Gill's specifications) an arsenal of machine guns, rifles, and tear gas. Sellin disliked these features, regretting that machine guns were to be found at Norfolk.[16] Gill, however, was without ambivalence, not only describing the wall as a necessary fact of prison life, but as an asset. The principle that custody did not infringe upon rehabilitation was no less valid, in his mind, in architecture than in social work. The wall provided the measure of external security that enlarged the inmates' liberties. "Objections have been raised by visitors," Gill acknowledged, "to the 'bristling' wall." But their opposition was mistaken. "If we make our wall impregnable . . . we not only reduce the danger to life, but we also make possible a fairly free community within the wall. . . . Places without a wall have to maintain such a stringent, strict system that psychological conditions are worse than with a wall."[17]

True to this claim, Norfolk did not repeat the standard state penitentiary design (an imposing administration building with radiating wings made up of cell blocks). Instead, it grouped a number of two- and three-story buildings around an open rectangular space. The majority of inmates lived in these dormitories, in single rooms or in four- to seven-bed cubicles; in some of the dorms, the interior space was open so that the men could move about freely; in others locked doors and wire mesh sealed off particular sections. Still, Norfolk did not depart altogether from a prison plan. In keeping with the idea that the Colony could simultaneously serve the ends of custody and rehabilitation, or, to use another kind of language, could be at once a minimum (open dorm), medium (closed dorm), and maximum security institution, Norfolk had a Receiving Building, what inmates and staff alike referred to as its "jail." Gill intended this structure to house

newly arrived prisoners and all disciplinary cases, and so fitted it
with 105 regular cells, using the best of steel and the latest in
locking devices ("tool proof" was the manufacturer's term). And
Gill defended the jail just as he had the wall: the isolation of the
few would enable him to treat the many.[18]

The organization of Norfolk's staff followed with remarkable
consistency from its guiding principles and physical design. Gill
divided the personnel into two separate groups: the custodians
(the guards) on the one hand, and the case workers (the House
Officers) on the other. Once again, security considerations would
be separated in order to allow for the implementation of a rehabilitative program. "In most prisons," Gill explained, there prevails "a peculiar mixture of personal relationship and custodial
function. . . . A prison guard is at one moment an officer, but at
another he is sympathizing with the inmate as a person. The
results are sometimes disastrous." Security could be weakened by
an overindulgent or too friendly guard, and at the same time, an
inmate could be hassled by a meddlesome one. Accordingly, Norfolk "set up a very sharp line of demarcation between the two."
Guards were forbidden to fraternize with the inmates, "not even
to check them up unless they are creating a disturbance." In
keeping with a community model, "they are like the policeman on
the beat. He doesn't interfere or accost persons who are going
about their business." Guards were to concern themselves exclusively with "escape, contraband, and disturbances. . . . In nothing
else do they enter into the institution's life." The ideal recruits to
these positions were "young unmarried men who wish to be
trained for the State Police." And Gill so treated them: they wore
uniforms, carried arms when on duty atop the wall, and lived and
slept in barracks just outside the wall, all in "semi-military organization." In both a literal and a figurative sense, they were to
be at the perimeter of the institution.[19]

At the core were the House Officers, those who lived with the
men in the dormitories and implemented the case work, educational, and vocational assignments. Their function was "to make
the ideal and the program of individual treatment effective in the
daily routine of the institution. . . . These House Officers instead of

being typical prison guards, are essentially caseworkers, charged with the difficult and responsible task of trying to understand the problems and needs of the inmate, and through the medium of scientific friendship to help them." Unlike the guards, they did not wear uniforms (by regulation they were to dress in "clean and tidy ordinary civilian clothes") and they carried no weapons (except, by regulation, "common sense, good judgment, alertness, fair dealing, firmness, tact, good will").[20] Thus Norfolk's design did have an internal coherence: border patrol along a defensible line which was to allow for therapeutic encounters everywhere else.

Which leads us to the most crucial and, not surprisingly, most difficult issue confronting Norfolk: how to bring a commitment to treatment into the daily life of the institution. Where to begin? Gill and all his Progressive colleagues knew the answer, and it came directly from the hospital model — with a system of classification.

But what type of classification should operate within a prison? The scheme that Gill brought to Norfolk represented the best thinking on the subject. In light of his own background (business school, prison industries, working with Herbert Hoover) he found himself most comfortable with Harvard Business School professor Elton Mayo, who was at this moment conducting his well-known experiments with worker adjustment at the General Electric plant at Hawthorne. There was little really that differentiated Mayo's categories from half a dozen other systems. Change a term or two and all of them divided inmates into one of the following five Norfolk categories, the SCAMP plan.

> 1. *Situational Cases:* Presenting little or no personality problems . . . domestic, vocational, financial, educational or other . . . the man whose circumstances and situation are at the bottom of his difficulties . . . Clear up the situation . . . and he no longer tends to be a criminal.
>
> 2. *Custodial Cases:* They are the subnormal, the very abnormal, the old, the senile, the unfit . . . beyond

treatment who will always need supervision . . . low
grade mentalities, inadequate personalities, the senile,
the hardened criminal.

3. *Asocial Cases:* They have a philosophy which is
anti-social . . . That group of professional criminals
who need to develop a new philosophy . . . those in
which . . . gangster activities, racketeering, professional criminal practices seem to be the chief factors . . .
The men who believe in belonging to the gang, who
are going to get theirs by hook or crook.

4. *Medical Cases:* Men who are primarily criminals
because they are physically unable to make the grade
. . . These are the handicapped, deformed, tubercular
. . . who have become criminals mainly by reason of
their afflictions.

5. *Personality Cases:* In this class come the psychotics,
neurotics, peculiar personalities, who have fallen into
crime . . . all cases where personality difficulties play
the major part in leading the man into crime . . . in
which the man's personal problem had tended to get
him crosswise with other people.[21]

Gill was perfectly clear on what SCAMP was not. It had nothing to do with the seriousness of the crime or the severity of the
punishment. "Certainly the murderer, the robber and the rapist
may be found in all groups." Second, it was not meant to serve as
a prison housing classification; Gill did not intend to put all the
asocial cases into one dorm and all the personality cases into
another. Most schemes, he argued, were too ambitious, attempting to "work out a single classification which will cover all needs.
As a result, the classification is apt to become a hodge podge of
administrative psychology and miscellaneous data." Nor were
these categories to be predictive of eventual adjustment or success on parole. Finally, *"It is not a classification for causation or
motivation*; the cause of a crime may lie back in the environment
of the individual and yet his present diagnosis may be asocial."[22]
What use then were these categories? "First and foremost this

is a *treatment* classification and designed primarily to indicate what is to be done at the moment about any case and by whom." With SCAMP, case work became "a significant, specific thing," and Gill comfortably returned to a medical analogy: it allowed the institution "to build up a therapeutic practice, just as a doctor builds up a practice. . . . We have a situational case, a situational disease, and we find that certain things have helped in treating the cases." Thus, in conceptual terms, the design solved the problem of making the prison into a hospital by identifying what the counterpart for disease was in the criminal. In practical terms, it indicated who was to do the actual treating. "These five groupings more or less will be the five techniques to be developed for dealing with human problems and their relations. The situational case rates the technique of the social worker, the medical case is obviously a problem for the doctor, the personality case is a problem for the psychiatrist, the asocial case is for education, and the custodial case for the supervisor, the police, the caretaker."[23]

Yet something of an intellectual shell game is going on; the categories are both more and less than they first appear. Gill insisted that SCAMP was not a classification for causation but for treatment — in other words, he implied that one could rehabilitate the deviant without first understanding the origins of the behavior. Commissioner Stearns made the point explicitly: "If we are in the dark as to the real underlying *cause* of the crime itself, yet we are confronted with any or all of these [SCAMP] conditions as a *result* of the crime, and can treat them if we will."[24] The argument, however, was spurious. The categories incorporated the very assumptions that Gill and Stearns denied that they were making. SCAMP was based finally not on results but on causes, and one need only look back to the definitions to confirm the point. The "situational" problem was "at the bottom" of the criminal activity; the "medical" condition was "mainly the reason" for it; the "personality" make-up "plays the major part in leading" men into crime. Admit to it or not, these categories were explanations, not mere descriptions of conditions.

Further, Gill proposed that rehabilitation at Norfolk proceed on many fronts, using the skills of psychiatrists, teachers, doctors, and social workers. Norfolk was not aiming to do all things to all men but to make its medicine specific to the disease. To use SCAMP in this way, however, was once again to make clear that these were causational categories. If personality was not at the root of the inmate's problems, then why would a psychiatric intervention prove effective? If the medical ailment was not the cause of the crime, why would a doctor's skills be relevant? This contradiction was a central problem for all Progressives, from William Healy to Adolf Meyer, and Gill's enterprise could not escape it.

The fallacies in the Norfolk scheme point not only to the inadequacy of social science concepts, but to an eagerness to do good that would not be thwarted by an ignorance of how to do good. Thus Stearns concluded his remarks on treating results, not causes, with the injunction: "Only when we can do nothing, may we regard a man as merely a custodial problem." Whatever our lack of understanding, we must be doing something. Or as Edwin Powers, who did the final evaluation of case work at Norfolk, concluded: "It must be admitted that neither psychology nor criminology has reached the point where it can answer questions of causality with any degree of assurance. Perhaps a research into this problem will someday be undertaken." Meanwhile the effort to treat had to continue, and it might well be successful. "At this point we must be dogmatic. We have certain convictions incapable of proof. We believe that we know these men."[25] In the end, the Norfolk system rested on faith.

Oddly, Norfolk's classifications and general design were never questioned very closely. Perhaps it was because all of the programs had the blanket justification of being part of an "experiment." In this sense, the Bureau's grant gave Gill not only funds but a useful source of legitimation. And the medical model helped to spare Norfolk from attack. Just as doctors tried one kind of medicine and then another, so Norfolk too would "build up" a therapeutic practice. The record of the institution, its *Diary*, like the record of the patient's progress, his chart, would reveal which interventions succeeded and which did not. Finally, and most significantly, those who might have been Gill's critics were his collaborators. So prestigious and innovative a sociologist as William Thomas visited the Colony, made a few queries about the categories (why were situational cases in prison at all?), but did not doubt their essential usefulness. A prestigious Norfolk committee on case work, chaired by Elton Mayo and composed of some of the leading figures in public health and medicine at Harvard, were also comfortable with the classification scheme — it was, for all practical purposes, their own. The contradictions and ambiguities that underlay Norfolk's design escaped comment because they were so essentially Progressive.[26]

While most of Gill's energies went into implementing the hospital treatment model he did in several ways attempt to realize the ideal of the prison as community. Dress for inmates was pants and shirts, not special uniforms; the Colony encouraged visits and letter writing. Gill also instituted inmate self-government modeled on Thomas Mott Osborne's Mutual Welfare League. The Inmate Council was to be more than a grievance committee, if less than a real governing body. But the most critical and revealing of all these arrangements was Gill's scheme for housing the inmates. It was almost as elaborate as the classification plan, and no less caught up in a web of contradictions.

Norfolk's system for assigning men to the dormitories was intended both "to facilitate the treatment objectives of the institution" (according to the *Manual* this was its "primary purpose") and to make the prison into a normal community. Men were to be grouped "upon the basis of their attitude and cooperation in carrying out their *individual programs*, and the extent to which they can be relied upon to take active part in the *community program*." Those who fulfilled the criteria were graded A-1 ("entirely cooperative and trustworthy") or A-2 (those "who are getting something out of Norfolk and supporting the community program"), and they enjoyed the greatest privileges (lights out at ten o'clock; the choice of rooms; more visits; and so on). In more traditional language, which Gill also used, they were the minimum security inmates. Next in rank were the medium security inmates: B-1 (who did not give "full cooperation") and B-2 ("not carrying out and not supporting the program, and who cannot be trusted in the dormitory units, or for whom there is no room in the dormitory units"). They were locked in their rooms at six, not allowed to participate in the Inmate Council, and limited to writing one letter and receiving one visit weekly. At the bottom of the ladder was the "C group" (the "disciplinary problems and who need custodial supervision"). These maximum security inmates were confined to the steel cells in the Receiving Building, "under severe restrictions."[27]

To Gill, this plan looked to reward men not for mere good conduct, for doing their time, but for receptivity to treatment: in his favorite phrase, for "what the man is getting out of the institution as the result of conscious endeavor." All inmates (except the C group) would enjoy a decent minimum of comforts; those who took advantage of Norfolk's opportunities would enjoy special privileges. The housing plan was also designed to emphasize "the constructive forces in each man"; the dormitories would encourage "self-respect, trust, privacy, that is freedom from the stigma of forced restraint . . . with various types of rooms covering individual needs." Lastly, it promoted an intelligent allocation of attention. Norfolk would devote its energies to those most eager to be helped.[28]

But again, all is not so simple as it first appears. More is at stake here than hyperbolic rhetoric (how would dormitories ever reduce the stigma of incarceration imposed by an outside public?) or vague concepts (just what does "getting the most" from Norfolk mean?). A housing system whose "primary purpose" ostensibly was "to facilitate treatment" in fact was a system whose primary purpose was to fill custodial needs. The discrepancy between the rhetoric of rehabilitation and the reality of the ABC ranking is apparent as soon as one begins exploring the reasons why the treatment categories were useless for making dormitory assignments. Why at just this point did Gill abandon the hospital model — which does not divide its wards by patient behavior — to adopt a far more conventional plan of separating inmates by minimum, medium, and maximum security designations? Gill himself supplied the answer: the ABC categories took into account the inmate's "general attitude which will be based

upon previous record and reputation and Institutional history."
Therapy aside, some men were more dangerous than others, more
troublesome than others; and to ignore this fact would undermine the good order of the institution. The housing classification
would protect "the safety and security of the institution."[29]

Had Gill been queried about the discrepancy (of course he was
not), his answer would have been that the housing system was to
resolve custodial questions so as to permit treatment. But his
response, however Progressive, cannot pass. Security at Norfolk
was supposed to be at the perimeters of the institution, at the
wall, with the guards; and now we find it at the core, internal to
the design. In effect, Gill was bringing in through the (back)
door all the considerations that he had claimed to be abandoning.
More, the assumptions implicit in the housing system represented
a significant scaling-down of the Norfolk promise. If we had initially believed that all or most of the situational or personality or
asocial cases could be cured, now we learn that only some of
them, the most cooperative, the best behaved, could profit from
treatment. If at first it appeared that the secret to successful
therapy was the right matching of inmate to counselor, now we
learn that the tough cases, the recidivists, the dangerous offenders,
those with the worst reputations, were probably outside Norfolk's treatment plan. In short, the hospital analogy broke down
completely. Rehabilitation was not like a medicine that could be
prescribed to an inmate. He had to be so open and receptive to
treatment as to be almost already cured.

Gill's housing scheme also indicated that when it was not rhetoric but reality that counted, treatment took second place to institutional needs. Therapy was the luxury grafted onto the institutional program. Norfolk's organization did not balance security
and rehabilitation. *Norfolk by design was first and foremost a
prison which delivered some treatment, not a hospital whose patients happened to be criminal offenders.* And turning the definition around is to make more than a stylistic revision; it puts the
entire enterprise in a very different context.[30] Perhaps Gill would
interject that even if dormitory arrangements reflected custodial
considerations, still security did not prohibit treatment. But in-

stead of pursuing how lame such an answer would be, let us keep
the tension unresolved and ask not if Norfolk could but if Norfolk did deliver on its rehabilitative promise.

The tension cannot be maintained for long because in the most
obvious ways, and by all accounts, Norfolk's effort to deliver
treatment was a total failure. The attempt to implement therapy
through case work bordered on the farcical. By mid-1933, one
disappointed staff member informed Commissioner Stearns:
"There is a vast difference between what Norfolk is on paper and
what it actually is in practice. . . . No social case work has been
applied at Norfolk which could be acceptable to any authorities
on casework practice. Fundamentally there is no set-up to carry
on casework method." Louis Balsam, one of Gill's oldest and
strongest supporters, put the matter in unmistakably authentic terms: "The House Officers are making 'perfunctory passes' at
casework. For the most part they are bored and indifferent about
it. Casework days are devoted in fair part to discussions about
salary increases, baseball games, swimming, women, and other
delightful institutions." Hence, Edwin Powers's report on treatment appropriately concluded that "Casework has fallen far short
of achieving its goal. . . . The casework objectives were too ambitious, or the difficulties . . . were too overwhelming. . . . We are
too ignorant of the essential ingredients in 'treatment.' "[31]
Yet the least interesting aspect of the Norfolk experiment is the
final outcome. That it failed is not nearly as intriguing as the
interesting ways in which it failed. Some of the causes were predictable, which is another way of saying that they are recurring,
and so we ought to pay all the more attention to them. And some
were surprising and could not have been anticipated, alerting us
to more covert but critical considerations that innovative efforts
in this field had better understand.

An analysis of the dynamics that shaped events at Norfolk
begins with the staff. It was at all levels ill-equipped to implement a treatment program. Gill himself had no special training in
psychology or casework, and perhaps his very faith in the approach was built upon his ignorance. In fact, enthusiasm for the

experiment became one of the most important criteria in selecting the staff. Take the choice of Louis Balsam, the first organizer of case work at Norfolk. Balsam had begun his career in advertising, and as one of the pioneers in the field in the 1920's, quickly made a good deal of money. But Balsam soon had his fill of the job and, quite literally, dropped out. After several years of globe trotting, he returned to the United States and bought a farm at Norfolk; at just this moment Gill arrived at the scene, the two men hit it off well (one adventurer to another?), and Balsam was soon setting up the social work system.[32]

If the rest of the staff had less exotic experiences, they had no more suitable credentials. The Deputy Superintendent was a former cook and night watchman at the Concord Reformatory. The Officers in Charge of the House Staff (OIC's), administrative charts notwithstanding, included a former taxi driver, a male nurse, a shoe salesman, and a former officer from the boys' reformatory. And as for the House Officers themselves, one story will suffice. At the first case work conference one of them was heard to exclaim "that he did not know what all this case work was about. He was a plumber."[33]

Why did Gill compile such a dismal record at recruitment? For one, he felt compelled to recruit OIC's from the officers who had first managed the inmates during the building time; no experiment, it would seem, ever begins totally from scratch. Gill undoubtedly hoped that their having been a part of that marvelous moment of unity and good will, would compensate for their lack of skills. For another, he was bound to recruit his staff from those who passed civil service examinations — and few of them would be social work school graduates. Then too, whatever Gill's sense of the job specifications for dormitory heads, in terms of salary and prerequisites the post was identical with custodial positions in other institutions. "Their real position," as one observer noted, "is comparable to that of attendants in a mental hospital."[34]

But how reconcile plumbers, shoe salesmen, and mental hospital attendants with such an ambitious design? What ever kept Gill, or all the others who visited Norfolk, from simply abandoning the whole project from the outset as overambitious? One common hope was that the House Officers would get on-the-job instruction in casework. The Bureau funds, in fact, did allow Gill to hire two men with some credentials in the field to head up the social work division. But the better trained staff simply could not communicate with the House Officers. Professional jargon was unintelligible to a group of men who lacked college degrees. The House Officers were also suspicious and critical of the professionals, calling them "theoretical" and "pedantic"; the social workers' explanations about inmate behavior seemed too vague to be helpful in practical ways. A diagnostic label did not enable a House Officer to solve daily problems.[35]

In fact, the friction between the House Officers and their social worker superiors was intense. The social workers complained that House Officers asked the men all the wrong questions at the wrong times, and thereby ruined their own attempts to compile meaningful case records; the Officers for their part turned casework conferences into occasions to vent their frustration, creating a dialogue where the two parties regularly spoke past each other.

> House Officer: We should be careful not to let the Research Department . . . [drown us in] its lengthy case histories.
> Psychologist: There was an inappropriate display of emotion, and the attitude of the House Officers seemed to border on antagonism. . . . A high emotional pitch was maintained. . . . It seemed that resentment arising out of low wages, long hours . . . had been vented upon a substitute object.[36]

However acute the division between these two groups, it was mild in comparison to the split between the House Officers and the security staff. Guards and would-be social workers could not coexist in the same institution. The antagonisms were continuous and pervasive, each group certain that the other was engaged in sabotage, each convinced that the other did not belong at Norfolk. The very petty quality of most of the incidents points to how emotionally charged the situation was. Since the House Officers were more comfortable with the *Diary*, their side gets recorded more often. But it takes little imagination to see the same incident from the guards' perspective. Thus, the House Officers complained that the guards did not open locked doors quickly enough for them; or that the guards searched the dorms and then proceeded to confiscate goods that the House Officers had explicitly allowed; or that the guards, against all orders and regulations, insisted on locking the doors of men classified A-1 and A-2. The House Officers generally had the support of their social work superiors, who also were convinced that the custodians were "tearing down the philosophy" of Norfolk, that a campaign had constantly to be mounted against "the advocates who seek to have us move back to the old principles of penology."[37] For their part, the guards complained among themselves ("Casework never did anybody any good. What they need is strict discipline. They are no damn good"), and leaked whatever scandal stories they could to the press. So it did not take long for Norfolk to gain the reputation of being poorly administered, of being unable to keep its own staff in line.[38] Ultimately, Norfolk was the scene of a fierce war between custodians and therapists, and Gill proved to be an inept peacekeeper. The staff could not balance custody and rehabilitation.

Norfolk's treatment ambitions, as we have noted, depended to a large degree upon inmate cooperation. The medicine that was case work demanded their active participation, but in all sorts of ways, and for good reasons, it was not forthcoming. As anyone who has raised children in a two-parent household will immediately understand, inmates were remarkably adept at playing off one staff member against another. Fully aware of the division among the administrators, prisoners skillfully manipulated the system for their own ends. "If you tell an inmate he can't do a certain thing," complained one House Officer, "he goes around to everyone else and gets permission." Thus, the man eager to get assigned to the Colony farm, who knew of his House Officer's reluctance, "runs around to get opinions from other members of the staff, and then comes back to the House Officer and says that the matter is all settled if he will O.K. him." And then what was the officer to do? A refusal seemed like a punishment. "There may be sufficient reason why you don't want a man to go out to the Farm, and you may not want to tell him." So in the end, you gave in, unwilling to be "the only one who is stopping him from doing what he wanted to do," and explaining it as the best way "to keep the confidence of the inmates."[39]

More important, Norfolk's prisoners proved to be particularly reluctant to confide in those who were supposed to be their therapists. Part of the reluctance undoubtedly reflected their belief that such treatment was suitable only for those considered mentally ill; the inmates, in their words, would not consent to be "psychoed." Indeed, among inmates there was a general ranking of institutions that was very sensitive to gradations of stigma: the prison was preferable to the workhouse (it was more honorable to be a criminal than one of the unworthy poor) and the prison and the workhouse were both preferable to the state hospital (better to be sane than insane).[40]

Still stronger reasons prompted inmates to distrust the case worker. From their experience, he seemed to be only the latest in a long line of officials who pried them for information, who wanted them to talk and tell all. Mark Roser, head of social work at Norfolk, complained a few months after his arrival that "the men . . . look upon the casework investigation with an attitude similar as they look upon a police investigation. . . . They must somehow realize the therapeutic value of frankness, and that the information about themselves which they give to caseworkers will not be used as such information is used by the police." But the inmates rejected this contention, certain that whatever they disclosed would be held against them both by the staff and, in even more damaging ways, by the parole board. To talk openly about one's actions and attitudes might well, to use the Norfolk jargon, reveal that one was not getting all that he should from the program; and the penalty might be a B or C classification. Worse yet, Norfolk was only one part of the larger criminal justice system, and staff assurances were no guarantee that the information divulged would not ruin their chances for parole. Despite the institution's claims to the contrary, the inmates understood that in one critical way the case worker did not approximate the doctor in a hospital: he did not hold the key to release.[41]

This problem, endemic to all such situations, was exacerbated at Norfolk by the staff's unwillingness to open up the files to inmates. From a case worker's perspective, no client ever examined his dossier. As Roser told an inmate: "These records were written for use by professional people and like professional medical records they are liable to misinterpretation if read by nonprofessional men." But to the inmates, the House Officers were compiling a secret dossier and the less they cooperated with the venture, the better. They interpreted the closing of the records as a sure sign that practically "all of the reports are unfavorable and . . . that casework consists of just that incriminating feature." (When, as a result of sloppy record keeping, files were left open on a desk or dropped on the floor to be picked up by the sweeper, the inmates did get to see their dossiers; and their suspicions were often confirmed.) Accordingly, cooperation seemed positively foolish. "It is generally conceded among them," concluded one case worker, "that the good things which they do while in the Colony are not recorded to their credit, but that all bum raps, lock ups, etc., go on record and spoil their chances for parole."[42]

Curiously, when Roser himself first arrived at Norfolk, he was particularly sensitive to the problem of the therapist as double agent, the case worker who was at once supposed to serve the institution and the inmate. In one of the first entries in the *Diary* in January, 1932, he noted that Norfolk was going to test "how far is one in an official capacity in the Institution able to gain the confidence of the men, and what use should be made of such confidence." This issue, Roser recognized, "has not yet been satisfactorily answered." Could case work take place within an incarcerative setting? In his words: "It involves a question as to whether or not, if ever, the psychological analysis of an individual connected with an Institution will be successful. Talking with such an individual will be quite hard, because he knows [and Roser here does not deny it] the information will be used both for and against him in securing a parole, and in his life here." He went on to suggest ever so casually that perhaps counseling should be carried on "by an individual who has no official capacity."[43] But whether because the administrative difficulties seemed insuperable (if the institution did not pay the counselor who would?), or because this was really no answer at all (the double agent bind was not avoided merely by getting the case worker a grant), or because the very statement of the problem was too anti-Progressive in its assumptions (this kind of conflict of interest could not be pursued), Roser soon dropped the matter. The inmates, for their part, did not. For them, a case worker remained a cop.

(A brief aside for those interested in parole board proceedings. The men's fears that the board would use the case workers' material against them was exaggerated, because the board was too busy ever to go through their dossiers closely and the case workers had difficulty in summarizing their reports. In fact, the Norfolk staff itself complained that it was not being consulted on parole decisions. The Massachusetts board, like all others, focused far more intently on past criminal record than on institutional behavior or responsiveness to programs. In this sense, the inmates worried excessively and took Norfolk's plans too seriously. Perhaps they just could not conceive that all this fuss and bother, insofar as release was concerned, was pointless.)

Inmates' distrust of case work was part of their hostility to Progressive innovations. To them, administrative discretion and indeterminate sentences meant discrimination and unpredictability. Gill, for example, reported an "interesting talk" with an ex-convict who showed "a true 'con' attitude. . . . Mr. Brown thought the only thing was uniformity, that is, treating everybody alike, and that this was the only system to use." Gill, of course, rejected this notion out of hand and went on to expound Norfolk's treatment philosophy; Mr. Brown, however, would have none of it. His conclusion, as reported by Gill, stood for his fellow inmates as well: "He just could not understand it all."[44]

But what of the treatment program itself? What did the commitment to the SCAMP system amount to in practice? Given the theoretical confusions that underlay the categories (not to men-tion the incompetence of the staff and the suspicions of the inmates), we need not belabor the point of how inept and ineffective rehabilitation actually was at Norfolk. But several points do warrant attention. For one, the all-inclusive character of the SCAMP classifications made it well nigh impossible to compile a dossier; the social worker had no idea of what to leave out. Every detail was seemingly relevant; one had to know the inmate's occupational history (was his a situational case?), the nature of his relationships (was he asocial?), his psychic make-up (did he fit into the grab-bag category of personality?) — and the system did not provide any way of differentiating the trivial from the important. "There is nothing too small to make note of," the chief of research told the staff. But such an assignment was impossible to fulfill. So at Norfolk one administrative rearrangement followed upon another. An initial division between a field worker (who went out to interview friends and relatives) and an institution worker (who interviewed the inmate) gave way to one case worker doing both jobs, which in turn gave way to the abandonment of field work altogether (the overload of information was staggering and only one or two cases a week were being completed), which in turn gave way to the creation of a diagnostic division apart from a treatment division. But shuffling the staff about was a symptom of the deficiencies in the plan itself, not a cure for them.[45]

SCAMP also provided no help in designing treatment strategies. Just as it instructed case workers to know everything about an inmate's history, so it told them to do everything to cure him, which was plainly no advice at all. Take, for example, the not atypical recommendations for Lee Sauls, a "personality" case: "Successful treatment . . . will depend upon intensive casework." The man "must be convinced that . . . 'crime does not pay.' In order to get this across to him his H. O. must gain his respect and confidence. . . . If the personality problems are discussed with him the man will be in a better position to adjust himself." In effect, the message amounted to an exhortation to talk him out of his criminality, not guidance in how to treat. And this case resembled many others. "On the whole," reported one staff member, "programs are vague, they suggest rather than specify. . . . Programs are made in mass production, and men have been termed worthless or worse as a result of a half-hour interview." With this as the coin of the realm is it not surprising to find Gill periodically exclaiming: "We must develop what I have come to call 'significant case work' as contrasted with just case work." It was "imperative that we begin to discriminate as to what particular thing it is which a man needs in order to help him eliminate his tendency to crime." But to change the jargon from "case work" to "significant case work" was really of little consequence; it was another symptom of the problem not a response to it.[46]

The staff at Norfolk knew just how dismal the situation was. One case worker who investigated treatment practices concluded that "programs have been inadequate and that — fortunately almost — they have been very partially carried out." The problem was exacerbated by a shortage of resources at Norfolk. Not only were the House Officers continuously protesting that the day-to-day tasks of running the units left them little time to talk with the men (so much for social work with the personality cases), but educational facilities, vocational training, and available employment were pitifully inadequate (so much for readjusting the situational cases). In all too many instances, the Norfolk job training program amounted to unskilled construction work, in essence ditch digging. "The jobs for the majority," conceded Mark Roser in November, 1932, "are limited to pick and shovel work, which doesn't involve much trade training." Six months later, the staff was still denouncing "the lack of interesting work," "the lack of diligence," "work crews too large to supervise," and two times as many men assigned to a job as were necessary. Gill, in an especially telling moment, suggested that ditch digging had its virtues. "It may be good experience for the men to dig in a ditch who have had vocational training, as it will help to teach them to meet emergencies that are bound to arise in their life outside when their term of incarceration is over. . . . It may well be that we have put too much emphasis on education."[47] But even the fact that these words were written at the onset of the Great

Depression does not make them persuasive. What a long and complicated route to get to a system that equated ditch digging with treatment.

Whatever Howard Gill or Leonard Dunham or Thorsten Sellin anticipated from Norfolk, they and everyone else associated with the experiment expected that the Colony would be administered fairly and humanely. It might not be able to rehabilitate all its inmates, but its failures would be instructive (clarifying which strategies did not work and maybe even some that did), and the amount of harm that it would do would be minimal. No one thought that Norfolk would breed its own kind of horror stories. Given all the fanfare that surrounded the experiment, surely it would not end up as one more miserable prison. But did this commitment to treatment at the very least produce decent conditions of confinement? Were Norfolk's inmates treated humanely? Was the goal of rehabilitation worth pursuing, not because it was realizable, but because it helped the institution avoid other evils?

At Norfolk, the commitment to rehabilitation did not substantially reduce coercion. Once more, treatment did not temper custody but fell victim to it. Not that Norfolk represented the worst brutalities in the American penitentiary system; inmates' lives were not in constant jeopardy. Nevertheless, the threat of substantial punishment was central to the administration of the program, and for a sizable minority of the inmates (around 15 percent) it was not a threat but a reality. For all the rhetorical allegiance to a medical model, Norfolk remained much more of a prison than a hospital. Worse yet, the processes by which custody took precedence over treatment had an inevitable and unavoidable quality about them.

Not only did Norfolk have its own jail but Gill was not uncomfortable about the use of solitary confinement within it. He did devise some school-like penalties, such as keeping inmates on the bench outside his office during recreation periods. But, he insisted, "Segregation in itself is valuable in calming down a man." Seemingly, Norfolk's use of solitary would be different: "The punitive attitude involves tying him up, which," Gill noted,

"may be good for a few, perhaps, but certainly not as a rule"; for
its part, Norfolk would confine men to a normal cell without
cuffs, and allow them a regular diet. To a number of visitors, such
as sociology professor Conrad Taeuber, the arguments were not
persuasive. "Somehow, there seems to me to be an anachronism
in the use of the lock-up as a means of punishment by an institution that denies the value of imprisonment per se. I admit I have
no suggestion. . . . It may be that in some cases no other language
is understood by the inmate." Nevertheless, "our whole system of
imprisonment seems to have grown up because it is such a simple
solution to problems from the standpoint of the individual confronted with them." But Gill did not share his concern. His final
answer was that Norfolk was being run for the 90 percent who
"can be won back to society," not for the 10 percent who need
"punitive measures." Since the institution was eager to rehabilitate the many, it need not concern itself with the well-being of
the few.[48]

Gill was no less certain that sentences to the lock-up at Norfolk,
like sentences to prison in the outside society, should be indeterminate. He noted that "the inmates do not like this type of individual treatment. It demands more of them than a definite
sentence which they can fulfill and then be done with." Still,
Norfolk's indeterminate sentence "gives treatment to fit the criminal rather than a punishment for the crime. . . . Release is controlled by a change in attitude," and "the change in attitude
should not be confused with lip service."[49] Gill was being consistent here; what is more unexpected is the fact that staff disagreed
with him (and the dialogue between them is so evocative of
current debate on sentencing as to tempt the conclusion that
occasionally history does repeat itself). To some of the social
workers, the indeterminacy of punishment at the Colony was
unfair and counterproductive. "We need some deterministic basis
for applying punishment," insisted Roser. "The application of
punishment should involve a due consideration for the seriousness
of the offense. . . . The inmate should feel that his punishment
comes almost automatically when he has transgressed a rule."
And Norfolk's chief psychologist agreed: "Our task is to avoid

antagonism by having a few definite rules, the infractions of which are immediately and automatically met with by punishments which tend to be definite. . . . It is only by a system of definite and automatic punishments that the men can be convinced that there is justice at Norfolk and in the world." Punishment and treatment should be kept separate; where punishment was concerned, one must focus on "individual deserts . . . to convince men that we have been fair," and be "satisfied with the benefits of a universal confidence in justice."[50]

The resolution of these disagreements (all too suggestive of what may be the outcome of today's debates), was less a compromise than a hardening of the rules. Gill established a fixed minimum term in the lock-up, but not a fixed maximum. The principle of indeterminacy was sacrificed and a floor was set for punishment, but no ceiling. All sentences to the jail at Norfolk were for no less than thirty days, with release allowed only after a change of heart was certified by the disciplinary committee and the superintendent himself. In defense of this procedure Gill announced that those in the lock-up "are to be considered as special problem cases for the casework department. It is the responsibility of the casework department to see that no opportunity for rehabilitation is overlooked for this group."[51] Not for the last time would discretion coupled with severity be cloaked in the garb of treatment opportunities.

The conflict over the duration of punishment within Norfolk was only one part of the larger controversy about placing inmates in the ABC categories, and about implementing the dormitory classifications. Once again Gill was at odds with some of his staff and once again the outcome moved Norfolk closer to an outright prison. The problem became acute in the closing months of 1932 in light of two particular developments. First, Norfolk's population was becoming more and more typical of an ordinary prison. During the "building time," Gill had taken in only the best of Charlestown's inmates, first offenders and most cooperative workers. Already, by the fall of 1930, he had skimmed off the cream of Charlestown; and by the fall of 1932, with construction just about complete, Norfolk was about to expand its size. Gill's decision, as had always been assumed by the Correction Department, was to admit more inmates from Charlestown (throughout these years, Norfolk did not receive any prisoners directly from the courts). The population climbed, from 300 at the end of 1931 to 540 by the end of 1933, and the "quality" dropped. Now complaints could be heard about the gangs that came down to Norfolk and particularly about one MacRaughry (of whom more later) who was "undisciplined, intemperate, a sexually promiscuous, boisterous, and thoughtless individual," who "shows little desire or effort to change."[52]

Simultaneously, the completion of its facilities meant that Norfolk had to go about filling its Reception Building, putting some inmates into the steel cells. Those who had heretofore been living in the dormitories, more or less on a first-come, first-served basis, were to be reassigned in accordance with their ABC ratings; those graded A would have their pick of rooms, but those graded B or C, who had been enjoying the freedom of the dorms, would now come under a restricted regimen. In effect, this procedure meant that the men who had been labeled B, who had not committed major infractions, who had done their day's work and obeyed the rules but were seen as not getting anything out of Norfolk, were to be penalized, and rather seriously so; they not only lost their choice of rooms but were to be locked up after 6 o'clock on weekdays, weekends, and holidays. Not surprisingly, they protested vehemently and Norfolk almost had a riot. Gill's response was uncompromising; since these men were not getting anything out of Norfolk they were not to enjoy what he defined as privileges. "Of course they can just do their time here, but they can't have the opportunities that the other men who do want casework have." Treatment, he insisted, was voluntary, yet those who did not take advantage of it could not expect rewards.[53] To other staff members, the procedures not only belied the notion of voluntary treatment but were patently unfair. "For men who have up to the present time been living similar lives to all others, it is quite impossible suddenly to comprehend why they should often arbitrarily be denuded of privilege and placed in a lower classification." And the classifications themselves were not so precise or accurate as to avoid injustices. Could one really differentiate between those who were and those who were not making progress at Norfolk?[54]

The protests did lead to some changes. A few of the B men were reassigned to A groups, and a new category, A-3, was invented so that men who had been obedient to the rules would not be locked up after work. But it was increasingly evident just how heavy a hand Norfolk was laying on its inmates. Gill was now defending his procedures with phrases that came dangerously close to double-talk: "A man is not under punishment because he doesn't have any privileges." The inmates were being subjected to arbitrary judgments. "I am afraid," reported Conrad Taeuber, "that very few of the House Officers and hardly any of the inmates understand the differences among the three A classes. . . . I will admit, that I had some difficulty in learning what the difference . . . was, and would hardly be able to stand questioning on it now." And finally, the staff itself was recording their own sense of the growing degree of coercion within the institution. "The emphasis," argued one of Norfolk's most loyal workers, "should be upon making institution programs sufficiently attractive, not upon locking-up participants. This latter is a sad retrogression, and singularly out of place in the Norfolk regime."[55]

No sooner did the controversy over the A and B categories quiet down than another one erupted over the C classification. Thirteen inmates were moved from the dorms to the steel cells of the Reception Building, to be confined there whenever they were not at work. In this instance, at least, there was something of a record to go on — each of them had a history of major disciplinary infractions. But the case worker assigned to the C men, Hans Weiss, was soon protesting that this classification constituted bad therapy: it created a stigmatized class and thereby exacerbated the very problem it was to solve. "These men," contended Weiss, "had developed an attitude of such bitterness and antagonism toward the institution as a result of this segregation in a group of 'outcasts' that rediagnosis and casework seemed impossible." He recommended that the C category be eliminated, that disciplinary cases be adjudicated quickly and those found guilty be confined for short periods of time. "A clear distinction should be made between punishment and housing classification. . . . A brief, stiff lock-up is more effective and more desirable as a method of dealing with behavior problems than prolonged segregation in a group."[56]

Gill held firm, not only arguing against "set rules of punishment," but bluntly insisting that "we don't care what happens to the 10 percent." The minority of troublemakers "does not mean a great deal to us." Practical political considerations were also relevant. "If we can have some successes with fifty or seventy-five percent of our men, we will be allowed to go on. . . . We must insure popular support, because in the last analysis, the public are running this." And with a confidence that moved over into arrogance, he concluded that if reform did not take place, "the fault is not with Norfolk but with the men." But his response only provoked more criticism. Harvard professor Carl Doering, a member of the case work advisory committee, observed, ever so properly: "It seems that if a man breaks down at Charlestown it is the fault of the system, but if he breaks down at Norfolk it is his fault." More, "the analogy in medicine is that the sick ones are the very fellows who are in need of medical attention — your C class or problem cases." Why was Norfolk deserting the medical model at just this point? Gill countered that a C category was not punishment but an opportunity for rediagnosis, and the debate went round on itself one more time.[57]

Gill was not only a victim of reformers' pride but of the architectural consequences of his willingness to give Norfolk a jail. The Receiving Building counted as part of Norfolk's capacity; the cells had to be filled with inmates. Weiss's successful efforts to reduce the antagonisms of some of the C men and get them back into the general population only made the problem more acute — who, then, was to go to the Receiving Building? In April, 1933, Gill ordered each of the House Officers to select three or four of their men who were not getting all that they should from Norfolk (even, he told them, if it was necessary to choose A-2 types) to be housed in the Receiving Building; in this way, dormitory space would be freed up for new inmates who had been in the Building waiting for reassignment for several months. Staff members objected: architecture was now determining treatment — men were being fitted to the facility, not the facility to the men.[58]

The *Diary* pages, reporting at length on this latest controversy, make obvious how impossible it was for Norfolk to carry out its dual mandate to treat and to punish. In a very real and tangible way the jail was taking over the institution; the specter of confinement in the steel cells now pervaded the Colony. If Gill was prepared to lock up A-2 men then clearly any inmate might well find himself in confinement. And Norfolk's staff was fully aware of this. "The question is," one of the House Officers asked in the *Diary*, "Shall Norfolk become a 'penal opportunity school' (with emphasis at least as much on the 'penal' as on the 'opportunity'), or shall it develop into a *treatment institution?*" A growing number of officers were beginning to suspect how Norfolk would answer that question.[59]

All the challenges and debates finally began to wear on Gill himself. On June 23 he wrote in the *Diary*: "It seems impossible that prisons will ever serve as an adequate means of handling the problems of crime. We think of them now as places in which criminals should be confined for reformation. . . . I wonder if we shall not come to another concept. . . . Reliance will be had upon supervision within the community itself as the real corrective. . . . The thought that we can build a community prison which approximates the normal is faint hope."[60] The designer was starting to abandon hope for his project, and incidentally, to discover the next reform movement.

Within a week of Gill's disheartened comments, Norfolk began the most tumultuous and chaotic six-month period in its history. One near escape by a group of inmates attempting to tunnel under the walls, followed by a successful escape by two other inmates going over the walls, set off a chain of events that culminated in Gill's removal as superintendent. It was almost as if he had recognized the victory of custody over treatment and begun to will his own destruction. More substantively, the disciplinary problems that provoked his despair became so much more acute, and the Colony grew so preoccupied with punishment, that Gill's dismissal is almost incidental to the larger point that Norfolk had become a full-fledged prison. Let one architectural change confirm the point. By January, 1934, twelve cells had had their windows boarded up, their plumbing stripped, and their beds removed. Norfolk had its hole.

The final act in the Norfolk drama began on June 28, 1933, when, acting on a tip from some inmates, the guards discovered the tunnel dug toward the prison walls. Although no evidence could be found implicating any particular inmates, the staff was not about to concern itself with procedural niceties or even elementary fairness. Twenty-three inmates were rounded up and put under twenty-four-hour lock-up in the Receiving Building. As one of the OIC's explained: whether they were guilty or not of the attempted escape, this was an opportunity to discipline those "with a negative attitude toward Norfolk treatment. . . . By picking up this group of aggressive non-cooperators . . . we would be getting a good portion of the men implicated, and at the same time we would be decreasing our behavior problem in the community."[61] (Incidentally, their move to the Receiving Building did free up space in the dormitories, and before the day was over, their beds went to other inmates.) Not unexpectedly, the twenty-three men set up a clamor, banging on their cells, shouting, and destroying whatever property they could. The administration responded by preparing tear gas, depriving them of smoking and reading materials, and forbidding correspondence or visits. "They would want to write to all sorts of people," Gill explained, "and people would be given an unfair picture of the whole situation. . . . He would be swamped with politicians asking questions."[62]

Cooler heads did prevail and a bargain was struck; some of the men confessed, and Gill went easy on them. Nevertheless, something critical had happened. The earlier doubts as to whether Norfolk would be a penal or a treatment institution were giving way to a recognition that "With all the comforts of Norfolk, its own limited freedom, its humane approach, its modern living conditions, etc., we have realized with something of a shock that it is still a prison." The guards now demanded stricter regulations over the men; and Gill began to offer explanations for the failure of his experiment. "It is evident," he declared, "that in a prison community, as in the outside community, minorities govern." That troublesome ten percent could not be isolated; sooner or later, the institution had to organize its entire regimen to handle them. Gill also began to sense an inevitable conflict between custody and rehabilitation, the full price that one paid for having a jail. "I am interested that the most serious trouble at Norfolk," he observed, "has come with the opening of the Receiving Building, but in part, I wonder if it is not due to the very nature of the building itself as a repressive agency. It seems that the more bars and locks we have, the more of a reaction against them is engendered." And so he concluded in very non-Progressive fashion: "A little restriction and a little freedom do not mix," that the inmates' "need is for a great deal of freedom or a great deal of repression." Norfolk (or any other institution?) could not have it both ways.[63]

Three months later, in September, 1933, two inmates (one of them the famous MacRaughry) who were known to be troublesome, went over the wall. Their escape prompted many staff members to insist along with Roser that "men with long terms and vicious anti-social traits should not be sent to Norfolk." More, they were now prepared to get tough with the hard core, to bring into Norfolk the kinds of punishments and disciplinary practices used in other prisons. To observe these changes is to have the feeling of watching a puppet show, with Norfolk captive of a force quite outside itself, moving to someone else's command. The dynamic of incarceration took the Norfolk staff from treatment to mild discipline to brutal discipline. Thus, one of the Colony's House Officers who had consistently promoted treatment goals now suggested: "We need a stronger discipline than we are giving at the present time. I would suggest that a separate cell block be built for the worst cases. . . . I would suggest that this type of 'bastille' building [remember when that was a dirty word at Norfolk?], should have the minimum of comforts and should be the most undesirable place for any human being to inhabit. . . . Only when we show them that we have fire to fight fire with will they be less inclined to play with fire." He had moved quite a distance from a rehabilitative rationale. And so had the institution. Norfolk has "changed its standards of sending men back to the Receiving Building," Mark Roser was soon explaining. "The criterion now is not so much 'What is the man doing on his program?' as 'How much of a risk is he to the security of the institution?' "[64]

Both of these men justified the new measures by telling about the recent case of one inmate, Seelington. This hapless fellow, who objected to being moved from the dorms into the Receiving Building for a disciplinary infraction, started throwing furniture around and broke a glass door; he refused to quiet down, even after being placed in the steel cell. "It seemed evident," recounted Roser, "that there was no alternative but to try to change the man's opinion by placing him in a situation in which, as long as his attitude continued, he actually felt physical discomfort, and more physical discomfort than he would normally feel when locked in a cell on the top floor of the Receiving Building." Accordingly, Seelington was handcuffed, locked in a basement cell with a mattress and two blankets, and put on a bread and water diet. After four days he begged to be released, in Roser's view a changed man — indeed, changed in a way that seemingly testified to the wisdom and efficacy of solitary on bread and water. Not only was Norfolk now breaking the hard case through cruel punishment; not only was Gill's earlier discrimination between locking up and tying up an inmate gone; but the process by which this declension had taken place was all too apparent. Few phrases out of Norfolk's history are more grim than Roser's final comments on the episode: "It is rather evident that once the men get into the Receiving Building they do not feel the discipline of merely remaining in their cells and we are more or less forced, for the morale of the group, to inaugurate a more rigid system of discipline." And to remember how caretakers can legitimate almost any action, ponder Roser's phrase: "for the morale of the group."[65]

As one would expect at this point, Gill was fully prepared to keep control at Norfolk by applying "some strong force and deprivation." The various schemes that had looked to treatment or to a normal community life within the institution gave way to an overriding concern for security. Thus Gill insisted that "grading according to social attitude be made equal to grading according to casework achievement," which was another way of saying that disciplinary considerations were to become the measure for all inmate classifications. Accordingly, prisoner Joseph Hadley was to be confined to the Receiving Building "because he has so much anti-administration influence, plus his general characteristics of a clever anti-social individual. This classification is made despite evidence of superficial institutional adjustment." By the same token, Gill was ready to commit to the Receiving Building any inmate who would not join the Inmate Council — whose members were now compelled to sign a pledge to break up any escape attempt and to turn in any contraband, although not necessarily to report the name of the offending inmate. That the Council, throughout these years at Norfolk, had never served as much more than a shadow committee, lacking any real authority and constantly manipulated by Gill for his own ends, is not as interesting as the fact that when the system did come under stress Gill immediately turned the Council into one more mechanism for maintaining obedience. The organization that was ostensibly to teach inmates the lessons of self-government became another instrument of coercion.[66]

Thus, it is hardly a shock to learn that in November, 1933, Norfolk converted twelve cells into "the hole," or to discover that in January, 1934, twelve cells were no longer considered enough. The report in the *Diary* on this change offers one last poignant text to study. The entry, written by the inmate editor of the prison newspaper, described a very novel meeting at Norfolk. The inmates and the staff were joined by no less an official than the state Commissioner of Correction to discuss the issue of discipline. "The Superintendent pointed out that this meeting with the Commissioner probably had never been duplicated in the history of penology." But however unprecedented the session, the outcome was all too familiar in the history of penology. "It was agreed that secure solitary cells should be installed in which bread and water punishment would be meted out in place of regular rations." The inmate went on to note that "there was considerable discussion as to which cells should be used as punishment cells. The top floor of the Receiving Building was suggested, also basement punishment cells, to which the Superintendent objected, because so many disgraceful things have happened in underground places of that sort and he didn't like it." But the reporter knew how to frame this point: "This was, of course, incidental detail in the discussion and agreement that there was a need for more secure cells and the facilities for solitary confinement which we do not have at present."[67] In the end what was left of Gill's ambitions and the Norfolk experiment was a last pathetic gesture, an incidental detail: in the Norfolk prison the hole would not be in the basement.

The closing events in Gill's administration need not detain us long. Inmates became less tractable, as evidenced by a drunken Christmas Eve party and a food strike two weeks later. The press played up all of Norfolk's problems, as relayed to them by disgruntled guards, and one eager Massachusetts politician set out to advance his career by "exposing" Norfolk. At the end of January, 1934, Gill was "withdrawn" as superintendent pending investigations; and several months later the withdrawal turned into a dismissal. Gill's replacement did for a time maintain a rhetorical commitment to treatment, but successive annual reports conceded that Norfolk had become just another penal institution, difficult to distinguish from Charlestown. By the end of 1936, the new superintendent admitted that "the State Prison Colony cannot be operated (as it was first intended) purely as a 'rehabilitative' institution, but must be administered to a very great extent as a 'custodial' prison."[68]

Although Gill was finally a victim of state politics, the critical elements in the Norfolk story were the internal ones. Once it had the hole, the experiment was over. That Gill left the scene when he did was probably to his good fortune. It could then appear, however misleadingly, that the final decline took place under someone else's authority; indeed, that Gill was removed may even have helped to blur the genuine significance of the events, making it seem that reform had fallen victim to politics, not to its own dynamic. The scapegoat could be Massachusetts and therefore the most vital considerations — the nature of Progressive assumptions and the reasons why they were incapable of successful application — could be ignored.

Perhaps the Norfolk story is clear enough not to need a final gloss. This text, in light of the previous chapters, may well speak for itself. But some of its implications are so compelling that they demand to be drawn out. The Norfolk experience reallocates the burden of responsibility and justification, from those who would be prepared to trust to the benevolent impulses of the reformer to those who would regard him with an acute suspicion. To recall George Eliot's dictum that it would be ignorant unkindness to be angry with ignorant kindness, if anger is not the appropriate response then extraordinary caution surely is. The problem with ignorant kindness is that we tend to let down our guard, to trust it too much. We are ready to suspend belief, to grant indulgences, on the wrong-headed notion that the resulting cruelties will necessarily be less severe, that the pledge to do good will somehow or other offer protection against disastrous results.

More, the events at Norfolk recall all the troubling points raised here about anyone's ability to deliver effective treatment within an institution. The narrative points to a series of particular questions that would demand solution. How will a trained staff be recruited? How will therapists live with caretakers? Do we have a conceptual framework that will produce meaningful treatment techniques? Are classifications merely descriptive statements or are they relevant to treatment?

Most critical, Norfolk too reveals the difficulty, even the impossibility, of a program that would at once cure and coerce, that would discipline and rehabilitate, that would mix reform with custody. Norfolk's fate recapitulates the issue we have explored in probation, parole, the juvenile court, and the mental health system — that to join assistance to coercion is to create a tension that cannot persist indefinitely and will be far more likely to be resolved on the side of coercion. The most problematic of all Progressive assumptions was embodied in Norfolk's first principle, that it could "guard securely" and return "better men."

Finally, the Norfolk experience does point to the extraordinary difficulties of administering a humane *system* of incarceration. An account of any one institution, or indeed the accounts here of many institutions, cannot finally resolve the matter; too many contingencies will inevitably remain. In the instance of Norfolk, one can at least imagine a series of different circumstances producing different outcomes. What if the custodial staff had been recruited from outside the system so as to share a greater affinity with a rehabilitative ethic? Or perhaps another chief administrator would have been more adept than Gill in settling disputes.

But the issue need not rest there. In the end, Norfolk is a text that should be interpreted with an eye to its "meaning" in the way that an anthropologist will find meaning in an immolation ceremony or in a cock fight. And since we have seen that the outcome at Norfolk was repeated in other prisons, training schools, and mental hospitals, this approach is all the more fitting. Thus, in incarceration, we inevitably confront the need for one more sanction. Not that we cannot here or there run one decent institution; rather, that the decency of any one place rests ultimately upon a coercive back-up, and that back-up in turn rests upon the presence of a still more coercive back-up. If the inmate will not behave at the minimum security camp, we have the threat of the maximum security penitentiary, and if he will not behave there, we have the threat of administrative segregation, and if that will not do, solitary, and if that does not break him, bread and water, or physical punishment. Is there any point short of brutality to stop? A system of incarceration seems incapable of maintaining decency throughout *all* its sectors.

The historical record does not provide an answer to the problem of punishment versus treatment. But in the end, Norfolk, in the context of the events of 1900–1940 that we have been analyzing, becomes a powerful parable. Its fall, its degeneration to the hole with bread and water, constitutes a final indictment of the Progressive system. To attempt today to perpetuate or resurrect one or another element of that system, to keep alive the

Progressive trust in the discretionary power of the state, its view of a harmony of interests, its readiness to treat the individual not the act, would appear to contradict whatever lessons an historical record can provide. We are now entering a post-Progressive period, in wholesale revolt against inherited procedures, perhaps too much in revolt in the sense that current solutions all too often assume that the obverse of a Progressive measure is necessarily a wiser measure. Whether the new programs will fare better than the old ones, whether due process protections for juveniles and mental patients will be an improvement over discretion, whether fixed sentences will be an improvement over indeterminate ones, whether a commitment to liberty will accomplish more than a commitment to equality, it is too soon to say — although these are some of the questions that I am now eager to explore. But what is clear is that the Progressive measures themselves, in terms of both conception and implementation, did not succeed in reforming the asylum, in elevating conscience over convenience.

Notes

Chapter One

1. Many of the sources for analyzing the changes in post–Civil War asylums are noted in my earlier volume, *The Discovery of the Asylum* (Boston, 1971), chs. 10–11; see also Blake McKelvey, *American Prisons* (Montclair, New Jersey, 1977), chs. 4–9; Gerald Grob, *Mental Institutions in America* (New York, 1973), chs. 6–8; Albert Deutsch, *The Mentally Ill in America*, 2nd ed. (New York, 1949).
2. New York State Prison Commission, *Investigations of the State Prisons and Report Thereon* (Albany, 1876), 2.
3. *Ibid.*, 329; New York Commission . . . to Investigate Clinton Prison, *Report* (New York, 1892), 10, 85.
4. New York Prison Commission, *Investigations*, 8–9, 329; Clinton Prison, *Report*, 10–11. See also Committee of the California Assembly, *Strait Jackets . . . in the State Prisons*, Feb. 10, 1903, California State Archives, Sacramento.
5. Clinton Prison, *Report*, 12.
6. "Investigation of the Lansing Kansas Penitentiary," Jan. 7, 1909, manuscript in Oklahoma State Archives, Oklahoma City, 40, 60.
7. Traill Green, "Functions of a Medical Staff of an Insane Hospital," *American Psychological Journal* 1 (1883), 226; Orpheus Everts, "The American System of Public Provision for the Insane and Disposition in Lunatic Asylums," *American Journal of Insanity* (*AJI*) 38 (1881), 116; "Proceedings of the Association," *AJI* 43 (1886), 39, 146.
8. New York Senate Committee to Investigate the Lunatic Asylum at Utica, *Report* (Albany, 1884), 102, 657 and passim.
9. *Ibid.*, 204.
10. See, for example, Commissioners of the Illinois State Penitentiary at Joliet, *Report for 1890* (Springfield, 1890), 60–64; California State Board of Prison Directors, *Fourth Annual Report* (Sacramento, 1883), 35–39. The Annual Reports of countless other institutions confirm this point.
11. U.S. Bureau of the Census, *Insane and Feeble-Minded in Hospitals and Institutions* (Washington, D.C., 1895), Table 154, 268–270; Illinois State Hospital at Elgin, *Second Annual Report* (1872), 10–11; Board of Trustees of the Connecticut Hospital for the Insane, *Twentieth Report* (Middletown, 1885), 19–21; cf. Massachusetts Board of Lunacy and Charity, *Report for 1890*, table XXV, pp. lxvii–ix.

12. New York Committee to Investigate Utica, *Report*, 736–738, 805–806.

13. U.S. Industrial Commission on Prison Labor, *Report* (Washington, D.C., 1900), vol. 3; see too, U.S. Bureau of Labor, *Convict Labor* (Washington, D.C., 1887). *Annual Report of the Auditor to the Governor of the State of Ohio . . . 1883* (Columbus, 1884), 5–6.

14. *Annual Report of the [Ohio] Auditor*, 1883, 6–8; cf. the *Annual Report of the Auditor of the State of Indiana*, 1883 (Indianapolis, 1888), 30–31, 34–36. See also John A. Fairlie, *The Centralization of Administration in New York State* (New York, 1898), chs. 3, 5.

15. Henry Wolfer, "The Prisoner's Rights, Past and Present," copy of speech of Oct. 21–23, 1897, Wolfer Letter Book, 462, Minnesota State Archives, St. Paul.

16. New York State Commission in Lunacy, *First Annual Report*, 1889 (Albany, 1890), 45–74.

17. *Transactions of the National Congress on Penitentiary and Reformatory Discipline*, reprinted in New York Prison Association, *Twenty-Sixth Annual Report* (Albany, 1871), 541–567.

18. *Ibid.*, 543, italics added.

19. New York State Reformatory, *Report . . . 1877* (Elmira, 1877), 8–15, quotation on p. 9; see Elmira's Annual Reports and Zebulon R. Brockway, *Fifty Years of Prison Service* (New York, 1912).

20. New York State Reformatory, *Report . . . 1879*, 12–14; *Report . . . 1882*, 88–89.

21. New York State Reformatory, *Report . . . 1891*, 3–4; *Report . . . 1886*, 20–21.

22. *Science* 7 (1886), 207; *North American Review* 140 (1885), 294–307; W. M. F. Round, "How Far May We Abolish Prisons?," *Journal* 25 (1897), 200–201.

23. *In the Matter of the Charges Preferred Against the Managers of the New York State Reformatory at Elmira* (Albany, 1894), esp. 1–13, quotation from p. 6.

24. Charles E. Rosenberg, *The Trial of Assassin Guiteau* (Chicago, 1968), 61.

25. Edward Spitzka, "Reform in the Scientific Study of Psychiatry," *Journal of Nervous and Mental Diseases (JNMD)* 5 (1878), 202, 204, 209, 223; see the 1883–1884 volumes of the *American Psychological Journal* for the views of the National Association for the Protection of the Insane and the Prevention of Insanity; for example, Clark Bell, "The Rights of the Insane and their Enforcement," 10–23; and its *Papers and Proceedings* (New York, 1882). The attack is reported well in Albert Deutsch, "The History of Mental Hygiene," in *One Hundred Years of American Psychiatry, 1844–1944* (New York, 1944).

26. William A. Hammond, *The Non-Asylum Treatment of the Insane* (New York, 1879), 2, 7–12.

27. Edward Spitzka, "Merits and Motives of the Movement for Asylum Reform," *JNMD* 5 (1878), 711–713. See also William Hammond, *A Treatise on Insanity in its Medical Relations* (New York, 1883), 718–732.

28. Richard Dewey, "Present and Prospective Management of the Insane," *JNMD* 5 (1878), 85.

Chapter Two

1. U.S. Attorney General, *Survey of Release Procedures*, vol. 2, *Probation* (Washington, D.C., 1939), ch. 1 (hereafter, Attorney General, *Probation*); Francis Hiller, *Adult Probation Laws of the United States* (New York, 1933), iv, 8–13. See the discussion in the opening pages of chapter three.

2. U.S. Attorney General, *Survey of Release Procedures*, vol. 4, *Parole* (Washington, D.C., 1939), ch. 1; U.S. Bureau of the Census, *Prisoners, 1923* (Washington, D.C., 1929), 123–125. See the discussion in the opening pages of Chapter Four; also, the Committee on Discharged Prisoners, "Report," National Prison Association, *Proceedings . . . 1902*, 288–289.

3. Emily Talbot, "Social Science Instruction in Colleges," American Social Science Association, *Journal* 22 (1887), 12–14.

4. Sheila M. Rothman, *Woman's Proper Place* (New York, 1978), 112–113; Allen F. Davis, *Spearheads for Reform* (New York, 1967), 27.

5. Robert Hunter, *Poverty* (New York, 1904; reprint ed., 1965), 25, 47.

6. *Ibid.*, 258–259.

7. John Dewey and Evelyn Dewey, *Schools of Tomorrow* (New York, 1915; reprint ed., 1962), 225. See also, David W. Noble, *The Paradox of Progressive Thought* (Minneapolis, 1958).

8. Herbert Croly, *The Promise of American Life* (New York, 1909, Capricorn reprint ed.), 5, 22–25.

9. Sophonisba Breckinridge and Edith Abbott, *The Delinquent Child and the Home* (New York, 1912), 15, 103, chs. 5–7; cf. Thomas Travis, *The Young Malefactor* (New York, 1908), passim.

10. City of New York Magistrate's Court, *The Probation Services, 1917–1918* (New York, 1918), 12.

11. C. S. Potts, "Some Practical Problems of Prison Reform," *University of Texas Bulletin*, no. 162 (Austin, 1911), 7–9, 12.

12. William Healy, *The Individual Delinquent* (Boston, 1915), quotations from 124–125, 130–132, 165, 284. To compare, for example, Healy and Freud see here, 407.

13. *Ibid.*, 130–132, 165.

14. *Ibid.*, 124–125 and chs. 6–7.

15. Warren Spaulding, "Possibilities of a Probation System," speech delivered at the 1907 Massachusetts Conference on Charities (Cambridge, 1908), 86–88; Edward Devine, "Proceedings . . . of Probation Officers," in New York State Probation Commission, *Fifth Annual Report* (Albany, 1912), 239.

16. Committee on Translations, "General Introduction" to Cesare Lombroso, *Crime: Its Causes & Remedies* (Boston, 1911), vi–vii; Charlton T. Lewis, "The Indeterminate Sentence," National Prison Association, *Proceedings . . . 1900*, 175.

17. Thomas Osborne, *Society and Prisons* (New Haven, 1916), 34–35.

18. Committee on Translations, "General Introduction" to Lombroso, *Crime*, vii; see too, Leon Radzinowicz, *Ideology and Crime* (New York, 1966).

19. Charlton Lewis, "The Indeterminate Sentence," 161, 174.
20. Ralph Ferris, "The Case History in Probation Service," in Sheldon Glueck, ed., *Probation and Criminal Justice* (New York, 1930), 137, 140 and passim; Attorney General, *Probation*, 157 for Sutherland quotation.
21. See Attorney General Survey of Release Procedures, Files (hereafter cited as *AG Files*), box 39, "Notes on Court Reports of Other Jurisdictions," May 21, 1936, National Archives, Washington, D.C.
22. Warren F. Spaulding, "Principles and Purposes of Probation," National Prison Association, *Proceedings . . . 1906*, 87–89.
23. Attorney General, *Probation*, ch. 8.
24. New York State Probation Commission, *First Annual Report* (Albany, 1908), 81 and *Seventh Annual Report* (Albany, 1914), 344–345; New York Magistrate's Court, *Probation Services, 1917–1918*, 29, 12–14.
25. Quoted in Rothman, *Woman's Proper Place*, 74; New York State Probation Commission, *Sixth Annual Report* (Albany, 1913), 137.
26. New York State Probation Commission, *Manual for Probation Officers in New York State* (Albany, 1913), 61.
27. *Juvenile Court Record (JCR)*, February, 1903, 5.
28. New York State Probation Commission, *Fifth Annual Report*, 271–275.
29. Edwin J. Cooley, "Current Tendencies in Adult Probation," National Probation Association (NPA), *Twelfth Annual Report* (Albany, 1919), 147–151.
30. Charlton Lewis, "The Indeterminate Sentence," 161; Charles Hoffman, National Prison Association, *Proceedings . . . 1919*, 19. See also Frank Sleeper, "A Twentieth Century Reform Movement," *Arena* 41 (1909), 476.
31. Roland Molineux, "The Court of Rehabilitation," *Charities* 18 (1907), 739, 741.
32. Warren Spaulding, "The Treatment of Crime," *Journal of Criminal Law and Criminology (JCLC)* 3 (1912–1913), 378, 381; Frederick Wines, "The Indeterminate Sentence," National Prison Association, *Proceedings . . . 1910*, 280–281.
33. Molineux, "The Court of Rehabilitation," 739–745; O. F. Lewis, "When The Prisoner Returns," *North American Review* 195 (1912), 427–491.
34. Burdette Lewis, *The Offender* (New York, 1916), 80; New York Prison Association, *Sixty-First Annual Report* (Albany, 1906), 113–114.
35. Warren F. Spaulding, "The Cost of Crime," *JCLC* 1 (1910–11), 90–94, 101.
36. Julia Jaffrey, ed., *The Prison and the Prisoner* (Boston, 1917), 25; Charles Hoffman, "Probation as a Judicial Policy," NPA, *Thirteenth Annual Report* (Albany, 1920), 22. See also, New York Magistrate's Court, *Probation, 1917–1918*, 26; New York State Moreland Commission, *Report on Prison Reform* (June 10, 1913), 8–9.
37. Jaffrey, *The Prison and the Prisoner*, 25, for the Glueck quotation; National Prison Association, *Proceedings . . . 1899*, 164; New York Prison Association, *Sixty-First Annual Report*, 114.
38. Hoffman, "Probation," 23.
39. National Prison Association, *Proceedings . . . 1900*, 373; *Proceedings . . . 1901*, 258; *Proceedings . . . 1903*, 77.

40. See the wardens' opinions expressed in Potts, "Prison Reform," 13–25; National Prison Association, *Proceedings . . . 1900*, 578; *Proceedings . . . 1902*, 166–167.
41. See the judges' remarks in New York State Probation Commission, *Sixth Annual Report*, 135–137, 146–147; *Seventh Annual Report*, 312–313; *Eighth Annual Report* (Albany, 1915), 260–264, 404–407.
42. *Geo. v. the People*, 167 Illinois 462 (1897).
43. *Miller v. State*, 149 Indiana 608, 615–616 (1898); *Peters v. State*, 43 O.S. 646 (1885); *People v. Cook*, 147 Michigan 132 (1907); *People v. Cummings*, 88 Michigan 254 (1891). See also, *Geo. v. the People*, 167 Illinois 458 (1897); *People v. Illinois State Reformatory*, 148 Illinois 421 (1894).
44. New York State Probation Commission, *Sixth Annual Report*, 126–128. See also Chapter Three, notes 27–34.
45. International Association of Chiefs of Police, *Proceedings of the 18th Annual Convention* (Grand Rapids, 1911), 113–115, 129. See also New York State Probation Commission, *Tenth Annual Report* (Albany, 1917), 320–326.
46. Chiefs of Police, *Proceedings of the 4th Annual Convention* (Grand Rapids, 1897), 48.
47. A Prisoner, "The Indeterminate Sentence," *Atlantic Monthly* 108 (1911), 330; Remarks of Charles Nott, Jr. in *JCLC* 1 (1910–1911), 117; Massachusetts Civil Alliance, Broadside, 1917, in Massachusetts State Library, Boston.
48. William Gemmill, "Crime and its Punishment in Chicago," *JCLC* 1 (1910–1911), 40. See also *JCLC* 3 (1912–1913), 119.
49. Sir Evelyn Ruggles-Brise, "An English View of the American Penal System," *JCLC* 3 (1912–1913), 360–361.

Chapter Three

1. U.S. Attorney General, *Survey of Release Procedures*, vol. 2, *Probation* (Washington, D.C., 1939), 80. (Hereafter, Attorney General, *Probation*.)
2. Charles Chute, "Probation and the Institutions," *Probation* 7 (1929), 3–6; Andrew Bruce, E. W. Burgess, and Albert J. Harno, "The Probation and Parole System," in the *Illinois Crime Survey* (Chicago, 1929), 546 (hereafter, Bruce, "Probation and Parole"); National Commission on Law Observance and Enforcement, *Penal Institutions, Probation and Parole* (Washington, D.C., 1931), 152–153 (hereafter, Wickersham Commission, *Penal Institutions*); Francis Hiller, *Adult Probation Laws of the United States* (New York, 1933), iv, 8–13.
3. Attorney General, *Probation*, 80–86; Sheldon Glueck, ed., *Probation and Criminal Justice* (New York, 1933), 7–14; Edwin Cooley, *Probation and Delinquency* (New York, 1927), 319.
4. *AG Files*, box 40, J. M. Brown report on Oregon (1936), 14–15; New York State Crime Commission (hereafter NYSCC), *Hearings, July, 1926*, 1022, New York State Library, Albany.
5. *AG Files*, box 56, Schedule on Chicago Criminal and Municipal Courts

(February, 1936); box 56 contains many other similar reports; Attorney General, *Probation*, 87–91; Wickersham Commission, *Penal Institutions*, 186.

6. Attorney General, *Probation*, ch. 3; *AG Files*, box 56; Miriam Van Waters, "Probation for Women and Girls," NPA, *Eighteenth Annual Report* (New York, 1924), 206.

7. NYSCC, *Hearings*, July, 1926, 1022; Hans Weiss, "Where Are We in Probation Work," NPA, *Eighteenth Annual Report*, 52–56.

8. Wickersham Commission, *Penal Institutions*, 155; *AG Files*, box 57 for the Newark schedule; Francis Hiller, *Probation in Wisconsin* (New York, 1926), 45. See also, New York Court of General Sessions, *A Decade of Probation* (New York, 1936), 17.

9. Attorney General, *Probation*, 181–182.

10. *Ibid.*, 183–193; Van Waters, "Probation," 210–211; Roscoe Pound and Felix Frankfurter, eds., *Criminal Justice in Cleveland* (Cleveland, 1922), 417.

11. The pre-sentence reports are to be found in the *AG Files*, box 56, Baltimore (February, 1937). In box 57: Detroit (December, 1936), quotation p. 2; Minneapolis (March, 1937), quotation p. 4; St. Louis (November, 1935), quotation p. 3; Erie-Buffalo (February, 1937).

12. New York Court of General Sessions, *Probation*, 41, 142–143; Hans Weiss, "The Social Worker's Technique and Probation," in Glueck, ed., *Probation*, 168–171; Attorney General, *Probation*, 281.

13. Attorney General, *Probation*, 222–246.

14. NYSCC, *Hearings*, Oct. 1, 1929, 860–861; Pound and Frankfurter, *Criminal Justice in Cleveland*, 417–418; Ruth Topping, "Social Treatment of the Sex Delinquent," NPA, *Sixteenth Annual Report* (New York, 1923), 155–156.

15. Hiller, *Probation in Wisconsin*, 46–47; *AG Files*, box 40, Brown report on Oregon, 15, 17; NPA, *Twentieth Annual Report* (New York, 1926), 146.

16. *AG Files*, box 56, Roxbury Municipal Court (January, 1937), see Remarks; Suffolk County Superior Court (January, 1937).

17. Attorney General, *Probation*, 336–339.

18. Glueck, ed., *Probation*, 10; NPA, *Twentieth Annual Report*, 31.

19. See discussions in Chapter Two and Chapter Nine.

20. New York State, *Proceedings of the Governor's Conference on Crime, the Criminal, and Society* (Albany, 1935), 1014–1015.

21. *AG Files*, box 39, Maryland, Joseph Ullman, "Probation in Baltimore," address, March 10, 1932; Virginia Commission to Study Prison Sentences, "Report," *Virginia House Document No. 3*, January, 1934, 12; NYSCC, *Hearings*, December 7, 1927, 3149–3150.

22. See notes 1 and 2 for this chapter.

23. NPA, *Twentieth Annual Report*, 129.

24. James Kirby, "Educating the Public on Probation," NPA, *Twenty-First Annual Report* (New York, 1927), 62.

25. NYSCC, *Hearings*, July 2, 1926, 451–452.

26. Charles Chute, "The 'Crime Wave' and Probation," NPA, *Fifteenth*

Annual Report (New York, 1922), 32; *Sixteenth Annual Report*, 176; Attorney General, *Probation, vii.*

27. Bruce, "Probation and Parole," 549; NYSCC, *Report . . . 1927* (Albany, 1927), 103. See also, Wayne L. Morse and Ronald H. Beattie, *Survey of the Administration of Criminal Justice in Oregon* (Eugene, 1932), ch. 7.
28. Bruce, "Probation and Parole," 550–551; *AG Files*, box 39, remarks of Carl May, "The Place of Probation," 9.
29. NYSCC, *Report . . . 1927*, 103, 135.
30. *AG Files*, box 41, Texas Probation Schedule, 25–26, Report of C. S. Potts.
31. Attorney General, *Probation*, 425–426.
32. *Ibid.*, 426–427; Bruce, "Probation and Parole," 550; NYSCC, *Hearings*, December 14, 1926, 2205–2207.
33. *AG Files*, box 57, Minneapolis 4th District and Juvenile Court, Probation Schedule, March, 1937; Bruce, "Probation and Parole," 550.
34. NYSCC, *Hearings*, December 21, 1926, 2522–2523.
35. Bruce, "Probation and Parole," 544.
36. Bruce, "Probation and Parole," 542–543; *AG Files*, box 34, Arizona Release Procedures, 1936, 10; Hiller, *Probation in Wisconsin*, 34; *AG Files*, box 40, Brown report on Oregon, 13–14.
37. *AG Files*, box 56, Schedules of U.S. District Court, New Haven; U.S. District Court, Brunswick, Georgia; U.S. District Court, Atlanta; Supreme Bench of Baltimore; Roxbury Municipal Court; Boston Municipal Court; Suffolk County Superior Court.
38. *Ibid.*, box 57, Erie County Supreme Court (February, 1937), 2; U.S. District Court, St. Louis, Investigation of November 11, 1935, 3–4.
39. *Ibid.*, box 40, Brown report on Oregon, 13; box 39, remarks of Carl May, "The Place of Probation," 12; box 39, C. G. Grason to Justin Miller, November 25, 1936.
40. *AG Files*, box 39, Ullman, "Probation in Baltimore," 7–10.
41. NPA, *Twenty-First Annual Report*, 14–15, 42–43.
42. NYSCC, *Report . . . 1927*, 37; NPA, *Twenty-Second Annual Report* (New York, 1928), 13–25; Bruce, "Probation and Parole," 542; Attorney General, *Probation*, 115–121.
43. *AG Files*, box 40, Brown report on Oregon, 13; NYSCC, *Hearings*, July, 1926, 969–970, 974; December 15, 1926, 2247–2253, 2330–2331.
44. New York State Probation Commission, *Eighth Annual Report*, 58–59.
45. Attorney General, *Probation*, ch. 10, esp. table XXIV, p. 395; Frank Wade, "The Relation and Coordination of Probation and Parole," NPA, *Seventeenth Annual Report* (New York, 1924), 257.
46. *AG Files*, box 39, Ullman, "Probation in Baltimore," 10; NYSCC, *Hearings*, July 14, 1926, 938; Wade, "The Relation of Probation and Parole," 256.
47. New York State Probation Commission, *Eighth Annual Report*, 59.
48. New York State Probation Commission, *Fifth Annual Report*, 10–11; *Eighth Annual Report*, 58–59; *Tenth Annual Report*, 36A, B; *Twentieth Annual Report* (Albany, 1927), 23, 46–47.
49. Wickersham Commission, *Penal Institutions*, 164–165.
50. NYSCC, *Report . . . 1927*, 102; NYSCC, *Hearings*, June 11, 1926, 144; December 15, 1926, 2429.

51. New York Court of General Sessions, *Probation*, 106; Massachusetts Commission on Probation, "Report on . . . the Permanent Results of Probation," Massachusetts *Senate Document* 431, March 15, 1924, 27; success here represented no record of subsequent incarceration.

Chapter Four

1. Charles Davis, "The Prisoner in the Road Camp," in Julia Jaffrey, ed., *The Prison and the Prisoner* (Boston, 1917), 157.
2. Frank Tannenbaum, *Wall Shadows* (New York, 1922), 41.
3. Thomas Osborne, *Society and Prisons* (New Haven, 1916), 125, 145, 128. See too his *Within Prison Walls* (New York, 1914).
4. Osborne, *Society and Prisons*, 141.
5. *Ibid.*, 150–153, including the Gladstone quotation. See also his "The George Junior Republic," American Social Science Association, *Journal* 36 (1898), 136–137.
6. Thomas Osborne, *Prisons and Common Sense* (Philadelphia, 1924), 35.
7. Tannenbaum, *Wall Shadows*, 73, 85; New York State Prison Survey Committee, *Report* (Albany, 1920), 149, 158–159.
8. Edwin Sutherland and Thorsten Sellin, *Prisons of Tomorrow*, American Academy of Political and Social Science, *The Annals* 157 (1931), 8–9, 78.
9. Cf. Sheila Rothman, *Woman's Proper Place*, 166–171.
10. William A. White, *Crime and Criminals* (New York, 1933), 10.
11. Ernest B. Hoag and Edward H. Williams, *Crime, Abnormal Minds, and the Law* (Indianapolis, 1923), 314.
12. William A. White, *Insanity and the Criminal Law* (New York, 1924), 228.
13. Hoag and Williams, *Crime*, xxiii.
14. William A. White, "The Need for Cooperation between the Legal Profession and the Psychiatrist," *American Journal of Psychiatry* 7 (1927), 504; *Crime and Criminals*, 234–235; *Insanity and the Criminal Law*, 221.
15. Massachusetts Civic League, "The Massachusetts Prison System, its Defects and Remedy" (Boston, 1922), 10; Wickersham Commission, *Penal Institutions*, 79, 170–171.
16. New York Prison Survey [Lewisohn] Committee, *Report* (Albany, 1920), 217, 187. Austin MacCormick, "Education in Penal Institutions," *National Conference of Social Work*, 1929, 205, 207–208.
17. Wickersham Commission, *Penal Institutions*, 114; Lewisohn Committee, *Report*, 187.
18. Davis, "The Prisoner," in Jaffrey, ed., *The Prison*, 157–158.
19. Illinois State Penitentiary at Joliet, *Report . . . 1896* (Springfield, 1897), 16; New Hampshire State Prison, *Report . . . 1906*, 5–6, 335, *Report . . . 1908*, 7; U.S. Attorney General, *Survey of Release Procedures*, vol. 5, *Prisons* (Federal Prison Industries, Leavenworth, Kansas, 1940), 98 (hereafter Attorney General, *Prisons*). The discussion here and the pages that follow draw heavily on the *AG Files* schedules, particularly for the institutions noted below in notes 48–49, 51.

20. New Hampshire State Prison, *Report . . . 1906,* 7.
21. California State Board of Prison Directors, *Biennial Report, 1921–1922,* 106–107.
22. *Ibid.,* 107; *AG Files,* box 80, schedule of Virginia State Penitentiary, 58.
23. New Hampshire State Prison, *Report . . . 1916,* 3.
24. See, for example, the schedules in the *AG Files* on such institutions as San Quentin (box 64); Eastern State Penitentiary (box 78); Sing-Sing (box 75); Auburn (box 75); Minnesota State Prison (box 72); see also the compilation on New Hampshire State Prison, *Report . . . 1916,* 25–35.
25. Attorney General, *Prisons,* 106–107.
26. John L. Gillin, *Criminology and Penology* (New York, 1945), 460–463.
27. *AG Files,* box 83, schedule on Lewisburg Penitentiary, 2–3.
28. Winfred Overholser, "Psychiatric Service in Penal and Reformatory Institutions . . ." *Mental Hygiene* 12 (1928), 808–810.
29. Wickersham Commission, *Penal Institutions,* 64–65.
30. Overholser, "Psychiatric Service," 806–807.
31. Attorney General, *Prisons,* 156–157; Alexander Patterson, *The Prison Problem of America* (Maidstone, England, n.d. [ca. 1935]), 48.
32. Wickersham Commission, *Penal Institutions,* 61.
33. Attorney General, *Prisons,* 59–61, 242–243; Wickersham Commission, *Penal Institutions,* 49; New York Prison Survey Committee, *Report,* 216; MacCormick, "Education in Penal Institutions," 202.
34. See *AG Files,* schedules on New Jersey State Prison (box 74), Auburn (box 75), Sing-Sing (box 75), San Quentin (box 64); Lewisohn Committee, *Report,* 216.
35. Attorney General, *Prisons,* 28–29; *AG Files,* box 65, schedule on Colorado State Penitentiary, 21–22.
36. Wickersham Commission, *Penal Institutions,* 15.
37. *Ibid.,* 14; Howard Gill, "The Prison Labor Problem," in Sutherland and Sellin, *Prisons of Tomorrow,* 85–88; Attorney General, *Prisons,* 50–53.
38. Wickersham Commission, *Penal Institutions,* 95; see also 82–87, 90–97.
39. *Ibid.,* 82; see also Fletcher Green, "Some Aspects of the Convict Lease System in the Southern States," in Fletcher Green, ed., *Essays in Southern History* (Chapel Hill, 1940), 112–123.
40. Texas State Penitentiaries, *Report for . . . 1888* (Austin, 1889), 7–10, 24–27; *Report for . . . 1898* (Austin, 1898), 16. The best starting point for analysis is the Texas Penitentiary Committee, *Report and Findings* (Austin, 1913).
41. Texas Penitentiary Committee, *Report,* 14–16; Texas Prison System, *Report for . . . 1911* (Austin, 1912), 7–8, 45.
42. Texas Penitentiary Committee, *Report,* 5; Gill, "Prison Labor," 86–88; Texas Prison Board, *Report for . . . 1928* (Austin, 1929), 8.
43. Wickersham Commission, *Penal Institutions,* 83–94; Gill, "Prison Labor," 86–87, 90–101; Attorney General, *Prisons,* 32–33, 210–211, 228–230.
44. Wickersham Commission, *Penal Institutions,* 93–94; Attorney General, *Prisons,* 32–33, 228–231.
45. New York State Moreland Commission, *Report on . . . State Prisons,* December 26, 1911 (Albany, 1911), 5–7; New York Prison Survey Com-

mittee, *Report*, 41–43, 143–145; NYSCC, *Hearings*, October 14, 1929, 1044 ff.; Wickersham Commission, *Penal Institutions*, 95.
46. Wickersham Commission, *Penal Institutions*, 6–7.
47. *AG Files*, box 75, schedule on Clinton Prison, 60.
48. The information here recapitulates the data in the *AG Files* on the wardens at the prisons in Oklahoma; Colorado; New York (Clinton, Attica, Auburn, Sing-Sing); Pennsylvania (Western); Massachusetts (Charlestown); Virginia; California (San Quentin and Folsom); Illinois (Menard and Stateville); Michigan (Southern); Indiana; Oregon; Arizona; North Dakota; and Tennessee, all in the mid-1930's.
49. The data here include most of the institutions listed in note 48 above, together with information from the Eastern State Penitentiary, Pennsylvania; and from Oklahoma, Connecticut, and Texas.
50. Wickersham Commission, *Penal Institutions*, 43–47; the Illinois investigation is quoted there, p. 44; Attorney General, *Prisons*, 69–70; Gill, "Prison Labor," 66.
51. Attorney General, *Prisons*, 64–65; Patterson, *The Prison Problem*, 41; Gill, "Prison Labor," 66–67; calculations from the *AG Files* on turnover in Pennsylvania (Eastern and Western); New York (Clinton, Auburn, Sing-Sing); Virginia; California (San Quentin and Folsom); Michigan (Southern); Massachusetts (Charlestown); and Colorado confirm these findings.
52. *AG Files*, box 64, schedule on Folsom prison, 21 ff.; Gill, "Prison Labor," 66.
53. Wickersham Commission, *Penal Institutions*, 43; Gill, "Prison Labor," 66.
54. Wickersham Commission, *Penal Institutions*, 18–19, 35.
55. Rules culled from Wickersham Commission, *Penal Institutions*, 25–32.
56. *Ibid.*, 34, 38; Attorney General, *Prisons*, 117.
57. Wickersham Commission, *Penal Institutions*, 19; New York State, *Duties of Keepers and Guards* (undated), New York State Library, Albany, 3, 9.
58. New York State, *Duties of Keepers*, 14–15; Wickersham Commission, *Penal Institutions*, 19–24; Attorney General, *Prisons*, 72.
59. Wickersham Commission, *Penal Institutions*, 27–40, surveys these general practices.
60. *Ibid.*, 30.
61. *Ibid.*, 31; Andrew A. Bruce, Ernest Burgess, and Albert Harno, *The Workings of the Indeterminate-Sentence Law and the Parole System in Illinois* (1928), 32–33.
62. The analysis here follows on the material at the California State Archives, Sacramento: "Hearings, Proceedings, Charges," by John G. Clark, Director of Penology, against the [California] State Board of Prisons Director, before Culbert L. Olson, Governor, November 3–9, 1939.
63. *Ibid.*, 37, 57, 55, 52.
64. *Ibid.*, 38, 36.
65. *Ibid.*, 481–483, 485.
66. *Ibid.*, 545, 576.
67. *Ibid.*, 2651.
68. Wickersham Commission, *Penal Institutions*, 29–30; Attorney General, *Prisons*, 122–123, 126–127.

69. David J. Rothman, "Decarcerating Prisoners and Patients," *Civil Liberties Review* 1 (1973), 8–9; quotation on p. 11, from *Stroud v. Swope*, 1951.
70. "Hearings . . . Against the [California] Prisons Director," 26–27.
71. Attorney General, *Prisons*, 96–97, 101–102; New York State Legislative Hearings, "Inquiry on Prisons," January 29, 1930, table p. 14A and pp. 66–68, New York State Library, Albany.

Chapter Five

1. Clair Wilcox, *The Parole of Adults from State Penal Institutions in Pennsylvania* (Part II of the Report of the Pennsylvania State Parole Commission to the Legislature, Philadelphia, 1927), 1; Bruce, Burgess, and Harno, *The Workings of the Indeterminate-Sentence Law and the Parole System in Illinois* (hereafter, Bruce et al., *Indeterminate Sentence*), iii–vi; U.S. Attorney General, *Survey of Release Procedures*, vol. 4, *Parole* (Washington, D.C., 1939) vii, 2–3.
2. *Chicago Daily Tribune*, November 9, 1936, November 16, 1936.
3. *Denver Post*, January 25, 1936, September 5, 1936; Martin Moody, *The Parole Scandal* (Los Angeles, 1939), 2–3.
4. *AG Files*, box 36, schedule on Wisconsin Release Procedures, 46–47; Attorney General, *Parole*, 54 ff. for details of other state practices.
5. *AG Files*, box 37, John Burroughs, "The Parole System in Minnesota," 55; box 36, Washington Release Procedures, 17–18, 57–59; box 70, schedule on Massachusetts State Prison, Charlestown, 91–92; schedule on Eastern State Penitentiary, 91; Wilcox, *Parole*, 116–117.
6. Attorney General, *Parole*, 140–146; Wilcox, *Parole*, 60.
7. Attorney General, *Parole*, 146–157; Bruce et al., *Indeterminate Sentence*, 68.
8. New York State Special Committee on the Parole Problem, *Report*, February 5, 1930, 16–17. Also New York County Grand Jury, *Parole Systems of the City and State of New York*, December 31, 1934, 40; Wilcox, *Parole*, 62; Wickersham Commission, *Penal Institutions*, 306–307; *AG Files*, box 36, Washington Release Procedures, 139–140, 144, 155; *AG Files*, box 34, *Proceedings at Meeting before the Idaho State Parole Board*, Boise, Idaho, April 15, 1937 (hereafter, *Idaho Proceedings*); Attorney General, *Parole*, 160.
9. Attorney General, *Parole*, ch. 5.
10. *AG Files*, box 168, "Oregon Parole Calendar," June, 1939, In RE J.C., number 13680. The correct initials of the persons are retained, but the names in text are fictive to protect confidentiality.
11. *Ibid.*, in RE C.H.H., number 13489.
12. *Ibid.*, in RE J.L., number 13665.
13. *Idaho Proceedings*, 18–19, 27–28, 56–58; Attorney General, *Parole*, 170; Wilcox, *Parole*, 33.
14. *Idaho Proceedings*, 38.
15. *Oregon Parole Calendar*, In RE F.H., number 12525.
16. *Ibid.*, In RE G.L.J., number 13437.
17. NYSCC, *Hearings*, November 23, 1926, 1728–1729.
18. See note 10 above.

19. *Oregon Parole Calendar*, in RE R.B., number 13362.
20. *Idaho Proceedings*, 52–54.
21. Wilcox, *Parole*, 122–123.
22. *Idaho Proceedings*, 54, 62.
23. *Ibid.*, 62–63.
24. *Ibid.*, 24–25.
25. *Ibid.*, 11, 18, 54.
26. Wilcox, *Parole*, 66–67, 71; Attorney General, *Parole*, 373.
27. *AG Files*, box 36, Washington Release Procedures, 57; Wilcox, *Parole*, 133; Attorney General, *Parole*, 417.
28. *AG Files*, box 36, Washington Release Procedures, 15.
29. Wilcox, *Parole*, 129–131.
30. *AG Files*, box 40, Oregon Schedules, J. M. Brown to Justin Miller, September 12, 1936, 7.
31. Quoted in Wilcox, *Parole*, 176; *AG Files*, box 34, State of Michigan, "Manual for Parole Agents," 1936, 26–27, 50.
32. Wickersham Commission, *Penal Institutions*, 305.
33. *AG Files*, box 36, Washington Release Procedures, 59, 70–73; Wilcox, *Parole*, 209.
34. *AG Files*, box 40, Oregon Schedules, J. M. Brown to Justin Miller, September 12, 1936, 4; box 37, Idaho Penitentiary Schedule, 105; Attorney General, *Parole*, 192–199.
35. *AG Files*, box 36, Washington Release Procedures, 33; Wilcox, *Parole*, 78, 175–177; Attorney General, *Parole*, 212.
36. *AG Files*, box 37, John Burroughs, The Parole System for Adult Offenders in Minnesota, 43, 76–77.
37. Bruce et al., *Indeterminate Sentence*, 192; Pennsylvania State Parole Commission, *Report, 1927* (Philadelphia, 1927), 25; Wilcox, *Parole*, 80–81, 199; *Boston Post*, June 29, 1936; *AG Files*, box 36, William Atherton, "Prisons, Prisoners, and Paroles" (ca. 1935), 9; Joint [Ohio] Legislative Committee on Prisons, *The Penal Problem in Ohio* (Columbus, 1926), 33.
38. New York State Special Committee on Parole, *Report*, 17–18; New York Grand Jury, *Parole Systems*, 38–39, 44; New York State, *Proceedings of the Governor's Conference on Crime, the Criminal, and Society* (Albany, 1935), 1068.
39. Bruce et al., *Indeterminate Sentence*, 197–198; Wilcox, *Parole*, 83.
40. New York State, *Governor's Conference on Crime*, 863; Wilcox, *Parole*, 67; Attorney General, *Parole*, 49.
41. National Prison Association, *Proceedings . . . 1926*; Attorney General, *Parole*, 148–153; *AG Files*, box 34, J. M. Brown, Parole in Montana, 2.
42. Wilcox, *Parole*, 67, 25.
43. New York State, *Governor's Conference on Crime*, 852.
44. *AG Files*, box 36, Washington Release Procedures, 16, 29; box 67, Stateville, Illinois Prison Schedule, 63; Henry Higgins, "Is Parole a Success?," National Prison Association, *Proceedings . . . 1923*, 267.
45. NYSCC, *Hearings*, November 23, 1926, 1727; December 6, 1928, 2111–2112.
46. See, for example, U.S. Bureau of the Census statistics, *Prisoners in State*

and Federal Prisons and Reformatories, 1927 (Washington, D.C., 1931), 8; *1928* (Washington, D.C., 1931), 8; *1929* (Washington, D.C., 1932), 5; *1936* (Washington, D.C., 1938), 8.

47. Bruce et al., *Indeterminate Sentence*, 46–47.
48. *Ibid.*, 47; New York Grand Jury, *Parole Systems*, 37.
49. Attorney General, *Parole*, 133.
50. NYSCC, *Hearings*, July 21, 1926, 790–792.
51. *Ibid.*, July 21, 1926, 790; November 23, 1926, 1780; October 16, 1928, 351–352.
52. *Ibid.*, October 21, 1926, 1107–1110, 1119.
53. New York State, *Governor's Conference on Crime*, 972, 1113–1114.
54. NYSCC, *Hearings*, July 21, 1926, 746, 750–765, 969–970; December 21, 1926, 2522–2523.
55. U.S. Bureau of the Census, *Prisoners . . . 1927*, 16–25, 46–51.
56. Wickersham Commission, *Penal Institutions*, 129; Wilcox, *Parole*, 23, italics added.
57. U.S. Bureau of the Census, *Prisons . . . 1923*, 124; David J. Rothman, "Doing Time," in Amitai Etzioni, *Policy Research* (Leiden, 1978), 130–138; Wickersham Commission, *Penal Institutions*, 129.
58. Bruce et al., *Indeterminate Sentence*, 49, 51, 245, 254.
59. *AG Files*, box 36, Washington Release Procedures, 126–129, 139.
60. *AG Files*, box 36, William Atherton, "Prisons, Prisoners, and Paroles" (ca. 1935), 3.
61. Wilcox, *Parole*, 22–23; see also pp. 58–59 on Pennsylvania; NYSCC, *Hearings*, December 20, 1926, 2432.
62. George Thomas and Adolph Ladree, *A Study of the Indeterminate Sentence, Probation and Parole in Utah* (Salt Lake City, 1931), 78; Memorandum of Sheldon Messinger, June 1977, prepared for Andrew von Hirsch's *Abolish Parole?* (Boston, 1979); U.S. Bureau of the Census, *Prisoners . . . 1926*, 51.
63. NYSCC, *Report . . . 1929*, 12.
64. NYSCC, *Report . . . 1927*, 13.
65. NYSCC, *Hearings*, October 20, 1927, 3033–3039; November 21, 1927, 2945–2949, 2991–2995.
66. *Ibid.*, December 14, 1926, 2448.
67. NYSCC, *Report . . . 1927*, 13; NYSCC, *Hearings*, December 14, 1926, 2440.
68. NYSCC, *Hearings*, November 22, 1926, 1566. See too, on Napanoch, 1546–1567, 1590–1592.
69. *Ibid.*, November 21, 1927, 3064–3066, 3100.
70. *Ibid.*, 3101, 3079–3080.

Chapter Six

1. For general surveys of the juvenile court see Herbert Lou, *Juvenile Courts in the United States* (Chapel Hill, 1927); Anthony Platt, *The Child Savers* (Chicago, 1969); Robert Mennel, *Thorns and Thistles: Juvenile Delinquents in the United States* (Hanover, N.H., 1973); Ellen Ryerson, *The Best-Laid Plans* (New York, 1978); Sanford J. Fox,

"Juvenile Justice Reform: An Historical Perspective," *Stanford Law Review* 22 (1970), 1187–1239; Evelina Belden, *Courts in the United States Hearing Children's Cases*, U.S. Children's Bureau Publication no. 65 (Washington, D.C., 1920). See also, on the immigrant, New York State Probation Commission, *Ninth Annual Report* (Albany, 1916), remarks of Frank Wade, 232–233.

2. Rothman, *Woman's Proper Place*, 98–100, 104–106; G. Stanley Hall, *Adolescence* (New York, 1904), vol. 1, and its condensed version, *Youth* (New York, 1904) are the appropriate texts here. The quotation is from *Youth*, 237.

3. Rothman, *Woman's Proper Place*, 104, 107–108.

4. *Proceedings of the [White House] Conference on the Care of Dependent Children* (Washington, D.C., 1909), 87, 92.

5. *Ibid.*, 141, 143–144. See too, Rudolph Reeder, *How Two Hundred Children Live and Learn* (New York, 1917), especially 56–57, 74.

6. Hall, *Youth*, 136.

7. *Ibid.*, 134–135.

8. *Ibid.*, 139; *Adolescence*, 342.

9. Richard Tuthill, "The Juvenile Court Law in Cook County," Illinois Board of Public Charities, *Report . . . 1900*, 338; Jacob Riis, *The Peril and Preservation of the Home* (Philadelphia, 1903), 173.

10. *Juvenile Court Record (JCR)*, December, 1900, pp. 6–7; *Survey*, 22 (1910), 638–639.

11. *JCR*, November, 1900, p. 11; New York State Probation Commission, *9th Annual Report*, 440–441; *Survey*, 22 (1910), 607.

12. *JCR*, February, 1903, 5.

13. *Ibid.*, January, 1903, 7; Summer issue, 1903, 14; Allan East, *A History of Community Interest in a Juvenile Court* (1943), 9–17.

14. Cf. Steven L. Schlossman, *Love and the American Delinquent* (Chicago, 1977), ch. 4.

15. New York State Probation Commission, *Eighth Annual Report*, remarks of Frank Wade, 127; Lou, *Juvenile Courts*, 25–29.

16. *Survey* 22 (1910), 607, 649; *Harvey Humphrey Baker, Upbuilder of the Juvenile Court* (Boston, 1920).

17. *JCR*, May, 1906, 21; Bernard Flexner, Reuben Oppenheimer, and Katharine Lenroot, *The Child, the Family, and the Court*, Children's Bureau Publication no. 193 (Washington, D.C., 1929), 21–22.

18. Flexner, Oppenheimer, and Lenroot, *The Child, the Family, and the Court*, 21–24; *JCR*, March, 1904, 4.

19. *Survey* 22 (1910), 608, 648.

20. *Ibid.*, 658; *JCR*, Summer, 1903, 10–11.

21. *JCR*, December, 1900, 4; June, 1902, 5.

22. *Ibid.*, December, 1900, 4.

23. Homer Folks, "The Probation System, its Value and Limitations," *Proceedings of the Child Conference for Research and Welfare, 1910* (New York, 1910), 228; *JCR*, June, 1902, 5.

24. Homer Folks, "The Probation System," 227–228; James Ricks, "Standards of Organization in Children's Courts," *Proceedings of the Child Conference, 1910*, 372; *JCR*, December, 1900, 5.

25. Louis Robinson, "Standards of Probation Work," *Proceedings of the Child Conference, 1910*, 378; *JCR*, October, 1901, 6; New York State Probation Commission, *Ninth Annual Report*, 235–236.
26. *JCR*, December, 1900, 4; June, 1902, 5.
27. *Ibid.*, September, 1906, 22; March, 1906, 15.
28. Victor Arnold, "What Constitutes Sufficient Grounds for the Removal of a Child from his Home," *Proceedings of the Child Conference, 1910*, 345.
29. *JCR*, June, 1902, 6.
30. National Congress of Mothers, *Fourth Annual Convention* (June, 1901), 187; *JCR*, Summer, 1903, 11.
31. *JCR*, May, 1906, 24; see too, November, 1900, 7; Arnold, "Sufficient Grounds for the Removal," 345–346.
32. *JCR*, August, 1901, 8; April, 1902, 9.
33. Franklin Hoyt, *Quicksand of Youth* (New York, 1921), 3–4, 54, 65; *JCR*, Summer, 1903, 11.
34. *JCR*, April, 1901, 6.
35. Breckinridge and Abbott, *The Delinquent Child*, 174, 177; Mabel B. Ellis, "How One Juvenile Court Helps to Make Child Labor Legislation Effective," *Child Labor Bulletin* 5 (1917), 3.
36. *JCR*, November, 1900, 11; June, 1901, 16–17; November, 1902, 9; Fox, "Juvenile Justice," 1222 ff.
37. *JCR*, June, 1901, 17; Mary Covell to Emma Lundberg, September 11, 1923, Children's Bureau Archives, 1921–1924, box 367, National Archives, Washington, D.C.
38. *JCR*, Summer, 1903, 13.
39. *Ibid.*, Summer, 1903, 9–14; October–November, 1904, 5; *Survey* 22 (1910), 634–635; cf. Thomas Eliot, *The Juvenile Court and the Community* (New York, 1911), 33–40.
40. *JCR*, February, 1901, 13.
41. Eliot, *The Juvenile Court*, 39–40; *Survey* 22 (1910), 634; *JCR*, Summer, 1903, 21; October–November, 1904, 5.
42. *JCR*, January, 1902, 10.
43. Roscoe Pound, "The Administration of Justice in the Modern City," *Harvard Law Review* 24 (1913), 302–328.
44. Edward Lindsey, "The Juvenile Court Movement from a Lawyer's Perspective," American Academy of Political and Social Science, *Annals* 52 (1914), 140–147.
45. *People v. Turner*, 55 Illinois 282–287 (1870).
46. *Commonwealth of Pennsylvania v. Fisher*, 213 Pennsylvania 50–55 (1905).
47. Lou, *Juvenile Courts*, 10 ff.; *In Re Sharp*, 15 Idaho 26 (1908); *Mill v. Brown*, 31 Utah 473 (1907); *JCR*, December, 1905, 11–13; *Marlowe v. Commonwealth*, 142 Kentucky 106 (1911).

Chapter Seven

1. Evelina Belden, *Courts Hearing Children's Cases*, 35 and appendix A, charts I–III; Katharine Lenroot and Emma Lundberg, *Juvenile Courts at*

Work, Children's Bureau Publication no. 141 (Washington, D.C., 1925), 4–16, 19, 126–127.

2. Belden, *Courts Hearing Children's Cases*, 11–13.
3. W. I. Thomas, "The Juvenile Court of Cincinnati," Bureau of Social Hygiene file, box 34, folder 473, pp. 3–9, Rockefeller Foundation Archives, New York. Italics added.
4. *JCR*, February, 1902, 9; December, 1903, 6; April, 1904, 10.
5. *Ibid.*, September, 1904, 13.
6. Neva Deardorff, *Child Welfare Conditions and Resources in Seven Pennsylvania Counties*, Children's Bureau Publication no. 176 (Washington, D.C., 1927), 107–117.
7. Illinois Committee on Child Welfare Legislation, *Report* (Springfield, 1931), 29; Belden, *Courts Hearing Children's Cases*, 55; New Jersey Juvenile and Probation Study Commission, *Report*, February 17, 1928, 14.
8. Philadelphia Bureau of Municipal Research, *Juvenile Division of the Municipal Court of Philadelphia* (Philadelphia, 1930), 20; Children's Division, County Court of Monroe County, *Annual Report, 1923* (Rochester, 1924), 28–29; Children's Court of the County of Westchester, *Annual Report for 1930*, 10–13; Thomas, "The Juvenile Court of Cincinnati," 6, 20, 33.
9. Lenroot and Lundberg, *Juvenile Courts at Work*, 22–31, 171–177, 193–195.
10. Overholser, "Psychiatric Facilities," 800–808.
11. Sheldon and Eleanor Glueck, *One Thousand Juvenile Delinquents* (Cambridge, Massachusetts, 1934), 30.
12. *Ibid.*, 111, 255, 281–283.
13. *Ibid.*, 119–120, 123.
14. *Ibid.*, 133–138.
15. *Ibid.*, 227, 201, 223. See also Philadelphia Bureau, *Juvenile Court*, 58–59.
16. *Juvenile Court Statistics, 1927*, Children's Bureau Publication no. 195 (Washington, D.C., 1929), 5–6; *Juvenile Court Statistics, 1929*, Children's Bureau Publication no. 207 (Washington, D.C., 1931), 17–18.
17. *Statistics of the Juvenile Court of the District of Columbia for Fiscal Years 1906–1926*, 69th Congress, 2nd Session, Senate Document no. 236 (1927), 91–149; see especially tables V (p. 194), XII (p. 105), XV (p. 125). Part I of this document is a reprint of a Ph.D. dissertation, Raymond W. Murray, *The Delinquent Child and the Law*, which ably surveys the history of the Washington, D.C., juvenile court.
18. Lenroot and Lundberg, *Juvenile Courts at Work*, 113–119.
19. *Juvenile Court Statistics, 1927*, 14–18; *Juvenile Court Statistics, 1929*, 12; cf., for example, Richmond (Virginia) Juvenile and Domestic Relations Court, *Tenth Annual Report, 1925* (Richmond, 1926), 22–23.
20. *Juvenile Court Statistics, 1929*, 8; *Juvenile Court Statistics, 1927*, 10–11; New York City Children's Court, *Annual Report, 1925*, 59, 69–70.
21. *Juvenile Court Statistics, 1927*, 20–21.
22. Philadelphia Bureau, *Juvenile Court*, 64, 60–61.
23. Deardorff, *Child Welfare in Pennsylvania*, 8–9.
24. *Dependent and Delinquent Children in Georgia*, Children's Bureau Publication no. 161 (Washington, D.C., 1926), 22; *Child Welfare in New*

Jersey, Children's Bureau Publication no. 180 (Washington, D.C., 1927), 27; *Juvenile Delinquency in Maine*, Children's Bureau Publication no. 201, (Washington, D.C.), 1930, 11–12; *Dependent and Delinquent Children in North Dakota and South Dakota*, Children's Bureau Publication no. 160 (Washington, D.C., 1926), 34.

25. U.S. Bureau of the Census, *Children Under Institutional Care, 1923* (Washington, D.C., 1927), 346–355; *Juvenile Delinquents in Public Institutions, 1933* (Washington, D.C., 1936), 59–62.

26. See, for example, J. B. Maller, *Maladjusted Youth*, Part II of the State of New York, *Report of the Joint Legislative Committee to Investigate the Jurisdiction of the Children's Court* (Albany, 1939), 128–129.

27. Philadelphia Bureau, *Juvenile Court*, 61; the chart appears first in Lenroot and Lundberg, *Juvenile Courts at Work*, 154.

Chapter Eight

1. Remarks of Edward Henry, National Conference of Juvenile Agencies (NCJA), *Twentieth Annual Session, 1923,* 8, 11.

2. See, for example, remarks of Sanford Bates, NCJA, *Twenty-First Annual Session, 1924,* 12–14, 16; and *Twentieth Annual Session, 1923,* 202.

3. *Facts About Juvenile Delinquency*, Children's Bureau Publication no. 215 (Washington, D.C., 1935), 37.

4. Remarks of William Slingerland, NCJA, *Twentieth Annual Session, 1923,* 193–194; Mary Palevsky, "An Ideal Program for an Institution Dealing with Delinquents," *Jewish Social Service Quarterly* 3 (1927), 32; White House Conference on Child Health and Protection, *The Delinquent Child*, Report of the Committee on Socially Handicapped-Delinquency, Frederick P. Cabot, Chairman (New York, 1932), 312 (hereafter, *The Delinquent Child*); William I. Thomas and Dorothy S. Thomas, *The Child in America* (New York, 1928), 110–111.

5. Remarks of Calvin Derrick at the NCJA, *Twenty-Fourth Annual Session, 1927,* 69, and remarks of Elizabeth Packard, 23; Carrie Smith, "The Elimination of the Reformatory," *National Conference of Social Work, 1921,* 131.

6. Smith, "The Elimination of the Reformatory," 131–132.

7. *The Delinquent Child*, 308; Calvin Derrick, "The Delinquent Adolescent," *National Conference on Social Work, 1926,* 204; Alida Bowler and Ruth Bloodgood, *Institutional Treatment of Delinquent Boys*, Children's Bureau Publication no. 228 (Washington, D.C., 1935), part 1, "Treatment Programs of Five State Institutions for Delinquent Boys," 288.

8. Jack M. Holl, *Juvenile Reform in the Progressive Era: William R. George and the Junior Republic* (Ithaca, New York, 1971), passim.

9. Remarks of Clinton McCord, NCJA, *Twentieth Annual Session, 1923,* 61; Palevsky, "Ideal Program for Delinquents," 30.

10. Palevsky, "Ideal Program for Delinquents," 30–34.

11. *The Delinquent Child*, 298–299.

12. Smith, "Elimination of the Reformatory," 131; Frank F. Nalder, *The American State Reformatory* (University of California Publications, Edu-

cation, vol. 5, March 10, 1920), 316–321; remarks by Roy McLaughlin, NCJA, *Twentieth Annual Session, 1923*, 25; National Committee on Mental Hygiene (NCMH), *Cook County and the Mentally Handicapped*, prepared by Herman Adler (New York, 1918), 60; Indiana Boys' School, *Fifty-Fourth Annual Report* (1920), 12.

13. Remarks of William Slingerland, NCJA, *Twentieth Annual Session, 1923*, 185–186; Alida Bowler and Ruth Bloodgood, *Institutional Treatment of Delinquent Boys*, Children's Bureau Publication no. 230 (Washington, D.C., 1936), part 2, "A Study of 751 Boys," 42–47.

14. Bowler and Bloodgood, "Treatment Programs," 200–201, 109–111; NCMH, *Cook County*, 61; Olive Hull, "State Care of Juvenile Delinquents in Illinois," in Illinois Committee on Child Welfare Legislation, *Report* (Springfield, 1931), 203.

15. Hull, "State Care of Delinquents in Illinois," 201–205.

16. Bowler and Bloodgood, "Treatment Programs," 179; William Slingerland, *Child Welfare Work in Oregon* (Salem, Oregon, 1918), 16.

17. Kansas Boys' Industrial School, *Thirteenth Biennial Report* (Topeka, 1940), 12.

18. Bowler and Bloodgood, "Treatment Programs," 184–186.

19. NCMH, *Cook County*, 57–59.

20. Remarks of Elizabeth Prescott, NCJA, *Twenty-Fourth Annual Session, 1927*, 29–30; Kansas Temporary Commission, *Public Welfare Report, 1933*, 96–98.

21. Bowler and Bloodgood, "Treatment Programs," 201–202; *Proceedings of the Third National Conference on the Education of Backward, Truant and Delinquent Children* (Philadelphia, 1906), 61–62; Colorado State Industrial School, *Tenth Biennial Report* (1899–1900), 13; and *Thirteenth Biennial Report* (1905–1906), 42–43.

22. Bowler and Bloodgood, "Treatment Programs," 30–31, 96–97, 152–153; NCMH, *Cook County*, 47–48; Slingerland, *Child Welfare Work in Oregon*, 14–21.

23. Max Winsor, "The Practice of Psychiatry in an Institution for Delinquents," paper read at the Annual Meeting, American Psychiatric Association, 1935, copy in the Bureau of Social Hygiene File, pp. 1–2.

24. Leonard Hanson and Pryor M. Grant, *Youth in the Toils* (New York, 1938), 112–113.

25. Indiana Boys' School, *Forty-Ninth Annual Report* (1915), 56–57.

26. Bowler and Bloodgood, "Treatment Programs," 43, 205.

27. Bowler and Bloodgood, "751 Boys," 44.

28. NCMH, *Cook County*, 60; Bowler and Bloodgood, "Treatment Programs," 42, 167, 205.

29. Bowler and Bloodgood, "Treatment Programs," 121; remarks of Superintendent Close, NCJA, *Twenty-First Annual Session, 1924*, 160–61.

30. NCMH, *Cook County*, 60; Kansas Temporary Commission, *Public Welfare, 1933*, 99.

31. Kansas Temporary Commission, *Public Welfare, 1933*, 99; Bowler and Bloodgood, "Treatment Programs," 205.

32. Bowler and Bloodgood, "Treatment Programs," 75; Austin MacCormick,

"The Michigan Boys' Vocational School, Lansing," report during the winter of 1941–1942, 121, 31.

33. MacCormick, "The Michigan Boys' School," 32–35.
34. *Ibid.*, 51–53.
35. *Ibid.*, 61–66.
36. NCMH, *Cook County*, 53; Winsor, "Psychiatry in an Institution," 8.
37. Kansas Temporary Commission, *Public Welfare, 1933*, 91.
38. Roy Wallace to George Darrow, March 8, 1916; Julia Lathrop to Walter Ufford, December 18, 1914; and Lathrop to Henry Thurston, March 24, 1916, Children's Bureau File, box 99, Washington, D.C.
39. Helen Jeter, *The Chicago Juvenile Court*, Children's Bureau Publication no. 104 (Washington, D.C., 1922), 88–90. See too, Fred Gross, *Detention and Prosecution of Children* (Chicago, 1946), 19–20, 56–59.
40. New York Joint Legislative Committee on Children's Court Jurisdiction and Juvenile Delinquency, *Hearings*, December 1, 1937, 26–28, 118–121, and passim; December 3, 1937, 395–396.
41. Glueck and Glueck, *One Thousand Juvenile Delinquents*, 151, 183.
42. Bowler and Bloodgood, "751 Boys," 124; William Healy and Augusta Bronner, *Delinquents and Criminals* (New York, 1926), 201–211.
43. Glueck and Glueck, *One Thousand Juvenile Delinquents*, 183; Massachusetts Child Council, *Juvenile Delinquency in Massachusetts as a Public Responsibility* (Boston, 1939), 1, 7, 149.
44. Bowler and Bloodgood, "751 Boys," 124–128; *Facts About Juvenile Delinquency*, 38–39; *The Delinquent Child*, 259, 310.
45. Van Waters, *Youth in Conflict*, 242–243; Thomas and Thomas, *Child in America*, 107.
46. Illinois Committee on Child Welfare Legislation, *Report*, 29; Harrison and Grant, *Youth in the Toils*, 152, 156–159; Van Waters, *Youth in Conflict*, 243.

Chapter Nine

1. S. Weir Mitchell, "Address Before the 50th Anniversary Meeting of the American Medico-Psychological Association," May 16, 1894, reprinted in *Journal of Nervous and Mental Diseases* (*JNMD*) 21 (1894), 414, 422, 424, 429–430. Before 1893, the Association went under the title, Association of Medical Superintendents.
2. *Ibid.*, 427, 420, 414, 433.
3. *Ibid.*, 433, 435.
4. Walter Channing, "Some Remarks on the Address . . . by S. Weir Mitchell, *American Journal of Insanity* (*AJI*) 51 (1894), 171–172, 175–176.
5. Livingston Hinckley, "Difficulties . . . of Doctor Mitchell's Ideal Hospital for the Insane," *JNMD* 21 (1894), 602–604.
6. *Ibid.*, 604. See also here, 512–515, for a response by H. A. Tomlinson.
7. Clifford Beers, *A Mind That Found Itself*, 4th edition (New York, 1917), viii.

8. *Ibid.*, 45, 172, 162, 117.
9. *Ibid.*, 68, 169, 154.
10. *Ibid.*, 280, 231–233, 237.
11. *Ibid.*, 255, 228, 317–318.
12. *Ibid.*, 247, 254–255, 257, 302.
13. The citations throughout are to the four volumes of *The Collected Papers of Adolf Meyer* (hereafter, Meyer, *Papers*), ed Eunice E. Winters (Baltimore, 1950–1952). For the quotation above see vol. 3, 422; on mind-body, vol. 3, 404–405.
14. Meyer, *Papers*, vol. 3, 15–16.
15. *Ibid.*, 39–41.
16. *Ibid.*, 54–56.
17. Meyer, *Papers*, vol. 4, 342, 71; vol. 2, 200.
18. Meyer, *Papers*, vol. 4, 169. See also Owen Copp, "Community Organization for Mental Hygiene," *National Conference of Social Work, 1917*, 391–393.
19. Meyer, *Papers*, vol. 4, 52, 227; vol. 2, 178.
20. Homer Folks and Everett S. Elwood, "Why Should Anyone Go Insane?," reprinted in New York State Charities Aid Association, *Twenty-First Annual Report* (New York, 1913), 2–4.
21. *Boston Medical and Surgical Journal* 146 (1902), 292–293.
22. Meyer, *Papers*, vol. 2, 198, 194; Frederick Peterson, "Some Problems of the Alienist," *AJI* 56 (1899), 3.
23. Meyer, *Papers*, vol. 2, 178, 206; vol. 4, 21.
24. Meyer, *Papers*, vol. 2, 190, 194–200.
25. *Ibid.*, 190.
26. Douglas Thom, "Results and Future Opportunities in the Field of Clinics, Social Service, and Parole," *National Conference of Social Work, 1922*, 376.
27. Meyer, *Papers*, vol. 4, 269–270; Peterson, "Problems of the Alienist," 3.
28. *Boston Medical and Surgical Journal* 116 (1887), 242; Julia Lathrop, "Village Care for the Insane," *Twenty-Ninth National Conference of Charities and Corrections* (1902), 199.
29. New York State Charities Aid Association, *First Annual Report of the Subcommittee on After Care* (New York, 1906), 10, 14; New York State Commission in Lunacy, *Eighteenth Annual Report* (1905–1906), 119 ff.
30. New York State Charities Aid Association, *Second Annual Report* (1907), 10–13; *Third Annual Report* (1908), 12–13; *Fourth Annual Report* (1909), 12–17 (quotations from p. 14).
31. Katharine Tucker, "Social Service for the Mentally Ill," *New York State Hospital Bulletin* 8 (1915), 75–76.
32. Lawson G. Lowry, "The Contribution of Mental Hygiene to the Differentiated Fields," *National Conference of Social Work, 1928*, 360–366; H. Douglas Singer, "The Function of the Social Worker in Relation to the State Hospital Physician," *National Conference of Social Work, 1919*, 632–637. See also Henry Stedman, "A Programme of Practical Measures for Mental Hygiene Work," *Boston Medical and Surgical Journal* 170 (1914), 187; C. M. Campbell, "The Mental Health of the Community,"

Forty-Fourth National Conference of Charities and Corrections (1917), 432–433; Thom, "Clinics, Social Service, and Parole," 376–378.

33. Beers, *A Mind that Found Itself*, 321–322; "Report of the Activities of the Rockefeller Foundation in Mental Hygiene, 1915–1918," 4–11, Rockefeller Foundation Archive, North Tarrytown, New York. See also Lewellyn F. Barker, "The First Ten Years of the National Committee for Mental Hygiene," *Mental Hygiene* 2 (1918), 557–581; Wilbur Cross, ed., *Twenty-Five Years After* (New York, 1934), on Beers and the National Committee.

34. New York State Hospital Commission, *Twenty-Eighth Annual Report* (1925–1926), 355–360.

35. Meyer, *Papers*, vol. 2, 73; vol. 4, 64, 74, 48–49.

36. Meyer, *Papers*, vol. 4, 71, 186–187; August Hoch, "The Manageable Causes of Insanity," *New York State Hospital Bulletin* 2 (1909), 351.

37. Meyer, *Papers*, vol. 4, 227; see also Mark H. Haller, *Eugenics* (New Brunswick, New Jersey, 1963).

38. *AJI* 73 (1916), 82–84.

39. *Ibid.*, 84–86.

40. *Ibid.*, 85–86; James May, *Mental Diseases: A Public Health Problem* (Boston, 1922), 81.

41. Barker, "First Ten Years," 559; Samuel Smith, "On the relation of Psychiatry to the State," *AJI* 72 (1915), 8–9.

Chapter Ten

1. Massachusetts State Board of Insanity, *Annual Report, 1910*, 30–31.

2. A substantial history of changing commitment laws remains to be written. Deutsch, *The Mentally Ill*, ch. 19, is an introduction to the material. See also the several articles in the American Social Science Association, *Journal* 19 (1884), 66 ff.

3. Meyers, *Papers*, vol. 4, 168, 186–187, 205, 230–231. See also Winfred Overholser, "The Voluntary Admission Law," *American Journal of Psychiatry* 2 (1924), 476–481; "Report of the Committee on Institutions," *First International Congress on Mental Hygiene* (1930), 58 ff.

4. Massachusetts State Board of Insanity, *Annual Report, 1915*, 92; *Annual Report, 1917*, 93–94.

5. *Idem*, Annual Report, *1914*, 93–94.

6. C. M. Campbell, "The Work of the Psychopathic Hospital," *First International Congress on Mental Hygiene* (1930), 358. See also Trustees of the Boston Psychopathic Hospital, *Annual Report . . . 1921*, 20; L. Vernon Briggs, *History of the Psychopathic Hospital of Boston* (1922).

7. Massachusetts State Board of Insanity, *Annual Report, 1914*, 94; Trustees of the Boston Psychopathic Hospital, *Annual Report . . . 1921*, 3.

8. Massachusetts State Board of Insanity, *Annual Report, 1914*, 14.

9. Campbell, "Psychopathic Hospital," 357–358.

10. Trustees of the Boston Psychopathic Hospital, *Annual Report . . . 1938*, 7, 37.

11. Trustees of the Boston Psychopathic Hospital, *Annual Report . . . 1931*, 9.

12. Syracuse State Psychopathic Hospital, *First Annual Report* (1931), 10; *Fifth Annual Report* (1935), 5.

13. Michigan Psychopathic Hospital, *First Biennial Report* (1908), 6–9; *Second Biennial Report* (1910), 8–9; *Third Biennial Report* (1912), 7.

14. *Idem, Fifth Biennial Report* (1918), 35; *Second Biennial Report* (1910), 9; *Fourth Biennial Report* (1916), 7.

15. NCMH, *Cook County,* 14–25, quotations from 21, 25.

16. New York State Psychiatric Institute and Hospital, *Eighth Annual Report* (1937), 9; *First Annual Report* (1930), 6–7; *Sixth Annual Report* (1935), 64. On Meyer's program see New York State Commission in Lunacy, *Nineteenth Annual Report* (1906–1907), 94–97.

17. New York State Psychiatric Institute and Hospital, *Sixth Annual Report*, 61–63, 66; *Tenth Annual Report* (1939), 6, 63–64.

18. New Hampshire Asylum for the Insane, *Report . . . 1900*, 17; James Russell, "Asylum Versus Hospital," *Proceedings of the American Medico-Psychological Association* 5 (1898), 242–244.

19. Burton Chance, "Needed Reforms in the Care of the Insane," *Outlook* 78 (1904), 1037; "Asylum or Hospital," *Literary Digest* 51 (1915), 153.

20. Russell, "Asylum Versus Hospital," 245.

21. Norwich (Connecticut) Hospital for the Insane, *Second Biennial Report* (1908), 14. See also William F. Lorenz, "Educational Value to the Community of Mental Hygiene Agencies," *National Conference of Social Work, 1921*, 380.

22. The records located in the Northampton State Hospital, Northampton, Massachusetts, are extensive. The material here refers to analysis of the case records, alphabetically arranged, patient by patient, stored in several rooms in the Hospital basement.

23. See, for example, Case 9863, admitted November 9, 1910; for the first year there are 30 entries (10 in the first two months); for 1912–1915, there are six entries.

24. Mr. L., admitted May 19, 1928, no case number; 5th Case in "L" file.

25. Mrs. H., admitted August 21, 1935, 5th Case in "H" file, entry of May 25, 1938; see too, entries December 13, 1938 and September 29, 1939. Miss H., admitted December 15, 1931, 6th case in "H" file, entries of January 2 and July 25, 1932.

26. Miss H., admitted April 26, 1930, 8th Case in "H" file, entries of April 29, May 3, May 14, and May 23, 1930.

27. Case 9863, admitted November 9, 1910, entry of May 14, 1913; Patient H, admitted December 26, 1929, entries of February 28 and April 10, 1936.

28. William James to John D. Rockefeller (Senior), June 1, 1909, Bureau of Social Hygiene Collection, Rockefeller Archive Center, North Tarrytown, New York; New York State Commission in Lunacy, *Thirteenth Annual Report* (1900–1901), 479–480.

29. Milton H. Erickson and R. G. Hoskins, "Grading of Patients in Mental Hospitals as a Therapeutic Measure," *American Journal of Psychiatry* 11 (1931), 105–106, condensed from original.

30. *Report of the Rhode Island Mental Hygiene Survey* (New York, 1924), 88–89; Samuel Hamilton et al., *A Study of the Public Mental Hospitals of the United States, 1937–1939* (Supplement no. 164 to United States, *Public Health Reports*), 57–60. At this time, shock treatment had just entered the treatments of the state hospital, but its full popularity would not come until after 1940.

31. Norwich (Connecticut) State Hospital, *Thirteenth Annual Report* (1930), 13.

32. Norwich (Connecticut) Hospital for the Insane, *Third Biennial Report* (1910), 16; Western (Virginia) State Hospital, *Eighty-Fourth Annual Report* (1911), 10; New York State Commission in Lunacy, *Nineteenth Annual Report* (1906–1907), 299.

33. Hamilton, *Public Mental Hospitals*, 57; Herbert J. Hall, "Neurasthenia," *Boston Medical and Surgical Journal* 153 (1905), 48; C. F. Haviland, "Discussion on 'Occupations for the Insane,'" *New York State Hospital Bulletin* 5 (1912), 25.

34. Haviland, "Discussion on 'Occupations for the Insane,'" 24; New York State Commission in Lunacy, *Nineteenth Annual Report*, 276–282.

35. Frank L. Warne, "Hospital Industries," *New York State Hospital Quarterly* 9 (1924), 230–233; Eugene Bogen, "Effects of Long Hospitalization on Psychiatric Patients," *Mental Hygiene* 20 (1936), 569–570.

36. Massachusetts Commissioner of Mental Diseases, *Annual Report . . . 1922*, 66; Arthur V. Gass, "Occupation as a Remedial Agent in the Treatment of Mental Disease," *AJI* 70 (1913), 481–482, 485.

37. Haviland, "Discussion of 'Occupations for the Insane,'" 147; Western (Virginia) State Hospital, *Ninety-Fourth Annual Report* (1921), 38–39; Elgin (Illinois) State Hospital, *Twenty-Fourth Biennial Report* (1916), 16.

38. Haviland, "Discussion of 'Occupations for the Insane,'" 14; C. R. Norgord, "Fundamental Problems of State Institution Farms," *New York State Hospital Quarterly* 9 (1924), 234; Massachusetts Commissioner of Mental Diseases, *Annual Report . . . 1922*, 66; Western (Virginia) State Hospital, *Eighty-Fourth Annual Report* (1911), 10; Bradford West, *Financial Aspects of State Care of the Insane in New York* (Philadelphia, 1930), 73–75.

39. U.S. Bureau of the Census, *Patients in Hospitals for Mental Disease, 1923* (Washington, D.C., 1926), 26–30, 36, 44–45; *Patients in Mental Institutions, 1939* (Washington, D.C., 1943), 16–21.

40. Massachusetts Commissioner of Mental Health, *Annual Report . . . 1939*, 115, 219, 228–230; New York State Hospital Commission, *Thirty-Seventh Annual Report* (1924–1925), 144–149, 156–159; Stuart K. Jaffary, *The Mentally Ill and Public Provision for their Care in Illinois* (Chicago, 1942), 99–102; Illinois Department of Public Welfare, *Fourteenth Annual Report* (1930), 472–473.

41. U.S. Bureau of the Census, *Patients in Hospitals, 1923*, 20; New York State Hospital Commission, *Thirty-Seventh Annual Report* (1925), 214; Massachusetts Commissioner of Mental Health, *Annual Report . . . 1939*, 161. See too, New York State Commission in Lunacy, *Eighteenth Annual*

Report (1905–1906), chart 4; Illinois Department of Public Welfare, *Fourteenth Annual Report* (1930), 465.

42. U.S. Bureau of the Census, *Patients in Institutions, 1939,* 159; see too, Hamilton, *Public Mental Hospitals,* 22.

43. U.S. Bureau of the Census, *Patients in Hospitals, 1923,* 92–93; *Patients in Institutions, 1939,* 8–9, 159.

44. New York State Hospital Commission, *Thirty-Seventh Annual Report* (1924–1925), 27, 183–184; New York State Commission in Lunacy, *Fifteenth Annual Report* (1902–1903), 79.

45. Massachusetts Commissioner of Mental Health, *Annual Report . . . 1939,* 134–137.

46. New Hampshire Asylum for the Insane, *Report . . . 1894,* 15–16, 21; New Hampshire State Hospital, *Report, 1922,* 5–6, and *Report, 1928,* 10–11.

47. Connecticut State Hospital, *Twelfth Biennial Report* (1928), 11, and *Fifteenth Biennial Report* (1934), 15. See also, *Report of the Rhode Island Mental Hygiene Survey,* 24. The examples could be compounded endlessly.

48. U.S. Bureau of the Census, *Patients in Hospitals, 1923,* 240–243; *Patients in Institutions, 1939,* 162–163; Hamilton, *Public Mental Hospitals,* 36–38; New York State Hospital Commission, *Thirty-Seventh Annual Report* (1924–1925), 44–45.

49. Hamilton, *Public Mental Hospitals,* 40–45; Massachusetts State Board of Insanity, *Report, 1908,* 75; *Report, 1909,* 63.

50. New York State Hospital Commission, *Thirty-Seventh Annual Report* (1924–1925), 46–47; Massachusetts State Board of Insanity, *Report, 1906,* 38; *Report, 1913,* 117.

51. Jaffary, *The Mentally Ill,* 85–86; William Mabon, "Proposed Legislation Regarding Wages and Pensions," *New York State Hospital Bulletin* 2 (1909), 711.

52. Norwich (Connecticut) Hospital for the Insane, *Second Biennial Report* (1908), 13; Jaffary, *The Mentally Ill,* 89; Massachusetts Commissioner of Mental Diseases, *Annual Report . . . 1920,* 85. The Willard quotation (and the ones that follow below from other New York State institutions) are in the records of the Boards of Managers of the several institutions, New York State Library, Albany. For this case, see the Willard file, August 3, 1911, 2.

53. Charles Page, *The Care of the Insane and Hospital Management* (Boston, 1912), 84–85; Ernest M. Poate, "The Management of Disturbed and Excited Patients," *New York State Hospital Quarterly* 2 (1917), 143–155.

54. Board of Managers, Hudson River State Hospital, April 18, 1914, 2, in New York State Library, Albany.

55. Board of Managers, Manhattan State Hospital, August 12, 1909; October 31, 1912; August 31, 1909.

56. Board of Managers, Hudson River State Hospital, March 18, 1911, 4.

57. Board of Managers, Hudson River State Hospital, September 19, 1914, 3.

58. Massachusetts Commissioner of Mental Health, *Annual Report . . . 1939,*

48–49; Board of Managers, Hudson River State Hospital, January 21, 1911; Board of Managers, Kings Point Hospital, May 27, 1911, 3.

59. Helen Crockett, "Boarding Homes as a Tool in Social Case Work with Mental Patients," *Mental Hygiene* 18 (1934), 194; Massachusetts Commissioner of Mental Health, *Annual Report . . . 1939*, 146; U.S. Bureau of the Census, *Patients in Institutions, 1939*, 8.

60. Northampton State Hospital, *Fifty-Seventh Annual Report* (1912), 14; *Fifty-Eighth Annual Report* (1913), 13–14.

61. Massachusetts State Board of Insanity, *Annual Report, 1912*, 190, 200.

62. *Ibid.*, 206.

63. *Ibid.*, 195, 203; Northampton State Hospital, *Fifty-First Annual Report* (1906), 12.

64. Horatio M. Pollack, "The Development and Extension of the Parole System in New York State," *Psychiatric Quarterly* 1 (1927), 53–56; M. B. Heyman, "A Plea for the Extension of the Parole Period," *New York State Hospital Quarterly* 2 (1916), 13–17.

65. U.S. Bureau of the Census, *Patients in Hospitals, 1923*, 17–18, 88–89; *Patients in Institutions, 1939*, 99; Hamilton, *Public Mental Hospitals*, 34–35.

66. Discussion of Russell Blaisdell, "What Patients May be Safely Paroled?," *New York State Hospital Quarterly* 7 (1922), 438; Aaron J. Rosaroff and Thomas Cusack, "The Parole System and its Relation to Therapy," *AJI* 7 (1920), 151. See also E. H. Howard, "The Parole System and After Care Treatment," *New York State Hospital Bulletin* 6 (1913), 150–157.

67. The study is reported in Jaffary, *The Mentally Ill*, 129–130; the full analysis is in Florence Worthington, *Suggested Community Resources for an Extensive Parole System for Mental Patients in Illinois* (Smith College Studies in Social Work, 1933).

68. Jaffary, *The Mentally Ill*, 130.

69. Massachusetts Commissioner of Mental Health, *Annual Report . . . 1939*, 132; June F. Lyday and Maida H. Solomon, "The Problem of the Supply of Psychiatric Workers for State Hospitals," *American Journal of Psychiatry* 7 (1928), 629–631; Hamilton, *Public Mental Hospitals*, 44–45; Illinois Department of Public Welfare, *Fourteenth Annual Report*, 161. See also, *First International Congress on Mental Hygiene*, 76.

70. National Committee for Mental Hygiene, *Research in Mental Hospitals* (New York, 1938), 99–101; Helen L. Witmer, *Psychiatric Clinics for Children* (New York, 1940), 108–111, 128; "Directory of Psychiatric Clinics in the United States, 1936," *Mental Hygiene* 20 (1936), 72–129. Only a handful of hospitals, no more than seven, set up clinics to serve only adults. In fact, there were many more clinics that accepted only children as clients.

71. West, *Financial Aspects of State Care*, 95–97; "Reports of Social Workers . . . 1916," *New York State Hospital Quarterly* 2 (1917), 205–206, 209; Elizabeth Greene et al., *Report of a Survey of Mental Hygiene Facilities and Resources in New York City* (New York, 1929), passim; Discussion, "Patients Safely Paroled?," 438; George W. Mills, "The Ac-

tivities and Uses of a Parole Clinic," *New York State Hospital Quarterly* 6 (1921), 325–327.

72. Illinois Department of Public Welfare, *Annual Report, 1925*, 130.

73. Records of the Springfield, Massachusetts, outpatient clinic, in the Northampton State Hospital; filed alphabetically. See also, the annual reports of the Hospital, which include a section on the clinics, with complaints of inability to serve clients; for example, *1935*, p. 7.

74. New York State Psychiatric Institute and Hospital, *First Annual Report*, 8–9; *Eighth Annual Report*, 8; Trustees of the Boston Psychopathic Hospital, *Annual Report . . . 1921*, 33.

75. Rothman, *Woman's Proper Place*, ch. 4; Jaffary, *The Mentally Ill*, 148–149; Witmer, *Psychiatric Clinics*, 97.

76. Witmer, *Psychiatric Clinics*, 87.

77. *Ibid.*, 182 ff.

78. *Ibid.*, 198–205; Secretary of Welfare of the State of Pennsylvania, *Second Biennal Report* (1924), 38–39; Paul Homer, "A State-Wide Mental-Hygiene Program for Pennsylvania," *Mental Hygiene* 18 (1934), 205–211.

79. Witmer, *Psychiatric Clinics*, 211–212; see also, *Report of the Boston Mental Hygiene Survey* (Boston, 1930), 90–94.

80. In addition to Witmer's *Psychiatric Clinics*, see the articles by Ethel Dummer and William Healy in *Orthopsychiatry, 1923–1948: Retrospect and Prospect*, and George S. Stevenson and Geddes Smith, *Child Guidance Clinics* (New York, 1934), which traces the pertinent work of the Commonwealth Fund. The child guidance movement, like so much else in this field, still lacks a competent history.

81. Council of State Governments, *The Mental Health Programs of the Forty-Eight States* (Chicago, 1950), 30–37.

Chapter Eleven

1. Carl Doering, ed., *A Report on the Development of Penological Treatment at Norfolk Prison Colony in Massachusetts* (New York, Bureau of Social Hygiene, 1940), 71–75. The Doering volume is made up of three parts, the *Official Manual*, compiled by Walter Commons; *A History of the State Prison Colony*, by Thomas Yahkub; and *Individualization of Treatment as Illustrated by Studies of Fifty Cases*, by Edwin Powers. Future citations will be to the particular section, as in this case, Yahkub, *History*, 71–75. See also Massachusetts Department of Correction, *Annual Report for the Year ending November 30, 1927*, 4–5.

2. Massachusetts Department of Correction, *Annual Report . . . 1929*, 2–3; Stearns's predecessor, Sanford Bates, resigned to head up the Federal Bureau of Prisons.

3. Massachusetts Department of Correction, *Annual Report . . . 1928*, 3. Norfolk *Diary*, Bureau of Social Hygiene Collection, Rockefeller Foundation Archives, New York, entry of August 8, 1932, manuscript page 262.

4. *Diary*, January 4, 1933, 354.

5. Howard Gill memorandum to Dr. George Vold, August 7, 1931, "Re: Research Project" (unless otherwise noted, all letters and memoranda are part of the Bureau of Social Hygiene Collection in the Rockefeller Archive Center, North Tarrytown, New York); Howard Gill memorandum to Dr. Warren Stearns, August 29, 1930, 1.
6. *Diary*, July 6, 1932, 179–180.
7. Howard Gill to the Bureau of Social Hygiene, January 14, 1930, to the attention of E. H. Sutherland; Edwin Sutherland memorandum to the Board, June 17, 1930, 1–2; Howard Gill to Edwin Sutherland, May 9, 1930.
8. Thorsten Sellin memorandum to Leonard Dunham, October 23, 1930; Sellin memorandum to Dunham, March 16, 1931, "Visit to Norfolk Prison Colony, March 10–12, 1931"; Thorsten Sellin to George Vold, November 6, 1930; George Vold memorandum to Howard Gill, ca. December 10, 1930, with carbon copy to the Bureau of Social Hygiene; Thorsten Sellin to Leonard Dunham, August 13, 1931.
9. Thorsten Sellin memorandum to Leonard Dunham, December 19, 1931, 1–3, "State Prison Colony at Norfolk."
10. *Diary*, May 9, 1932, 101; April 15, 1932, 73.
11. Commons, *Manual*, 3; *Diary*, November 2, 1933, 587.
12. Commons, *Manual*, 3; see also *Diary*, May 1, 1933, 447.
13. *Diary*, July 6, 1932, 181–182.
14. Commons, *Manual*, 3; *Diary*, May 1, 1933, 447; July 6, 1932, 183.
15. *Diary*, July 6, 1932, 183.
16. Thorsten Sellin to Leonard Dunham, October 23, 1930, 8.
17. *Diary*, August 21, 1932, 265–266; August 3, 1933, 513–514.
18. *Diary*, August 21, 1932, 262–263; Commons, *Manual*, 6–7, describes all the buildings and the layout.
19. *Diary*, August 3, 1933, 515; August 21, 1932, 266.
20. Commons, *Manual*, 8–9, 32–33; *Diary*, August 21, 1932, 267.
21. The definitions that follow are a composite of the various definitions that were issued over 1932. See Commons, *Manual*, 30; *Diary*, July 12, 1932, 135–139 and May 17, 1932, 119–120. Compare too, May 15, 1932, 156–160, and the Massachusetts Department of Correction *Annual Report . . . 1932*, 19.
22. Yahkub, *History*, 138, quoting from the *Diary* of June 14, 1932; Massachusetts Department of Correction, *Annual Report . . . 1932*, 19.
23. Yahkub, *History*, 137–138.
24. Stearns's memorandum on this point was sent by Thorsten Sellin to Mrs. Florence Taylor, February 15, 1933. Quotation is from page 2.
25. Powers, *Treatment*, 222.
26. *Diary*, May 25, 1932, 148.
27. Commons, *Manual*, 30–31; *Diary*, June 15, 1932, 162.
28. *Diary*, May 17, 1932, 120; March 10, 1932, 37; May 18, 1933, 443; May 11, 1933, 448. See also Yahkub, *History*, 140–141.
29. *Diary*, May 17, 1932, 120.
30. Cf. the comments of Mark Roser, head social worker at Norfolk, in the *Diary*, April 18, 1932, 78; Powers, *Treatment*, 240.

31. Julian Hadley to Warren Stearns, March 28, 1933, 5; *Diary*, July 28, 1933; Powers, *Treatment*, 240.
32. Thorsten Sellin to Leonard Dunham, October 23, 1930, 3–5; cf. Sellin to Dunham, March 16, 1931, 1, for the story of how an ex-minister joined the Norfolk group.
33. Julian Hadley to Warren Stearns, March 28, 1933, 6–7; *Diary*, January 2, 1932, 1; see also Dr. Edwin Wilson to Leonard Dunham, April 1, 1932.
34. *Diary*, May 9, 1932, 100–101; Thorsten Sellin to Leonard Dunham, October 22, 1930, 2–3, 5; Julian Hadley to Warren Stearns, March 28, 1933, 7.
35. See the entry of the chief psychologist, *Diary*, August 3, 1933, 511–512; the remarks of Gill, July 12, 1932, 136.
36. *Diary*, April 18, 1932, 78; March 28, 1932, 46; August 1, 1933, 508.
37. *Diary*, May 5, 1932, 136; January 15, 1933, 383; March 9, 1932, 43; May 17, 1932, 99; July 22, 1932, 219–220; March 9, 1932, 43.
38. *Diary*, May 20, 1932, 137; January 4, 1933, 356; Thorsten Sellin to Leonard Dunham, December 19, 1931, 1–2 and March 16, 1931, 2. Cf. *Diary*, May 18, 1933, 439.
39. *Diary*, May 20, 1932, 136; November 16, 1933, 613.
40. *Diary*, November 23, 1932, 304.
41. *Diary*, May 11, 1932, 116.
42. *Diary*, December 12, 1933, 645–646; November 2, 1932, 291; March 29, 1932, 54.
43. *Diary*, January–March 1932 (as yet unnumbered in its initial pages), first entry of Mark Roser.
44. *Diary*, March 10, 1932, 37–38; cf. October 28, 1932, 289. I have altered inmates' names but kept the correct initials.
45. *Diary*, July 26, 1932, 232; August 18, 1933, 438–440; April 15, 1932, 75.
46. *Diary*, May 1, 1933, 577; April 13, 1932, 69; November 2, 1933, 584.
47. *Diary*, September 26, 1933, 561; January 15, 1932, 12; November 22, 1932, 302; March 24, 1933, 418; March 4, 1932, 34.
48. *Diary*, October 26, 1932, 294. Cf. March 16, 1933, 412, 415; August 28, 1933, 528.
49. *Diary*, October 26, 1932, 294.
50. *Diary*, November 22, 1932, 303; November 27, 1932, 311–314.
51. *Diary*, January 25, 1933, 374–376.
52. Thorsten Sellin to Leonard Dunham, October 23, 1930, 2, 9; *Diary*, July 27, 1933, 503; September 25, 1933, 538.
53. *Diary*, May 18, 1933, 443, in review of the incident.
54. *Diary*, January 20, 1933, 367; February 6, 1933, 384–385.
55. *Diary*, May 18, 1933, 444; August 28, 1933, 528; January 20, 1933, 367.
56. *Diary*, March 16, 1933, 409–412.
57. *Diary*, March 16, 1933, 409, 412, 413; March 29, 1933, 424, 426.
58. *Diary*, April 17, 1933, 433–436.
59. *Diary*, April 17, 1933, 437.
60. *Diary*, June 23, 1933, 467.
61. *Diary*, July 9, 1933, 477–478.
62. *Diary*, July 25, 1933, 493.

63. *Diary*, July 13, 1933, 493–501; July 7, 1933, 470; July 12, 1933, 472; July 9, 1933, 481. (In the *Diary*, later entries sometimes precede earlier ones in pagination.)
64. *Diary*, September 25, 1933, 537–538; October 30, 1933, 580–581.
65. *Diary*, September 25, 1933, 540–541.
66. *Diary*, November 2, 1933, 585–587; October 30, 1933, 581 (b).
67. *Diary*, January 6, 1934, 680–681.
68. Massachusetts Department of Correction, *Annual Report . . . 1936*, 16.

Index

Abbott, Edith, 365; *The Delinquent Child*, 51–52, 211, 226

Addams, Jane, 47, 214, 313

After-Care: design of, 301, 312–316, 321; in practice, 360–373. *See also* Psychiatric clinics; Meyer, Adolf

Alcoholism: and mental illness, 308, 320–321, 349–350, 374

Allison, H. E., 123

Almshouses, 110, 375–376

American Academy of Political and Social Science, *Annals*, 231–232

American Institute of Criminal Law and Criminology, 57–58

American Psychiatric Association, 353

American Social Science Association, 46

Arnold, Victor, 223–224

Attendants: in mental hospitals, 300, 318–319, 333, 353–355; and patient abuse, 356–357; and aftercare, 362, 365–367, 371–372. *See also* Guards

Attica State Prison, 133, 157

Attorney General *Survey of Release Procedures*: on probation, 84–85, 87, 91, 98, 100, 108; oppose plea bargaining, 100; on prisons, 129, 132 135, 137–138, 147, 149–151, 156; on parole, 160, 162, 165, 173, 184, 189

Attorneys: and juvenile courts, 216, 241

Auburn State Prison, 119, 123, 136, 146, 157

Augustus, John, 44

Baker, Harvey, 215, 239

Balsam, Louis, 398, 399

Baltimore: probation in, 95, 105, 109; juvenile court in, 230

Barrows, Samuel, 72

Bates, Sanford, 197

Baumes, Caleb, 186–187, 198–200

Beers, Clifford: *A Mind That Found Itself*, 298–301, 319; and Adolf Meyer, 317

Blair, James, 229

David J. Rothman is Professor of History at Columbia University and Senior Research Associate at the Center for Policy Research. Born in New York City, he graduated from Columbia College (1958) and received his Ph.D. from Harvard University (1964). Research for his first book, *Politics and Power: The United States Senate, 1869–1901* (1966) was conducted under a Frederick Sheldon Traveling Fellowship. His next book, *The Discovery of The Asylum* (1971) won the Albert Beveridge prize of the American Historical Association. In 1973–1974 he served as Robert Pinkerton Visiting Professor at the School of Criminal Justice, SUNY, Albany; in 1977, he delivered the Samuel Paley lectures at Hebrew University, Jerusalem, where he had earlier served as Fulbright Professor. David Rothman serves on the board of directors of the New York Civil Liberties Union and the Mental Health Law Project. He has collaborated with his wife, Sheila M. Rothman, in editing several books in American social history. They are now co-directors of the Project on Community Alternatives, analyzing the deinstitutionalization of the mentally disabled.